1985

University of Pennsylvania Publications in
# Conduct and Communication
ERVING GOFFMAN *and* DELL HYMES, *General Editors*

# SPEECH PLAY

ANTHONY E. BACKHOUSE

VICTORIA REIFLER BRICKER

GARY H. GOSSEN

BARBARA KIRSHENBLATT-GIMBLETT

RICHARD PRICE

SALLY PRICE

MARY SANCHES

DINA SHERZER

JOEL SHERZER

BRIAN SUTTON-SMITH

EDITED BY
BARBARA KIRSHENBLATT-GIMBLETT

# Speech Play

*Research and Resources*

*for Studying Linguistic Creativity*

UNIVERSITY OF PENNSYLVANIA PRESS

1976

# Contents

## III. Creativity: Institutional and Individual

## IV. Conclusion

*one hen*

*two ducks*

*three cackling geese*

*four corpulent porpoises*

*five limerick oysters*

*six pairs of Don Alfredo's favorite tweezers*

*seven hundred Macedonian warriors dressed in full battle array*

*eight brass monkeys from the ancient sacred secret crypts of
    Egypt*

*nine lyrical spherical heliotropes from the high plains of
    Heliothemia*

MARCIE WEIMER, age 9, c. 1964
*Suburbs of Philadelphia*

# Acknowledgments

I WOULD like to express my gratitude to Kenneth S. Goldstein for making his superb library available to me when I was compiling the bibliography, for his efforts in reprinting classic collections of children's lore and nursery rhymes, and for his unstinting help and encouragement. Peggy MacLeish and Tony Moffett kindly sent me bibliographic materials from the Western Kentucky University Folklore Archive and showed me their rich collections of children's lore. Requests for bibliographic information were graciously answered by Dan Ben-Amos, Robert Georges, Scott Hambly, Wayland Hand, Mick Maloney, Shelly Posen, Dina Sherzer, Brian Sutton-Smith, and John Szwed. Of great help in the task of checking bibliographic citations were Toby Blum Dobkin, Christine Heck, Basil Kopey, Dina Miraglia, and Harriet Rubin. I am grateful to Claire Ferguson for her generous assistance with the preparation of bibliographic entries and to Barbara Bliss and Victoria Bromberg for help with the typing. Tina Phipps kindly checked the Spanish entries. Harriet Rubin proved to be a veritable sleuth in the library and was indispensable in all phases of the preparation of the manuscript.

This volume owes much to Joel Sherzer, whose insights and encouragement have been so important from the start. Robert Erwin's sensitive reading of the manuscript and astute suggestions are much appreciated. Conversations with Andrew Levitt, when we taught Children's Folklore together, stimulated me to rethink the subject. Jean Toll and John McGuigan provided expert editorial assistance.

The impact of Dell Hymes on this volume is a reflection of his formative influence on the fields of folklore and sociolinguistics more generally. His thoughtful reading and detailed remarks at several stages during the preparation of the manuscript were invaluable.

Most of all, I am indebted to Max, for his unqualified support and his way with words.

# BARBARA KIRSHENBLATT-GIMBLETT
## AND JOEL SHERZER

# Introduction

I

Like kidding, teasing, joking around, and related play activities, speech play is a part of everyday interaction probably in all societies. Consistent with the approach of ethnography, we assume that each community, each culture, may have its own definition of speech play, relative to other uses of speech. Our aim is to elucidate such concepts and to avoid imposing definitions of speech play that may prove arbitrary. Nonetheless, certain general patterns do emerge, corresponding to common usage of the term, but broadening and deepening our understanding of it. To encompass these patterns, speech play can be conceived as any local manipulation of elements and relations of language, creative of a specialized genre, code-variety, and/or style. A key word, of course, is "manipulation." It implies a degree of selection and consciousness beyond that of ordinary language use. Such a conception could be taken to implicate all forms of verbal art; indeed, we want to stress the continuity between what is usually called "speech play" and all verbal art, but stop short of so comprehensive a definition. The substitutions of sounds used to mark characters in Nootka myths (Sapir, 1915), for example, would readily be considered speech play, but the poetic organization of the myths as wholes would not. In effect, "speech play" occupies a central, essential sphere between individual expressive features and major literary forms.

In a given case, the number of languages made use of may be more than one; the elements and relations manipulated may be of one or of several levels, including the contextual; and the ends served may be various, indeed multiple—comic, to be sure, but also religious, artistic, mnemonic, competitive, rehearsal and practice, and, as the term itself implies, sheer play with verbal resources for its own sake. The study of speech play obviously requires an approach to language broader than

1

that characteristic of most linguistic work.[1] Basic to speech play is the expressive, stylistic potential of language, which requires recognition of language structure as embodying a variety of functions[2] (see Jakobson, 1960; Stankiewicz, 1964; Hymes, 1974b). It is furthermore crucial to investigate language and speech in the context of their role in social interaction and in patterns of speaking, ultimately in terms of the ethnography of speaking of the community in question (see Bauman and Sherzer, 1975).[3]

This volume is directly concerned then with the aesthetic and expressive uses of language, understood in terms of the five key notions Hymes (1975) proposes as the foundation of folklore as a discipline: genre, performance, tradition, situation, and creativity. The comprehensive view adopted by the papers in this volume facilitates the analysis of speech play as part of the larger universe of human activity. Adults, children, literate and nonliterate, Western and non-Western societies, all engage in linguistic creativity and playfulness, not only in oral discourse but also in written literature. Ethnographic, empirically-oriented studies of particular cases like those provided here are necessary for the emergence of a cross-cultural perspective on how various speech communities select and group certain features from their linguistic and social resources in order to produce speech behaviors they define as playful, and on how they use such speech patterns in social life.

[1] In the bibliographic guide in Chapter 10, the paucity of contributions by linguists to the study of speech play is striking. See Fish (1973) on the narrowness of concepts of "ordinary language."

[2] Jakobson (1960) provides a classic statement on the "poetic function." See Stankiewicz (1964) on emotive language, where he distinguishes between emotive and poetic language and surveys "the varieties of emotive language which can be rendered through the message and those which constitute a part of the phonological and grammatical levels of language." (259) An important recent contribution to an expanded notion of language is Hymes's 1974 presidential address before the American Folklore Society:

... verbal means are based on not one, but two interdependent elementary functions. Although most linguists and many other fields have attended only to referential function, the features, units, and patterns to be discovered are based on socio-expressive, or stylistic function as well. . . . From the standpoint of structure, all levels of language show means based on stylistic (socio-expressive), as well as referential, function.

Speech play reveals the rich possibilities within the stylistic function so defined.

[3] See especially Goffman (1974), which investigates the role of 'frame' in social interaction: frame and play are closely related concepts. Goffman is indebted to Huizinga (1955), who sees play, ritual, theater, work, war, poetry, philosophy, art, and law as framed worlds, set apart and governed by special rules.

Our aim here is to analyze speech play in all its forms as intrinsic to social life in various societies around the world. Play languages, riddles, proverbs, mnemonics, verbal dueling, and various adult and children's speech play forms drawn from North, Central, and South America, Europe and Asia, and from oral tradition and written literature, form the basis for analysis. We stress that speech play is not restricted to marginal areas of the world, among the nonliterate, or among children. It is important to social and aesthetic life everywhere it has been studied. The studies in this volume describe a variety of speech play genres in their ethnographic context, formulate the rules involved in generating them, establish typologies, and discuss the relevance of speech play to current issues in folklore, psychology, anthropology, linguistics, and literature.

Folklorists in the past have made important contributions to the study of speech play but have tended to emphasize the collection of texts, genre definitions, and classification schemes designed to facilitate the storage and retrieval of the material. Recently, innovative studies of children's lore have been stimulated by the work of Sutton-Smith on play and games. Psychologists have tended to stress experimental studies of children's comprehension and appreciation of riddles and jokes and how this reflects their cognitive and psychosocial development. Few folklorists or psychologists have stressed an ethnographic approach to speech play as a social phenomenon. Anthropologists have reported instances of speech play, but have rarely devoted serious analysis to it. (Exceptions include the recent interest in nicknaming; see Collier and Bricker, 1974; Brandes, 1975; Dorian, 1970.) Linguists have shown even less interest in the ludic aspects of language. Some literary scholars have made important contributions and their works are cited on page 8 and in Chapter 10, where the scholarship pertaining to the study of speech play and many of the issues raised in this volume are surveyed. An extended bibliography is appended.

This book began as a "Symposium on Linguistic Play" at the 1971 Annual Meeting of the American Anthropological Association in New York City. The aim of the symposium was to explore the ways in which speech play and linguistic theory might illuminate each other. The productivity of the combination was evident, and we have been led to prepare this volume as a further effort to overcome what Sutton-Smith (1970) aptly calls "the triviality barrier" that has inhibited serious study of play. We view speech play as a domain worthy of research in its own right and of great potential value for a wide variety of problems of acknowledged importance in several disciplines.

## II

How do contributors to this volume express their common concern with conceptualizing speech play as a special kind of activity? We will place their notions of speech play in the context of theories of play more generally and then attempt a synthesis. The work of Huizinga (1955) and his follower, Caillois (1961), is still useful in this regard despite refinements which have since been made on their concept of play and its breadth of application. Huizinga defined play as:

a free activity standing quite consciously outside "ordinary life" as being "not serious," but at the same time absorbing the player intensely and utterly. It is an activity connected with no material interest, and no profit can be gained by it. It proceeds within its own proper boundaries of time and space, according to fixed rules and in an orderly manner. It promotes the formation of social groupings which tend to surround themselves with secrecy and to stress their difference from the common world by disguise or other means. (Huizinga, 1955: 13)

Following Huizinga, Caillois characterizes play as *free*—people engage in it voluntarily; *separate*—play is bounded in space and time and these boundaries are fixed in advance; *uncertain*—the result is not known beforehand; *unproductive*—nothing new is created by way of goods, wealth, or "new elements of any kind"; *governed by rules*—ordinary laws are suspended and new ones established which are the only ones which hold for the time play is in operation; *make-believe*—play is "accompanied by a special awareness of a second reality or of a free unreality, as against real life" (Caillois, 1961: 10). Caillois then distinguishes four types of "games" on the basis of whether the activity is focused on competition, chance outcome, mimicry, or the experience of vertigo.

Huizinga and Caillois have profoundly influenced the study of play (see Berlyne, 1969 for a survey of the field). Among the refinements which have been made on their conceptualizations are the attempts to distinguish clearly games from other kinds of play activities. Roberts, Arth, and Bush argue that the term *games* has been used too broadly to include activities that are strictly speaking "amusements," "group pastimes," "stunts," "model play," and other "noncompetitive recreational types of activity." Games, they argue, are "recreational activities characterized by organized play, competition, two or more sides, criteria for determining the winner, and agreed-upon rules" (Roberts,

Arth, and Bush, 1959: 597). While play is a cross-cultural universal, games, as they define them, are not. They then classify games on the basis of whether the outcome depends primarily on physical skill, strategy, or chance.

Sutton-Smith (1974b) argues that play and other forms of inversion make the existing system more tolerable and promote flexibility in its members which help them deal with the present social order as well as with change. Nietzsche might have included play when he said, "We have art not to die of the truth." For Sutton-Smith, play is the precursor of innovative forms and the source of new culture, a view borne out by the speech play data in several articles in this volume and consistent with Bateson (1953), who relates the presence and acceptance of paradox and the freedom to change the system of thought to humor, mental health, and human amenity. Fry (1968: 119–172) explicates Bateson's position and suggests that "play depends on paradox for its essential structure." Recent developments in the theory of play are discussed in Chapter 10 of this volume.

## III

How do these concepts of play and games illuminate the nature of speech play as it figures in this volume? First, while all the contributors are concerned with speech play, few deal with games, in the strict sense of the term, because only some of the activities they consider are competitive, organized in terms of sides, and accompanied by criteria for determining a winner (for examples of speech play in the form of games, see Basso, 1972; Fock, 1958; M. R. Haas, 1957; Frake, 1964). Second, regarding speech play, the contributors generally agree that it is voluntary, rule-governed, and "carried on for its own sake."

They differ however on the status they assign the other characteristics of play outlined by Caillois. For example, the native concepts of speech play in several Maya languages as discussed by Bricker for the Zinacantecos and Gossen for the Chamula, stress what Caillois called the "make-believe" quality of play, its tendency to create a "second reality" distinct from though related to "real life." In Bateson's terms, the "this is play" message signals the presence of a play frame, within which special premises and rules operate (Bateson, 1955). "Frivolous language," the English gloss for the native term in several Maya languages for a category of speaking which contains many types of speech play, is defined primarily in terms of the hypothetical, nonserious, specifically nonfactual status of what is being said.[4] The Chamula add the further requirements that the speech be funny and invert norms. In contrast, the statements made in the play languages analyzed by J. Sherzer and R. and S. Price are not necessarily funny or hypothetical. Indeed, the users of play languages are preoccupied with the *means,* in this case, the code, rather than with the *message.*

The analytic or etic concepts of speech play used in the other papers in this volume stress to varying degrees the importance of playing with the expectations of ordinary conversation and also offer variations of Caillois's make-believe criterion of play, Huizinga's requirement that play be accompanied by a "consciousness that it [play] is different from ordinary life," and Bateson's "this is play" message. Sutton-Smith's discussion of children's riddles is based on the notion that riddles are expected to differ from questions in ordinary conversation by having arbitrary but not idiosyncratic answers. And even these expectations about riddles may be played with and violated in a genre called "parody riddles."

The papers on play languages by J. Sherzer and the Prices are the only ones to focus on play activities that may be used to promote "the formation of social groupings which tend to surround themselves with secrecy and to stress their difference from the common world by disguise or other means," a process which Huizinga (1955: 13) includes in his definition of play. Although the function of some play languages is "concealment and a corresponding delimitation of social groups and subgroups," J. Sherzer makes clear that not all play languages and certainly not all speech play operate in this way (see also Polsky,

[4] Brukman (1972: 150) explains that "for the Koya, 'joking' like 'festival' or 'ceremony' is an act that is labelled, either by the term *Paraaskam* (E = 'joking') or *NaalumaaTa* (E = 'tongue play')." Brukman (115) adds that "one of the attributes of joking is that it be non-serious," a feature which is culturally relative. Huizinga (1955: 33) cites Uhlenbeck on Blackfoot terminology for play: "A very singular feature is the possibility of giving any verb a secondary meaning of 'for fun,' 'not seriously' by adding the prefix *kip,* literally 'merely so,' or 'only.' Thus, for instance, *aniu* means 'he says'; *kipaniu,* 'he says for a joke,' or 'he only says.'" Newman (1955 in Hymes, 1964b: 399) identifies a category "frivolous language" among the Zuni: "Old people are supposed to ignore such 'nonsense talking'—*penakʔammeʔ peye,* literally 'not-fit-to-be-spoken is-talking,' an expression which covers slang, punning, telling tall stories, and frivolous uses of language. Slang, however, does not carry strong disapproval. It is merely one of the types of foolish behavior normally indulged in by young people, and among members of this age group it can be tolerantly excused." In contrast with Zuni sacred language, their slang vocabulary changes rapidly and "a large proportion of slang words and expressions are denotatively meaningless or indeterminate and possess a communication function that is largely intentional" (401).

1971: 105–114). In the case of verbal dueling among the Chamula, the presence of a special social group or dyad, one of peers, is a prerequisite for the duel, and the duel, in turn, enhances feelings of male peer group solidarity.

The conception of speech play underlying the analyses of D. Sherzer, J. Sherzer, Sanches and Kirshenblatt-Gimblett is consistent with Huizinga's notion that play "has its aim in itself." Restated by Miller (1973: 97),

. . . play is activity, motor or imaginative, in which the center of interest is process rather than goal. There are goals in play, but these are of less importance in themselves than as embodiment of the processes involved in attaining them. Process in play is not streamlined toward dealing with goals in the shortest possible way, but is voluntarily elaborated, complicated, in various patterned ways.

Also called "over-motivation" (Curti, 1930), "deliberate complication" (Piaget, 1962), "psychical damming up" (Groos, 1901), this process, when it figures in speech play, involves the manipulation of language for its own sake, what Jakobson (1960) calls "poetic function of language" and defines as "situations in which the *shape* of the message becomes a focus of attention, perhaps exploited for its own sake" (Hymes, 1964: 291). Or as Todorov (1971: 14–15) puts it: "Linguistic signs stop being transparent instruments of communication or understanding and they acquire an importance in themselves." Furthermore, D. Sherzer, Sanches, and Kirshenblatt-Gimblett also stress that any of the components of speech (and relationships among components) may be played with. (For a discussion of the components of speech, see Hymes, 1971: 47–93.) With reference to code, phonological, morphological, syntactic, and semantic levels all lend themselves to manipulation for the sake of manipulation. Sociolinguistic rules may also be played with. Indeed, we may distinguish various genres of speech play found in different cultures on the basis of what and how components of speech are manipulated (see D. Sherzer, in press). A question we must ask then is, "To what extent, in what ways, and for what purposes is speech manipulated for its own sake or for kinds of effect recognized as play and art?" (Hymes, 1964: 293).

The problem of distinguishing speech play from other ways of speaking, especially from verbal art, is worthy of considerably more attention than it has received to date. Miller's definition of play in terms of a priority of process over outcome is intended to distinguish play from work but could also provide a basis for understanding the relationship among speech play, verbal art, and other kinds of discourse. The preoccupation with process, whether it be expressed in a high degree of phonological patterning, syntactic embedding, or a long list of semantic oppositions, clearly dominates the children's speech play productions analyzed by Sanches and Kirshenblatt-Gimblett. In contrast, they found that process is generally not allowed to dominate adult verbal art to the extent that it does in speech play,[5] although in verbal art, process and outcome vary in relative priority depending on genre, individual performer, setting, and other factors. At the other extreme from speech

---

[5] For instances of literary works where speech play does become a primary focus, see studies of Raymond Roussel by Heppenstall (1967) and Foucault (1963), as well as of James Joyce (Beckett et al., 1929; Burgess, 1973). The French *nouveau roman* is also important in this regard; writing for this school is not "l'écriture d'une aventure mais l'aventure de l'écriture." See Robbe-Grillet (1963), Ricardou (1967, 1971), Heath (1972), D. Sherzer (1976), and such works on concrete poetry as Solt (1970). We are indebted to D. Sherzer for bringing these works to our attention. See Hollander (1975) on Dante's use of baby talk.

See also Morrissette (1971: 160) who views both language and literature in a play frame and suggests that the premising of a novel on game principles may lead away from the serious thematics so long associated with the novel.

For Mukařovský, Frye, Todorov and others, the play element is central to their concept of literature and literary meaning. Frye suggests that "in literature, questions of fact or truth are subordinated to the primary literary aim of producing a structure of words for its own sake, and the sign values of symbols are subordinated to their importance as structure of interconnected motifs" (Cited by Todorov, 1971: 14). Todorov (1971: 14) suggests that for Mukařovský "two main functions of language oppose each other: the first is the function of representation, of reference, the second is the aesthetic function, the function of the autonomous sign." See also the recent contributions of Babcock-Abrahams.

The cultural relativity of concepts of literature and attitudes to speech play is especially clear in discussions of mannerism. Curtius (1963) and others have suggested that in literature, playing with language and giving propositional or referential meaning second priority, leads to decadence and mannerism when carried to extremes. He argues that medieval mannerists were artificial and excessive in their play with rhetorical figures and with language more generally (Curtius, 1963: 282–292), a feature which Strecker considered essential to medieval Latin mannerism: "The fact that the language was learned in school led in itself to a particularly strong emphasis on the formal. This predilection for form, or one may often say for trifling, is characteristic and must be studied by anyone who would understand the Middle Ages" (cited by Curtius, 1963: 291). The penchant for form is equally essential to modernist literature. Morrissette (1971: 167) asks: "Is the predilection for games and game structures evidence of excessive formalism in Robbe-Grillet?" He concludes that, for Robbe-Grillet, game "has come to mean structural freedom, absence of traditional rules of transition, viewpoint, chronology, and other parameters of previous fiction, and, on the constructive side, an invitation to create new models, to develop new combinations, to push ahead even further the aptly termed *nouveau roman*." Whether deplored or praised, speech play thus emerges as an important, even essential, aspect of both literary and cultural history.

play, for example, in the exchanges between an airplane pilot and the control tower, outcome takes definite priority over process as every effort is made to streamline communication, to maximize efficiency and minimize complication, this *not* being an end in itself but rather the way to land a plane safely. Verbal art and conversation fall along a broader range of the continuum, indicating that they may involve greater and lesser degrees of speech play, in given instances. In the following diagram, process and outcome are presented as two poles on a continuum. At the far left, process has priority over outcome. At the far right this relationship is reversed.

Process . . . . . . . . . . . . . . . . . . . . . . . . . . . . . . . . . Outcome
————————verbal art————————
speech play                                   purely instrumental talk
————————conversation————————

## IV

A further general notion, especially associated with language, needs to be considered—the notion of nonsense. In his study of La Rochefoucauld, Lewis (1971: 137) argues that "playing with words may, then, involve more than juggling them about, reorienting their relationships; it may compromise their very status as linguistic signs, revealing their inadequacy to relay accurately or completely the 'realities' they purport to designate."

Jan (1974: 62) suggests that the March Hare's tea party, in *Alice's Adventures in Wonderland*, illustrates especially well the "intractability and inadequacy of language as experienced by a child in adult company. . . . It is not so much that words do not mean anything; on the contrary, their significance is preserved too literally—so that language becomes impenetrable. When words are taken literally we are the prisoners of language and of the insuperable barriers of its logic."[6]

---

[6]A play on words in Rabelais illustrates the points made by Lewis and Jan and provides a beautiful example of Huizinga's (1955) theory that such domains as legal proceedings are really a form of play. Rabelais' description of Judge Bridlegoose's dice decisions actually invokes an archaic form of legal procedure, that of oracular decision and the association of justice, fate, and chance. But in this case, the decision to use dice is linguistically motivated:

The second important episode built on the imagery of games is the scene in which the old Judge Bridlegoose solved all lawsuits by casting dice. The legal term, *alea judiciorum* (meaning the arbitrariness of court decisions) was understood by the judge literally since *alea* means "dice." Basing himself on this metaphor, he was fully convinced that since he pronounced his judgments by dicing, he was acting in strict accordance with legal requirements. He gave a similar interpretation to the term in *obscuris minimum est sequendum*, "in obscure matters it is better to make the minimum

Nonsense, though only one variety of speech play, epitomizes the linguistic manipulation characteristic of speech play: "language in nonsense is thus a seamless garment, a pure cover, absolute surface" (Holquist, 1972: 163). Like play languages, nonsense involves a transformation of a source language. The differences have to do with the levels at which the transformations take place, their complexity, how they are implemented, and to what purpose. Play languages generally involve operations performed regularly on the morphophonological level of a base language (see Laycock, 1972: 1–3). Nonsense involves other operations as well. Furthermore, Sewell's and Holquist's definitions suggest that true nonsense involves operations performed on the discourse rules: "Nonsense 'is a collection of words or events which in their arrangement do not fit into some recognized system,' but which constitute a system of their own" (Holquist, 1972: 150, citing Sewell). To the uninitiated, play languages seem like nonsense, but the critical difference is that play languages, while designed to conceal, are readily and consistently decipherable. Nonsense is not translatable: it is hermetic to hermeneutics; it achieves coherence through inherence (Holquist, 1972: 156; see also Shibles, 1969, on Carroll's language).

Nonsense and other forms of speech play thus represent a radical alternative to the tyranny of propositional meaning and instrumentality. Jablow and Withers (1965: 255) quote an eighteen-year-old girl as saying: "We like nonsense because all the squares think something has to *mean* something all the time." In such cases as

---

decision" (as the most prudent one). Following this rule, Bridlegoose solved obscure matters by using the smallest dice. The entire order of this peculiar court procedure is built on the metaphors used by the judge in his court decisions. When induced to weigh the testimony of both parties, he places the plaintiff's file opposite the file of the defendant and then casts his dice. (Bakhtin, 1968: 238)

Rabelais is playing with language and using the traditional motif of the literal fool (Thompson Motifs J2450–J2499). This motif exploits the problematical nature of the referential function of language, a tactic which is essential to the workings of nonsense, literature, and nonsense as literature.

Numerous examples of speech play informing linguistically motivated customs and rituals may be found in Yiddish:

Folk etymology also belongs here. The custom of *tashlekh* . . . "casting the sins into a river on Rosh Hashana," which originated in Ashkenazic Jewry, is associated with *teshlekh*, "small pockets," because the pockets are turned inside out. *Mern*, "carrots," are eaten on Rosh Hashana because the same word, as a verb, means "to multiply." Among the western Ashkenazim there was established the custom of eating on Hoshana Raba *koul mit vaser*, "cabbage (cooked) with water" with reference to the Hebrew expression . . . (pronounced *koul mevaser*) "the announcing voice," which appears in the liturgy of that day. (M. Weinreich, 1968: 406)

Phonological convergences are here given priority. Liede (1963, vol. 2: 266–278) devotes an entire chapter to speech play in magic and mysticism, and Bertholet (1940) examines the roles of onomatopoeia and folk etymology in religious belief and practice.

glossolalia and other instances of ritual language, incomprehensibility is institutionalized and acquires a special value and function as an indication of inspiration or contact with the supernatural (see Samarin, 1973). When used in children's poems or Carroll's verse, nonsense calls attention to language, making us aware again that "language is not something we know, but something alive, in process—something to be discovered" (Holquist, 1972: 161). In nonsense, "the system itself provides the rules for giving meaning to itself, beginning with no content, ending with no content, pure process which has no end other than itself. It does what it is about" (Holquist, 1972: 159).[7]

Carroll apparently saw children as being more willing than adults to let strange things remain strange, a phenomenon confirmed by Shultz's (1974) riddle studies, which showed that younger children have a high tolerance for unresolved incongruity. Carroll, in his verse for children, did exploit morphophonologically determined forms, using rhyme not to aid meaning but to subvert it. Sanches and Kirshenblatt-Gimblett who find that much children's nonsense is also phonologically determined, attribute this feature to the child's developing language structure, which provides the system that makes peculiar "sense" of the nonsense. In this respect, children's nonsense and much of their speech play in general is similar in its systematicness to play languages and adult nonsense, though differently motivated.

## V

The papers which follow have been organized under three headings. The first, "Speech Play as Language Structure," brings together three

---

[7]This approach to nonsense as a semiotic system is developed by Kirk and illuminated by Shibles. Working out of Wittgenstein's language philosophy, Shibles (1959) examines the language of *Alice's Adventures in Wonderland* to show what happens "when ordinary language goes on a holiday." In a suggestive study, Kirk (1965) shows how all of Carroll's work, whether mathematical, logical, or literary, was dominated by his semiotic interests and playfulness: ". . . reality for the modern semeiotician, *qua* semeiotician, is primarily the linguistic system, not what lies beyond it." Indeed, "Dodgson's everyday life consisted of thinking about words and mathematical symbols, rules and axioms, postulates and theorems, proofs and manipulation of signs. His everyday world was the meta-linguistic environment of a semeiotician, whether at work or at play" (p. 70). According to Kirk, Carroll explored in his literary works the pitfalls of language and their humorous consequences. In so doing, Kirk feels that Carroll anticipated fundamental principles of modern logical positivism later developed by Charles Sanders Peirce; for example, using experience as a test of meaning (p. 59). Kirk suggests that Carroll was ahead of his time in questioning the arbitrary quality of postulates and the reality of language, in distinguishing between "analytic and synthetic statements" (p. 59), and in showing "a strong intuitive feeling for the distinction between 'structural' and 'lexical' meaning in language" (p. 57).

papers which show how speech play can illuminate questions of language structure and cognitive reality. J. Sherzer particularly suggests that manipulation of language in play may reveal crucial aspects of the representation of linguistic structure by native speakers. Both Sherzer and Bricker provide evidence of more than one underlying representation, and psychological reality, within a community. In Bricker's case, incongruities between terms for reference and terms for address within the kinship system provide a basis for repartee among Zinacantecan males. Her careful description of joking shows that analysis of both types of terms is necessary, within the context of a certain verbal genre, if one is to understand the knowledge members of the community have of the terms, and the use they make of them. In her study, one sees how rules are actually implemented—a desideratum of all studies of speech play.

The Prices are also concerned with the manipulation of the morphophonological sector of language, and reveal another aspect of linguistic creativity. They show that speakers may generate new linguistic material solely for the purpose of deriving play forms from it. They describe three play languages "for which there is an implicit 'base language' created solely as an analytical (non-spoken) stage for these *akoopina*s." This implicit base language is formed from three play languages in the community, plus "things of its own." The criterion of "sweetness" is used for selecting lexemes from one or another of the three possible sources. The base language so formed would provide an excellent opportunity for exploring the notion of "sweetness" as an aesthetic of language in this community. The Prices further indicate that one of the play languages is based on syllable rearrangement of French Guiana Creole, although many of its speakers have no knowledge of French Creole. This suggests that the play language may have originated in the application of a set of rules to a known, spoken base, but that it has been later learned, in its own right, by others for whom it is independent of its source. The Prices also report native explanations of the origin of these play languages.

There is an interesting link here to Sherzer's finding that all the play languages he examined derive from an extremely colloquial variety, so that more than one step separates the language of interpretation from its source. To decipher the play language, a speaker must infer from the play form an argot form, and then from the argot form the standard usage. Such double coding is of course an effective way to disguise speech, and disguise is indeed an important motivation in several cases. The Prices suggest that Creole societies may be especially rich in such uses of speech play for verbal disguise, and that their multilingual setting may be a factor in such creativity. Sex-role differences within the societies tend to support this view, since women, who tend not to know foreign languages, also do not know the play languages.

In the second section, "Initial and Continuing Acquisition," are three studies of how children and adolescents play with language and develop competence in genres of aesthetic discourse. Sanches and Kirshenblatt-Gimblett examine a variety of speech play forms found from age five to fourteen and relate the speech play preferences of children to the development of their language competence. The speech play forms involve varying degrees of manipulation of phonological, morphological, semantic, syntactic, and sociolinguistic aspects of language. Recent research on children's acquisition of language is used to illuminate the character of speech play at different developmental points. The findings have implications in turn for the study of child acquisition of language, and specifically for study of the acquisition of poetic or artistic discourse. In general, children in their speech play are found to focus on components of language in which they are already competent.

Sutton-Smith focusses on one genre—riddles—and, working with an age range similar to that examined by Sanches and Kirshenblatt-Gimblett, relates riddle production to cognitive development and the child's changing concept of the riddle genre as new riddle forms are mastered. Play with both semantic structures and sociolinguistic rules is involved. Piaget's observation that children are most interested in riddles at the age at which they show initial competence in problems of classification provides the basis for Sutton-Smith's typology of riddles. However, Piaget's scheme, while it helps us to understand the relation of some riddle preferences to a child's cognitive development, does not explain the popularity among older children of riddles not involving classificatory problems, for example, parody riddles. To account for this development and the interest in riddling *per se,* Sutton-Smith discusses this activity as a game of arbitrary power in which children gain experience in dealing with interrogation, ambiguity, and humiliation. Riddling is thus seen as contributing to the child's social development.

Gossen also focusses on one genre, verbal dueling, but draws his data from a traditional Mexican culture, the Chamula, and examines the nature of acquisition and socialization among adolescents rather than young children. Gossen examines the phonological, semantic, and sociolinguistic rules involved in mastering Chamula verbal dueling—a genre which requires strict economy of phonological and semantic means in conjunction with the uses of metaphor and the couplet form in carefully defined social contexts—and provides a detailed ethnographic description of this genre, formulates its rules, discusses its psychosocial and cultural functions, and specifies the developmental sequence involved in mastering verbal dueling in Chamula. First, minimal sound shifts are mastered, but without semantic continuity. Then semantic continuity is achieved through the memorization of rote sequences. Finally comes skillful improvisation of metaphoric couplets satisfying both the minimal sound shift and semantic continuity requirements. Because of the phonological requirements of this genre, verbal dueling in Chamula constitutes an impressive living catalog of phonological minimal pairs. Since verbal dueling involves the systematic cataloguing of deviance, expertise in this genre also provides the player with a thorough knowledge of Chamula social norms. The expert player acquires through dueling general language proficiency, the basis for formal adult verbal art forms, and social competence, both of which are essential resources for a Chamula adult.

Gossen, and Bricker as well, contrast with earlier analyses of the nature and function of joking relationships by Radcliffe-Brown (1965) and others who have argued in terms of joking as occurring between persons standing in a specified relationship within a given structure. As Brukman (1972: 168) notes:

. . . this specification of the potential field of actors involved can tell us virtually nothing about the way in which this potential may be actualized in any concrete situation of face-to-face interaction. It tells nothing in short about the content [and form] of the interchange, nor the rules which appear to govern the interaction itself. It also tells nothing of the *consequences* of this kind of verbal behavior for the actors.

Gossen and Bricker examine how social relationships are continually being defined in particular social situations, and how the structure of the relationships of the participants affects the content and organization of the interchange.

The third section of the book, "Creativity: Institutional and Individual," consists of two papers. Backhouse's study of Japanese number mnemonics shows how speech play can expand the resources of a language and pervade the everyday life of a modern industrialized nation where speech play is institutionalized to serve such practical needs as the remembering of telephone numbers and historical dates. The principles in the construction of the mnemonics include an extended punning technique, known as *goroawase*, "matching of sounds." Word play is used here to extend the repertoire of numeral forms. The prerequisites for this type of word play are language-bound homophony and the presence of forms with initial vowels, so that pronounceable acronyms can be formed. Because these mnemonics are based on orthography, they provide an opportunity to use a writing-spelling system to infer native understanding of phonological structure. (J. Sherzer's Javanese data also show how the orthographic representation of a word can perform a role in play languages.)

Playing with discourse rules is central to D. Sherzer's typology of gnomic expressions created by Beckett in *Molloy* and to her examination of their role in a literary text. Beckett uses gnomic expressions to call attention to the act of writing, and plays with these sayings by using a conventional form to make unconventional statements. He combines unlikely elements, for example, mixing registers, and exploits the possibilities of text-context relations. Beckett may make a phonological rather than semantic relationship between a gnomic expression and its context primary, or he may use a weighty gnome in a trivial context, or he may make the context shape the meaning of the gnomic expression.[8] Here is an instance of playing with language which occurs in the work of a widely acclaimed Nobel prize winner. Thus speech play is not restricted to children or to nonliterate societies. It is found as an important principle in the most respected published literature. It is by playing with language, and especially by playing with a popular form of verbal art, that Beckett tells us both explicitly and implicitly that he is writing.

Sutton-Smith and D. Sherzer both curb a tendency in the analysis of verbal art to conceive of "poetic" or "literary" language in terms of "distortions" of and "deviations" from the norms of "language as a whole" (Bloch, 1953: 42) or of given registers, dialects, or genres of verbal art, whether these norms be statistical or of some other kind (see Leech, 1965; Freeman, 1970: 5–10). A positive alternative to the "style as deviation school" is the notion of a "poetic grammar" (Bierwisch, 1965, 1967), aesthetic norms, and the concept of "foregrounding" (Mukařovský, 1964, 1970).[9] Sutton-Smith and D. Sherzer thus stress the creative exploitation of available linguistic and sociolinguistic

[8]Beckett's use of phonological convergences between a gnomic expression and its context may be seen as a kind of pun. Indeed, any proverb in context is a situational pun given Milner's extension of the concept of pun beyond phonological and lexical convergences to syntactic and situational ones (Milner, 1972: 17 ff.).

[9]As Fish (1973: 44) so gnomically says, "Deviation theories always trivialize the norm and trivialize everything else. (Everyone loses.)" See also Hymes's comments in Sebeok (1960: 109–110, 335) on the concept of style and Burke's (1931) essay on the psychology of literary form.

systems and thereby affirm the potential for creativity inherent more generally in language systems and broaden the scope for future analysis.

Together, the papers in this volume contribute uniquely to cross-cultural perspective, and an eventual typology and general theory. First of all, they closely analyze the linguistic features of their materials, and take care to integrate descriptions of speech play forms with accounts of their use. They attend to the relations between the internal structure of speech play forms and other structures, such as the organization of performance events, the place of participants within a social structure, the developing structure of a child's language system, the cognitive organization of a semantic domain such as kinship terminology. In sum, they forward the basic task of specifying what kinds of speech play are found and preferred in individual communities; how they are used; how they fit into ways of speaking; and their consequences. The papers by J. Sherzer and the Prices on play languages, and by Gossen and Bricker on ritual insult, are especially helpful to the comparative goal, because they provide examples of comparable forms in a variety of cultures. Gossen, moreover, locates forms in a detailed taxonomy of Chamula speaking. In addition, the contributors find that an investigation of speech play brings to light more general cultural patterns, important to the societies in question. The volume concludes with suggestions for further research and a bibliographic guide intended to facilitate future studies of speech play.

# Speech Play as Language Structure

PART I

JOEL SHERZER

# Play Languages:
# Implications for (Socio) Linguistics

CHAPTER ONE

SPEECH PLAY defines a broad area of language usage in which linguistic forms at any level are purposely manipulated. Speech play thus defined can be understood in terms of what Jakobson (1960) calls the poetic function of language. For Jakobson, this poetic function, which occurs in many verbal genres in addition to poetry, involves the projection of paradigmatic linguistic axes onto syntagmatic axes, resulting in a focus, foregrounding, and/or manipulation of any aspect of language (phonetics, lexicon, syntax, etc.) for its own sake. In speech play, the poetic function of language becomes so predominant that one might say it is on display. There is an interesting relationship between speech play and verbal art. Verbal art often, but not always, involves speech play. On the other hand, speech play also occurs in speech usages which particular societies may not consider to be verbal art, for example, play languages.[1] Furthermore, the play involved need not necessarily be humorous; for example, serious messages are communicated in the play languages described in this paper. It is the task of the investigator to analyze and describe not only the linguistic properties of speech play, but the precise social functions as well.

Play languages are a type or subclass of speech play. They typically involve the creation of a linguistic code based on the language usually employed by the participants and derived from the language by a series

---

[1] For further discussion of the definition of speech play and its relationship to verbal art, see the Introduction to this volume and the paper by Sanches and Kirshenblatt-Gimblett.

of definable rules.[2] (For an exception, see Price and Price in this volume who describe how new linguistic material is created for the express purpose of deriving a play language from it.) In the scholarship, *play languages* are also called "disguised speech" (M. Haas, 1967, 1969); "linguistic games" (Burling, 1970; Sherzer, et al., 1971); "ludling" (Laycock, 1965; Laycock, Lloyd, and Staalsen, 1969); "pig latins," "secret codes," "secret languages" (Opie and Opie, 1959; Berkovits, 1970); "speech disguise" (Conklin, 1956); and other names. I prefer the term *play language* (which I borrow from Price and Price, this volume) as a general term because, first, play languages are not games strictly speaking. They do not necessarily involve competition, two or more sides, and criteria for determining the winner (see Roberts, Arth, and Bush, 1959: 597). Second, play languages are not necessarily or exclusively used for purposes of secrecy. They may be widely understood and used primarily for fun. Third, not all methods of disguising speech need produce play languages.

Although play languages have attracted the attention of folklorists, they have not been a central concern of linguists. Halle (1962) uses *pig latin* to argue for the necessity of ordered rules in phonological descriptions. Conklin (1956, 1959), Hale (1971), and M. Haas (1957, 1969) describe play languages in non-western societies. M. Haas (1967) suggests a typology of play languages (see also Laycock, 1965). Burling (1970) argues that investigation of play languages would provide data for the analysis of the linguistic structures on which they are based. The folklorists Opie and Opie (1959) and Berkovits (1970) describe play languages used by English-speaking children in England and the United States respectively.

In this paper, I will discuss play languages from three points of view: first, their inherent properties, that is, the kinds of linguistic rules that are involved in the generation of play languages; second, the relevance of play languages to theoretical linguistic concerns, both within particular languages and concerning language in general; third, what play languages reveal about the ethnography of speaking and sociolinguistic patterns of a community.

Since a play language is a coded version of a particular variety of a language, the rules for each play language are derivations from that variety to the play language forms. In contrast with some other types of

[2] Native speakers of play languages can often articulate the language's rules, as they have to, for example, in teaching the language to others. The native version of the rules is usually simpler than that which a linguist would construct. The native version enumerates the major linguistic transformations or derivations involved in the play language, while the linguist's version, in addition to these, enumerates minor morphophonemic adjustment rules.

speech play, for example, counting out rhymes, play languages are used by speakers to transfer novel messages to one another. Examples of play languages from three different speech communities, Cuna, French, and Javanese, will illustrate the types of phenomena involved.

## Five Cuna play languages[3]

The first play language is called *sorsik summakke* or *arepecun-makke*,[4] "talking backwards." It consists of taking the first syllable of a word and placing it at the end of the word. The following rule generates the forms used:

$$\#S1 \ S2 \ S3 \ldots . \ Sn \ \rightarrow \ S2 \ S3 \ldots . \ Sn \ S1\#$$

where S signifies syllable and # signifies word boundary.
Some examples are:[5]

| | | |
|---|---|---|
| *osi* "pineapple" | > | *sio* |
| *ope* "to bathe" | > | *peo* |
| *takke* "to see" | > | *ketak* |
| *take* "to come" | > | *keta* |
| *ipya* "eye" | > | *yaip* |
| *uwaya* "ear" | > | *wayau* |

The rule for this first play language is written above in terms of syllables and the language is indeed based on the syllable. Let us consider another possibility for describing it. Cuna words have the following properties with regard to permitted consonant clusters. No more than one consonant can begin or end a word. Word internally, i.e., intervocalically, clusters of two consonants, but no more than two, can occur. Canonic shapes for Cuna words include, for example:

| VC | : | *an* | "I, my" |
|---|---|---|---|
| CVC | : | *nek* | "house" |
| VV | : | *ia* | "older brother" |

---

[3] The Cuna data for this paper were gathered on the islands of Mulatupu and Niatupu in San Blas, Panama. The research was supported by NSF Grant GU-1598 to the University of Texas.

[4] *arepecunmakke* is derived from Spanish *al revés*, "backwards," plus Cuna *sunmakke*, "to speak." This play language and especially its implications for sociolinguistic theory is investigated in greater detail in Sherzer (1970).

[5] The examples represent but one way of forming words in this play language. (See Sherzer, 1970.) They are represented in a more phonological than phonetic form. Cuna phonemes are *p, t, k, k$^w$, s, m, n, w, y, r, l, a, e, i, o, u. c* results from a cluster of *s* plus *s*. Stress usually falls on the penultimate syllable of the word.

| CVV | : | *poe* | "to cry" |
|---|---|---|---|
| CVCV | : | *kape* | "to sleep" |
| CVCCV | : | *warpo* | "two pole-like objects" |
| CVCCVC | : | *sorsik* | "backwards" |

The maximal canonic shape with regard to consonant clusters is:

$$\#C1 \ V \ C2 \ C3 \ V \ C4 \ . \ . \ . \ VCn\#$$

It is possible to represent every Cuna word as having this maximal phonological structure if those places where consonants can potentially occur but happen not to are filled in with zeros: $\emptyset$ This would not entail a boundless or unstructured use of $\emptyset$ but rather a logical one based on the canonic shape of Cuna words.[6] In the following examples the $\emptyset$ will be placed *in front of* single, intervocalic consonants. This will enable the proper generation of play language forms in the rules to be stated below.[7] Examples are:

| *ia* | "older brother" | ($\emptyset i\emptyset\emptyset a\emptyset$) |
|---|---|---|
| *ope* | "to bathe" | ($\emptyset o\emptyset pe\emptyset$) |
| *kape* | "to sleep" | ($ka\emptyset pe\emptyset$) |
| *uwaya* | "ear" | ($\emptyset u\emptyset wa\emptyset ya\emptyset$) |

The rule for play language 1 can now be rewritten in terms of the canonic shape of the Cuna word; i.e., in terms of a shifting of consonants and vowels and without reference to syllables.

$$\#C1VC2C3VC4 \ . \ . \ . \ VCn\# \ \rightarrow \ \#C3VC4 \ . \ . \ . \ VCnC1VC2\#$$

Repeating the examples of the play language from above with inserted zeros:

| *osi* | "pineapple" | ($\emptyset o\emptyset si\emptyset$) | > | *sio* |
|---|---|---|---|---|
| *ope* | "to bathe" | ($\emptyset o\emptyset pe\emptyset$) | > | *peo* |
| *takke* | "to see" | ($takke\emptyset$) | > | *ketak* |
| *take* | "to come" | ($ta\emptyset ke\emptyset$) | > | *keta* |
| *ipya* | "eye" | ($\emptyset ipya\emptyset$) | > | *yaip* |
| *uwaya* | "ear" | ($\emptyset u\emptyset wa\emptyset ya\emptyset$) | > | *wayau* |

The resulting "backwards" words for the most part fit the phonological canons of ordinary Cuna speech. They could be and at times actually are perfectly good words in Cuna. This gives the hearer of the

---

[6] I suggest then another use of nothing, following Hoenigswald (1959).

[7] The placing of the $\emptyset$ is of course directly related to the fact that single, intervocalic consonants serve as the first consonant of the following syllable and not the final consonant of the preceding syllable.

play language the superficial impression that the player is speaking normal Cuna.

The second Cuna play language is called *ottukkuar sunmakke*, "concealed talking" and consists of inserting a sound sequence after the initial consonant-vowel sequence of each syllable. The inserted sequence consists of *pp* plus the vowel of the preceding syllable. In terms of the canonic shape of Cuna words, the rule for play language 2 is:

$$\#C1V1C2C3V2C4 \ldots Cn\# \quad \rightarrow \quad \#C1V1ppV1C2C3V2ppV2C4 \ldots Cn\#$$

Some examples are:

| | | | | |
|---|---|---|---|---|
| *merki* | "North American" | (*merki∅*) | > | *mepperkippi* |
| *pia* | "where" | (*pi∅∅a∅*) | > | *pippiappa* |
| *ua* | "fish" | (*∅u∅∅a∅*) | > | *uppuappa* |
| *perkʷaple* | "all" | (*perkʷaple∅*) | > | *pepperkʷappapleppe* |

Although the forms used in this play language theoretically fit Cuna phonological canons, they are marked by alliteration and rhyme because of the constant repetition of *ppV*.

The third Cuna play language has no name; it is the same as the second except that the inserted sound sequence is *r* plus the vowel of the previous syllable. The rule is thus:

$$\#C1V1C2C3V2C4 \ldots Cn\# \quad \rightarrow \quad \#C1V1rV1C2C3V2rV2C4 \ldots Cn\#$$

Examples are:

| | | | | |
|---|---|---|---|---|
| *merki* | "North American" | (*merki∅*) | > | *mererkiri* |
| *pe* | "you" | (*pe∅*) | > | *pere* |
| *pia* | "where" | (*pi∅∅a∅*) | > | *piriara* |
| *tanikki* | "he's coming" | (*ta∅nikki∅*) | > | *taranirikkiri* |

Like those of play language 2, the forms of play language 3 fit Cuna phonological canons but exhibit marked alliteration and rhyme.

The fourth Cuna play language has no name and involves the prefixation of *ci-* before every syllable. Furthermore, each syllable in the source or original Cuna word receives primary stress in the play language form. The rule for this play language, stated in terms of syllables, is:

$$\#S1 \ S2 \ S3 \ldots Sn\# \quad \rightarrow \quad \#ciŚ1 \ ciŚ2 \ ciŚ3 \ldots ciŚn\#$$

or stated in terms of the canonic shape of Cuna words:

$$\#C1VC2C3VC4 \ldots VCn\# \quad \rightarrow \quad \#ciC1V́C2ciC3V́C4 \ldots Cn\#$$

Examples are:

| | | | | |
|---|---|---|---|---|
| *ina* | "medicine" | ($\emptyset i\emptyset na\emptyset$) | > | *ciíchiná* |
| *ai* | "friend" | ($\emptyset a\emptyset\emptyset i\emptyset$) | > | *ciáchii̇́* |
| *naipe* | "snake" | ($na\emptyset\emptyset i\emptyset pe\emptyset$) | > | *cináchii̇́chipé* |
| *maceret* | "man" | ($mace\emptyset ret$) | > | *cimácicécirét* |

The forms of this play language ring quite differently from ordinary, spoken Cuna, because of both the repeated *ci* and the positioning of the stressed syllables.

The fifth Cuna play language, like the first, is called *sorsik sunmakke*, although it is actually quite different from the first. It is the only one of the five Cuna play languages which is not based on the syllable. Rather it is based on the vowel.[8] In this instance, every vowel becomes *i*. Stated in terms of the canonic shape of Cuna words, the rule is:

$$\#C1V1C2C3V2C4 \ldots Cn\# \rightarrow \#C1iC2C3iC4 \ldots Cn\#$$

or, more simply, without reference to context:

$$V \rightarrow i$$

Examples are:

| | | | |
|---|---|---|---|
| *pia* | "where" | > | *pii* |
| *pe* | "you" | > | *pi* |
| *tanikki* | "he's coming" | > | *tinikki* |
| *iki* | "how" | > | *iki* |
| *nuka* | "name" | > | *niki* |

The forms used in this play language have a strange ring to them due to the fact that *i* is the only vowel used.

## Two variants of a complicated French play language

French backwards talk is called *langage à l'envers*, "backwards language," *parler à l'envers*, "speak backwards," or, in the code itself, *verlen* or *larper*. There are variants of this play language, one of which involves a switching of syllables. Dubois et al. (1970: 65) describe this version. In it:

---

[8] It is important to note, however, the following relationship between Cuna vowels and syllables. Each short vowel forms the nucleus of a single syllable. Long vowels are phonologically two vowels and are two syllables in length. There is variation within the Cuna speech community, however, in the treatment of long vowels. For a discussion of this variation see Sherzer (1970: 346–347).

| | | | |
|---|---|---|---|
| *l'envers* | "backwards" | > | *verlen*[9] |
| *pédés* | "pederast" | > | *dépés* |
| *mari* | "husband" | > | *rima* |
| *copains* | "friends" | > | *painsco* |
| *cul* | "ass" | > | *luc* |

Notice that French orthography plays a role in this play language. The *s* of *copains,* for example, is not pronounced in ordinary French but it is pronounced in the backwards *painsco.* Similarly with regard to the *l* of *cul.* Some function words, such as prepositions, are not affected and are deleted in the play language outputs. Thus *peau de balle,* "nothing," becomes *balpeau.* This variant of the play language has three rules, which operate in the following order:

1. Delete those words not to be affected.
By this rule, *peau de balle > peau balle*
2. Number the pairs of syllables which are to be switched.
By this rule, *peau balle > peau balle*
<sup>1</sup> <sup>2</sup>
3. Switch each syllable numbered *1* with the following syllable numbered *2.*

By this rule, *peau balle > balpeau,* which is the desired play language output.

Another version of this play language is even more complicated. Basically, it consists of switching the initial consonants or consonant clusters of two consecutive syllables.[10] *Pàrler,* "to speak," for example, becomes *larper.* In words of a single syllable, it is the initial and final consonants or consonant clusters of this syllable which are switched. Thus: *boire* "drink" > *roib* and *mec* "guy" > *quem.* As in the Dubois version described above, certain classes of words are not affected; in this version, however, they still appear in the play language outputs. Thus *je bouffe pas*[11] "I'm not eating" > *je foub pas,* only the verb being affected. Pronouns and definite articles are generally not affected, except when they are phonetically linked with the next form by vowel elision (*j'* and *l'*):

| | | | |
|---|---|---|---|
| *le mec* | "the guy" | > | *le quem* |
| but *l'école* | "the school" | > | *qu'élole* |

[9] All French play language forms are written here in normal French orthography and the ordinary orthographic to pronunciation canons can be followed in reading them.
[10] The examples which appear here were collected by the author in August, 1970.
[11] This play language is derived from an extremely colloquial variety of French. (See discussion below.) Thus the rather formal negative *ne* is not involved.

| | | | |
|---|---|---|---|
| *je bouffe pas* | "I'm not eating" | > | *je foub pas* |
| but *j'entends* | "I hear" | > | *t'enjends* |

This variant of talking backwards requires the following ordered rules:

1.　Mark all words as to whether or not they are to be affected. By this rule (using parentheses to mark unaffected words), examples are:

| | | | |
|---|---|---|---|
| *je vois* | "I see" | > | *(je) vois* |
| *je parle* | "I speak" | > | *(je) parle* |
| *le mec* | "the guy" | > | *(le) mec* |
| *je te pissais à la raie* | "I pissed in your face" | | |
| | | > | *(je) (te) pissais (à) (la) raie* |
| *passe moi la bouteille* | "pass me the bottle" | | |
| | | > | *passe (moi) (la) bouteille* |
| *je te crache à la gueule* | "I spit in your face" | | |
| | | > | *(je) (te) crache (à) (la) gueule* |

2.　Assign the number *1* to the initial consonant or consonant cluster of each affected word and the number 2 to the initial consonant or consonant cluster of the second syllable of each affected word. If the affected word has only one syllable, assign the number 2 to the terminal consonant or consonant cluster of this syllable.

By this rule,

| | | |
|---|---|---|
| *(je) vois* | > | *(je) $\overset{1}{v}$ois* |
| *(je) parle* | > | *(je) $\overset{1\ 2}{parle}$* |
| *(le) mec* | > | *(le) $\overset{1\ 2}{mec}$* |
| *(je) (te) pissais (à) (la) raie* | > | *(je) (te) $\overset{1\ 2}{pissais}$ (à) (la) $\overset{1}{r}$aie* |
| *passe (moi) (la) bouteille* | > | *$\overset{1\ 2}{passe}$ (moi) (la) $\overset{1\ 2}{bouteille}$* |
| *(je) (te) crache (à) (la) gueule* | > | *(je) (te) $\overset{1\ 2}{crache}$ (à) (la) $\overset{1\ 2}{gueule}$* |

3.　If any affected word has only one number, erase the first set of parentheses to its left and renumber, beginning with the newly affected word.[12]

By this rule,

| | | |
|---|---|---|
| *(je) $\overset{1}{v}$ois* | > | *$\overset{1\ 2}{je\ vois}$* |
| *(je) (te) $\overset{1\ 2}{pissais}$ (á) (la) raie* | > | *(je) (te) $\overset{1\ 2}{pissais}$ (à) $\overset{1\ 2}{la\ raie}$* |

---

[12]Notice that the rules for this play language are then cyclic in the sense that this notion is currently used in transformational grammar. I am grateful to Lawrence Foley for calling this fact to my attention.

4. Switch each consonant or consonant cluster numbered *1* with the next consonant or consonant cluster numbered *2*.
By this rule,

$$
\begin{array}{lll}
\overset{1\ \ 2}{je\ vois} & > & ve\ jois \\
\overset{1\ \ \ 2}{(je)\ parle} & > & je\ larpe \\
\overset{1\ 2}{(le)\ mec} & > & le\ quem \\
\overset{1\ 2}{(je)\ (te)\ pissais}\ (\grave{a})\ \overset{1\ \ 2}{la\ raie} & > & je\ te\ sipais\ \grave{a}\ ra\ laie \\
\overset{1\ 2}{passe}\ (moi)\ (la)\ \overset{1\ \ \ 2}{bouteille} & > & sap\ moi\ la\ toubeille \\
\overset{1\ \ \ 2}{(je)\ (te)\ crache}\ (\grave{a})\ (la)\ \overset{1\ \ 2}{gueule} & > & je\ te\ chacre\ \grave{a}\ la\ lueugue
\end{array}
$$

# Seven Javanese Play Languages
## of increasing complexity

The following Javanese play languages are described by Sadtono (1971). In the first Javanese play language, every vowel of the source word is followed by a syllable which consists of *f* plus a repetition of the vowel. The rule for this play language is as follows:

$$V \rightarrow VfV$$

An example is:

*aku arep tuku klambi* "I want to buy a dress"

> *afakufu afarefep tufukufu klafambifi*

Like many play languages, this one is based on the syllable. Here, every open syllable is followed by *f* plus the vowel which is the nucleus of the syllable. Every closed syllable inserts such a new syllable (eg., *fV*) before its final consonant.

The second Javanese play language is identical to the first, except that the inserted syllable begins with *p*.
The rule is thus:

$$V \rightarrow VpV$$

Example:

*kikik anak nakal* "kikik is a naughty boy"
> *kipikipik apanapak napakapal*

The third Javanese play language is similar to the first two Javanese ones although it is somewhat more complicated. Analogous to the first two, each non-initial syllable of each word adds *s* plus a repetition of the vowel which is the nucleus of the syllable. The first syllable of the word is treated as follows. If the syllable is open, it is closed with *s*. If the syllable is closed, the closing consonant is replaced by *s*, the replaced consonant in turn becoming the initial consonant of the following syllable, sometimes preceding the original initial consonant of this syllable, sometimes replacing it. This play language may be described in terms of the following two rules:

1. $\#CV - CVC \ldots \# \rightarrow \#CVs - CVsVC \ldots \#$

where $-$ signifies syllable boundary and $\#$ signifies word boundary.

2. $\#CVC^a - C^bVC \ldots \# \rightarrow \#CVs - C^a(C^b)VsVC \ldots \#$

where parentheses signify that $C^b$ is sometimes deleted.

Example:

*aku arep tuku klambi karo sepatu kembaran karo bocah akeh* "I want to buy a dress and a pair of shoes which are identical with those of my friends"

$>$

*askusu asresep tuskusu klasmbisi kasroso sespasatusu kesmbasarasan kasroso boscasah askeseh*

The two rules are not ordered with respect to one another but rather deal with two different possibilities. The first accounts for initial syllables which are open. The second accounts for initial syllables which are closed. The two rules could of course be conflated into a single one. Regardless, this play language involves more complicated operations than the first two Javanese ones described.

In the fourth Javanese play language, every syllable of every word except the initial one is deleted. Furthermore every syllable in the play language output must be closed; this is done by retaining the initial consonant of the second syllable of the source word, if needed. The two rules for this play language are:

1. $\#C1V1 - C2V2C3 \ldots \# \rightarrow \#C1V1C2 \ldots \#$
2. $\#C1V1C2 - C3V2C4 \ldots \# \rightarrow \#C1V1C2 \ldots \#$

Example:

*aku arep luŋo* "I am going to go" $>$ *ak ar luŋ*

The fifth Javanese play language involves a switching of the kind already encountered in one version of French backwards talk. The consonant or consonant cluster (or $\emptyset$) which begins each word is switched with the consonant or consonant cluster which begins the second syllable of the same word.

The rule for this play language is:

$$\#C1VCC2V \ldots \# \quad \rightarrow \quad \#C2VCC1V \ldots \#$$

where $C$ signifies consonant or consonant cluster.

Examples are:

$$\begin{array}{lll} nduwe & \text{``have''} & > \quad wunde \\ rupiah & \text{``rupees''} & > \quad puriah \end{array}$$

The sixth Javanese play language is based on the word; in it every word is pronounced completely backwards. The rule is:

$$\#C1V1C2C3V2C4 \ldots Cn\# \quad \rightarrow \quad \#Cn \ldots C4V2C3C2V1C1\#$$

Example:

*bocah iku dolanan asu*   "the boy is playing with a dog"
$$> \quad hacob \; uki \; nanalod \; usa$$

The seventh Javanese play language is based on the order of the Javanese consonant alphabet. This alphabet is as follows:

1.*h*   2.*d*   3.*p*   4.*m*   5.*n*   6.*t*   7.*ḍ*   8.*g*   9.*c*   10.*s*   11.*j*
12.*b*   13.*r*   14.*w*   15.*y*   16.*ṭ*   17.*k*   18.*l*   19.*ñ*   20.*ŋ*

The play language associates with every consonant an equivalent derived by superimposing the alphabet in reverse order onto the normal order. Play language equivalent consonants are thus

*h*:ŋ   *d*:ñ   *p*:*l*   *m*:*k*   *n*:*ṭ*   *t*:*y*   *ḍ*:*w*   *g*:*r*   *c*:*b*   *s*:*j*

In the play language, vowels are unaltered and all consonants are replaced by their alphabetically derived equivalents.

Example:

*aku gawe layaŋ*   *"I'm writing a letter"*   :   *ŋamu rade pataŋ*[13]

At first glance, this play language seems so complicated that it is hard to believe that individuals actually speak it rapidly. However, there are several facilitating factors. First, the alphabet contains twenty letters; therefore only ten interchanges must be learned. The second ten

---

[13]In Javanese orthography *aku*, "I," is written *haku*. Therefore in this play language *aku* > *ŋamu*.

are merely the reverse of the first ten. Second, if all twenty sounds are grouped into two classes,

    (1)   all non-nasal stops

    (2)   all other sounds: nasal stops, semivowels, affricates, fricatives, and *r* sound,

then eight of the ten interchanges involve exchanges from class (1) to class (2) or vice versa. The exceptions are *s:j* and *h:ŋ*, both within class (2). These involve, however, shifts from fricative to homorganic voiced affricate and from fricative to almost homorganic nasal stop. The remaining eight interchanges involve some homorganic or almost homorganic shifts and some not at all homorganic shifts. Finally, all but three interchanges (*d:ñ ḍ:w g:r*) involve shifts in voicing. Thus, although this is undoubtedly an intriguingly complicated play language, there are, nonetheless, some regular patterns which facilitate its learning.

    All of the play languages described here are rule-governed in the precise sense that this notion is currently used in generative phonology. The rules operate on a particular phonological or phonetic input, changing the order or sequencing of sounds and/or their nature (constituent features), thereby producing new outputs.[13a] Furthermore, the order in which the rules apply may be crucial. (For a discussion of generative phonological rules and their occurrence in play languages, see Halle, 1962 and M. Haas, 1960.)

    Haas (1967) provides a taxonomy of the mechanisms or rules generally involved in play languages. These are addition, subtraction, reversal, and substitution. Of the Cuna play languages, play language 1 illustrates reversal; play languages 2, 3, and 4, addition; and play language 5, substitution. French backwards talk is a reversal play language. Javanese play languages 1 and 2 involve addition; play language 3, addition and subtraction; play language 4, subtraction; play languages 5 and 6, reversal; and play language 7, substitution. But other phenomena are also involved in these play languages. In French backwards talk, for example, there is first a rule which marks which categories of words are to be affected by the later reversal rule and which not. It is interesting that this rule must operate after the ordinary French rules of elision. The seventh Javanese play language depends on knowledge of the Javanese alphabet and an ability to associate with

---

[13a]Although the play languages described here (and most of those discussed in the literature) involve relatively superficial and essentially phonological aspects of language, Hale (1971) describes a play language which operates at the level of underlying semantic contrasts.

each consonant in this alphabet another consonant, derived by super-imposing a backwards order of the alphabet onto the normal order. The substitution rule applies after the alphabetic operation. That the or-thographic representation of a word (rather than its pronunciation) sometimes plays a role in play languages is demonstrated by the first version of French backwards talk described above. (See also Foley, 1971; N. Johnson, 1971; and C. Johnson, 1971.)

Although the forms that the rules for play languages take are very much like those written by generative phonologists in their descriptions of language (whether synchronic or diachronic), the actual substance or details of the rules are unlike those typically found in ordinary lan-guage (again, viewed from either a synchronic or a diachronic perspec-tive). That is, there are no documented cases of ordinary linguistic processes in which the syllables of all or most words are reversed or the same sound sequence is prefixed to all or most syllables of words. The explanation for this difference between ordinary linguistic processes and those that occur in play languages cannot be given in purely linguistic terms. Rather it has to do with one of the common social functions of play languages: concealment. Most ordinary phonological rules (e.g., the voicing of intervocalic consonants or the merger of two similar vowels) do not result in a new language so different from the original as to be difficult for native speakers to understand. On the other hand, most play languages are unintelligible to persons who do not know them (even if they are native speakers of the source language). Thus one major linguistic task of a play language is to produce distinct and hard-to-recognize forms by means of one or two relatively simple rules. This is done most efficiently by making use of the rule structure or rule format of ordinary language but at the same time filling in this structure or format with possibilities not exploited in ordinary lan-guage. This is a particularly striking case of creativity in language use, especially when one considers that the play languages in question are usually played by relatively young children.[14] It is also interesting that although the play languages typically involve only one, two, or three rules, these rules can be somewhat complex, as is illustrated above in the French and Javanese examples.

Play languages are relevant to the concerns of theoretical linguists for a number of reasons. First, they are a valuable source of data crucial to the solution of such basic problems as the structure of syllables, the

[14]This kind of linguistic creativity is not discussed by Chomsky, who wants to limit the concept of creativity to the ability to produce novel sentences. For a more original approach to the problem of creativity in language use, see Hymes (1971: 52–59).

abstract representation of sounds, and the grouping of morphemes and words into classes. Many play languages are based on the syllable. The permutation of syllables or the insertion of a sound sequence at the boundaries of syllables aids the analyst of a particular language to arrive at a definition of this basic phonological unit. For example, the Cuna play languages discussed above demonstrate that the Cuna syllable has a basic *CVC* structure; and that words of the shape *CVCCVC* are always syllabically *CVC#-#CVC;* and words of the *CVCVC,* *CV#-#CVC.* Thus in Cuna talking backwards, which moves the first syllable of every word to the end of the word, *ipya,* "eye," becomes *yaip* and *ome,* "woman," becomes *meo.*

By throwing sounds into new environments, in which they usually undergo the ordinary morphophonemic rules of the particular language,[15] the play languages provide rich evidence of the kinds of patterned phonetic alternation used by linguists to posit abstract phonemes or morphophonemes. The Cuna word *in·a* "chicha," when pronounced backwards, becomes *nain.* We have here evidence for the argument that a lengthened *n* at the surface phonetic level is represented by two short *n:    nn,* at a more abstract phonological level. At this abstract level *in·a* is represented *inna.*

Play languages, such as French backwards talk, which affect certain words in sentences and not others, effectively group all words into two classes. It is interesting that in the French play language the affected words are *major* or *content* words (nouns, adjectives, verbs, and adverbs) while the unaffected words are relatively *minor* or *function* words (articles and prepositions) but also pronouns, which straddle the content-function boundary. The distinction between major and minor classes of words is of course one that has been made by many theoretical linguists. (See, for example, Weinreich, 1966: 432; Lyons, 1968: 435–442 discusses the related question of grammatical vs. lexical meaning.)[15a]

Play languages also provide insights concerning the psychological reality of linguistic descriptions, a subject which is of increasing interest to linguists and psychologists. Much of the discussion of this issue has tended toward a circular trap. The most popular view is probably that the best or in some sense the most economical linguistic description *must* be the one employed by native speakers. (See, for example, Chomsky, 1964, 1965.) This argument must be accepted or

[15]But see M. Haas (1969: 283) for a Burmese play language in which no morphophonemic rules can be applied after the play language rule.

[15a]The speaking style which Hale (1971: 473) describes as a "type of semantic pig-Latin" is most revealing of semantic structures which exist in the Walbiri language of central Australia.

rejected on faith. Play languages, on the other hand, in which native speakers manipulate such linguistic units as syllables and abstract phonemes, offer direct evidence of how the speakers themselves actually represent these units.

It is rather interesting then that careful investigation of variation in the speaking of play languages strongly suggests the possibility that there is a corresponding variation in native speaker linguistic models, from the perspective of both the individual speaker and the speech community at large. Thus, for example, there is in Cuna a surface distinction between voiceless and voiced stops intervocalically: *dage* "to come"; *dake* "to see." In talking backwards (Cuna play language 1), all speakers say *geda* for *dage;* but for *dake* some speakers say *gedag* and others *geda* or *keda.* It is as if some speakers represent voiceless stops as underlying or abstract sequences of two identical voiced stops, while others do not. The first model is probably a more efficient and economical one from the point of view of Cuna grammar as a whole; both models, however, are descriptively adequate.[16]

A particularly interesting example of the existence of variation in underlying models of linguistic structure is the following, revealed by an investigation of two Cuna play languages. The Cuna word for "mangrove" is *aili.* It does not alternate with any other form. There are three possible underlying phonological representations (written here with dashes to indicate syllable boundaries):

(1)  *ak-li* (since *k* becomes *i* before any consonant other than *k*),
(2)  *ai-li,*
(3)  *a-i-li.*

In *sorsik sunmakke* (Cuna play language 1) there are two ways of saying *aili: liak,* which supports solution (1) above, and *liai,* which supports solution (2). In Cuna play language 4 there are also two ways of saying *aili: ciaícilí,* which supports solutions (1) or (2), and *ciáciícilí,* which supports solution (3).

In French backwards talk, there is variation with regard to which words are affected and which are not. For all speakers, nouns, verbs, adjectives, and adverbs are always affected; articles,[17] prepositions, object pronouns, emphatic pronouns, and the negative particle *pas* are typically not affected. An interesting category of words in this play language includes subject pronouns, possessive pronouns, and demon-

[16]See Sherzer (1970) for additional examples of variation in the speaking of this play language.

[17]Notice though that according to the rules for the play language articles *are* affected when they are linked by elision to the noun or when the noun consists of a single, open syllable. I am talking here then about the initial marking rule.

strative adjectives. For some speakers these are affected; for others, they are not. Furthermore the same speaker will sometimes treat them as affected, sometimes as not. Thus, *ce conard*, "that idiot," becomes either *ce nocard* or *que sonard*. *Mon pinard*, "my booze," becomes either *pon minard* or *mon nipard*. Thus, at least as far as this play language is concerned, subject pronouns, possessive pronouns, and demonstrative adjectives straddle the boundary between the major and the minor word classes. Linguists have alternated between treating these morphemes as prefixes (thus more grammatical, functional, or minor) and as separate, independent words (thus more content or major); it is not surprising that the same variation exists in the minds of native speakers.

The data from play languages thus enable us to reformulate the problem of psychological reality in a way that is socially more sensible. The *socio*linguistic reformulation asks, for a particular speech community: what are the areas and aspects of linguistic structure for which there is variation in native speaker models? One suspects that such variation occurs in aspects of rather superficial linguistic structure (such as those made use of in play languages) and not in aspects of deeper structure.

Any investigation of play languages should pay attention to the social functions that the play languages serve. All of the play languages discussed here are derived from an extremely colloquial variety within the repertoire of linguistic varieties in use in the speech community. Thus no Cuna play language forms are derived from words used in the formal historical-political-religious or curing varieties. (See Sherzer and Sherzer, 1972, for a discussion of the various linguistic varieties in use among the Cuna.) The Javanese play languages are played at the *ngoko* level, the lowest level of Javanese varieties on the scale of formality. (See Geertz, 1968, for a description of Javanese linguistic varieties.) French talking backwards is based on the extremely colloquial slang of French adolescents. When used by French gangs, many of the source words are in an argot limited to the particular gang. Thus a double code is involved: in order to decipher what is said in the play language, one must first move back up the play language derivation rules to the source word and then translate the source word from the special gang argot into standard French.

A common function of play languages is concealment and a corresponding delineation of social groups and supgroups.[17a] That is, a

---

[17a]The play language described by Hale (1971) plays an important role in Walbiri male initiation rituals.

major and public means of demonstrating that one is a member of a particular group is the fluent use of its play language. Children often use such play languages to keep secrets from other children and at times from their parents. Play languages may also play a role in language learning. Some Thai play languages are used by Thai children to help them learn new words and generally improve their competence in speaking. (See M. Haas, 1957; Palakornkul, 1971.) Another possible social function is pure fun. For the Cuna, the primary purpose of the play languages described above is not concealment. They are not used by certain groups of children to keep secrets from others. Rather, the play languages seem to be a form of linguistic play for play's sake.

Finally, play languages provide insights into general patterns and themes of speech use and into the role of speaking in the community. Parisian youth gangs are extremely concerned with publicly marking their distinctness as a group. (See Monod, 1968.) A major way of doing this is through language, by means of both a special and elaborate argot and the frequent use of the complicated talking backwards play languages, often based on the argot. For the Cuna, play and creativity with language are highly valued. With regard to adults, this play and creativity include expressively altering Cuna sounds, introducing non-Cuna sounds, making use of foreign words, altering the names of people and things, developing metaphors, and inserting relevant jokes and anecdotes.[18] Although adults do not use the play languages and usually claim not to understand them, they generally consider them acceptable behavior for children and seem amused when they are used. It is as if they recognized them to be a children's variety of Cuna linguistic play. Some traditional ceremonial leaders are against the use of such play languages, however, especially if they think that obscene words are being concealed in them.[19]

[18] One way to classify Cuna genres of speaking is according to the types and degrees of linguistic creativity and play (both serious and humorous) involved in them.

[19] At the traditional congress held in Mulatupu-Sasardi in June, 1970, a visiting official from an extremely traditional village complained publicly about one of the play languages and claimed that it was obscene. Since then I have at times heard Mulatupu parents stopping their children from using the play languages, reminding them that village officials had declared them obscene. The traditional leaders might have been struck by a similarity between play languages and Cuna *sekretos. sekretos* are short, charm-like utterances which are used to control objects in nature, animals, and human beings. They are considered both powerful and dangerous. Their effectiveness resides in language, by means of which the origin of the object or individual to be controlled is revealed. The language of each *sekreto* (considered obscene because it deals with sexual origins) is not comprehensible to anyone who has not learned it because it is a secret code—usually containing nonsense syllables or words from languages other than Cuna.

I have argued here that play languages, although interesting in and of themselves, also have relevance for various issues that students of language confront today—the nature of linguistic rules, the psychological and sociological reality of linguistic descriptions, and the ethnographic patterns involved in speech use.

# Secret Play Languages in Saramaka: Linguistic Disguise in a Caribbean Creole*

## CHAPTER TWO

ALTHOUGH LINGUISTIC games and play languages have been receiving increasing scholarly attention of late, they have been almost completely ignored by students of Creole languages and societies. There are, however, good sociohistorical reasons to believe that Caribbean Creoles may be particularly rich in such games of verbal disguise (see, for example, Abrahams, 1970e: 86–96; Brathwaite, 1971: 237–239; Herskovits, 1958: 153–158; T. Price, 1970; and Reisman, 1970).[1]

This paper presents a description and partial analysis of several play languages spoken by the Saramaka Maroons ("Bush Negroes") in Surinam, and called by them *akoopína,* "secret play language(s)." Although mentioned only briefly in the literature on Bush Negroes (Hurault, 1961: 68, reprinted in Hurault, 1970: 19; and van der Elst, 1970: 11–12), these play languages warrant serious attention; they reflect fundamental Saramaka values regarding creativity, play, and

* Two years of field research in Surinam were supported by a United States Public Health Service Fellowship (MH-22, 007) and an attached research grant. After having completed this paper in 1972, we deposited our field recordings of play languages and other verbal data in the Archives of Traditional Music, Indiana University. We are grateful to Roger D. Abrahams, Harold C. Conklin, George L. Huttar, Jan Voorhoeve, and especially to Paul Newman for helpful comments on this paper. Unfortunately our data were insufficient to allow us to act on several of their suggestions for improvement.

[1]For recent work on play languages, see the discussion and bibliography in the paper by Joel Sherzer in this volume. The only such study known to us which deals with a Caribbean Creole is Alexis (1970).

performance which influence a much wider range of linguistic contexts, from greetings and riddles to the rhetoric of ritual.

In the history of Afro-America, the Bush Negroes hold a special
place; of all the groups of runaway slaves in the New World, only they
succeeded in establishing viable, independent societies which are still
flourishing today. The ancestors of the major tribes escaped from the
plantations of coastal Surinam in the late seventeenth and early
eighteenth centuries and, after more than half a century of guerrilla
warfare against European and colonial troops, signed peace treaties
with the government in the 1760s. Until well into the nineteenth
century, they were allowed to develop more or less in isolation, and
even today, although all men engage in periodic wage labor on the
coast, these societies are still in many respects "states within a state."

The Saramaka, who number between fifteen and twenty thousand,
are one of the two largest Bush Negro tribes. They now live in about
seventy villages most of which are located along the Surinam River and
its tributaries, the Gaánlío and the Pikílío (see R. Price, 1970a and
1970b for maps; for general background on the Saramaka, see R. Price,
1975b and 1976). Saramaccan (*Saamákatŏngò*), the Saramaka language, is one of the few Creoles of the world in which tone is clearly
phonemic. Although there are strong syntactic similarities between
Saramaccan and the other Creoles of Surinam, of which Sranan and
Ndjuka are the most important, their phonemic systems differ considerably and Saramaccan contains many more words of Portuguese
and African origin (R. Price, 1975a). Saramaccan and these related
languages are not mutually intelligible.

Saramaka men spend many years at a time engaged in wage labor
outside of tribal territory and come into contact with a number of
foreign languages: Sranan, the coastal Creole; other Bush Negro languages, most frequently Ndjuka; French Guiana Creole (*patois*); and
sometimes Dutch, English, or French. In contrast, Saramaka women
have only recently begun making trips of more than a few days to the
coast (see R. Price, 1970a) and rarely have knowledge of any language
but their own; some women do however use esoteric ritual language in
possession and other religious contexts. The ability to "get along" in a
foreign language is a central male value. Men who have worked in
French Guiana commonly show off and amuse themselves by con-
ducting boisterous conversations in *patois*, and groups of boys frequently imitate them, shouting out sounds they remember from their
own visits to the coast. This deep appreciation of linguistic adaptability
certainly has its roots in the past: "It was in language that the slave was
perhaps most successfully imprisoned by his master, and it was in his

(mis-) use of it that he perhaps most effectively rebelled" (Brathwaite, 1971: 237). We would suggest that Saramakas and their slave ancestors have always utilized languages (and had them used against them) for purposes of deception and secrecy.[2]

Saramakas love to play with words, and there is a genuine admiration for the skillful speaker, what Abrahams, referring to Afro-America more generally, has called "the man of words" (1970b: 164–166). Elsewhere (Price and Price, 1972), we have discussed the importance of linguistic play in Saramaka name-giving and name use. Similar arguments could be made with regard to reference or address usages, formal rhetoric, and many other linguistic contexts as well.

Our oldest informants spoke of the existence of *akoopína*s in their parents' youth, during the late nineteenth century, and we have no reason to believe that they were not spoken even earlier. One *akoopína*, the only one we know of that is spoken by some women as well as men, is said to be several generations old and to be used by almost an entire village. At any one time during the past half-century at least, a number of different *akoopína*s were in use in different villages along the Surinam River. The phenomenon has been reported for Djuka, Aluku, and Matawai as well (George L. Hutter: personal communication; Hurault, 1970: 19; Edward Green: personal communication). There is undoubtedly a good deal of intertribal cross-fertilization when Saramaka men spend time in villages with Djukas or other Bush Negroes. During the twentieth century, most *akoopína*s seem to have originated among small groups of teenage boys or young married men as part of the establishment of peer group solidarity, often while these youths were away from tribal territory. Some continued to be used occasionally among friends well into old age and have been passed on to younger generations.

Our data were elicited largely from three male informants, aged sixty-five, forty-five, and twenty-six, and are confined to seven *akoopína*s. Because no *akoopína*s were spoken in the village in which we lived during the time of our fieldwork, we were unable to make

[2]Special ritual languages, such as Papá, Komantí, and Púmba, provide an additional dimension to the linguistic environment of Saramakas, but are beyond the scope of this paper. It is interesting that "disguise" in these languages also seems to be achieved in part by drawing on "foreign" languages; Sranan-speaking *kromanti* mediums from Paramaribo are said to make use of "Bush Negro" words and pronunciation when possessed (Voorhoeve, 1971; 313); the speech of Saramaka *komantí* mediums is heavily infused with borrowings from Ndjuka; and Djuka and Aluku *kromanti* mediums are said to draw heavily on Saramaccan. (Saramaka *komantí* and Sranan, Aluku, and Djuka *kromanti* are closely related sets of dieties which, when possessing a human medium, speak in the ritual language of Komantí [Saramaccan] or Kromanti [Sranan, Aluku, Ndjuka], respectively.)

observations in natural situations. This seems especially unfortunate given the high value placed on verbal performance in this society and the stress our informants gave in discussion to individual variation among speakers of any *akoopína*. However, the rapidity and elegance with which our informants were able to speak these play languages more than a decade after they had last used them are certainly suggestive of very high expectations for fluency by speakers of *akoopína*s and reflect the great value placed on verbal virtuosity among Saramakas generally.

For four of the seven *akoopína*s recorded, we discussed the basic rules with a speaker and elicited both word lists and texts with Saramaccan translations. All our recorded texts were transcribed first by us while in the field and later by Adiante Franszoon, a Saramaka living in New Haven. We then listened again to passages in which the two transcripts differed and discussed discrepancies with Mr. Franszoon before arriving at the final versions.

In this paper, we adopt the orthography proposed for Saramaccan by Voorhoeve (1959, 1961; see also Donicie and Voorhoeve, 1963; for bibliographical references on Surinam Creoles, see Voorhoeve and Donicie, 1963, and Grimes, 1972). In this orthography, long vowels are indicated by double letters (è = ɛ, ò = ɔ). A nasalized vowel is indicated by V*m* before labial consonants and by V*n* before nonlabial consonants. Single prenasalized consonants are indicated by *mb, nd, ndj, ng,* and *nj.* Both *kp* (*kw*) and *gb* (*gw*) are single consonants. An acute accent ( ´ ) indicates high tone. Low tones are unmarked. Words are written as pronounced in isolation; tone-sandhi is not indicated.

## Akoopína 1

The simplest *akoopína* on which we have data was spoken in the early 1950s by a group of teenage boys in the Pikílío region. It served mainly to disguise the group's activities from younger boys and was generally limited to several-phrase exchanges—to arrange a meeting, comment on a passing girl, and so forth.

This *akoopína* transforms normal Saramaccan by shortening long vowels and by a combination of repetition and insertion of extra syllables; each syllable is repeated and then followed by an optional insert which consists of *1V1V*, where the vowel is that of the preceding syllable. (Saramaccan syllables can take the form CV or V; "dipthongs" are conceptualized as two syllables.) The basic rules which generate the forms used in this play language can be written:

1. $\bar{V} > V$
2. $\#S_1 \ldots S_n\# > \#S_1S_1 (1V_11V_1) \ldots S_n S_n (1V_n1V_n)\#$

where S signifies syllable, $\#$ signifies word boundary, and ( ... ) signifies optional insert, and where the number of inserts in words of more than one syllable must be at least one. Moreover, nasalization is not repeated; tone, which is phonemic in Saramaccan, is ignored; and stress falls on the first syllable of each repeated pair, producing a machine-gun-like effect, quite different from spoken Saramaccan.

There are other types of operations taking place in this *akoopína* as well, though we do not feel that our small corpus permits elaboration of the basic rules at this time. For example, there are recurrent shifts in the placement of nasalization and in voicing, e.g., *-banda* > *bambalalatata* (not, for example, *\*babalalandanda*); nasalization is sometimes simply added (*de* > *dendelele*); and there are occasional cases of substitution (rather than insertion) of *1V* for a CV syllable (*pampía* > *pampalilijaja;* *(w)óto* > *wowololo*). In general, our informant stressed the great importance of individual flexibility and variation in speaking this *akoopína*. For example, a single speaker might render Saramaccan *máu*, "hand," as either *mamalalalulu* or *mamalulu*. Moreover, the speaker's ability to produce variant forms is taken as one indication of his skill in the *akoopína*.[3]

We illustrate this *akoopína* with a few sentences from our texts.

*Akoopína* 1:  *Bobolologogo a wowololo bambalalatata.*
Saramaccan:  *Mbó-u-gó a (w)óto bánda.*
English:  Let's go to the other side [of the river].

*Kokololo a-alalakiki* OR *Kokololo ala tatalilikiki.*
*Kó akí.*
Come here.

*Dede mumujejelele mimi kokololo a gangalaladada.*
*Déé mujěè-miíi kó a gandá.*
The girls came back to the village.

*Nana seselele dedelele mamalala tata dudululumimi?*
*Ná sě déé mmá tá duumí?*
Where do those mamas [girls] sleep?

[3]We would speculate, without firm evidence, that just as in everyday speech verbal play sometimes involves ellipsis carried nearly to the point of unintelligibility, two *akoopína* speakers might well, at times, play similar games. This would result in constantly expanding and shifting complexities, in plays on plays, as the language was used.

> *Dendelele anan tata dudululumimi kuku dedelele mama?*
> *De án tá duumí ku de mmá?*
> They don't sleep with their mothers?

## Akoopína 2

A similar but more complex *akoopína* was spoken by a group of boys in the Lángu region during the same time period as *akoopína* 1, and served identical social functions. In addition to syllable repetition and *1V* infixation, this *akoopína* requires syllable rearrangement. We did not collect texts in this *akoopína* in the field. Examples of isolated words include *nanapipilili* < *pína,* "a palm species," and *mimilolowowo* < *wómi,* "man."

## Akoopínas 3, 4, and 5

The following three *akoopínas* were described by a forty-five-year-old man who learned and spoke them about 1940 in the large village of Santigoon on the Saramacca River, which has a mixed population of Saramakas and Djukas with some Matawais. In these three *akoopínas*, unlike *akoopínas* 1 and 2, Saramaccan is not the base upon which operations such as rearrangement, repetition, and insertion are performed. Rather, there is an implicit "base language" created solely as an analytical (nonspoken) stage for these *akoopínas*. For all Saramakas in Santigoon, Ndjuka and Sranan are a constant aspect of the linguistic environment, and they understand these languages with ease, although they do not necessarily speak them. But the analytical "base" for these three *akoopínas* draws even more on Ndjuka and Sranan than does the everyday language of Santigoon Saramakas. Because of the syntactic similarities of the three parent languages, mastery of the "base" for these *akoopínas* mainly involves learning which specific lexical items are drawn, by convention, from Ndjuka, Saramaccan, or Sranan.

As our informant explained for one of these *akoopínas*: "It turns around [rearranges] in Ndjuka; it turns around in Sranan; it turns around in Saramaccan. So it is mixed . . . [and also] it has things of its own." He then went on to discuss the conventions of the implicit base language by means of an example:

When you say *"mbakú"* that's [reversed] *kumbá* . . . which is how Djuka people say "navel." While [if one reversed] in Saramaccan, it would be *gonbi* [from Saramaccan] *bíngo.* But when you are really talking the language, you have to say *mbakú*. Because it's Ndjuka that is used [in this case]. The language with the sweetest name for a thing is what you must take. If Saramaccan is sweeter, you use that; if Ndjuka, you use that; if Sranan, you use that.

This last sentence suggests, incidentally, an avenue of research which we unfortunately did not explore in the field. Since the concept of "sweetness" plays a crucial role in the evaluation of speech behavior by Saramakas, as by other Afro-Americans (see, for example, Abrahams 1970c: 294), the base language" of these *akoopínas* would provide an excellent opportunity for analyzing semantic properties of this concept. And this would seem to be a different kind of example from those outlined by Sherzer (1970, 1971) of the ways that linguistic play can provide insights into language more generally.

*Akoopína* 3 is illustrated by excerpts from our informant's text accompanied by the "base" for each word, which we elicited from him in the field. In writing the "base language," we do not indicate tone unless a word is unambiguously in Saramaccan. We also provide a Saramaccan translation, to indicate the degree of difference between the base language and Upper River Saramaccan, and a literal English translation.

| Akoopína 3: | *Dugá* | *èdi* | *keemi* | *nisá:* | *kabalá,* |
|---|---|---|---|---|---|
| Analytical stage: | *Gadu* | *e* | *meki* | *sani:* | *bak(a)la,* |
| Saramaccan: | *Gádu* | *tá* | *mbéi* | *soní:* | *bakáa,* |
| English: | God | [*] | makes | things: | Westerners, |

| *ngènĕ,* | *ngií,* | *lahá* | *nisá.* | *Mem* | *edi* | *keemi* |
|---|---|---|---|---|---|---|
| *nenge,* | *ingi,* | *ala* | *sani.* | *Hen* | *e* | *meki* |
| *nĕngè,* | *íngi,* | *híi* | *soní.* | *Hĕn* | *tá* | *mbéi [déé soní]* |
| Blacks, | Indians, | all | things. | He | [*] | makes |

| *tipó* | *a o* | *goon balí.* | *Fobó* | *edi* | *a* | *sib,* | *ngopí,* |
|---|---|---|---|---|---|---|---|
| *poti* | *a* | *goon liba.* | *Bofo* | *de* | *a* | *busi,* | *pingo,* |
| *butá* | *a* | *goón líba.* | *Bófo* | *dĕ* | *a* | *mátu,* | *pingo,* |
| puts | on [the] | earth. | Tapirs | are | in [the] | bush, | wild pigs, |

| *mono,* | *ed* | *time* | *nisá* | *gana* | *edi* | *sifí.* | . . . . . |
|---|---|---|---|---|---|---|---|
| *nomo,* | *de* | *meti* | *sani* | *nanga* | *de* | *fisi.* | . . . . . |
| *nŏò* | *déé* | *mbéti* | *soní* | *ku* | *déé* | *físi.* | . . . . . |
| well, | the | animal | things | and | the | fish. | . . . . . |

| *De* | *nóon* | *edi* | *fu* | | *ogo* | *a* | *tofó* | *gu* | *libá* |
|---|---|---|---|---|---|---|---|---|---|
| *De* | *no* | *de* | *fu* | | *go* | *a* | *foto* | *go* | *bali* |
| *De* | *án* | *dĕ* | *fá u* | | *gó* | *a* | *fóto,* | *gó* | *bái* |
| They | not | are | [able] to | | go | to | [the] city, | go | buy |

* progressive form

| | | | | | | | |
|---|---|---|---|---|---|---|---|
| *nisá* | *ekile* | *a fa* | *u* | *wedi u* | *ogu* | *libá* | |
| *sani* | *leki* | *fa* | *wi* | *e* | *go* | *bali* | [a] |
| *soní* | *kuma* | *fá* | *u* | *nán-* | *gó* | *bái* | [soní a] |
| things | like | how | we | [*] | go | buy | [in] |

| | | | | | | |
|---|---|---|---|---|---|---|
| *tofó* | *a* | *edi* | *alikú.* | | *Elá* | *likee* |
| *foto* | *a* | *de* | *akuli.* | | *De* | *akuli* |
| *fóto* | *a* | *déé* | *akulí.* | | *Déé* | *akulí* |
| [the] city | from | the | East Indians. | | The | East Indians |

| | | | | | | |
|---|---|---|---|---|---|---|
| *likee* | *kemi* | *asilí* | *tipó* | *a* | *kusá* | *kusá* |
| *akuli* | *meki* | *alisi* | *poti* | *a* | *saku* | *saku* |
| | [*tá*] *mbéi* | *alísi* | *butá* | *a* | *sáku* | |
| East Indians | make | rice | put | in | sacks | sacks |

| | | | | | | |
|---|---|---|---|---|---|---|
| *kusá* | *a* | *tofó. . . .Lofó* | *oni* | *ed* | *os.* | *Sifí* |
| *saku* | *a* | *foto. . . .Folu* | *no* | *de* | *so.* | *Fisi* |
| | *a* | *fóto. . . .Fóu* | *án* | *dě* | *sǒ.* | *Físi* |
| sacks | in [the] | city. . . .Birds | not | are | thus. | Fish |

| | | |
|---|---|---|
| *onu* | *ed* | *os.* |
| *no* | *de* | *so.* |
| *án* | *dě* | *sǒ.* |
| not | are | thus. |

* progressive form

It should be clear from this fragment that what the speaker calls simply "reversal" involves several types of rearrangement. Our limited texts include the following types, which certainly do not exhaust the repertoire of this *akoopína*.

(1) Complete inversion of the order of syllables in a word. Examples are *tofó* < *fóto*, "city," *silivá* < *valisi*, "valise," *dogas-rama* < *masragado*, "supreme deity." This is the most frequent operation in this *akoopína*.

(2) Rearrangement, but not complete inversion, of the syllables in a word. Our corpus includes rearrangements of the form 1-3-2, 2-1-3, 2-3-1, 3-1-2, and 3-1-4-2, e.g., *alikú* < *akulí*, "East Indian," *kabala* < *bakala*, "Westerner," and *filibi* < *bilifi*, "letter."

(3) Complete inversion of the order of phonemes in a word. In our corpus this is limited to words of the form CV, e.g., *os* < *so*, "so," *ed* < *de*, "to be," *og* < *go*, "to go." Less frequently, such words appear in the *akoopína* with a terminal vowel, e.g., *edi, ogu*.

(4) Rearrangement, but not complete inversion, of the order of phonemes in a word. Our corpus includes only two cases; in both, vowel order is retained while consonants are rearranged. In these cases, the

initial vowel is also lengthened: *keemi* < *meki*, "to make," and *kaati* < *taki*, "to talk."

In addition, a number of phonetic shifts are evident in our texts. Some produce invariant, conventionalized forms, what our informant called the *akoopínas* "things of its own," e.g., *nao* < *na* (Sranan definite article), *ed*, *edi* < *e* (Sranan progressive marker), and *mem* < *hĕn* (Saramaccan third person singular pronoun). But there are also phonetic shifts which vary from speaker to speaker or even within a single utterance, and the ability to play with words in this way is highly appreciated. Examples from our text include *kamosi* < *mŏkísi* (Saramaccan "to mix"), *kalawa* < *watra* (Sranan "water," which Saramakas pronounce *watala*), *sebala* < *prati* (Sranan "to share," which Saramakas pronounce *palati*), *kezi* < *taki* (Sranan "to take"), *deda* < *drape* (Sranan "there"), or *Wasakala* < *Salamaka* (Sranan "Saramaka"). Finally, this *akoopína* retains certain "function words" without changing them; e.g., *fa* (Sranan/Ndjuka/Saramaccan "how") or *fu* (Sranan/Ndjuka/Saramaccan "for," "of").

The effect of disguise in this *akoopína* is undoubtedly achieved in part by its unusual phonetic configurations. For example, words in the form VC, which are frequent in this *akoopína* because of complete phonemic reversal, do not occur in Saramaccan, and sound strange and "foreign."

Even our limited data on this *akoopína* suggest that detailed comparison of its principles of disguise with features of everyday Saramaccan would be productive. For example metathesis is common in Saramaccan speech: *musiní* = *misinú*, "fishing basket," *bakisi* = *bisaka*, "fish trap," and *makisá* = *masiká*, "crush." One might wish to relate its general incidence to its use in this *akoopína*.[4] It seems likely that a full analysis of this *akoopína* would yield useful data on problems in Saramaccan linguistics more generally. For example, forms in this *akoopína* may be able to indicate the native speakers' perception of syllable boundaries (*íngi*, "Indian" > *ngií*, not *\*iíng*), word boundaries (*masragado* [Sranan "supreme deity"] > *dograsrama*, not *\*srama doga*), and underlying phonological representations (*máu*, "hand" > *umá*, not *\*aúm*).

*Akoopína* 4, which uses the same implicit base as *akoopína* 3, is

---

[4]One might even speculate that similar rearrangements occur implicitly without verbalization; the conventional symbol in dreams for the major village deity (*gádu*), whose sacred color is white, is a white dog (*dágu*), suggesting an associational inversion of the type alleged by Leach, in an interesting but controversial paper, for English *god* and *dog* (1966: 27).

considered easier to speak and understand. Our informant explained that here

> You change [words in] Saramaccan . . . Sranan . . . [and] Ndjuka, [but] you change them in an entirely different way. Each thing you say twice. Each thing you say, it must say *edóo*. *Edóo* must be in it always. But that *edóo* there is not [inserted] in any single [natural] language; it is [inserted] in the *akoopína* [base language] itself.

In this *akoopína*, each word is followed by the infix *edó* (alternatively *edóo, edi, edu,* or *e*) and then repeated. However, certain single-syllable "function words" are left unelaborated. In addition, a suffix, *-at,* is used to mark phrase endings. The basic rules could, then, be written:

$$W_1 W_2 \ldots W_n > W_1 edó(o) W_1 \quad W_2 edó(o) W_2 \ldots W_n edó(o) W_n at$$

where W signifies word. We present an illustrative text fragment:

| *Akoopína* 4: | *Mekiedemeki* | *u* | *goedógo* | *a* | *DjumuedéDjumuat.* |
|---|---|---|---|---|---|
| Analytical stage: | *Meki* | *u* | *go* | *a* | *Djumu.* |
| Saramaccan: | *Mbó-* | *u* | *gó* | *a* | *Djuumú.* |
| English: | Let | us | go | to | Djumu. |

| *Bakaedóbakaat.* | *Miedóbie* | *nangaedónanga* | *juedójuat.* |
|---|---|---|---|
| *Baka.* | *Mi* | *nanga* | *ju.* |
| | *Mi* | *ku* | *i.* |
| Again. | Me | and | you. |

| *A* | *saniedésani* | *miedúmie* | *nangaénanga* | *i* | *bi* |
|---|---|---|---|---|---|
| *A* | *sani* | *mi* | *nanga* | *i* | *bi* |
| *Dí* | *soní* | *mi* | *ku* | *i* | *bi* |
| The | thing | I | and | you | have |

*takiedótakaat.*
*taki.*
*táki.*
talked [about].

When spoken, *akoopína* 4 has a distinctive sound. There is greater regularity of accent, rhythm, and tone than in Saramaccan, which creates a monotonous singsong quality. As in *akoopína* 3, the form VC (here the suffix *-at*) which does not occur in Saramaccan gives it a strange ring.

More information would be required to define the exact nature of the phrase-like units terminated by -*at*. But just as operations of syllable rearrangement in some *akoopína*s yield data about Saramakas' perception of syllable and word structure in Saramaccan, so the use of the suffix -*at* may provide important leads toward understanding their perception of how their language is segmented into phrase-length units.

*Akoopína* 5 is even simpler than *akoopína* 4, yet its distinctive rhythm is the most different from normal speech of any *akoopína* known to us. Like *akoopína* 4, it involves infixation in the implicit "base language." One-syllable words are followed by the infix *fu* and then repeated; two-syllable words are simply broken by *fu*. These operations can be written as a pair of ordered rules:

1. $\#S\# > \#S\ S\#$
2. $\#S_1\ S_2\# > \#S_1\ fu\ S_2\#$

We cannot generalize these rules to words of more than two syllables on the basis of our brief tests. As in the previous *akoopína*s, some "function words" are left unelaborated. In the following text fragment, pauses are indicated by slashes, and stress by non-italicization.

| *Akoopína* 5: | Baá*fu*ja/ | meén*fuki*/ | u taá*fuki*/ | *wan* |
|---|---|---|---|---|
| Analytical stage: | *Baja,* | *meki* | *u taki* | *wan* |
| Saramaccan: | *Bája,* | *mbó* | *táki* | *wán* |
| English: | Man, | let | us talk [about] | one |

| toón*fuli*/ | . . . . .*We* goó*fugo*/ | taá*fuki*/ | *na* deé*fude*/ | oó*fuma*/ |
|---|---|---|---|---|
| *toli.* | . . . . . . . .*Wi e-go* | *taki* | *na fu* | *uma* |
| *sonî.* | . . . . . . .*U nángó* | *táki* | *déé* | *mujĕè* |
| thing. | . . . . . .We are going | to tell | | women- |

| toó*fuli*/ | foó*fufo*/ | Daán*fudan*/ | goó*fugo*. |
|---|---|---|---|
| *toli* | *fu.* | *Dangogo.* | |
| *sonî.* | *fu* | *Dángogo.* | |
| stories | about | Dangogo. | |

The most striking feature of this *akoopína* is its rhythm. The rhythmic requirements tend to reshape the vowels in CV initial syllables, lengthening them, raising the tone, and nasalizing them; e.g., *meki* (Sranan "to make") > *meénki*, *toli* (Sranan "story") > *toónli*. In addition, whole sentences (or long phrases) have a general falling tone contour; that is, they begin high and descend gradually.

## Akoopína 6

This *akoopína* was described to us by a sixty-five-year-old Pikílío man who was involved in its original development during the 1920s. While he and several classificatory brothers were working in French Guiana, one of them dreamed that a man greeted him in a strange language; when he awoke, he told his brothers those words which he remembered, and together they invented an *akoopína* which included them.[5] Each of the speakers was given a special name; one of these names, *Alepá*, came to refer to this *akoopína* as a whole. Today, the surviving members of the small group of speakers still enjoy using *Alepá* from time to time. It is worth noting that our informant for *akoopína*s 3, 4, and 5, who has some knowledge of *Alepá* as well, considers it far superior. We have brief texts with rough translations from two speakers, but no discussion of specific rules. The following partial analysis, done after we left the field, is extremely speculative. It attempts to relate this *akoopína* chiefly to French Creole and French, with which we know its inventors were acquainted. These men, however, were also well-versed in certain Saramaka ritual languages, particularly Komantí, which may play an important role here as well.

Possible direct borrowings from French Creole include:

*kanalihotó* "pot" < *canali*
*feli* "leaf" < *feuille*
*ki* "which" < *qui*.

Words which seem to be rearrangements of French Creole include:

*leega* "go" < *(ka)allé*
*wapé* "meal," "to eat" < *wepa*
*ozina* "light skinned" < *wozé*
*lamái* "to tie" < *mawé*
*dabaté* "to chat" < *bavadé*.

Other words seem to involve infixation, using a French Creole base:

*kabozu* "house" < *case* (which Saramakas pronounce *kazu*)
*bejĕènge* "to bathe" < *baigné*
*kinifí* "young girl" < *ti fi*.

A speculative but interesting etymology involves the word for tribal chief, *pavión*. If this were derived, as we suspect, from French or

---

[5] Dreams are a standard source for many kinds of innovation in Bush Negro societies; in the field of language, it is interesting that the mysterious writing system of Afaka is also said to have originated in a dream. (See Price, 1972: 98, for references.)

French Creole *pavillon*, it would represent a shift based on semantic content, a kind of metonymy, because the tribal chief alone is privileged on ceremonial occasions to sit under a canopy. Perhaps the strongest evidence that French Creole and French have influenced this *akoopína* is the negative, which is *pa* (or *pala*), as in *mon mivě otó*, "I see"; *mon pa mivě otó*, "I do not see."

Some words in this *akoopína* seem to involve phonetic shifts from Saramaccan (e.g., *baléésa* "to embrace" < *baasá*). Others involve semantic play in Saramaccan (e.g., *wetifánn* "salt" < *wéti fáán* "white" + intensifier).

Finally, there is a suffix, *-otó* (*-hotó, -utú, -hutú*), which figures repeatedly in this *akoopína* and which may be either a phrase-terminator similar to the *-at* in *akoopína* 4, or simply an embellishment similar to the *-ini* which Voorhoeve has observed among coastal Afro-Surinamers speaking Kromanti (1971: 314).

To conclude these speculations on this still-mysterious *akoopína*, we present a small sample from our texts, with a loose translation based on information provided by a not-always-reliable informant.

| *Tu galifelíi* | *ajunube* | *logoso-otú.* | *Alepáa,* |
| Brother, let's go | [water] | upstream. | Alepaa, |

| *lesankohotó?* . . . . . .*Sankó bálahotó.* . . . . . *Ma leega* | *sabláhotó.* |
| do you hear? . . . . . .Yes, I hear. . . . . . . . I went | downstream. |

| *Moki* | *dendu falama* | *leega* | *sabláhotó.* |
| Me and | man-white | went | downstream. |

## Akoopína 7

The most potentially interesting *akoopína* we heard about was mentioned by all three of our informants, although none of them could speak or understand it. It originated perhaps one hundred years ago in the village of Kámpu, and has been passed on exclusively to Kámpu inhabitants since then. All men and boys in the village, as well as a few of the older women, are said to speak it fluently.

Unlike the other *akoopínas* we have described, this one is used for extended conversations. It is apparently based on syllable rearrangement of French Guiana Creole, but interestingly, many of its speakers have no knowledge of French Creole itself. One of our informants, who had been told a few words of this *akoopína*, explained that it disguised French Creole *Koté u tuvé?* "Where did you find it?" as *Tékoe vé-utu;* he claimed, moreover, that *ventre*, "belly," pronounced by *patois*-speaking Saramakas as *vanti*, became *tívan* and was used to mean "family"

(Saramaccan *bèè*—both "belly-womb" and "[matrilineal] family").

The following table summarizes the major operational principles of the seven *akoopína*s we have discussed. In addition, those *akoopína*s we have heard spoken (nos. 1–6) all involve marked rhythmic variation from Saramaccan. We would assume that a study of additional *akoopína*s would reveal other principles of disguise as well.

### Principles of disguise

| | foreign base | syllabic and/or phonemic rearrangement | syllable or word repetition | infixation |
|---|---|---|---|---|
| *Akoopína* 1 | − | − | + | + |
| *Akoopína* 2 | − | + | + | + |
| *Akoopína* 3 | + | + | − | − |
| *Akoopína* 4 | + | − | + | + |
| *Akoopína* 5 | + | − | + | + |
| *Akoopína* 6 | +? | +? | −? | + |
| *Akoopína* 7 | + | + | ? | ? |

VICTORIA REIFLER BRICKER

# Some Zinacanteco Joking Strategies*

CHAPTER THREE

ORDPLAY is called "frivolous talk" (*ʔištol loʔil*) in Zinacantan, a Tzotzil-speaking Maya community in the highlands of Chiapas, Mexico. Wordplay is "frivolous" because it is usually hypothetical and therefore not serious. In one type of Zinacanteco "frivolous talk," the words in play are certain kinship terms whose meanings are ambiguous.

Comparison of Figure 1 with Figure 2 reveals that there are many more reference than address terms in the Zinacanteco terminological system. The address terms clearly have greater ranges of meaning and are therefore more ambiguous than the reference terms. The relationship between address and reference terms is not, however, simply one of inclusion; the address terms differentiate among some affinal relatives lumped by reference terms. It is this lack of congruence between the reference and address terms that creates opportunities for wordplay.

All Zinacanteco kinship terms are defined in terms of relative age or generation. Referential terms clearly express generational differences in the first two ascending generations in all lines; speakers of both sexes distinguish among older and younger relatives within the same generation. Ego classifies all his lineal relatives by generation, but distinguishes between older and younger siblings in his own generation only. In the collateral line, Ego lumps members of the first ascending generation with older cousins, and members of the first and second descending generations with younger cousins. Address terms override generational differences but classify kin in terms of relative age of

*The fieldwork for this paper was supported by NIMH Predoctoral Fellowship MH-20,345, the Harvard Chiapas Project directed by Professor Evon Z. Vogt, and a grant from the Harvard Graduate Society. I am deeply grateful to these institutions for their generous support which made the research possible. I would like to thank Professor Dell Hymes for his valuable comments on an earlier draft of this paper.

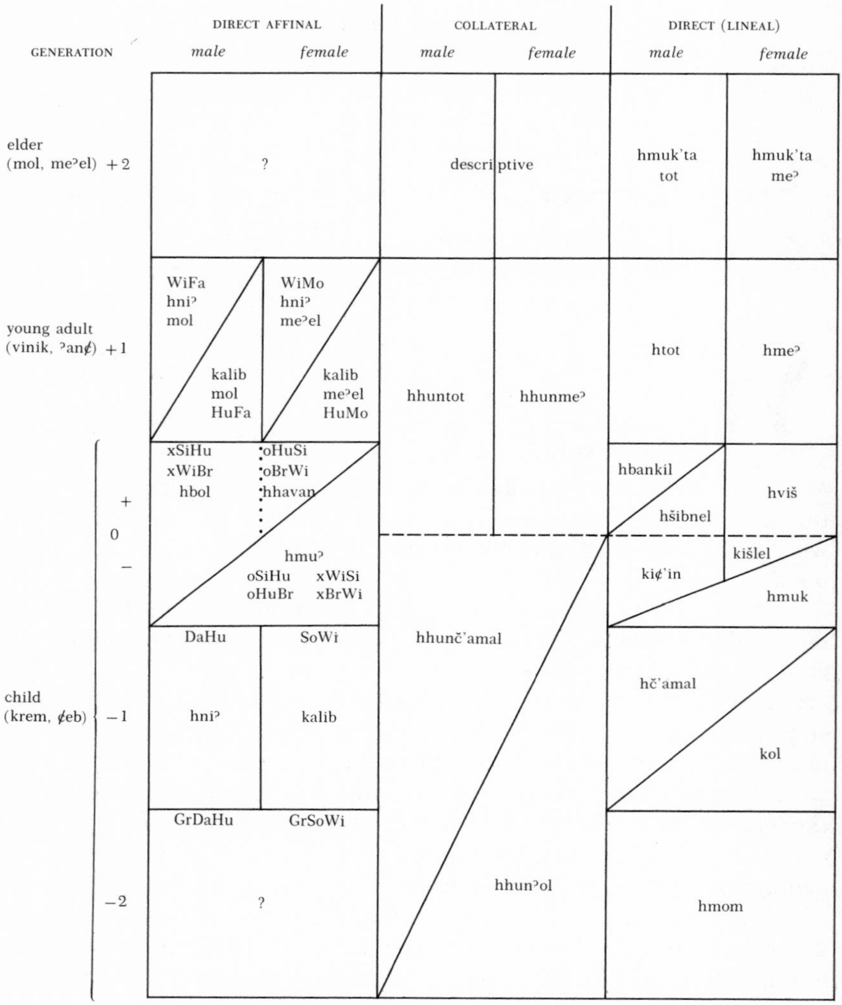


KEY:

- - - - - relative age marker; above is older, below is younger
/ sex of speaker marker; above is male, below is female
| sex of referent marker; left is male, right is female
. . . . . . . sex of intervening relative marker
x male
o female

FIGURE 1. *Zinacanteco Reference Terms* (after Collier, n.d.)

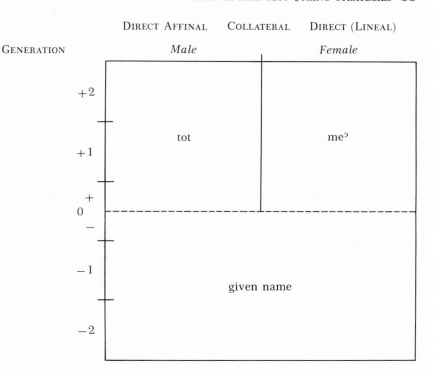

DIRECT AFFINAL     COLLATERAL     DIRECT (LINEAL)

FIGURE 2. *Zinacanteco Address Terms*

speaker and referent, or relative age of referent and intervening kin. Ego addresses all younger kin or relatives younger than the one through whom he is related with their proper names. Ego differentiates among his older relatives on the basis of their sex: he (or she) addresses all older male relatives as *tot* and all older female relatives as *meʔ*.

Almost all Zinacanteco kinship terms connote unequal status relationships with respect to Ego. In private life, status is a function of two variables: (1) relative age, calculated by birth order, and (2) sex. Older people outrank younger people, and men rank higher than women. In ritual contexts, all men rank higher than all women, but ranking within the sex categories is based on relative age. Formal expressions of age and sex ranking include walking, seating, and drinking order. The oldest (male) always walks at the head of the line when two or more Zinacantecos walk together; he sits at the head of the table during formal meals and is served first in drinking ceremonies. The youngest person (female) always walks at the end of the line, sits at the foot of the table, and is served last during drinking ceremonies. Other males arrange themselves in order of their age between the oldest male and the oldest female, while other females arrange themselves in age order between the oldest and youngest females.

Zinacantecos recognize three status levels in private life: child, young adult, and elder. The status terms for the lowest level are *krem,* "boy," and *ǯeb,* "girl"; for the middle level they are *vinik,* "man," and *ʔanǯ,* "woman"; and for the highest level they are *mol,* "elder man," and *meʔel,* "elder woman." Differential treatment is accorded to people depending on which of the three statuses they have attained.

Within the family, these status distinctions correspond to generational differences among the members. The zero generation and all descending generations would be equivalent to the status level *child;* the first ascending generation corresponds to the status level *young adult;* the second ascending generation matches the status level *elder* (Figure 1). Change of status from child (*krem* or *ǯeb*) to young adult (*vinik* or *ʔanǯ*) is marked by marriage. By the time individuals of the zero generation have children of their own (represented by the first descending generation), they will have changed status and have assumed membership in the first ascending generation, their children now moving up to the zero generation.

The boundary between young adult (*vinik* or *ʔanǯ*) and elder (*mol* or *meʔel*) is not so sharply defined as that between child (*krem* or *ǯeb*) and young adult (*vinik* or *ʔanǯ*). There is no rite of passage, such as marriage, which marks the transition. It is clear, though, that by the time men and women have grandchildren, they will have assumed the status of elder.

Tyler (1966: 693–94) has pointed out that it is the nominative stem of a term that is usually called the kin term in the analysis of kinship terminologies. Zinacanteco wordplay, however, is based on verb stems which are derived from the nominal stems of kinship terms in combination with the desubstantivizing suffix *-in.* With terms of reference the *-in* suffix is equivalent in meaning to the English desubstantivizing suffix *-ize* (i.e., *idolize, idol*) and may be glossed as "to become someone's _____," "to acquire someone as a _____," or "to make someone one's _____." For example, *-krem* is the nominal stem of the reference term which denotes "son"; *-kremin* is a transitive verb stem meaning "to acquire someone as a son," "to become someone's son," or "to make someone one's son"; in other words, "to adopt." With address terms the *-in* suffix means "to address someone as _____."

The nominal stems *-tot* and *-meʔ* are shared by the two address terms and by the reference terms for *father* and *mother.* In reference *-tot* denotes only "biological father," while in address *-tot* denotes any older male relative, including "grandfather," "uncle," "father-in-law," "stepfather," and "spouse of older sister," as well as "father." Similarly, in reference -me° is limited to "biological mother," but in address this noun stem may be used also for "grandmother," "aunt," "mother-in-law," "stepmother," and "spouse of older brother." The uses of these stems are therefore in complementary distribution with respect to the two types of contexts. The verbal forms -totin and -me°in, which are derived from these noun stems, are correspondingly ambiguous in meaning with respect to the two contexts. Thus -totin may mean either "to acquire as a father" or "to address as tot." Similarly, -me°in may be glossed as either "to acquire as a mother" or "to address as me°."

Constructions with the -in suffix are commonly used to express the formation of affinal relationships, functionally in the case of marriage, and hypothetically in joking interactions. An affinal relative is a relative acquired through marriage. Included in this category are spouses, in-laws, and apparently also step-relatives (see below).

Joking interactions are primarily a male activity in Zinacantan, where men use wordplay as an opportunity to prove or reaffirm their masculinity. Typically a joking interaction begins when one of the participants suggests that he and his joking partner form an affinal relationship as brothers-in-law, father-in-law and son-in-law, or stepfather and stepson. This offer, however phrased, implies sexual relations with the other's female relative: his sister, daughter, or mother, respectively. The response to this request should be a counter-proposal which both denies the implied sexual privilege to the man who initiated the joking interaction and demands of him sexual access to a female relative of his own. The interaction continues with one proposal and counter-proposal after another until one of the participants is left without a counter-proposal and must accept his opponent's last suggestion.

The number of joking strategies available to the participants is limited by the age and generation-based status inequalities which pervade kinship terminology and private life; the age relationships implied by the chosen affinal relationships must be consistent with the relative ages of the participants. (The sex variable need not be considered here because only males are participants in these interactions.) The relationships stepfather and stepson and father-in-law and son-in-law imply generational inequality. Even in the hypothetical situation defined by joking interactions there must be a significant age difference between the participants who use these relationships as ploys. Brothers-in-law, on the other hand, may be either age-mates or of different generations. Therefore, the choice of this relationship in joking is not determined by the relative ages of the participants.

The Zinacanteco reference term for "brother-in-law" (*-bol*) is a reciprocal term which implies social equality. The address system, on the other hand, differentiates among brothers-in-law in terms of the relative ages of the referent and the intervening relative. The rule is that the spouse of an older sibling outranks the spouse of a younger sibling. The former is addressed respectfully as *tot*, while the latter is addressed familiarly by his given name.

Thus the words in play in Zinacanteco joking interactions all imply status inequality whether or not the participants are age-mates. If the participants are of greatly different ages, they may propose any of the three affinal relationships: stepfather and stepson, father-in-law and son-in-law, or brothers-in-law. Age-mates are restricted to the brothers-in-law relationship as a joking theme.

Zinacanteco joking strategies involve playing off the reference system against the address system. This is possible because of the meaning ambiguity of the verb stem *-totin* which spans both systems but has a wider range of meanings in the address system than in the reference system. The verb stem *-meʔin*, although equally ambiguous, is not mentioned in joking. A man could possibly use this term to imply that his joking partner had homosexual tendencies (i.e., *čahmeʔin*—"I will make you my mother" or "I will address you as *meʔ* [aunt, mother, grandmother, etc.]") and that he, by contrast, was more masculine, but to my knowledge Zinacantecos have not considered this possibility.[1]

---

[1] I did, however, obtain one joke text in which homosexuality was implied, but not with the verb stem *-meʔin*:

| Manvel: | *voʔon ʔatoton, voʔon ʔamalalon, ti hayib* |
| | I am your father, I am your husband, for |
| | *k'ak'al kušulotike.* |
| | as long as we live. |
| Romin: | *voʔot kanǵot ti hayib k'ak'al kušulon ʔuke.* |
| | You are also my mistress for as long as I live. |

Here, too, the theme is status inequality. The father outranks the son because of his greater age, and the husband outranks the wife, if not because of age, then because males enjoy superior status in Zinacantan. But if Manvel is Romin's husband, then Romin must be Manvel's wife, a suggestion that Romin has homosexual tendencies. Confronted with this allegation, Romin's only alternative is to fling the accusation back by calling Manvel his mistress.

The word in play in this example is not a kin term, but the adjective *kušul*, which means both "alive" and "sober." When it is understood in the sense of "sober," the allegations of homosexuality become merely "frivolous talk": the men will not long remain sober because they are drinking together.

The following is a typical joking interaction between age-mates:

Manvel: *hbolin hbatik yuʔun toh lek ʔamikootik.*
Let's become brothers-in-law because we are such good friends!

Romin: *bveno stak' čeʔe.*
Well that will be fine then.

*hbolin hbatik.*
Let's become brothers-in-law!

*čakak'be li kišlele pero čavak'bon laviše.*
I will give you my younger sister if you will give me your older sister.

*ʔi mu persauk htohbe hbatik huhun-tal ʔun.*
And it won't be necessary to pay each other for them.

Implicit in Romin's response is the fact that the address system gives differential recognition to spouses of older and younger siblings. In this case, Manvel was not able to suggest a better counter-proposal and had, therefore, to agree to address Romin respectfully as *tot.*

Age-mates, then, use two joking strategies:

(1) The person who initiates the interaction suggests that he and his joking partner become brothers-in-law so that he will be entitled to sexual privileges with his opponent's sister.

(2) The appropriate response strategy is to agree to the proposal but to demand the other's *older* sister in return because older sister implies superior status in respect of age for oneself.

If the two joking partners are not age-mates, the older man will try to acquire the younger man as a stepson, and the younger man will try to acquire the older man as a father-in-law or brother-in-law. The stepfather-stepson relationship gives the older man the younger man's mother as a wife and enables him to assume a position of parental authority over the younger man. The father-in-law–son-in-law relationship entails a similar status inequality, but the father-in-law must give up his daughter in exchange for his position of authority. The strategic possibilities of the brothers-in-law relationship are the same as for age-mates.

In the following example, a joking exchange between an old man and an unmarried boy whose father is dead, the old man initiates the interaction by claiming to be the boy's stepfather:

Old Man: *pero ti ʔačaʔ-toton yaʔel ʔune.*
But I seem to be your stepfather.

*mu šač'unbon hmantal yaʔel ʔun.*
You don't seem to obey me.

Young Man: *bveno šuʔ šahtotin ti mi čavak'bon laǵebaʔa.*
Well I can address you as *tot* if you will give me your daughter.

*ta hman voʔon ʔun bi ʔa, komo yuʔun*
I myself will buy her, because

*hniʔ-molot ʔune.*
you are my father-in-law.

Old Man: *pero mu bu čakalbe ta šahniʔin,*
But I didn't tell you that I would make you my son-in-law,

*yuʔun ta šahkremin,*
because I will make you my son,

*yuʔun ʔatoton.*
because I am your father.

Young Man: *yeč ʔo me ʔun bi ta šahtotin ʔun—*
That is just why I am going to make you my father—

*pero yuʔun ta šavak'bon kahnil ʔun.*
because you are going to give me my wife.

*ta šinupunotikotik hčiʔuk laǵeb ʔun.*
For I am going to marry your daughter.

*mi čak'anbe stohole, ta htoh noštok ʔun, tot.*
If you want a bride-price, I will pay it, sir.

Old Man: *bveno šuʔ pero yuʔun naka noš ta hheltik*
Well all right, but then we'll just

*yaʔel ʔun bi ʔa.*
exchange them.

*haʔ ta škik' lameʔe,*
I'll take your mother,

*ʔi haʔ čakak'be li hǵeb ʔune,*
and I'll give you my daughter,

*ʔi mu persauk htohbe hbatik huhun-tal ʔun.*
and it won't be necessary to pay each other for them.

*ǵak ši noš yuʔun k'al tem ʔun.*
We can just take them to bed.

*k'al lok' habile,*
At the end of the year,

*yuʔun ʔayanem ʔoš hunuk yol lameʔe,*
your mother will have given birth to a child,

*pero ʔavuǵ' nan škaltik ʔun.*
probably your younger sibling shall we say.

Here the boy jokingly turns the tables on the old man, referring to him as "father-in-law" (rather than "stepfather") and asking to marry his daughter (instead of agreeing to give the old man his mother). The wordplay centers on the ambiguity of *ta šahtotin* (optionally contracted as *čahtotin*), which can mean either "I will make you my father" or "I will address you as *tot*." In terms of its reference meaning, this response indicates that the younger man agrees to acquire the older man as a father (i.e., as his mother's husband). But in terms of its address meaning, the response indicates only that the younger man will address the older by the term appropriate for older male relative, not necessarily mother's husband. In fact, the young man clearly wants to interpret *ta šahtotin* in the sense of the appropriate address term for father-in-law as his subsequent remark shows:

> *pero yuʔun ta šavak'bon kahnil ʔun.*
> because you are going to give me my wife.

The older man protests:

> *pero mu bu čakalbe ta šahniʔin,*
> But I didn't tell you that I would make
> you my son-in-law,
>
> *yuʔun ta šahkremin,*
> because I will make you my son,
>
> *yuʔun ʔatoton.*
> because I am your father.

The two men have used *tot*, which seems to be the same verbal stem with three different meanings: "father" (address term), "father-in-law" (address term), and "father" (reference term). Each insists on the interpretation which will be most to *his* advantage.

When the younger man initiates a joking interaction, he usually suggests that the older man become his father-in-law. The ideal affinal relationship for a younger man is brother-in-law, but if he opens the interaction with the suggestion: "Let's become brothers-in-law!" (*hbolin hbatik*), the older man will probably respond with: "Yes, let's become brothers-in-law! Give me your older sister!" (*bveno stak' čeʔe hbolin hbatik ʔak'bon laviše*). This places the younger man in a subordinate position without receiving anything in return. The younger man would benefit from the brothers-in-law relationship only if the older man made the mistake of proposing it and the younger man countered by offering his *younger* sister.

The older man clearly has the advantage in joking interactions, because two of the three possible affinal relationships automatically place him in a position of authority over the younger man. If the younger man cannot win, however, he can at least improve this situation by obtaining the older man's daughter as a wife. If the older man is stupid, the younger man may trick him into a subordinate social position by getting him to accept the younger man's younger sister as a wife.

The joking strategies of the older man are, in order of preference:

(1)   He suggests that the younger man become his stepson in order to gain sexual privileges with the youth's mother.

(2)   He offers to make the younger man his son-in-law, thereby assuming a position of authority over him.

(3)   He agrees to become a brother-in-law providing that the woman entailed by this relationship is the younger man's *older* sister.

The younger man's joking strategies are complementary:

(1)   He rejects the stepfather-stepson relationship, substituting for it the father-in-law–son-in-law relationship in order to obtain a wife in exchange for his loss of status.

(2)   He suggests that the older man become his father-in-law so that he can obtain a wife.

(3)   He agrees to the brothers-in-law relationship, if proposed by the older man, providing that the intervening relative in question is the younger man's *younger* sister.

Ultimately, each of the eight Zinacanteco joking strategies is based on the lack of congruence between the reference and address systems. See Figure 3. The discrepancy is most clearly seen in the case of brother-in-law terminology, where the reference system treats all brothers-in-law as equals, but the address system discriminates between brothers-in-law married to older siblings and those married to younger siblings. The strategies which employ the brothers-in-law relationship play the address system off against the reference system. Thus whenever a joking request is phrased in terms of the reference verb stem *-bolin* ("to acquire someone as a brother-in-law"), the response should be phrased in terms of discriminations made by the address system: *hbolin hbatik pero ʔak'bon laviše* ("Let's become brothers-in-law, but give me your *older* sister!").

Both the father-in-law–son-in-law strategy and the stepfather-stepson strategy rest on the previously mentioned ambiguity of the verb stem *-totin,* which is ambiguous because of another discrepancy between the reference and address systems: the root *-tot,* which denotes only "biological father" in the reference system, may be used as a term

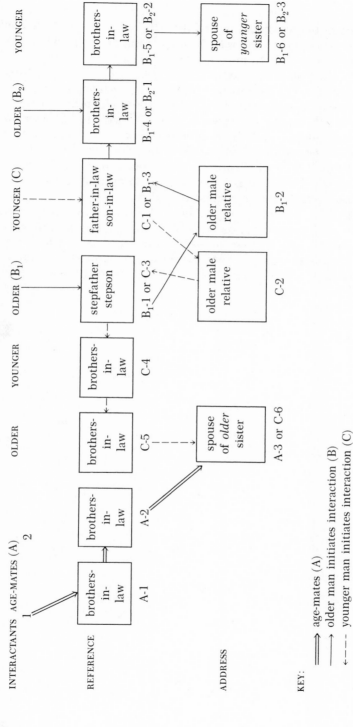

FIGURE 3. *Zinacanteco Joking Strategies*

KEY:

⟹ age-mates (A)

→ older man initiates interaction (B)

---→ younger man initiates interaction (C)

61

of address for any older male relative. In joking interactions, one of the participants prefers the reference meaning of -*totin*, while the other insists on the address meaning of the term.

My analysis of Zinacanteco joking strategies raises an interesting question about the cognitive saliency or psychological reality of kin terms (see Romney and D'Andrade, 1964). In order to understand Zinacanteco joking strategies, it was necessary to consider both the reference and the address terminological systems. It is clear that these systems present the Zinacanteco with two very different cognitive structures, both of which are equally "salient" in joking contexts. Their psychological reality is revealed in the joking strategies which play off one cognitive structure against the other.

The two systems share some of the same kin terms (-*totin* and -*me³in*). Which of the two ranges of meaning for each term is the more "salient"? I suspect that neither is. Zinacantecos use both reference and address terms daily. They live with two cognitive structures which divide up the world differently and, what is more, they often joke about it.

# Initial and Continuing Acquisition

PART II

MARY SANCHES AND
BARBARA KIRSHENBLATT-GIMBLETT

# Children's Traditional Speech
# Play and Child Language*

CHAPTER FOUR

WHILE IT has long been recognized that children's speech play is significantly different from adult verbal art, studies to date of the traditional speech play of children have been based for the most part on psychological and functional models. The aim of this paper is to show that the characteristic features of children's speech play can be accounted for in terms of the child's language model. We present a review of studies of children's speech play, a summary of findings about the nature of the child's language model, and an analysis of instances of children's speech play forms which illustrate how this kind of model can account for both the major characteristic features of these forms and the shifts in children's repertoires at various ages.

## Studies of children's speech play in English

The terminology for genres of children's speech play varies depending upon the historical period, the region, and dialect in which the genres appear, as well as on the individual collector's classification. In printed collections previous to the eighteenth century, children's rhymes were often referred to as songs and ditties; in the eighteenth century as songs for the nursery, Mother Goose rhymes or Tommy

* This paper has benefited from the careful reading and helpful suggestions of Roger Abrahams, J. L. Haines, Dell Hymes, R. J. Kaufman, Christopher Middleton, Joel Sherzer, and Beatrice Silverman-Weinreich. We would also like to thank the Center for Intercultural Studies in Folklore and Oral History at the University of Texas for so kindly making their archival materials available to us.

65

Thumb songs; and in the nineteenth century as popular rhymes, nursery rhymes, nursery pieces, nursery lore, or jingles. All these terms refer to the general class of speech play for *or* by children. The work of Ariès (1962, 1972) and the discussion of nursery lore and nonsense in Chapter 10 in this volume help to clarify why distinctions in terminology arise when they do, a matter related to the emergence of the concept of child and the development of lore for and by "children." Terms for smaller subcategories were few in nineteenth century collections and were usually formed by specifying the subject matter of the rhyme, for example, "rhymes upon natural objects," "rhymes on places" (Chambers, 1842). In twentieth century collections children's speech play has been differentiated into numerous genres, and the terminology has tended to focus upon the activity with which the rhyme is associated: counting out rhymes, jump rope rhymes, ball bouncing rhymes, dandling rhymes, tickling rhymes, teasing rhymes, derisive rhymes, divination rhymes, jeers, torments, insults, taunts, tangletalk, tongue twisters (Brunvand, 1968; Opie and Opie, 1959; Brewster, 1952). Although relatively little attention has been paid to the terms which children themselves use, the Cooperative Research Project in Tri-University (1968: 48) found that American children often refer to their speech play as "songs" or "poems" and the Opies indicate that British children often use the general term "rhyme" as well as special labels for particular genres: counting out rhymes may be called "dips" or "grace" (Opie and Opie, 1969: 28–61).

This relatively recent proliferation of terms for genre categories within the larger class of children's speech play results partly from twentieth century collectors having gathered more materials directly from children in contrast to their predecessors who depended largely on the memory of adults, and partly by an important distinction now made between *nursery lore*—traditions transmitted from adults to children— and *children's lore*—traditions transmitted from child to child (Opie and Opie, 1959: 1). Although mode of transmission has been the main distinguishing feature between these two types of traditions, there are also significant stylistic, thematic, and functional differences (see Opie and Opie, 1959; Wolfenstein, 1954; Bernstein, 1960). *Nursery lore,* which is discussed further in Chapter 10, would seem to be justifiably included in the same kind of cultural speech event as baby talk which results from a set of stylistic adjustments observed in the speech of adults for (not by) children (see Ferguson, 1956). Twentieth century scholars have paid more attention than their predecessors to the category of *children's lore,* the type of speech play to be investigated in this paper.

Most analytic classifications of children's rhymes are based upon a categorization of the games with which the rhymes are associated (Brunvand, 1968; Brewster, 1952) and this tendency is evident in the terminology discussed above. The rhymes have been further classified on the basis of the subcategories of each game (Buckley, 1966; Browne, 1955; Pinon, 1965a; Hall, 1940–1941; Hawthorne, 1966); the formal features of the rhymes (Hawthorne, 1966; Pinon, 1965a); and the thematic content of the rhymes (Pinon, 1965a; Buckley, 1966). Thus, jump rope rhymes may fall into such categories as rhymes for accompanying plain jump, call in/call out, speed jumps, and action jumps (Buckley, 1966). Each of these categories could be further subdivided according to formal features of the rhymes, such as single-lined verse, short unrhymed verse, longer rhymed verse (Hawthorne, 1966) or according to such features as counting, enumeration, nonsense, divination, thematic formula (Pinon, 1965a). Pinon breaks the thematic formula category down even further into twenty-nine topics such as infancy, clothing, love, history, plants (1965a: 78–79).

One of the problems in existing categorizations of rhymes is that the taxonomies which they could produce are not predictive. For example, the problem with categorizing rhymes according to the games with which they are associated is that "In one play group a rhyme may accompany the jump-rope; in another group the same rhyme may accompany a bouncing ball; or one child may use one rhyme for jump rope, ball bouncing and for taunting a playmate" (Cooperative Research Project, 1968: 47; see also Leach, 1949–50: 1016). Existing categorizations based upon formal stylistic features, though potentially a productive approach, have been inadequate because the features considered are generally limited to length of utterance, a feature that can differ widely from one variant to another, and the presence or absence of rhyme. These features alone are not sufficient for predicting the occurrence of these particular rhymes. Classifying rhymes by thematic content has presented problems because in addition to being so diverse, content is one of the more unstable features of the utterance: for example, in the variants of one jump rope rhyme, touching the ground and turning around are variously associated with humans or non-humans, with Teddy Bear, Butterfly, Lady, or Betty (Abrahams, 1969b: 180).

Some classifications involve a developmental scheme. Browne uses complexity, both of rhymes and jumps, as the basis for his scheme:

The inexperienced jumpers generally prefer the simpler forms and take up the more complicated forms as their experience grows. The very beginners often do not jump to rhymes oʳ any kind, but count 1, 2, 3, 4, . . . , until they miss. The simplest kind of rhyme is a short verse used to introduce this counting. . . . In another very simple rhyme the letters of the alphabet are recited to determine the name of the jumper's sweetheart. . . . As the jumpers gain skill, the complexity of the rhymes and jumps increases. . . . The final degree of intricacy comes when the jumper must practice pantomime. The pantomime varies in degree of complexity. . . . The more experienced jumper often chants intricate rhymes in which the rhymes and not the jumps are important. These I have grouped in the category "Straight Narrative." The preceding classification can be reduced to three categories: (1) counting, reciting the alphabet, and pepper; (2) pantomiming; (3) "Straight Narrative," which offers primarily a chant for the children to jump to. (1955: 4–5)

Other developmental schemes are related to thematic features in addition to formal features and will be discussed further below (see Cooperative Research Project, 1968; Muir, 1965; Wolfenstein, 1954).

Most of these attempts at classification have been largely the result of the collectors' efforts to find systematic ways of filing collected texts in archives or of arranging the materials for publication and have thus been a reflex of the collecting impulse which has dominated the study of children's speech play.

English language collections of speech play by or for children appeared as early as the seventeenth century although isolated examples had been appearing sporadically in literature for hundreds of years previous (see Opie and Opie, 1951). To this day collections far outnumber studies or analyses, as is evident from the Bibliography. Unfortunately, most collections indicate neither the age nor the sex of the child and therefore cannot be used for developmental studies. Many collectors do indicate the date the items were recorded and the places they were found. As a result, these collections lend themselves to historical and distributional studies. Appropriately, the earliest and most numerous studies are historically oriented. In their search for origin and meaning, scholars traced the appearance of nursery rhymes through earlier adult historical and political writings, collections of ballads, broadsides, popular songs or dramas (Chambers, 1841; Eckenstein, 1906; Opie and Opie, 1951); speculated about the diffusion of the rhymes; or followed the survivalist route to postulate mythological or ritual origins for the rhymes (Spence, 1947) or to hypothesize about their descent from "higher levels of culture" (see also Georges, 1969: 1–6). In each case children's rhymes were viewed as a degeneration of earlier utterances. Some attention has been focused upon empirically investigating questions of distribution and variation (Opie and Opie, 1959, 1969; Bolton, 1888; Brewster, 1952; Ainsworth, 1961; Enäjärvi-Haavio, 1932); although, with the exception of the Opies and Enäjärvi-

Haavio, this has often meant little more than annotations which cite previous, printed collections where the item appeared.

More recently, the historical approach has been directed toward the study of change in the game repertoire and game preferences of children over a period of several generations or decades (Yoffie, 1947; Sutton-Smith, 1968a; Sutton-Smith and Rosenberg, 1961; Jablow and Withers, 1965; see also Knapp and Knapp, 1973). One important trend is away from games involving physical skills and toward verbal games or the verbal aspects of older games (Sutton-Smith, 1968a: 188). Sutton-Smith has shown that the singing games and dialogue games so popular among young girls at the turn of the century have almost disappeared, but that:

The part of the old singing games that have continued most abundantly in other game forms, however, are the rhythm and rhymes. Grade-school children still have as many rhyming and rhythmic games as did children in the nineteenth century, but the major vehicles of expression are now the jump-rope, ball bouncing, and counting-out rhymes, rather than the singing games, as used to be the case. The girls in most schools can still provide the collector with some twenty to thirty jump-rope rhymes, and about the same number of other rhymes of various sorts. . . . (1968a: 184)

The old singing games to which Sutton-Smith refers are the same as the ones described by Willa Muir, who remembers that at the turn of the century in Scotland, working class girls between eleven and thirteen years of age used to play singing games in the school playtime (1965: 13–14). Participation in these games coincided with puberty. By the age of fourteen the children generally left school to enter the adult world. Muir points out that the lyrics to these singing games resemble the ballads sung by adults in the community. She also notes that middle class girls in the fee-paying school she later attended did not play these games. Thus age, sex, and social class were important factors in determining which children played this type of game (see also Sutton-Smith, 1959c).

As Bess Hawes has documented in her film, "Pizza Pizza Daddy-O" (1969), these singing games are still very popular in rural and urban areas among Afro-American girls, nine to ten years of age. In her discussion of the origins of these singing games, Hawes suggests that in over half the cases the lyrics are British, the other half being American, but that "stylistically, especially in terms of musical and kinesic elements, they seem equally clearly African, or at least Afro-American" (1969: 3). According to Hawes, "The total tradition [of singing games] is at present the exclusive cultural property of black American children" (1969: n.p.).

To account for the demise of the singing games among white American children, Sutton-Smith observes:

It is clear that if the modern American playground is less turbulent than its forerunners with respect to physical skills, it does seem to be a much freer place with respect to its *verbal games*—or to the verbal aspects of older games as we have already seen in the case of jump-rope. If one were to point out a single feature that distinguishes today's children from their forebearers, it would have to be their verbal facility. Encouraged by a more permissive form of education, by a greater freedom in their homes, and by the stimulation of movies, comics, radio, and television, today's children are both socially more mature and verbally more sophisticated. Which means that the collector of child lore often gets many more riddles, rhymes, and jokes than he does games. One is tempted to say that children today do not, to the same extent, need to have games to structure their social relationships. They are socially so much more mature that many of their relationships can be carried on in conversational terms. (1968a: 188)

That today's white children do not continue to play the old singing and dialogue games so popular years ago can be easily documented but more problematic are assertions regarding what nineteenth century children did not do. As indicated above, nineteenth century collections are highly selective because they were based for the most part on the memory of adults regarding their childhood; no distinction between nursery and true children's lore was observed; and only examples which were aesthetically pleasing and inoffensive by the standards of Victorian England were selected for publication. Hence the absence of obscenity in early collections. However, our sample does confirm Sutton-Smith's comments regarding the nature of the repertoire of white children today.

In addition to analyzing changes in the childlore of English-speaking children over a period of several decades, Sutton-Smith has examined the play repertoire and preferences of children in various age groups (1968a), socioeconomic strata and subcultures (1959c; n.d.), and cultures (Roberts and Sutton-Smith, 1962). See also Seagoe (1962). On the basis of such comparisons he has found, for example, that the presence of and emphasis upon speech play, competitive games, and imaginative play can vary considerably from one culture or subculture to another. Sutton-Smith (n.d.) cities Smilansky's study, *The Effects of Socio-Dramatic Play on Disadvantaged Pre-School Children* (1968), which compares three- to five-year-old American children from achievement-oriented middle class groups on the one hand and from tradition-oriented Asiatic groups on the other. Smilansky found:

whereas only 3 percent of the achievement group showed no play at all, 60 percent of the traditional group showed no play. The differences in imitative role play were not great with approximately 20 percent of each group showing play of this sort. On the other hand, when compared for sociodramatic play (which involves others, talking, and make believe with situations, etc.) only 11 percent of the traditional group and 78 percent of the achievement group participated. The verbalization differences were equally striking. The achievement group used more words, a greater variety of words, longer sentences, longer statements. (Cited by Sutton-Smith, n.d.: 14)

More comparative work is needed on the speech play of children in different socioeconomic strata and subcultures.

A classic study of the age factor in children's speech play is Martha Wolfenstein's *Children's Humor: A Psychological Analysis* (1954) in which she analyzes how children's joke preferences and performances vary according to their age. Wolfenstein interviewed 145 children in two New York City private schools. The children ranged in age from four to seventeen and were mainly from Jewish professional families. Wolfenstein's developmental scheme accounts for changes in the joke's overall form and style, in what she calls the "joke facade," in type of wordplay as well as in children's increasing understanding of jokes as they gradually learn to discriminate between joking and nonjoking discourse. With reference to the joke's form, she found that an important transition occurred "from improvisation of original joking fantasies to the learning and telling of ready-made jokes" when the child is about six years old and the latency period has begun (1954: 16). According to Wolfenstein, the characteristic joke form of the latency period is the riddle:

> With striking punctuality children seem to acquire a store of joking riddles at the age of six. As one six-year-old girl remarked: "We didn't know any of these jokes last year." At six or seven about three times as many joking riddles are told as jokes in any other form. In the following three years the percentage of riddles is a little over half. At eleven and twelve it is reduced to a third; riddles are being discarded in favor of anecdotes. Children from six to eleven are apt to use the terms "riddle" and "joke" interchangeably. Asked to define a riddle a seven-year-old boy says: "If people have riddles—like the moron jokes, jokes are riddles." (1954: 94)

The joking riddle tends to be a short verbal formula requiring only verbatim repetition: "the words spoken rather than the manner of speaking tend to be exclusively important" (Wolfenstein, 1954: 145). When the child is eleven or twelve years old he tells jokes in anecdotal form with greater frequency and joke telling shifts from verbatim repetition of a formula to artistic performance. The ingenuity of the teller comes increasingly into play as he develops a sense of tale structure and learns to handle reported dialogue, mimicry, timing, and other narrative skills (Wolfenstein, 1954: 144; see also Pitcher and Prelinger, 1963). The shift from the joking riddle form to the anecdote, from formulaic question to traditional narrative, is also accompanied by important stylistic changes; in developing their skill as narrators, children are observed to express themselves more indirectly, to use more allusion in order to maximize this indirectness, and to elaborate more.

Increasing indirectness of expression is part of the child's growing skill in formulating the joke facade which, in turn, is a way of maintaining the separation between the narrator and the characters in the joke. The joke facade gradually increases in complexity as the child develops:

Let us sum up the phases in the development of the joke facade which we have observed. For a four-year-old, throwing water on someone is a joke. The only indirectness is the substitution of water for urine. A five-year-old tells a "dirty joke" in which a little boy makes a pee-pee all over the floor. A seven-year-old tells the story of the little bear, in which the urgency to make water is justified by the unreasonable restrictions of the adults. The conflict with, and rebellion against authority enters into the joke content. An earlier element is retained in the actual wetting, which, however, is performed in a surprising way towards a victim who has been beguiled into foolish unwariness by the story. (Wolfenstein, 1954: 167)

The indirectness of the joke can be further maximized by wordplay, both puns and rhyme. *Punning,* or playing on double meanings, allows the child to say something tabooed while appearing to say something harmless: "An allusive formulation insures immunity since nothing objectionable has been said. The teller may disclaim responsibility for what the hearer thinks" (Wolfenstein, 1954: 168). In such joking attacks as "I'm the king of the castle and you're the dirty rascal" the use of *rhyme* is supposed to reduce the speaker's responsibility for what he is saying because of the tendency of the first rhyming word to have "the effect of compelling the utterance of the second" (Wolfenstein, 1954: 182). This is especially easy when the rhyme induces other children to chime in so that the attacker is not alone. These two kinds of speech play—rhyming and punning—are placed in a developmental scheme by Wolfenstein, who observes that young children enjoy playing with sounds for their own sake and only later appreciate punning.

Wolfenstein thereby anticipates what will be major points in our analysis of children's play:

The amusement with rhymes illustrates the early pleasure in playing with words better than puns. Young children enjoy the discovery of sound similarities, but when a shift of meaning is forced on them they are more apt to be distressed, as we have seen. It has been told of Keats that at an early age he used to reply to anything that was said to him by producing a rhyming word and laughing. These early reactions are later reversed. Rhyme becomes mainly a means of serious poetry, intensifying rather than reducing emotion, while it is the shift of meanings which becomes the major verbal gambit of jokes. (Wolfenstein, 1954: 182)

Both the development in children's speech play from the interest in playing with sounds to playing with meaning and Wolfenstein's observation regarding the reversal which takes place in adulthood will be discussed further below.

Six years after Wolfenstein's book was published, Basil Bernstein's review of the Opies' *The Lore and Language of Schoolchildren* appeared. The similarities between Bernstein's and Wolfenstein's discussion of children's lore are striking considering that Wolfenstein adopts a predominently psychoanalytic approach and Bernstein a sociolinguistic perspective. They both stress that the traditionality or "ready-made" character of the rhymes, jokes, taunts, or insults makes the utterances impersonal and therefore helps to insulate or protect the child from full responsibility for what he says. Bernstein views the kind of speech play we will be examining in this paper as "a public language in its pure form" (1960: 180), meaning by "public" that it

continuously signals the normative arrangements of the group rather than the individual experiences of its members.
The language does *not* facilitate the unique verbalization of subjective intent. Its use reinforces solidarity with the group, its functions, roles and aims. (Bernstein, 1960: 179)

According to Bernstein, then, children's traditional speech play influences the organization of the child's experiences and his subsequent behavior, making him "sensitive to role and status and also to the customary relationships connecting and legitimizing the social positions within his peer group" (1960: 179). Consistent with his sociolinguistic approach, Bernstein's concern is with the appropriate use of the various items in the child's repertoire and how the child learns to choose correctly the situation, the timing, tone, and fitness of an utterance (1960: 179). Bernstein's review, although general, is very suggestive and needs to be followed up with an application of his hypotheses to a particular body of data (see also Bateson, 1955).

By and large, however, psychologists and anthropologists have in recent years paid far more attention to games than to speech play even though these games often involve verbal play which could profitably be viewed from similar perspectives. For example, games in general are analyzed as mechanisms for ego development, for socialization (Roberts and Sutton-Smith, 1962), and for the development of strategic competence (Roberts, Sutton-Smith, and Kozelka, 1967). Correlations between game preferences on the one hand and social complexity and type of socialization processes on the other have been analyzed by Roberts, Arth, and Bush (1959) and Roberts and Sutton-Smith (1962).

The analysis of speech play could benefit from the notion of play as a means of enculturation, of games as buffered models of power within which the child can acquire some of the basic performances required by the adult culture (Sutton-Smith, n.d.: 3). This notion is discussed by Bernstein (1960) in more general terms in his review of the Opies and developed by Abrahams (1964; 1968; 1969a; 1969b; 1970e), who explores the idea that expressive behavior in the form of play and games, both verbal and nonverbal, is important in building up and widening the child's repertory of potential future responses (see also Sutton-Smith, 1968a: 181). Abrahams focuses on Afro-American speech play with special reference to such genres as the proverb, riddle, and verbal dueling.

Relevant here is Goldstein's specific analysis (1971) of the strategies which children use to control the chance element in counting out rhymes. Because Goldstein examines the activity of counting out *as it is actually played* by a given group of children, he can show how "the stated rules relate to the actual rules used in playing the games" (Goldstein, 1971: 169). Similarly, the Gump and Sutton-Smith analysis (1955) of the *It* role in children's games grounds more general, theoretical concerns in empirical observation of how certain types of games are *actually* played in order to show the effect of the power of the *It* role and other factors on the experience of the game participants. Such empirical studies of games as played in fact, rather than in principle, provide the basis for examining precisely *how* games affect the development of children.

Anthropological linguists have addressed themselves occasionally to the speech play and verbal art of adults and children mostly as it exists in non-Western societies (Hymes, 1964a: 291–381), although studies specifically of children's speech play are sadly lacking. One exception is

Mary Haas's study of Thai word games (1957) which shows the importance of speech play in the socialization of children in a bilingual setting. Her work on Burmese disguised speech (1969) and her taxonomy of disguised speech (1967) are important contributions to the identification, classification, and linguistic analysis of these forms of speech play (see also Sherzer, et al., 1971). Conklin's analysis of Hanumoo and Tagalog methods of modifying the normal patterns of speech for purposes of entertainment or concealment (1956, 1959) are of special importance because of the emphasis upon cultural context in the analysis of the relationship of modes of speech to social roles. Recently, Sherzer's work on Cuna play languages (1970) explores the implications of modifying the normal pattern of speech, for problems in linguistic theory such as the sociological reality of phonological descriptions. Nevertheless, with some exceptions, the emphasis has been placed upon adult speech play rather than that of children and upon languages other than English.

Problematic, although suggestive, is R. Burling's (1966) cross-cultural analysis of the meter of nursery rhymes and his conclusions that 16-beat verses are extraordinarily widespread if not universal, being found in English, Chinese, Bengulu, Yoruba, Cairo Arabic, and Serrano. Unfortunately, Burling does not differentiate *children's rhymes* from *nursery rhymes* and uses the terms synonymously. More important, overgeneralizations, selectivity of examples, and an overly simplified analysis of meter make his findings problematic. (For a careful analysis of English language meter in poetry and nursery rhymes, see Malof, 1970: 92–137; see also Guéron, 1974.)

The social scientific approaches to the study of children's speech play described above are based for the most part on functional-psychological models. We would like to consider here an approach in which children's verbal play is viewed in relation to the formal language model on which it is based. Accordingly, we will now discuss the structural features of the child's language.

## Characteristics of the child's developing language system

Children's speech play may be fruitfully analyzed in light of studies on phonological and semantic or conceptual structure and on the child's emerging syntax. To account for the speech of the adult native-speaker of any language, we need a generative description based on his underlying competence (e.g., Chomsky, 1957, 1965). Just what such a description must include is still in the process of being worked out (see, for example, the papers and references in Bach and Harms, 1968; Silverstein, 1972; and Postal, 1974). However, we do know some of the features which they must have. The following is a brief summary of the main points concerning the nature of the component parts of an adequate description of any language.

The language competence which will generate an infinite set of well-formed sentences or discourses in any language is represented as consisting first of levels or components. These may be called morpho-phonological, syntactic, semantic, and sociolinguistic. An adult speaker constructing an utterance puts together elements from the different levels of the language according to the rules that organize them in his model. There are two kinds of relations which organize elements on each of these levels: syntagmatic and paradigmatic. Syntagmatic relations govern the concatenation of elements on each level or the linear organization of elements, for example, noun phrase + verb phrase or modifier + modified. Concatenation order rules govern the syntagmatic organization of lexemes on the syntactic level within the larger unit customarily called a "sentence." In contrast, paradigmatic relations hold among members of a class which have the same syntagmatic function on any level of the language; for example, *mother, brother, sister, father* are all members of a paradigm. They all have the same syntactic function and are defined and distinguished by different combinations of semantic features.

Until recently, traditional Transformational-Generative theory has recognized the "sentence" as the largest unit of language production and the semantic as the "highest" component in the language system. In terms of this conceptualization, the "sentence" is the largest syntagmatic plan that people need to organize. However, work in ethnoscience (e.g., Metzger and Williams, 1963), narrative analysis (Propp, 1968; Labov and Waletsky, 1967; Sacks, 1972), the ethnography of communication (Hymes, 1964a, 1967, 1971a), and sociolinguistics (Ervin-Tripp, 1967; Schegloff, 1968) suggest that we must recognize units larger than a sentence—perhaps a "topic," "speech event," or "theme"—to account for adult language productions adequately. In terms of the priority of organization, an individual seems to choose first some overall semantically determined topic or theme, then its syntactic expression, and finally the morphophonological realization it will take.

Much of what characterizes children's language and its variation from adult language can be expressed quantitatively; for example, children's language is syntagmatically both shorter and less complex than adults'. Thus, if we make a series of "generative" models on which to base the child's speech productions, we find that the first of these, appropriate for a child who is about two, will only have to generate one word per "utterance." A short while later, we will have to expand the model in order to generate two-word and three-word utterances, that is, to incorporate more syntactic classes into the generative machinery. Both the length of the child's utterances and their complexity will increase rapidly until, by about age three or four, he has mastered much of the basic syntactic structure of the language. The earliest syntactic structure involves only the concatenation of two, then three and more syntactic classes as defined by distributional privileges of occurrence. As these simple syntactic structures gradually differentiate, the child gains mastery of devices like subordination and embedding.

Studies of children's emerging grammars indicate the complexity of language acquisition. As Blount (1975) explains in a review of recent studies of child language, researchers working on the earliest phases of grammatical development now recognize the importance of early semantic development as a basis for acquisition of syntax. Somewhat later the child begins the process of developing productive competence in the word-internal, morphological features of his language, for example, inflection and derivation. These features are only partially developed long after the child has mastered the essentials of syntax. As semantic relations and syntactic classes expand, the child's lexicon increases, and with it the complexity of his semantic structure. From early on, the child has begun to master rules and structures of the "sociolinguistic component" of the language. This involves not only features which encode social information but also features and rules for appropriate style and sometimes code-switching between languages. (See Halliday [1974] for an approach to the whole of language development in terms of social functions, and Keenan [1974] for observations stressing the social, and playful, character of early speech.)

According to the kind of model outlined above, the primary difference between adult and child language is *quantitative* and involves the *number* of rules and elements in the system. However, other evidence, much of it indirect, indicates that the child's "storage" system is *qualitatively* different from adults' and that to generate "child speech," the language model must contain design features which are not just quantitatively different from those of an adult.

Firstly, for a young child—and progressively less so for older children—the *phonological* component of language is much more strongly organized than the syntactic, semantic, or sociolinguistic. Supporting evidence comes from a variety of studies, some of it as an incidental by-product of investigations motivated by a view of language quite different from that acceptable to current linguistic theory. Exemplary are studies of "semantic conditioning" (for example, Razran, 1961; Riess, 1946). In these types of experiments, investigators trained subjects to produce a standard physical response to a given word, for example, to salivate when they heard the word *cat*. Then they observed how the conditioned response (salivation) would generalize to other words, that is, the extent to which subjects salivated to words which were phonologically similar to *cat*, for example, *mat* and *hat* as compared to *dog* or *lion*, words which are semantically similar to *cat*. They found that for young children and feeble-minded persons as contrasted to normal adults, the conditioned responses tended to generalize to words whose similarity to the original stimulus word was determined by features of *sound* rather than by grammatical and semantic features.

There is also evidence in support of this view from studies consciously aimed at exploring the language structure of children. Stross (1970) administered an elicited imitation test to children from ages two to thirteen who learned Tzeltal Mayan as their first language. He concluded:

The Tzeltal imitations include many mistakes that are the result of interference from sounds and sound sequences. . . . These are inversely correlated with the age of the child. . . . The mistakes are often triggered by sound, particularly for younger children. The older ones do sometimes exhibit interference from previous sentences, but more often than not they are triggered by similarities of meaning or from words and phrases belonging to earlier models. . . . (1970: 323)

That children enjoy playing with sound for its own sake has long been recognized as a prominent feature of child speech. Weir's 1962 study of her own son's bedtime monologues demonstrates this beautifully. Her analysis of the function and importance of the phonological structure as a generating principle in the child's speech is worth quoting in full. She first says that "there are a great number of instances in the child's monologues where play with the sounds of the language is basic in the hierarchy of language functions . . ." (Weir, 1962: 103). Her analysis of several monologues illustrates and supports her point:

We have to explain the history of our next example before analyzing it. Anthony was particularly fond of his blankets, and they seemed to mean a good deal to him. He was rarely seen without carrying one around with him or being near one. He also liked to watch his mother grooming herself and he knew all the necessary items for it. The lipstick left a very definite impression on him, and he decided that a certain corner of a certain blanket was like a lipstick. He knew exactly which corner it was, and he never made a mistake. He asked for or identified spontaneously *the blanket like a lipstick* during the day, a sentence which occurs frequently in the monologues as well, without apparent connection with preceeding or following context. To assign this a primarily referential function would be a mistake. That this expression is sound play becomes apparent upon closer examination. Breaking the longer sentence down into three units each starting with a strong stress, we arrive at a striking picture of interplay of stops and /1/, diagrammed as follows:

|         |    |   |     |
|---------|----|---|-----|
| blanket | bl | n | kt  |
| like a  | l  |   | k   |
| lipstick| l  | p | stk |

The occurrence of /1/ and /k/, in this order, is central to this sentence, occurring in every one of its parts, and it is what ties the shorter phrase. The longer one is tied even more intricately in that in the first part the bilabial /b/ precedes the /1/ and the alveolar /t/ follows the /k/ whereas in the third part the bilabial /p/ follows the /1/ and the alveolar /t/ precedes the /k/, reversing the order. The feature of voicing in the bilabial is lacking here due to its neutralization before the voiceless /s/. Two identical vowel phonemes also occur in /blEnkEt/ and /lIpstIk/, giving the sentence even more internal unity. (Weir, 1962: 104)

Therefore we would have to account for the priority of the phonological structure over both the semantic and grammatical in order to generate a "child" utterance, particularly that of a young child as distinct from an adult, and to determine the "connectedness" of the parts of the utterance.

Secondly, evidence from several studies suggest that children's *semantic* storage is significantly different from adults'. Bruner and Olver (1963) presented lists of "concept items" to children of different ages and told them to group together all the ones they thought were "similar." Then they asked the children *why* they put together the particular items they did and considered the children's responses as "grouping strategies." The most important strategies proved to be "superordinate," "complex formation," and "thematic grouping":

(1) "Superordinate: Items are grouped on the basis of one or more attributes common to them all" (Bruner and Olver, 1963: 32).

(2) "Complex formation: in which the subject uses selected attributes of the array without subordinating the entire array to any one attribute or to any set of attributes" (Bruner and Olver, 1963: 32).

(3) "Thematic grouping: The child puts things together according to the construction of functionally or temporally arranged activity. For example: the sequence, *coat, sweater, umbrella, house, infection,*

yielded the following . . . thematic grouping: 'If you get an infection, you wouldn't go out of the house but if you did, you'd take an umbrella if it were drizzling and wear a coat and sweater'" (Bruner and Olver, 1963: 132).

TABLE 1 *Children's Grouping Strategies*

|  | Grade | | |
| --- | --- | --- | --- |
|  | 1 | IV | VI |
| superordinate | 65 | 103 | 121 |
| complex | 57 | 30 | 18 |
| no grouping | 18 | 7 | 1 |

Bruner and Olver found that the kind of strategies children used varied with age. Younger children were more prone to use no grouping strategy or a strategy based on association complexes, while older children used superordinate groupings more. A quantitative summary of these findings from their data is shown in Table 1 (Bruner and Olver, 1963: 134).

Vygotsky also established a developmental sequence for the child's semantic system, but based his conclusions on observation rather than hypothesis testing. His categories involve the relations holding between signs and their referents. According to Vygotsky, the "stages" in the process of developing "true" concepts, that is, semantic categories defined in terms of criterial attributes, include "unorganized congeries," "complexes," and "concepts."

(1) The "unorganized congeries" or "heap" stage. At this stage, a word's meaning denotes to the child nothing more than "a vague syncretic conglomeration of individual objects that have somehow or other coalesced into an image in his mind. Because of its syncretic origin, that image is highly unstable" (Vygotsky, 1962: 60).

(2) "Thinking in complexes." Vygotsky distinguishes five types, including pseudo-concepts.

(a) Associative complexes. These "may be based on any bond the child notices between the sample object and some other. . . . In building an association complex, the child may add one block to the nuclear object because it is of the same color, another because it is similar to the nucleus in shape or in size, or in any other attribute that happens to strike him. Any bond between the nucleus and another object suffices to make the child include that object in the

group and to designate it by the common 'family name'"
(Vygotsky, 1962: 62).

(b) Collections. "Objects are placed together on the basis of some one trait in which they differ and consequently complement one another" or "on the basis of their participation in the same practical operation—or their functional cooperation. . . . The child would pick out objects differing from the sample in color, or in form, or in size, or in some other characteristic. He did not pick them up at random; he chose them because they contrasted with and complimented the one attribute of the sample which he took to be the basis of grouping" (Vygotsky, 1962: 63).

(c) Chain complexes. These are "a dynamic, consecutive joining of individual links into a single chain, with meaning carried over from one link to the next. The chain complex has no nucleus (unlike the associative complex); there are relations between single elements, but nothing more" (Vygotsky, 1962: 64).

(d) Diffuse complexes. In this case, "perceptually concrete groups of objects or images are formed by means of diffuse indeterminate bonds. To go with a yellow triangle, for example, a child would in our experiments pick out trapezoids as well as triangles because they made him think of triangles with their tops cut off. Trapezoids would lead to squares, squares to hexagons, hexagons to semi-circles, and finally to circles" (Vygotsky, 1962: 65).

(e) Pseudo-concepts. In these, "the generalization formed in the child's mind, although phenotypically resembling the adult concept, is psychologically very different from the concept proper; in its essence, it is still a complex" (Vygotsky, 1962: 66).

(3) "Concepts." As with complexes, Vygotsky distinguishes several bases for concepts. Complexes and concepts are differentiated by Vygotsky as follows:

The principal function of complexes is to establish bonds and relationships. Complex thinking begins the unification of scattered impressions; by organizing discrete elements into groups, it creates a basis for later generalizations.

But the advanced concept presupposes more than unification. To form such a concept it is also necessary *to abstract, to single out* elements apart from the totality of the concrete experience in which they are embedded. (Vygotsky, 1962: 76)

The development from thinking in complexes and pseudo-concepts to using true concepts is successfully accomplished when "the fusion of the two planes of speech, semantic and vocal, begins to break down as the child grows older and the distance between them gradually increases" (Vygotsky, 1962: 129).

Three other studies, using methods different from Bruner and Olver (1963) and Vygotsky (1962), who stressed grouping strategies and concept formation, also corroborate the idea that the structure of the child's semantic system is different from adults'. The first of these is the Feifel and Lorge (1950) study, in which investigators asked nine hundred children age six through fourteen for "definitions" of a group of forty-five words from the Form L Stanford-Binet Vocabulary test. They classified the children's responses into four types: (1) synonyms; (2) use and descriptions (e.g., something you do with it or a characteristic feature); (3) explanation (e.g., "priceless = it's worth a lot of money"); and (4) responses consisting of "demonstration, illustration, inferior explanation, and repetition." These were included together because "empirical analysis indicated that they occurred at about the same developmental level" (Feifel and Lorge, 1950: 4).

Viewed in terms of their underlying language structure, these response strategies indicate that the first type of response, providing a synonym, involves selecting a lexeme from the same grammatical class as the stimulus-word and referring to a higher node in a taxonomic structure for a superordinate category, or specifying the features, often distinctive, of the category: for example, responding to *orange* with *a fruit* or to *gown* with *long dress*. In the second type of response, "use and description," the child selects a functional feature, such as how it is used, or a noncriterial attribute as the most salient aspect of the category represented by the concept being defined. A response to *orange* might be *you eat it* (Feifel and Lorge, 1950: 4). As in this example, these features are not necessarily criterial attributes of the concepts. The third type of response, "explanation," resembles the "synonym" type except that instead of just one-word definitions, the child gives a phrase, possibly mentioning several features of the concept. The authors found that the type of responses varied over age as indicated in Figure 1 (Feifel and Lorge, 1950: 9).

As Figure 1 shows, even though some children of the youngest age group used the "synonym" response and some of the oldest responded in terms of "use and description" of the stimulus word, the overall frequency of each type of response changed from one age group to another. Therefore, although all four types of responses occur at about the same developmental level, they vary in frequency. Response types 1

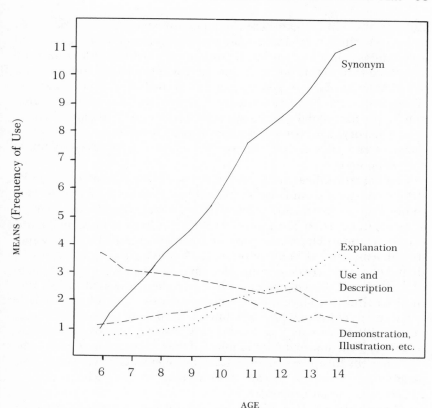

FIGURE 1: *Mean frequency of use of four qualitative categories by age (adapted from Feifel and Lorge, 1950: 9)*

("synonyms") and 3 ("explanations"), which represent referral of the stimulus concept to a structure based on both grammatical and semantic categories, are used very infrequently at first and then more often as the child grows older. In the case of the synonym type of response, the increased frequency is very dramatic. In contrast, the most frequent responses for the younger children were in categories 2 ("use and description" definitions) and 4 ("demonstration, illustration, . . ."), that is, those which required referral to a complementary grammatical class or associated nonessential characteristic of the category.

The word-association studies of Woodworth (cited in Brown and Berko, 1960) provide some data which replicate part of the Feifel and Lorge study. Woodworth reports that in word-association tests with both children and adults there were two types of responses: (a) associations to lexemes which were drawn from the same grammatical class and (b) associations to lexemes whose relations to the stimulus word could only be defined in terms of complementation in a grammatical construction. Stated in terms of the response categories of the Feifel and Lorge study, Woodworth's first kind of response is the "synonym" and "explanation" type; his second resembles Feifel and Lorge's "use and description" category. The results of Woodworth's word-association studies showed that children favor the second type of response while adults prefer the first.

Additional verification of this finding was made by Brown and Berko (1960), who were stimulated by the findings of Woodworth and devised an innovative experiment. They calculated that given first the changes in associations from those determined by reference to phonological features to those determined by reference to grammatical structure and, second, a new speech element presented in the context of a sentence, it should be possible to determine what an individual is going to do with it. They found, in agreement with the studies discussed above, that children tended to store the new element on the basis of its syntactic function in a construction, e.g., stimulus = *to send;* response = *away, a card.* With increasing age, the children gradually approximated adult responses. This approximation indicated they were learning to store the new element in a class along with other elements having the same paradigmatic features instead of with elements with which they occurred in grammatical constructions.

These studies on phonological and semantic or conceptual structure, along with what we know about the child's emerging syntax, can provide a fruitful background for the analysis of children's speech play. We will try to specify how and why this should be so.

Although functional and psychological studies are of value, they do not give us the necessary and sufficient conditions for the occurrence of the particular form taken by children's speech play productions, that is, they do not explain just how and why, in a mechanical, predictable way, children's speech play forms are different from adult verbal art. In addition, although there has been some interest in writing generative statements of adult verbal art (Propp, 1968; Köngas-Maranda, 1971; Bremond, 1966; Lord, 1960; Rosenberg, 1970), these formulations are not quite adequate for children's productions. It never seems to have been recognized that the differences between children's speech play and adult verbal art productions are determined primarily by the differences in the language structures upon which they are based.

What we want to show in the following section is that examples of children's speech play, in contrast with corresponding examples of adult verbal art, can be best understood in terms of characteristics of the children's language models uncovered in the studies described above.

## Children's speech play from the perspective of child language structure

Although child language, as contrasted with adult language, has been investigated in its own terms, as we reviewed above, children's speech play productions continue to be viewed from the same perspective as adults'. Several scholars have noted that children's speech play shares with adult forms the characteristics of all verbal art, what Jakobson calls the *poetic function* of language (1960) and defines as "situations in which the shape of the message becomes the focus of attention, perhaps exploited for its own sake" (Hymes, 1964b: 291). The poetic function is said to operate at all levels of language —morphophonological, syntactic, semantic, and sociolinguistic. Literary scholars commonly discuss the poetic function in terms of "figures of speech" and "rhetorical devices"; more specifically, they analyze alliteration, repetition, rhyme, meter, punning, metaphor, imagery, etc. Being rich in such features, children's rhymes are said to have "their own complete little beauty if looked at closely" (de la Mare in Opie and Opie, 1951: 2) and to be "nearer to poetry than the greater part of the *Oxford Book of English Verse*" (Graves in Opie and Opie, 1951: 2). In fact, the poetic function has even been cited as being responsible for the major characteristics of child speech as it differs from adult speech. Weir's analysis of the bedtime monologues of her two-year-old son exemplifies this notion (Weir, 1962), as discussed above. Although children's speech play forms obviously do exhibit the poetic function, as does all verbal art, we do not think that it is the poetic function per se which distinguishes child and adult speech productions, whether "ordinary" or "artistic." First, the *degree of poetic function* in child as opposed to adult *ordinary discourse* is an open question. Second, the *form of children's speech play* is significantly different from adult verbal art and these contrasts can be accounted for by differences in the language structure upon which they are based.

In sharing the poetic function with adult verbal art forms, children's speech play uses principles which, with important modifications, are employed by adults in more extended productions. These are the same basic devices which have been codified and labeled in rhetoric handbooks whose purpose was to teach adults to speak and write effectively: the rhetoric handbook constituted an adult metalanguage. Corroboratively, there are some instances where it can be shown that particular children's rhymes are derived historically from adult productions such as a popular song or broadside ballad. In such cases the resulting children's rhyme often tends to be changed in ways which resemble the systematic reduction of child language noted by Brown and Fraser (1964), for example. In discussing how children vary traditional rhymes, the Opies observe:

Thus, we find that variations, even apparently creative ones, occur more often by accident than by design. Usually they come about through mishearing or misunderstanding, as in the well-known hymnal misapprehension:

> Can a woman's tender care
> Cease towards the child she-bear?

A line in the song "I'm a knock-kneed sparrow" quickly becomes "I'm a cockney sparrow." "Calico breeches," no longer familiar to youth today, become "comical breeches." "Elecampane" becomes "elegant pain." "Green gravel, green gravel" becomes by association "greengages, greengages." And the unmeaning "alligoshee, alligoshee," in the marching game is rationalized to "Adam and Eve went out to tea." At one school the pledges "die on oath," "dianothe," and "diamond oath" were all found to be current at the same time. . . . Indeed the corruptive influence of the pun on language and custom is more considerable than might be supposed. (Opie and Opie, 1959: 8)

It has been shown that similar modifications occur in adult ballads (Coffin, 1963: 1) and folk songs containing words which have lost currency. The point is not that adults do not modify phonological sequences which are unfamiliar to ones which are familiar, but that (a) the younger child's structure contains fewer lexical and morphological forms on which to map newly heard phonological sequences; and (b) adults and older children, when rendering foreign or archaic sequences into something more familiar, will generally strive to "make sense" of the sequence while young children will sooner accept nonsense.

In the discussion which follows we will summarize the major formal differences between child and adult verbal art and attempt to account for them in terms of the features of child language outlined above: that is, the lesser degree of syntagmatic development, as related to overall lesser short-term memory span; the feature of undeveloped semantic classification; and the relatively greater importance of phonological structure. Our discussion will be divided into two parts: (a) the summary and explication of formal differences between adult and child verbal art in terms of their different language structures, and (b) a comparison of major structural foci of concern in the productions of children of different ages. The second perspective will demonstrate that, as he grows older, the child's concern shifts in the direction of the particular level of the linguistic system he is currently bent on mastering and that the span of his syntagmatic organization increases.

One major characteristic of children's verbal art forms is a rather direct reflection of the limited nature of the child's developing *syntagmatic organization:* in contrast with adult speech play, which ranges from the shortest possible utterances to extended productions lasting for hours, children's verbal art productions are all relatively *short,* ranging from as few as seven words, or even less, to sixty or seventy words at the upper limit. In addition, the stylistic devices children use tend to be structured over shorter spans than those of adults; complex rhyme schemes and complex stanzaic structures are not sustainable. Therefore, a very frequent form found in the children's productions is the rhyming couplet.

There are also occasional striking *irregularities* in rhyme scheme and stanza structure, two features which tend to be highly regular in traditional adult verbal art. These irregularities in children's productions, when they do occur, may be the result of limits on syntagmatic organization of the child's language.

The following traditional rhyme is irregular[1] because, in terms of metrical organization, the couplet structure begins with the second line. The internal rhyme in the first line produces a pseudo-couplet out of two half-lines:

(1)  Caroline Pink, she fell down the sink,
      She caught the scarlet fever
      Her husband had to leave her.
      She called in Doctor Blue
      And he caught it too—
      Caroline Pink from Chinatown.
                    (Abrahams, 1969b: #56)

A regular and common rhyme scheme would be aaaa, aaba, aabb, aabbccdd, whereas in this verse, the scheme is abbccd. Most important, for a regular rhyme scheme the basic couplet structure is maintained,

---

[1]Hymes (personal correspondence, September 16, 1974) suggests that in this rhyme two pairs of 3-beat lines are enclosed by two pairs of 2-beat lines. The repetition of the first line of the first pair sets up the expectation of a rounding off of not only meter but rhyme, but this expectation is defeated. The problem remains in dealing with oral verse of defining the metrical unit or "line."

with the possible exception of the final line which serves to terminate the verse. It would seem as though the child originator(s) of "Caroline Pink" saw its component parts as "Caroline Pink" plus "she fell down the sink" as complete unto itself. "She caught the scarlet fever" plus "Her husband had to leave her" would be the second unit. They apparently did not see the organization of the six lines, each a four-stress metrical unit, as a totality. If the composer(s) of this verse had had sufficient syntagmatic organization to conceptualize the whole form at once, the rhyme scheme would likely have been regular couplets, as is the case in the following typically regular verse:

> (2) Mable, Mable, strong and able,
> Get your elbows off the table.
> We've told you once, we've told you twice,
> We'd never tell you more than thrice.
> (Abrahams, 1969b: #323)

Or the verse would consist of couplets and an odd last line, usually the fifth or the third:

> (3) Mademoiselle went to the well,
> Combed her hair and brushed it well.
> They picked up her basket and vanished.
> (Abrahams, 1969b: #326)

In all three examples, there is internal rhyme in the first line. But in the regular verses, (2) and (3), the couplets proceed from the first four-stress metrical unit, rather than from the second, as in (1).

There are two other features of children's speech play forms which are related to the shorter span of their syntagmatic structure: (a) *concatenations* and (b) *expansion*. Concatenation involves joining a rhyme with another rhyme or with a series or list. These rhymes and series can also occur independently. Most common is the use of fixed-order series, such as the alphabet, numbers, days of the week, months of the year, or lists of members of classes (names of people, places, occupations, kinds of fruit, etc.). These series get attached to the end of a verse by means of such formulas as:

(a) How many (doctors did it take?) / (kisses did she get?) 1, 2, 3, 4, . . .
(b) What's the initial of my sweetheart? A, B, C, D, . . .
(c) It happened on: Monday, Tuesday, . . .
(d) And this is where I went: London, Paris, Saigon, . . .
(e) Tell me when your birthday comes: January, February, . . .

A series of verses which have nothing in common semantically or thematically can get linked together by means of such formulas as:

(a)   And this is what it said to me:
(b)   And the harp began to sing:

Built into many of the children's rhymes are points at which the reciter has an option either to terminate the rhyme or through the use of one of a series of devices, to link it to another rhyme, for example:

(4)   I went downtown
      To see Mrs. Brown.
      She gave me a nickel
      To buy a pickle.
      The pickle was sour,
      She gave me a flower.
      The flower was dead,
      She gave me a thread.
      The thread was thin,
      She gave me a pin.
      The pin was sharp,
      She gave me a harp.
      The harp began to sing. . . .
          (Withers, 1948: 141)

At this point the reciter can (a) finish the rhyme with "Minnie and a minnie and a ha ha ha" or (b) inaugurate another rhyme. For example:

(5)   [And on this harp I played:]
      I love coffee, I love tea.
      How many boys are stuck on me?
          (Brewster, 1952: 177)

(6)   [And on the card it said:]
      "Spanish dancer do the splits,
      Spanish dancer give a high kick,
      Spanish dancer turn around,
      Spanish dancer get out of our town."
          (Speroni, 1942: 1)

In addition to being easily "tacked on" at the end of a verse, series and lists are based on an unalterable memorized sequence and therefore allow the child to generate an extended production composed of repeated small segments, for example:

* (7) A hundred bottles of beer on the wall,
A hundred bottles of beer,
If one of those bottles should happen to fall
There'd be ninety-nine bottles of beer on the wall.

Ninety-nine bottles of beer on the wall,
Ninety-nine bottles of beer,
If one of those bottles should happen to fall
There'd be ninety-eight bottles of beer on the wall.

Ninety-eight bottles of beer on the wall, . . .

This type of device enables a child to produce a form longer than one which his syntagmatic span would normally allow by as many times as there are items in the sequence. In some cases, as with the set of natural numbers, this could extend to the upper limit of the child's counting capacity. In other cases, as with the days of the week or months of the year, the series has its own limitations. In still others, the lengths depend on the number of participants present and the extent to which children are prepared to call upon the same people repeatedly, for example:

* (8) On a mountain stands a lady.
Who she is I do not know.
I will ask her hand in marriage,
Will she answer yes or no?
O, rise [name of child], rise,
And close both your eyes,
And turn to the east,
And turn to the west,
And point to the very one that you love best.

The child named proceeds to select someone from the circle of players, who takes his place in the center. The verse is then repeated with the name of the child now in the center being used. Indeed, Browne (1955: 4–5), as mentioned above, proposes a developmental scheme: the younger children rely on these series, especially counting and the alphabet, much more than do older children, who recite more intricate rhymes involving pantomime and narrative.

---

* Those verses marked with an asterisk are ones which B. Kirshenblatt-Gimblett remembers from her childhood.

Another feature of the child's language structure which determines differences between the child's speech play forms and that of adults lies in the organization of the semantic system. The technical figure of speech employed in example (4) above ("I went downtown/To see Mrs. Brown") is *gradatio*, "linked repetition of words leading to a climax". However, if we compare this production to an adult example utilizing the same rhetorical device we will see a number of critical differences:

(9)   Now what remnant of the hope of liberty survives, if those men *may* do what they *please*, if they *can* do what they *may*, if they *dare* do what they *can*, if they *do* what they *dare*, and if you *approve* what they *do*?

The emphasized words are those which receive cumulative stress from the speaker and create the rhetorical effect of *gradatio*. These lexemes are all members of a semantic paradigm or set, "verbs of volition":

(10)   may
       please
       can
       dare
       do

The speaker plays with the discrete semantic features which determine the differences in meaning between the lexemes in this semantic paradigm and orders them so as to reach a climax.

Omitting for the present the feature of rhyme and the final line in example (4), let us look at the child's example in terms of the kind of associations among the elements in the series. The lexemes which are linked are not members of any semantic paradigm but are associated on the basis of their functioning as complementary parts of speech in a phrase: pickle–sour; flower–dead; thread–thin; pin–sharp; harp–sing. The relations between the various components of this children's rhyme resemble closely the principles upon which children's responses are determined in the word association tests administered by Brown and Berko (1960), which were discussed above: when asked to associate to stimulus words, children will respond more frequently with forms which function complementarily grammatically to the stimulus word in contrast to adults who will respond more frequently with a word which belongs to the same syntactic category as the stimulus word.

Another example in which this type of response is possibly even clearer is the riddle, "Why are fire engines red?" The answer is:

** (11)　One and one are two.
　　　　　Two and two are four.
　　　　　Three times four is twelve.
　　　　　There are twelve inches in a ruler.
　　　　　Queen Mary was a ruler.
　　　　　Queen Mary ruled the sea.
　　　　　There are fish in the sea.
　　　　　The fish have fins.
　　　　　The Finns fought the Russians.
　　　　　The Russians are red.
　　　　　Fire engines are always rushin'.
　　　　　That's why fire engines are red.

The similarity between this riddle and a child's response to why he grouped together an assemblage of semantically unrelated items in a concept formation task is striking: in both, the associations are structurally unmotivated. Rather than a structural feature like same class membership determining a response, chance hearing of the two words used in the same sentence provides the basis for association.

The third characteristic of child language, the importance of *phonological structure*, may be the strongest influence on the shape of early preferred children's speech play forms. In example (4), the selection and sequence of items in the list are also motivated by phonological convergences; each object in the list rhymes with the complement to the preceding object—thread–*thin, pin*–sharp. In example (11), several links are determined by homonomy—$ruler_1$/$ruler_2$, fins/Finns, Russian/rushin'. The child's interest in phonology also helps to account for the high degree of morphophonological patterning generally found in children's speech play productions and for the greater incidence of nonsense in the productions of young children. Let us distinguish between such forms of nonsense as *gibberish* and *jabberwocky*. In gibberish, which is relatively rare in adult verbal play, only the phonological rules are observed: the phonological sequences neither form units which have grammatical function nor lexemes with semantic reference. The following is an example of gibberish:

(12)　Inty, ninty tibbety fig
　　　　Deema dima doma nig

---

** B. Kirshenblatt-Gimblett (Toronto), Dell and Gorwin Hymes (Portland, Oregon), and Carol Silverman (New York City) remember this riddle from their childhoods.

Howchy powchy domi nowday
hom tom tout
Olligo bolligo boo
Out goes you.
　　　　　(Abrahams, 1969b: #254)

In jabberwocky, however, both phonological and syntactic rules are maintained although most of the individual pseudo-lexemes have no meaningful reference. A classic example is Lewis Carroll's poem:

(13)　'Twas brillig, and the slithy toves
　　　　Did gyre and gimble in the wabe;
　　　　All mimsy were the borogoves,
　　　　And the mome raths outgrabe.
　　　　　　　　(Gardner, 1963: 191)

Jabberwocky, unlike gibberish, does seem to appeal to adults rather than to young children and cannot rightfully be included in the latter's speech play productions. Although we have found no examples of jabberwocky in our corpus of children's speech play, older children do play with forms which resemble it, for example, tangletalk, which depends on jumbled syntactic co-occurrence rules. The Opies (1959: 24) recorded an example from a twelve-year-old girl:

(14)　'Twas in the month of Liverpool
　　　　In the city of July,
　　　　The snow was raining heavily,
　　　　The streets were very dry.
　　　　The flowers were sweetly singing,
　　　　The birds were in full bloom,
　　　　As I went down the cellar
　　　　To sweep an upstairs room.
　　　　　　　　(Opie and Opie, 1959: 24)

It is not accidental that young children should employ gibberish which is rhythmic and highly patterned phonologically to a much greater extent than adults, who prefer nonsense that is syntactically determined. Gibberish is purely phonologically motivated and it appeals to younger children because phonology, as compared to semantics and syntax, is far more highly developed in the younger child's language.

　　The importance of phonological structure is manifested in other ways in children's rhymes:

*(15)　Did you eever, iver, over,
　　　　In your leef, life, loaf,

See the deevel, divel, dovel,
Kiss his weef, wife, woaf?

No, I neever, niver, nover,
In my leef, life, loaf,
Saw the deevel, divel, dovel,
Kiss his weef, wife, woaf.

To an adult, this would probably not be thought worth memorizing and producing over and over again. What makes it attractive to a child is the phonological elaboration of the basic statement, "Did you ever in your life see the devil kiss his wife?" followed (in some but not all versions) by, "No, I never in my life saw the devil kiss his wife." *Life* and *wife* rhyme in the second and fourth phrases. On this rather simple rhyme and meter structure is the following embellishment: the consonant frames provided by the last words of lines 1 and 3 [v ɹ] and lines 2 and 4 [f] are triplicated varying the vowel glides [iy], [ay], [ow] in place of the original vowels occurring in the words of the underlying sentences. Thus to understand the message, the hearer must unravel its derivation.

Another example of phonologically determined interest in form is playing with homonyms:

* (16)   Hello, Bill.
  Where you going, Bill?
  Downtown, Bill.
  What for, Bill?
  To pay my gas bill.
  How much, Bill?
  A ten dollar bill.
  So long, Bill.

To an adult, this verse seems rather simple. To a child, however, it may be hilarious. Its appeal stems from the conjunction of (a) the homonymity involved and what this represents to the child and (b) the final position of the homonymous lexemes in the phrases. The emphasis of the child's language on phonology makes disambiguation of these lexemes a far greater problem for him than for an adult, who attends to the grammatical clues or phrases. That $Bill_1$ "personal name," $bill_2$ "an account," and $bill_3$ "a form of currency" are all possible and that more than one instance of $Bill_1$ "personal name" can occur in the world present the child in the process of mastering English with a problem to work out. It may be easy for an adult to keep the referents of these homonyms straight when they co-occur in one speech act, but the child, for whom "similarity" is determined largely by sound, finds it an enticing puzzle.

Pleasure in the incidental resemblance of sequences similar in sound but different in meaning is another indication of the importance of phonology in children's speech play:

* (17)   I scream.
         You scream.
         We all scream
         For ice cream.

The similarity between *I scream* and the casually articulated *ice cream*, in addition to the rhythm, makes funny to a child what hardly seems noteworthy to an adult:

[ayskriym]
[yuwskriym]
[wiyɔlskriym]
[fərayskriym].

In addition to the phonologically determined ambiguity, this verse produces an apparent inflection of the paradigm of person for *scream*, with one pseudo-member, * [fərayskriym], created by a deletion of juncture in casual speech.

The relative overdevelopment of phonology in the child's language would also seem to be responsible for the existence of imperfect puns in their play forms. In the following example, the grammatical functions of the lexemes in the phrases eliminate ambiguity for an adult, but not for a child:

(18)   Do you carrot all for me?
       My heart beets for you.
       With your turnip nose
       And your radish face
       You are a peach.
       If we cantaloupe,
       Lettuce marry,
       Weed make a swell pear.
               (Withers, 1948: 193)

An adult would immediately recognize that *carrot* vs. *care at*, *cantaloupe* vs. *can't elope*, *lettuce* vs. *let us*, *turnip* vs. *turned up*, and *weed* vs. *we'd* are not ambiguous. The members of each pair are not of equal lexemic status: the first member of the pair is a single lexeme while the second is two lexemes. In addition, each member of the pairs listed above are different "parts of speech" and function differently syntactically: they could not be used interchangeably. Only one reading, the second one in each case listed above, will qualify syntactically as part of a well-formed sentence in the language.

In contrast to example (18), with its "children's puns," "true puns" require that perfectly homonymous elements be used to produce two well-formed syntactic representations and thus two possible semantic interpretations

(19)  "Many a blonde $\begin{Bmatrix} \text{dies} \\ \text{dyes} \end{Bmatrix}$ by her own hand" (Esar, 1952: 77).

We know of no example of a "true pun" which is both intelligible and interesting to a young child (see also Wolfenstein's corroboration of this point, 1954: 182): on the contrary, example (18) suggests that *close phonological resemblance* (combined here with the iteration of members of a botanical taxonomy) satisfies the child. Since his language structure is as yet relatively undeveloped at the syntactic and semantic levels, the young child would likely find the disambiguation of a true pun too difficult, even distressing (Wolfenstein, 1954: 182).

The foci of children's speech play, that is, whether the form is dominated mainly by phonological, grammatical, semantic, or sociolinguistic concerns, reflect an exercise in whatever part of the language structure the child is currently mastering. Accordingly, different levels of the language structure are "played with" in the different instances. In a number of the examples presented here—(12), (15), and (17)—phonological relations dominate, especially the segmental features of phonology. The following rhyme shows the child's concern with suprasegmental features, namely, stress and juncture:

*(20)

pi co lo mi ni pi co lo mi ni     pi co lo mi ni pi co

lo mi ni pi co lo mi ni pi co lo mi ni pi co lo mi ni pi

co lo mi ni pi co lo mi ni pi co lo mi ni pi co lo mi ni

The metrical pattern is not congruent with the normal juncture and stress pattern of the word *picolomini,* which must be adjusted to accommodate the meter. Since each syllable is sung to a separate note and only one word is used throughout the entire song, deviations from the normal stress and juncture patterns of the word are foregrounded. First, *picolomini* is five syllables while the metrical unit consists of six beats, —ʋʋ—ʋʋ. Second, since in ordinary discourse only *pi* and *mi* are stressed (*pícolomíni*), when this five-unit word is superimposed on a six-unit metrical pattern, *each* syllable in the song gets stressed at some point. Third, and for the same reason, normal juncture is also modified. New metrical lines begin in the middle of the word. The trick in singing this song is for the final note to coincide with the final syllable of *picolomini* and for the performer to sing very fast without tripping up.

In the following example, a number of structural features are manipulated to achieve the total form:

* (21)   How much wood would a woodchuck chuck if a
      woodchuck could chuck wood?
      (See Opie and Opie, 1959: 30; Withers, 1948: 80.)

First, syllabic structures are alternated: VCV between two vowels [ʋ] and [ə], in combination with four consonants, [w] [k] [č] [d]. Of these, [w] [k] and [č] occur initially and [d] and [k] finally. Second, the syllabic sequences are organized in the following way:

$$\#\,hau\,\#\,məč\,\#\,wUd\,\#$$
$$\#\,wUd\,\#\,ə\,\#\,wUdčək\,\#\,čək\,\#$$
$$\#\,If\,\#\,ə\,\#\,wUdčək\,\#\,kUdčək\,\#\,wUd\,\#$$

Syllables $_k^wUd$ are juxtaposed with *məč* and *čək* in a pattern of increasing complexity: in the first line, there is one *məč* and one *wUd*; in the second line two each of both *wUd* and *čək*; and in the third line two each of both *wUd* and *čək* plus one *kUd.* Third, a problem in disambiguation is posed by the following homonyms:

(a)   $wUd_1$   *wood*         =   noun
      $wUd_2$   *would*        =   verb
      $wUd_3$   *wood* (*chuck*)  =   bound morpheme
(b)   $čək_1$   *chuck*        =   verb
      $čək_2$   (*wood*) *chuck*  =   bound morpheme

The next example is an exercise of competence in syntactic complexity. In this case embedding is the primary concern:

(22)   Are you the guy
      That told the guy

That I'm the guy
That gave the guy
The black eye?

No, I'm not the guy
That told the guy
That you're the guy
That gave the guy
The black eye.
    (Withers, 1948: 194)

Underlying the verse are four separate sentences:

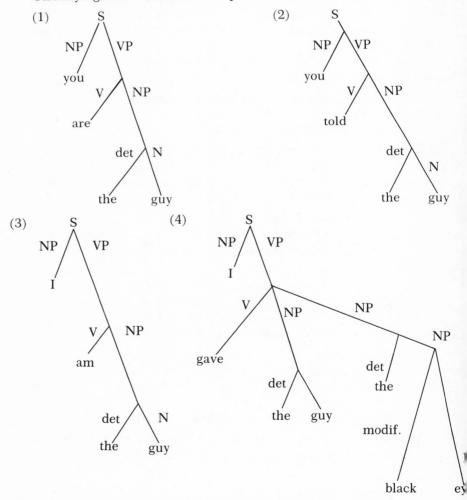

These four sentences are conjoined in the following manner:

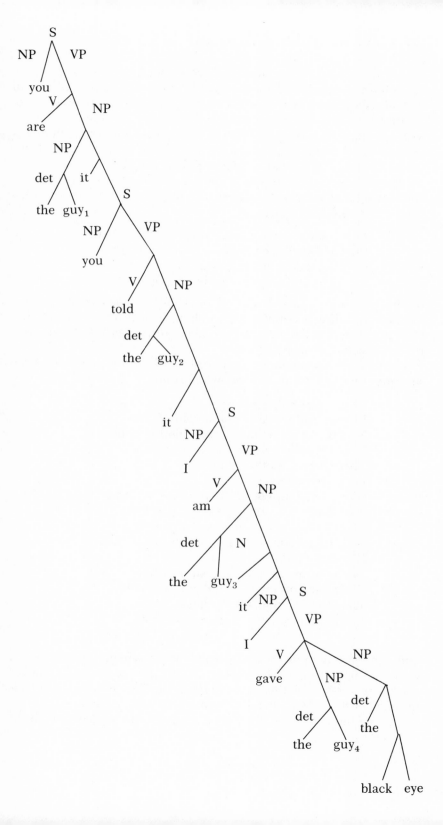

The child must recognize that first, everywhere the *it* marker occurs, the subject is raised and replaced with *that₁;* second, the two main sentence complexes, each involving the concatentation of both an identity relation and a transitive operation are conjoined by *that₂,* which is a subordinating conjunction, as distinct from *that₁,* which is a pronoun; and third, there is homonymy involved in the four occurrences of *guy,* which refer to four different people.

Attention is drawn to the child's concern with inflection, derivation, and syntactic class membership in the following example, recorded from a twelve-year-old girl:

(23)   As I walked down to the wayrail station, I met a
       bark and it dogged at me. I pulled a hedge
       out of a stake and necked its knock out.
                               (Opie and Opie, 1959: 24)

In this utterance, there is one example of reversed compounding, *wayrail,* and three examples of switching lexical class membership: bark/dog, hedge/stake, neck/knock. Derived from this is the inappropriate inflection of *dog* and *neck.*

Other forms seem to be exercises which focus primarily upon semantic relations, as in the following example of antithesis:

(24)   Ladies and jelly spoons:
       I come before you to stand behind you
       To tell you something I know nothing about.
       Last Thursday which was Good Friday,
       There'll be a mother's meeting
       For fathers only.
       Wear your best clothes if you haven't any
       And if you can come please stay at home.
       The admission is free so pay at the door.
       Pull up a chair and sit on the floor.
       It makes no difference where you sit.
       The man in the gallery is sure to spit.
       We thank you for your unkind attention.
       The next meeting will be held
       At the four corners of the round table.
                               (Withers, 1948: 199)

Almost every other phrase in this sequence is a semantic contradiction of the one preceding it. This verse calls attention to semantic rules of co-occurrences by violating them. In itself, this device would be of little amusement to one who has long ago mastered the system.

In the following examples from a ten-year-old's repertoire both the sociolinguistic rules of appropriate style levels and semantic co-occurrence restrictions are foci:

* (25) I presume that your presumptions are precisely incorrect. Your sarcastic insinuations are too obnoxious to be tolerated.

* (26) If you insinuate that I tolerate such biological insolence from an inferior person like you, you are under a misapprehended delusion.

"Precisely incorrect," "biological insolence," and "misapprehended delusion" mark the speaker as someone unfamiliar with the context of these lexemes. Although phonological features of alliteration and vowel harmony are used, they are subordinated to the focus of the utterances which is sociolinguistic and semantic in contrast with the utterances of young children in which concern with phonological structure dominated.

Since the particular formal features of the child's speech play productions reflect the structural concerns of his developing language—dominance in young children of phonological features which later are supplemented by an elaboration of syntactic, semantic, and sociolinguistic concerns—we should be able to see this development reflected, albeit very roughly, in a corpus of children's productions.

The collection we are using consists of jump rope rhymes, counting out rhymes, ball bouncing rhymes, taunts, songs, and odd verses which were collected from children in Austin, Texas, during the years 1967 to 1971 by undergraduate students in folklore classes at the University of Texas. The children ranged in age from five to fourteen (no thirteen-year-olds). We have averaged the number of forms collected from the

TABLE 2

| Age | Number of children | Mean number of items per child |
|---|---|---|
| 5 | 15 | 1.0 |
| 6 | 18 | 1.6 |
| 7 | 25 | 3.7 |
| 8 | 50 | 6.0 |
| 9 | 93 | 2.9 |
| 10 | 39 | 0.9 |
| 11 | 32 | 3.5 |
| 12 | 23 | 1.5 |
| 14 | 6 | 1.0 |

children in each age group (see Table 2), in addition to coding for sex and age of the child and for parents' occupation and ethnic group. While there is no standardization of the age groups, we feel that the differential distribution in mean number of forms collected from each represents a differential concern with this type of speech on the part of children of different ages.

In the development of a child's repertoire of speech play forms, (a) the child gradually adds verses to his repertoire until about the age of eleven at which point interest in many of these kinds of productions drops off sharply and other kinds of verbal art which we are not considering in this paper, for example, prose narrative, appear to be of greater interest; (b) there are principles of selectivity whereby the older children reject some verses as "babyish" and refuse to recite them; and (c) verses focusing on certain features of language structure appear to enter the repertoire at certain ages. An analysis of the collection at our disposal indicates that the child's concerns shift from phonological to grammatical to semantic and finally to the sociolinguistic level of language.

Although these data were collected without correlation with IQ or other determinants of ability to learn and produce rhymes, their characteristics are striking enough to demand discussion. The only "gibberish" in the whole sample appears in the five-to-seven age group. The following jump rope rhymes are from a five- and a seven-year-old respectively:

(27)  Okka bokka soda crokka
      Okka bokka boo;
      In comes Uncle Sam
      And out goes Y O U.

(28)  Onna wanna tat ta nee a,
      See a wee a compa nee a;
      Silva rack a tick a tack,
      I see a wee a one.

Although gibberish has also been found among older children, especially in their counting out rhymes (Opie and Opie, 1969), we found that gibberish and other phonologically determined rhymes figure in the repertoire of the youngest children in our sample. Verses based upon the manipulation of semantic and sociolinguistic rules are more prevalent among our older children.

For the five-to-seven age group, most of the instances of speech play are simple verses which are fairly short, none being more than five lines long. The following rhyme from a seven-year-old illustrates how attractive playing with phonological relations is for younger children:

(29)   A skunk sat on a stump.
       The stump said,
       "The skunk stunk."
       The skunk said,
       "The stump stunk."

The following is a representative example of one of the longest verses recited by the seven-year-old in our sample:

(30)   I asked my father for fifteen cents
       To see the elephant jump the fence.
       She jumped so high, she reached the sky.
       And didn't come back till the last of July.

The eight-year-olds, while still focussing on simple verses, start to play with social rules:

(31)   My eyes have seen the glory of the burning of the school.
       We have tortured all the teachers. We have broken all the
          rules.
       We will try to kill the principal tomorrow afternoon.
       His truth is marching on.

(32)   Teacher, teacher, I declare.
       I see someone's underwear.
       They're not white. They're not blue.
       They're not pink, but they sure do stink!

This trend continues until about eleven, when we find some play with semantic relations, especially antithesis, and much longer utterances:

(33)   Ladies and jelly-beans, hobos and tramps,
       Cross-eyed mosquitos and bow-legged ants.
       I come before ye to stand behind ye
       To tell ye something I know nothing about.
       There's going to be a ladies' meeting
       Friday, Easter Sunday.
       Men admitted free.
       Pay at the door.
       Pull up a chair and sit on the floor.
       We're going to talk about the four corners of the round table.

When Columbus sailed the Missisolopy River in a punch-
bowl,
With the Star Strangled BANANA in one hand,
And the Declaration of Indigestion in the other.

At about this time we also get parody-rhymes based on sex themes:

(34)   Violets are blue
And I turned red
As soon as I saw you
Nude in bed.

Social parodies of adult productions also begin to appear:

(35)   Winston tastes bad
Like the last one I had
No filter no taste
It's a forty-cent waste
W I N S T O N.

The parody themes culminate in the following contribution by a
fourteen-year-old:

(36)   Jesus loves me, this I know,
For the Bible tells me so.
I am Jesus' little lamb.
Yes, you're goddamned right, I am.

Children of this age are delighted by the obvious violation of the
sociolinguistic rule of style level: one does not use profanity in a
religious speech act. The beautiful "pure pun" in the following example from a fourteen-year-old, combined with the sex theme and the
perversion of the original "Mother Goose" into a "goose mother"
rhyme, make this rhyme attractive to the older child who will enjoy his
ability to disambiguate a true pun:

(37)   Jack and Jill went up the hill riding on an elephant.
Jill got off to help jack off the elephant.


## CONCLUSION

We have attempted to relate two bodies of data in the literature on
child language and performance, one being children's speech play and
the other child acquisition of language. Although each area has been
investigated, the two bodies of data have received very little scholary
attention together. Because of the nature of our data—limited to

English, and in the case of the data in the last section, to English spoken by a rather limited subgroup of middle-class white American children—our contribution is of the hypothesis-generating type. We offer it as such in the hope that it will stimulate further research in this area.

This enquiry should be broadened to include children being socialized into other languages to see if the hypotheses set forth here hold cross-culturally. In languages where the phonological, syntactic, and semantic relations determine structurally different realizations of "poetic devices," do the children's speech play forms still evince stages of concern with the different components of the language even if in different ways? We would expect that children will demonstrate the same concern with phonological structure and later with syntactic and semantic features although the poetic devices incorporated into their speech play forms will be different in languages where meter is based on principles different from English meter and in those which do not have rhyme, for example, Japanese.

Further research should also consider the discrepancy between the age(s) noted in the language acquisition literature for achieving competence in the various components of language and the ages at which each component serves as the child's focus of interest in terms of speech play forms. Language acquisition studies generally indicate that by about the age of four years, the child is competent syntactically in his native language. Our analysis of children's speech play forms indicates that, for example, phonological dominance is maintained long after the child is theoretically competent syntactically and semantically.

Also worthy of investigation is the relationship among linguistic competence, improvised speech play, disciplined speech play, and verbal art. Spontaneous, improvised speech play, as in babbling, provides several interesting contrasts with the disciplined, controlled speech play examined in this paper. Just as babbling is essential to the acquisition of language, the acquisition of language may be essential to controlled and disciplined speech play which may in turn be essential to the acquisition of poetic discourse. Therefore, it is not surprising that babbling precedes speech and that linguistic competence precedes disciplined playing with aspects of language structure. The control of rhythm, meter, rhyme, and stanzaic forms built upon the couplet provide the basis for traditional adult verbal art; so too with the disciplined extension of semantic categories in the form of puns, metaphors and similes, and the orderly patterns which are built upon morphophonological and syntactic repetition. That speech play is instrumental to the acquisition of adult verbal art is supported by (a) the fact that children's ordinary discourse does not exhibit the same degree of disciplined formal patterning as do their speech play productions; and (b) that when analyzed closely children's speech play does exhibit many of the rhetorical figures appropriate to adult eloquence and codified in the rhetoric handbooks (see Appendix at the end of this paper). These handbooks were developed through observations of effective adult oral discourse and intended for teaching adults to speak and write effectively. Therefore, the types of children's speech play considered in this paper may be important in the acquisition of poetic discourse, what Jakobson would call acquiring the poetry of grammar as preparation for the acquisition of the grammar of poetry (1968).

Not all the ways that children play with language later figure significantly in adult verbal art. Some of the speech play which fascinate children are openly shunned or negatively evaluated by American adults today as being silly or gross or not appropriate adult speech. For example, puns, in particular obvious puns, customarily evoke groans or hisses from adult audiences or formulaic responses such as "that's two-thirds of a pun: PeeYu" or "that's a groaner" or "puns are the lowest form of humor." Despite the pleasure taken, even the punster will try to protect himself with "pardon the pun" or "no pun intended." This difference in the way adults and children view puns today suggests that the major structural concerns evidenced by these forms are intuitively recognized by adult speakers of the language as typically being the property of children. Such an attitude, in conjunction with the fact that English speakers tend to share the idea that adults should not behave like children, discourages adults from using or, at the least, from showing their enjoyment in obvious puns or other features associated with childish speech.[2] Is this true in other languages? Along with alternative values and attitudes toward the role of children and the appropriateness of an adult behaving "like a child" do the characteristic features of children's speech play have differential survival in adult verbal art?

## APPENDIX

### Rhetorical Patterns in Children's Rhymes

*gradatio* (linking repetition of words leading to a climax)

> I went downtown
> To see Mrs. Brown.

---

[2]See Chapter 10 for a discussion of English punning in earlier periods.

She gave me a nickel
To buy a pickle.
The pickle was sour,
She gave me a flower.
The flower was dead,
She gave me a thread.
The thread was thin,
She gave me a pin.
The pin was sharp,
She gave me a harp.
The harp began to sing,
"Minnie and a minnie and a ha ha ha."[3]

*conversio* (repetition of the last word[s] in successive phrases)

I scream
You scream
We all scream
For ice cream.

A lady was chasing her boy around the room,
She was chasing her boy around the room.
And while she was chasing her boy around the room,
She was chasing her boy around the room.

*similiter desinens* (repetition of word endings)

Lift the nozzle
To your muzzle.
And let it swizzle
Down your guzzle.

*similiter desinens and articulus* (staccato effect achieved by single words set apart by pauses—also called a *comma*)

Did you eever, iver, over,
In your leef, life, loaf,
See the deevel, divel, dovel,
Kiss his weef, wife, woaf?

No. I neever, niver, nover,
In my leef, life, loaf,

---

[3]The principle of linked repetition is a common feature of the structure of "chain" stories and cumulative tales. Indeed, it is not uncommon to find the overall structure of tales patterned upon the same principles as rhetorical figures for details of verbal style.

> Saw the deevel, divel, dovel,
> Kiss his weef, wife, woaf.

*complexio* (repetition of both the first and last words of successive phrases)

> Are you the guy
> That told the guy
> That I'm the guy
> That gave the guy
> The black eye?
>
> No, I'm not the guy
> That told the guy
> That you're the guy
> That gave the guy
> The black eye.

*repetitio* (repetition of the initial word in successive phrases)

> Some write for pleasure
> Some write for fame,
> But I write only
> To sign my name.

*conduplicatio* (repetition of one or more words for the purpose of amplification or appeal to pity)

> Needles and pins, needles and pins,
> When you get married your trouble begins.

*contentio* (antithesis: opposite ideas juxtaposed)

> Ladies and jelly spoons:
> I come before you
> To stand behind you
> To tell you something
> I know nothing about.
> Last Thursday
> Which was Good Friday
> There'll be a mother's meeting
> For fathers only.
> Wear your best clothes
> If you haven't any,
> And if you can come
> Please stay at home.

The admission is free
So pay at the door,
Pull up a chair
And sit on the floor.
It makes no difference
Where you sit
The man in the gallery
Is sure to spit.
We thank you for your unkind attention.
The next meeting will be held
At the four corners of the round table.

*commutatio* (two discrepant thoughts so expressed by transposition that the latter follows the former although contradictory to it)

Algy met a bear
The bear was bulgy,
The bulge was Algy.

*adnominatio* (pun or wordplay)

Do you carrot all for me?
My heart beets for you,
With your turnip nose
And your radish face.
You are a peach
If we cantaloupe,
Lettuce marry;
Weed make a swell pear.

Mississippi said to Missouri,
"If I put on my New Jersey
What will Delaware?"
Virginia said, "Alaska."

*adnominatio* (pun or wordplay) and *conversio* (repetition of the last word in successive phrases)

"Hello, Bill."
"Where you going, Bill?"
"Downtown, Bill."
"What for, Bill?"
"To pay my gas bill."
"How much, Bill?"
"A ten dollar bill."
"So long, Bill."

*translatio* (metaphor)

> Margaret, Margaret, has big eyes,
> Spread all over the skies.

*distributio* (itemizing or assigning specific roles among a number of things or persons)

> One for the money,
> Two for the show,
> Three to get ready,
> And four to go.

Most dandling rhymes for the fingers and toes take this form.

BRIAN SUTTON-SMITH

# A Developmental Structural
# Account of Riddles

## CHAPTER FIVE

**M**ANY YEARS ago when I was teaching third graders, I was impressed with the fact that most teachers spoke in terms that were fairly incomprehensible to children a great deal of the time. It appeared to me that much adult conversation must have the character of an arbitrary series of puzzles to young children. Against that background, the regular practice in which children stood up in front of a classroom and teased each other with incomprehensible riddles struck me as both a model and a mockery of the adult-child process of communication. Some years later I hypothesized that riddles would appear cross-culturally in a context in which adults quizzed children orally and in which the children were required to be attentive and responsive to such quizzing. The underlying assumption formulated by John M. Roberts and myself was that conflict induced by child training procedures leads to the development of expressive models within which children both restate the paradox and gain buffered experience in dealing with it (Sutton-Smith, 1972: 338).

In a recent cross-cultural study of riddles, Roberts and Forman (1971) have gained considerable evidence for this point of view. In a survey of 146 cultures in the Human Relations Area Files, they found that riddles exist in cultures where rote learning from authority figures is emphasized, as well as oral interrogation by those figures. In addition, there is evidence of high compliance training of the children and of highly developed sensitivity to ridicule (Roberts and Forman, 1971).

The fun of the riddles on this account derives from the fact that their incongruities model, in a safe way, the larger process of adult interrogation and ambiguity. As a model of this process, the riddle appears to be a contest in which one central person competes with another or others for the possession of the role of arbitrary authority. Riddling is not strictly speaking a game of strategy because victory is not achieved by rational choice; Roberts found that riddling was not highly associated with games of strategy cross-culturally. It is rather a game of rhetoric or arbitrary power in which victory is achieved by prior access to arcane knowledge. The semantic logic of the riddles, like the power they convey, is also arbitrary. The group formation of this game, when it is played by children, is most like those other arbitrary games, such as "Mother May I" and "Redlight," in which one player exercises control over the others and acts like a referee rather than as another player. She tells them when they may move, what moves they may make, when they must start again, etc. (Sutton-Smith, 1972: 66).

In this paper I wish to consider an approach to the *structure* of the riddles themselves. Presumably the structures should mediate the types of ambiguity with which the children must deal in the larger child-adult process. I am here ignoring content, although one could point out that, in general, content involves an embodiment of some form of stupidity by morons or others, as if to echo the very predicament or character of the person who does not comprehend ambiguity.

My attention to the structural aspect of riddles was prompted by an article of Georges and Dundes (1963) entitled "Toward a Structural Definition of the Riddle," in which they distinguish categories of riddles on the basis of whether the riddles are metaphorical or literal, oppositional or non-oppositional. *Oppositional riddles* are those in which there is some kind of contradiction (antithetical, privational, or causal) between at least one pair of descriptive elements, for example, "What turns and never moves? A road." In the *non-oppositional riddles,* the descriptive elements are not contradictory, for example, "Got some yellow inside and green outside. A pumpkin." Both these examples are also *literal riddles* because the riddle referent or answer and the topic of the descriptive elements in the riddle question are identical. In *metaphorical riddles,* the riddle referent and the topic of the descriptive elements are different, for example, "Two rows of white horses on a red hill. Teeth." (See Georges and Dundes, 1963: 114.) The riddle answer "teeth" is the riddle referent, whereas the topic of what is described by the riddle statement is "horses on a hill." More recently, Abrahams (1968) and Abrahams and Dundes (1972) have pointed out techniques of confusion besides opposition and metaphor by which "the image (or *Gestalt*) presented in the riddle-question is impaired and therefore is, in most cases, undecipherable." In addition to opposition, they discuss "incomplete detail," "too much detail" (especially when the important features are buried in inconsequential detail), and "false *Gestalt*" in which the details in the riddle image suggest an answer, often embarrassingly obscene, which is not the "right" answer (Abrahams and Dundes, 1972: 131).

In contrast with riddles current among adults cross-culturally and found in Taylor's classic collection (1951), most of the children's riddles in the corpus used in this study are like moron riddles and do not fit into the above types. However, the strategies identified by Georges, Dundes, and Abrahams also involve various forms of classification. I decided, therefore, to collect a large sample of children's riddles, which are known to peak in popularity at about the third grade, and to see if they could be handled as a problem in classification. Piaget and others have indicated that, at about the age when riddles peak, children show their initial competence in problems of verbal classification, reclassification, and multiple classification. The limited focus in this paper, then, is on the specific semantic devices that give the riddler the materials for his exercise of arbitrary power in the rhetorical context. More specifically, it is an attempt to see if the Piaget categories of classification provide an adequate basis for the analysis of the structure of riddles.

Riddles were collected from a sample of 623 children in the predominantly small towns of northwestern Ohio in the early 1960s. Table 1 indicates the grade and sex of the respondents. There were three or four different schools involved in the contributions at each grade level.

TABLE 1 *Subjects*

| Grades: | 1 | | 2 | | 3 | | 4 | | 5 | | 6 | | 7 | | 8 | |
|---------|---|---|---|---|---|---|---|---|---|---|---|---|---|---|---|---|
| Sex: | m | f | m | f | m | f | m | f | m | f | m | f | m | f | m | f |
| N: | 10 | 15 | 38 | 41 | 47 | 62 | 47 | 58 | 56 | 56 | 35 | 34 | 17 | 17 | 46 | 45 |

Children in grades one and two were asked to contribute their favorite jokes orally. From grade three onward, they wrote their jokes down. In the first three grades, the contributions were predominantly riddles, whereas by the eighth grade, they were predominantly jokes. The collection yielded a total of 316 riddles and 455 joke responses.

The riddles in this collection have been classified as pre-riddles,

TABLE 2 *Joke and Riddle Responses*

| Grades: | 1 | 2 | 3 | 4 | 5 | 6 | 7 | 8 | Total |
|---------|---|---|---|---|---|---|---|---|-------|
| Riddles | 17 | 31 | 76 | 57 | 44 | 28 | 20 | 43 | 316 |
| Jokes | 9 | 6 | 32 | 50 | 90 | 40 | 76 | 132 | 455 |

TABLE 3 *Types of Riddles*

| Grades | 1 | 2 | 3 | 4 | 5 | 6 | 7 | 8 | Total |
|--------|----|----|----|----|----|----|----|----|-------|
| Pre-riddle | 7 | 12 | — | 1 | 2 | 1 | 1 | — | 24 |
| Implicit | 6 | 15 | 50 | 33 | 31 | 18 | 12 | 31 | 196 |
| Parody | 3 | 3 | 8 | 5 | 5 | 9 | — | 5 | 38 |
| Inverted r. | — | 1 | 6 | 14 | — | 1 | 6 | 4 | 32 |
| Expl.-reclas. | 2 | — | 9 | — | 4 | — | — | — | 15 |
| Non-crit. a. | — | — | 4 | 4 | — | — | — | — | 8 |
| Multiple | — | — | 1 | 2 | — | — | — | — | 3 |
| Total | 18 | 31 | 78 | 69 | 42 | 29 | 19 | 40 | 316 |

implicit reclassifications, riddle parodies, inverted relationships, explicit reclassifications, classifications on the basis of non-criterial attributes, and multiple classifications. Their frequencies in the children's responses are shown in Table 3.

TYPE 1. *Pre-riddles*

> Why did the man chop down the chimney?
> He needed the bricks.

About 7 percent of all responses were pre-riddles. These non-riddles actually constitute about a third of all responses in the first two grades. In a study of riddles given by four-year-old children, the percentage of such responses rises to as much as 80 percent (Park, 1971). Although these questions and answers would not generally be recognized as riddles, they are all couched in question and answer form and presented as if they constitute some sort of puzzle. Furthermore, in all of these pre-riddles, there is no systematic way of knowing what the answer might be. It depends on the riddler's idiosyncratic experience. Shultz (1974) also found that six-year-olds preferred incongruous riddles to congruous ones. The incongruity that gets a +1 for funniness at this stage requires no resolution. Nevertheless, the diffuse perception of these younger children perhaps actually highlights some of the salient or more obvious characteristics of the riddle, even if its subtler logic escapes them. From their "primitive" viewpoint, it seems that the riddle is a *puzzling question with an arbitrary answer*. While we hesitate to put this definition ahead of the more sophisticated ones which will follow, it certainly bears some attention, particularly if it emerges that the only difference between pre-riddles and true riddles is that in the latter the contrariness of the answers takes on a systematic rather than an idiosyncratic character. Additionally, if a riddle is indeed a contest and a way of sowing confusion among one's antagonists as Abrahams (1968) suggests, these idiosyncratic examples would serve that purpose. The definition certainly epitomizes the child-adult relationship mentioned earlier.

It is not always possible to tell whether one is dealing with a pre-riddle or a riddle parody. In some cases, it is only the well-established character of the "idiosyncratic" answer that establishes it as a traditional riddle rather than a purely personal response. In other cases, the pre-riddle is a degeneration of a real riddle.

TYPE 2. *Implicit Reclassifications (Homonymic Riddles)*

> Why did the dog go out into the sun?
> He wanted to be a hot dog.

The largest class of children's riddles across the grades from one to eight (over 60 percent in this collection) are those in which a word, term, letter, etc., is presented in one way, but then implicitly reclassified in some other way so as to produce an anticlimax. In the example here, a class (dogs) and a class attribute implied by the question (dogs of high temperature) are reclassified in the answer to form a new class (frankfurters) with the same attribute (high temperature). The arbitrariness of the connection between question and answer consists in treating a homonym (hot dog) in both classes as if it were one term with one meaning. If any principle stands out from this large corpus of children's riddles, it is that a *homonym is not a single term with a single meaning.* We may now amend our original definition of a riddle as a puzzling question with an arbitrary answer. We can define the riddle of Type 2 as *a puzzling question, the answer to which preserves the question's terminology, but reclassifies its significance, by foiling the expectation that one term will mean the same thing each time it is used. Instead, one term is shown to have two meanings.*[1]

This implies that answers to riddles are not completely arbitrary. They are restricted by the diversity of use allowed by particular words and letters. The linguistic play of children as manifested in riddles is in these terms an exploration of semantic diversity. This view corresponds neatly with Frank Kessel's recent conclusion that, as early as kindergarten, children can understand lexical ambiguities (Kessel, 1970).

Although the riddles of Type 2 are structurally like those of the classical Type 5 below, the requirement to guess the homonym in Type 2 riddles is not explicit as it tends to be in typical riddles, but is veiled

[1]See the discussion of riddles in Chapter 10 for alternative views of the riddle.

in the story-like form of moronic and other happenings. In another type of traditional riddle, the Wellerism, of which there are no examples in this sample, homonymic confusion is central, but instead of the subject guessing how the object in the question might be reclassified, a pseudo-homonym or imperfect pun is created by taking one or more unbound morphemes from the question and mapping them onto a sequence of similar sounding bound morphemes in the answer. Thus: "What did the bull say when it swallowed a bomb? Abominable"; "What did the window say when the tree fell through it? Tremendous."

## TYPE 3. *Riddle Parodies*

> Why did the chicken cross the road?
> He wanted to get to the other side.

While the bulk of riddles in this corpus (Type 2) first set up the expectation that the terms in the answer will be given the semantic significance they carry in the questioning statement and then proceed to upset that expectation, riddle parodies upset the expectation of such a relationship between question and answer by giving a straightforward answer: "How much dirt in a hole 5 by 3 by 3 feet? None."

After the implicit classifications, these are the next largest class in this collection (12 percent). The arbitrariness here does not involve reclassifying particular words or letters, but defeating the expectation that such a verbal logic will indeed occur. Instead of a complicated answer, we get a direct one. What seems like a riddle turns out to be an "obvious question." Some of the riddle parodies are straight puzzles masquerading as riddles, while others are pseudo-puzzles, for example, the question about dirt in the hole. In such pseudo-puzzles, the answer, instead of fulfilling the expectation that it will resolve contradictions or ambiguities in the question (dirt in a hole), points them up (there is no dirt in a hole), and thereby shows that there is something wrong with the question. Rather than showing the logic of the apparent illogical-ness of the question, as in Type 5, the answer *exposes* the illogic of the apparently logical question. What looks like a riddle turns out to be a "stupid question."

## TYPE 4. *Inverted Relationships*

> What does one flea say to another as they go strolling?
> Shall we walk or take a dog?

Like the reclassificatory riddles, Type 4 riddles (about 10 percent), do not meet the expectations set up by the first statement. In Type 4 riddles, however, the meanings of words or letters are not reversed.

Rather, to use Barker and Wright's terminology, the *standing patterns of behavior are changed.* Human behavior in most cases is highly conventional. For a given culture, we can predict with considerable certainty both the range of behavior within which most people will act in any given conventional behavior setting and how most people will think about relationships within any such setting. There are certain criteria for thinking about relationships. Thus when thinking about fleas and dogs, most people will think of the dogs having fleas and not of fleas having dogs. But in this riddle our conventional expectation is upset and the part-whole relationship between flea and dog is inverted. The answer suggests a new relationship between these critters which is either improbable or of low order probability for the usual way of thinking about them and their actions.

TYPE 5. *Explicit Reclassifications (Homonymic Oppositional Riddles)*

>   What has an ear but cannot hear?
>   Corn.

In Type 5 riddles (4 percent), a classification is presented and then one of its criterial attributes denied. The denied attribute may be a normal part of the object, a basic function of the object, or a usual consequence of the function. In Type 5 riddles, a homonym also figures. The *ear that hears* and the *ear of corn* are not really the same *ear,* even though they take the same linguistic form.

In contrast with Type 2 riddles (implicit reclassifications), Type 5 riddles, sometimes known as oppositional riddles, present the reclassificatory puzzle *explicitly,* that is, the hearer is given the *class* and is then questioned about an *attribute* of the class, which does not fulfill conventional expectations for attributes of that class. Ears are expected to hear. Type 2 riddles present similar problems but not explicitly as a lexical puzzle. Rather, Type 2 riddles bury these problems in the crazy and moronic goings on of beasts and idiots. Perhaps at the earlier age at which Type 2 riddles are found, the moronic type of content is as important to the riddler as lexical problems, if not more so.

TYPE 6. *Classifications on the Basis of Noncriterial Attributes*

>   White inside and red outside?
>   An apple.

In Type 6 riddles (2 percent), two contrasted attributes provide the basis for the classification C, but are not criterial attributes because they do not distinguish the category *apple* from other things which are also white inside and red outside. Furthermore, the classification is some-times literal, sometimes metaphorical, and homonyms are not involved. Although Types 5 and 6 constitute only 6 percent of the present collection, they comprise the bulk of most traditional collections and are what Archur Taylor has termed *true riddles*.

TYPE 7. *Multiple Classifications*

What is the difference between a teacher and an engineer? One trains the mind, the other minds the train.

Riddles in this category usually take the form: "What is the differ-ence between X and Y?" Here the homonymic relationship is often a double one. These are known traditionally as *conundrums* and consti-tute 1 percent of the present corpus.

## DISCUSSION

Approaching this corpus of riddles as problems in classification, reclassification, and multiple classification, implicit or explicit, does account for most of the present data (about 70 percent), but does not cover it all. Since the rest (Types 1 and 3) are formulaic questions and answers of an idiosyncratic or obvious sort, a definition of the riddle which would include these will be more general than the one provided for the largest subclass (Type 2) in this collection. Redefined, the riddle is a *puzzling question with an answer that seems arbitrary because the hearer receives meaning B in the riddle answer while expecting to react to meaning A in the riddle question; but the riddle question and answer are compatible because meanings A and B share some semantic rela-tionship.*

Developmentally speaking, we have noted a number of trends. Like Shultz (1974), we also find that riddles told by six- to eight-year-olds demonstrate a shift from a stage of pure incongruity (the pre-riddle) to a stage of resolvable incongruity. Pre-riddles are a third of the jokes in the first two grades. By the third grade, the riddles of implicit reclas-sification are dominant and they remain so throughout this collection to the eighth grade. A Piaget view of riddle structure as an exercise in classificatory ambiguities accounts for the major portion of this devel-opmental phenomenon. By the fourth grade, however, the non-criterial riddles which have more to do with part-whole relationships and expected behavior patterns come into play. Also, by the fourth grade and clearly thereafter, riddles give way to other joke forms in which questions of human relationships dominate over questions of the lexicon and classification. (See Sanches and Kirshenblatt-Gimblett in this volume for a discussion of speech play preferences of different age groups.)

Three major periods are typified in this material. There is the preoperational period when a child thinks of objects or sentences in an unidimensional way: when he is asked how many words there are in the sentence, "The man has twenty chocolates," he says there are twenty words (Beilin, 1972). By grade three, however, he knows that a sentence can contain two dimensions (possession of twenty chocolates can be communicated by only five words), just as objects can have two dimensions (number and extension) and words can have two meanings (hot dogs and hot dogs). By the fifth grade, his interest in ambiguities, at least as reflected in jokes, focuses dominantly on behavioral expectancies. But that is the subject of another study.

Given the child-adult relationship of oral interrogation, ambiguity, and humiliation, and the riddle as a working model of this relationship, the present developmental materials help to focus attention on the particular ambiguities that are the center of attention across various age levels. But the ambiguities as highlighted in this paper will not always be the center of children's attention. A similar survey done today might give higher importance to the riddle parodies, which are inclined to mock *any* form of expectancy rather than merely the classificatory ones. For example, today one often finds a succession of riddles which provides its own set of expectancies and then reverses them for anti-climax.

How do you shoot a pink elephant?
With a pink elephant gun.
and
How do you shoot a blue elephant?
You dye it pink and shoot it with a pink elephant gun.

GARY H. GOSSEN

# Verbal Dueling in Chamula*

CHAPTER SIX

T HE PRESENT description and analysis of an important genre of
Chamula verbal behavior, *baȼ'i ʔištol loʔil*, "truly frivolous talk," will
contribute data from a Maya society to supplement the strikingly few
reports of verbal dueling and other verbal games in native North and
Meso-America (see Dundes, 1967). Adopting an emic, holistic, and
performance-centered approach in the spirit of the "ethnography of
speaking" (see Hymes, 1962; Paredes and Bauman, 1971), I will discuss
*truly frivolous talk* as part of the Chamula folk taxonomy of *all* verbal
behavior (*k'op*), describe typical performance contexts, and subject the
data to linguistic and sociological interpretation. Approaching verbal
dueling as part of the continuum of information, style, and social
interaction which comprises Chamula oral tradition will facilitate the
identification of this genre's unique and shared qualities and its role in
the acquisition of adult social and linguistic competence.

Chamula is one of the eleven *municipios* in the state of Chiapas, in
southern Mexico, in which Tzotzil is spoken. Tzotzil is a member of the
Tzeltalan group (Tzotzil, Tzeltal, Tojolabal) of Maya languages. Some
forty thousand Chamulas live patrilocally in over one hundred scattered hamlets near the top of the Chiapas Highlands, at an average
elevation of about 7,600 feet.

The Chamula community has been described in detail elsewhere

* My research in Mexico was carried out over a period of fifteen months between 1965
and 1969 as a part of the Harvard Chiapas Project, under the direction of Evon Z. Vogt. I
am grateful to him and to many other members of the Project for help and criticism at
various stages of my fieldwork and analysis of data. I particularly want to thank Victoria R.
Bricker and Robert Laughlin for their assistance with technical and interpretive aspects of
Tzotzil humor. The members of the symposium of which this paper was a part also
contributed valuable support and criticism. My research was supported by grants from the
National Institute of Mental Health.

121

(Gossen, 1970, 1972a, 1972b, 1974; Pozas Arciniega, 1959, 1962; see also Laughlin, 1968). Since oral tradition is instrumental in maintaining the social order as the Chamulas know it, a few remarks concerning Chamula world view will suffice here. Chamula religion and cosmology form a complex syncretistic system which is the product of sixteenth century Spanish Catholicism and pre-Columbian Maya cults of nature deities. Basic to Chamula cosmological belief is that they live in the center of the universe. They view their home *municipio* as the only truly safe and virtuous place on the earth. The sun-Christ deity originally established order on the earth and continues to delimit the spatial limits of the universe as well as the temporal units (days and solar years) by the duration and position of his path. The sun created the first three worlds one by one and then destroyed them because people behaved improperly. Chamulas say that behavior equivalent to that of the people in the first three creations may still be found at the edges of the universe and, occasionally, among bad Chamulas. It is only the fourth creation which has been successful. This is a moral world which Chamulas must constantly strive to defend from bad behavior and evil people. Language, particularly the oral tradition, is a crucial tool for the defense, continuity, and ritual maintenance of the fourth creation, the social order as the Chamulas know it.

## Verbal dueling within a folk taxonomy of Chamula verbal behavior

Having described a complete folk taxonomy of *k'op*, "language," elsewhere (Gossen, 1970, 1972a), I will sketch it here only briefly in order to identify the place of verbal dueling within it. As part of a generic, stylistic, and behavioral totality (*k'op*), verbal dueling shares features of structure, content, and context of performance and acquisition with other kinds of Chamula discourse.

The word *k'op* refers to nearly all forms of verbal behavior, including oral tradition, and can be glossed as "word," "language," "argument," "war," "subject," "topic," "problem," "dispute," "court case," or "traditional verbal lore." Chamulas recognize that correct use of language (the Chamula dialect of Tzotzil) distinguishes them not only from nonhumans, but also from their distant ancestors and from other contemporary Indian groups and Spanish-speakers. According to Chamula narrative accounts, no one could speak in the distant past. That was one reason why the sun-creator destroyed the experimental people of the first and second creations. The more recent people learned to speak Spanish and then everyone understood one another. Later the nations and *municipios* were divided because they began quarreling, and the sun deity created different languages so that people would learn to live together peacefully in small groups. Chamulas consider their language the best one and refer to Tzotzil as *baȼ'i k'op*, "true language." They consider language the distinguishing trait of social groups and attach importance to correct verbal behavior as a defining feature of their own identity.

The taxonomy of *k'op* in Figure 1 was elicited several times from six male informants ranging in age from eighteen to sixty-five over a period of one year. I used both formal question frames and informal discussion to discover these categories (see Gossen, 1970, 1972a, and 1974 for more detail on method). The taxonomy is not represented as a grid of uniform and/or symmetrical criteria and distinctive features because this would distort the Chamula view of the taxonomy. For example: *time* is a relevant criterial attribute for distinguishing the level 3 categories of *recent words* and *ancient words* from each other; for other categories at the same level (3) of the taxonomy, *place* of performance is a defining feature (*court speech*); for still others at the same level (3), *performer* of the words is the relevant feature (*children's improvised games*). In this scheme "level" has no uniform "deep structure" information attached to it. "Level" is used only as a descriptive convention.

"Ordinary speech" (*loꞌil k'op*) is restricted in use by the dictates of the social situation and grammaticality and/or intelligibility of the utterance. The Chamulas consider *loꞌil k'op* idiosyncratic and without noteworthiness in style, form, or content; it is everyday speech. As one moves from left to right in Figure 1, progressively more constraints are apparent in *what* a person says (content), *how* he says it (form), and *where* he says it (social setting). The intermediate category, *speech for people whose hearts are heated*, involves restrictions on form but relatively few restrictions on content and social setting. This kind of discourse "comes from the heart of each person," according to a common Chamula explanation. Like *ordinary speech*, it is individual and idiosyncratic in content. It shares with *pure speech* stylistic features and an excited, elevated quality but differs from *pure speech* with respect to idiosyncratic content and relatively unrestricted secular settings for performance.

For *pure speech* to occur, *predictable content and prescribed formal features must appear jointly in genres associated with specific behavioral settings* (see right-hand side of the continuum in Figure 1). Within *pure speech*, the criterion of time association is primary in distinguishing the secular forms (*recent words*) from those of greater ritual and etiological significance (*ancient words*). *Ancient words* are associated

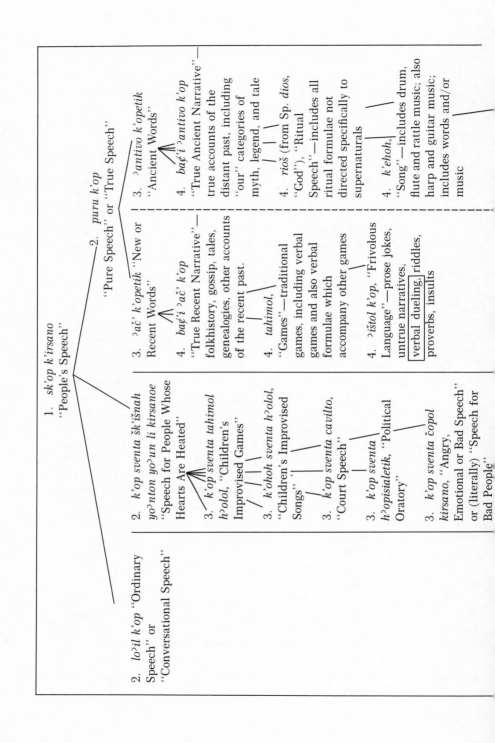

1. sk'op k'irsano "People's Speech"

2. lo'il k'op "Ordinary Speech," or "Conversational Speech"

2. puru k'op "Pure Speech" or "True Speech"

3. 'ač' k'opetik "New or Recent Words"

3. 'antivo k'opetik "Ancient Words"

4. bač'i 'ač' k'op "True Recent Narrative"—folkhistory, gossip, tales, genealogies, other accounts of the recent past.

4. tahimol, "Games"—traditional games, including verbal games and also verbal formulae which accompany other games

4. 'ištol k'op, "Frivolous Language"—prose jokes, untrue narratives, verbal dueling, riddles, proverbs, insults

4. bač'i 'antivo k'op "True Ancient Narrative"—true accounts of the distant past, including "our" categories of myth, legend, and tale

4. rioš (from Sp. dios, "God"), "Ritual Speech"—includes all ritual formulae not directed specifically to supernaturals

4. k'ehoh, "Song"—includes drum, flute and rattle music; also harp and guitar music; includes words and/or music

2. k'op sventa šk'išnah yo'nton yo'un li kirsanoe "Speech for People Whose Hearts Are Heated"

3. k'op sventa tahimol h'olol, "Children's Improvised Games"

3. k'ohoh sventa h'olol, "Children's Improvised Songs,"

3. k'op sventa cavilto, "Court Speech"

3. k'op sventa h'opisialetik, "Political Oratory"

3. k'op sventa čopol kirsano, "Angry, Emotional or Bad Speech" or (literally) "Speech for Bad People"

4. *resal* (from Sp. *rezar*, "to pray"), "Prayer"—all ritual speech addressed to supernatural

→

Associated with distance time-space coordinates; First, Second and Third Creations

Chamula exegesis: *mu sna? shel sbaik*, "They do not know how to change themselves."

Associated with close time-space coordinates; Fourth Creation

Increasing Formalism, Redundancy, and Invariance

Chamula exegesis: *ta šlok' ta yo?nton huhune*, "It comes from the heart of each one."

Chamula exegesis: *ta šk'opoh no?oš ti kirsanoe*, "The people simply talk."

→

FIGURE 1. *A Folk Taxonomy of Chamula Verbal Behavior.*

with the first three creations and, in ritual contexts, often transcend and manipulate the established order in a formal manner. In contrast, *recent words* were given in and are associated with the fourth creation. Both temporally and spatially (the behavioral settings of *recent words* are close to the center of the moral universe), *recent words* deal informally with the present social order, as the Chamulas know it.

The Chamulas classify verbal dueling as a kind of *frivolous language* which, in turn, belongs to *recent words*. They see verbal dueling (*truly frivolous talk*) as sharing more with proverbs (*obscure words*), riddles (*question words*), prose jokes (*lies*), and insults (*buried words*) than with *games* or *true recent narrative* (see Gossen, 1972a and 1972c for brief descriptions of these genres and an extended discussion of Chamula proverbs respectively).

The humorous and playful quality of all *frivolous language* is suggested by *ʔištol,* a noun meaning "toy," which is the key descriptive term in both "frivolous language" (*ʔištol k'op*) and verbal dueling (*bač'i ʔištol loʔil,* "truly frivolous talk"). The emphasis on play and humor in Chamula terminology for verbal dueling raises the question, "What is playful and funny in Chamula?"

As in other societies, humor in Chamula involves deviance. It is always the breach, whether planned, customary, or accidental, which elicits laughter. All five subgenres of *frivolous language* therefore set up deviant situations and/or respond to them with laughter, thereby drawing attention to the norm that is violated. This humorous strategy and the subject matter used unify for Chamulas kinds of verbal behavior whose analogues in other cultures may have little in common. The subgenres of *frivolous language* function as an informal charter for behavior because first, they are not performed in formal settings, that is, ones of ritual or religious significance, and second, they characteristically state norms negatively by providing models to avoid rather than emulate. By setting forth, alluding to, or acting out deviant behavior in the form of *frivolous language,* the speaker implies the normative opposite. For example, in Chamula society a man and his brothers-in-law typically do not get along well together. In fact, this affinal stress often leads to bitter feuds and sometimes to murder. However, a verbal duel which ridicules this stress by setting up a fictive brother-in-law relationship between players is uproariously funny. While appearing to make light of the tension, the verbal duel affirms its reality. Since brothers-in-law do not interact playfully in real life, their laughter in the course of a familiar, playful verbal duel is a way of saying, "This is not proper behavior for brothers-in-law." The humor of all *frivolous language* is based then on the recognition, expressed through laughter, that normative patterns have been inverted. In this way, the Chamulas affirm and defend their social universe. (For an extensive discussion of ritual humor in Zinacantan, a Tzotzil-speaking community which shares a long boundary with Chamula, see Bricker, 1968.)

## Truly frivolous talk

### TEXT AND CONTEXT

"Truly frivolous talk" (*baȼ'i ʔištol loʔil*) is a verbal game in which two players, typically adolescent males, exchange as few as two or as many as 250 verbal challenges. The sequence of permissible words and phrases follows strict rules of minimal sound shift and optimal derogatory or obscene meaning. There is always a winner, he who says the last word, and a loser, he who cannot answer the challenge. Typically, there is an audience of other males who encourage the players with their laughter. Although most typical of bachelors and young married men, even the most sober elders burst into laughter at a well-timed sequence of *truly frivolous talk*. This subgenre is particularly important to the Chamula. I have attended few Chamula social settings in which I did not hear *truly frivolous talk* in some form, however abbreviated.

*Truly frivolous talk* may occur in almost any physical setting. It is performed anywhere that conversation occurs provided the participants are in the correct joking relationship. Chamulas consider *truly frivolous talk* inappropriate to ritual settings although I have seen ritual officials complete a prayer and begin drinking *poš* (a powerful aguardiente) to the happy accompaniment of *truly frivolous talk*. Chamulas say that there are no sex or age restrictions governing who may verbally duel with whom and before whom. My own observation did not support this judgment. I have never heard men speak the genre directly to women. In fact, I am familiar with only two kinds of mixed sex performances of *truly frivolous talk*. One occurs among siblings below the age of seven or eight. Nonkin members of the play group may also be included although residence patterns usually place kinsmen together in these informal groups. Even in this mixed-sex setting, the genre is used by boys to taunt the girls. The boys exchange the loaded words and the girls listen in. Girls are supposed to pretend that they do not understand the intended meanings, most of which are sexual puns. A male-female exchange, therefore, does not actually occur.

A second mixed-sex setting occurs when bachelor men verbally duel in groups by themselves and intentionally speak loudly enough to be overheard by passing nubile girls. Although the girls may in fact understand the intended double entendre, they should not giggle or acknowledge in any way that they have heard the exchange; to do so would label them as sexually available women. I have heard that adolescent girls and women, particularly "bad" women (*čopol ⁊anȼ*), use *truly frivolous talk* to joke among themselves. However, neither my wife nor I heard females perform the genre although we frequently heard women laugh at suggestive puns in dialogue. Any pun, intended or accidental, which provokes laughter because of suggestive meanings can be classified as "frivolous talk" (*⁊ištol lo⁊il*). Verbal dueling (*baȼ'i ⁊ištol lo⁊il*), however, is far more fixed in form and setting than the occasional pun, as the adjective *baȼ'i*, "real," "true," "genuine," indicates.

Boys' and men's groups provide the most typical setting for performance of the genre. Players tend to be between twelve and thirty-five years old. This is the time in the male life cycle when adulthood is being asserted and established, but when full ritual masculinity is often not possible, usually for financial reasons. To be successful, that is, to extend the verbal duel to its limits of suggestiveness, the two people involved should have a joking relationship, which means they must interact in a familiar, open way, unobstructed by such barriers to communication as age and rank. Therefore verbal dueling often occurs as "filler" in idle moments of ritual sequences between players who would otherwise not have a joking relationship. Within the ritual setting, there are what Victor Turner (1969) calls occasions of liminality and *communitas,* that is, transitional "egalitarian" periods in ritual sequences when the regular rules of respect and rank are stripped away, later to be ritually reasserted. This is when clever young men may challenge and often beat respected elders at the game. The secular setting, however, is the more typical. In both ritual and secular cases, a joking relationship, whether temporary or permanent, exists.

The special joking relationship which participants in the verbal duel must have in order to play involves a fictive brother-in-law tie, the pretense of sexual availability of one's female relatives, and both overt and covert suggestion of homosexual familiarity. The reciprocal term *bolito* (a combination of the Tzotzil term for "brother-in-law," male speaking, *bol*, with a Spanish diminutive) is used by participants. For the purposes of the duel, they assume that each male has a nubile sister who is sexually available without charge of bride-price. In contrast, brother-in-law relationships in real life are typically formal, if not openly hostile. Furthermore, custom dictates formal bride petitioning ceremonies, formal bride-price negotiation, and premarital chastity. All of these rules are flaunted openly in the verbal duel, as they are, generally, in all male joking relationships.

These joking relationships also entail much public physical contact. Boys and men between twelve and thirty-five years of age typically hold hands, in couples, and dance embraced together at fiestas. They also engage publicly in playful grabs at one another's genitals and rub and stroke each other's shoulders, legs, and groins. Such familiar behavior frequently accompanies verbal dueling as well. Furthermore, the homosexual nuances of this behavior carry over into the themes of the exchanges. When not accusing each other's female relatives of being promiscuous or male relatives of being stupid, the duelers tend to impute feminity and passivity to each other.

Thus, two themes of considerable stress for young Chamula males prevail in these exchanges: *social immaturity* and the *prospect of bad affinal relationships which they will experience as adults.* Many men are forced to marry relatively late in life, usually due to lack of money for the expensive petitioning ceremonies and bride-price. Until they do marry, they should not even speak to a nubile woman who is not a relative. Unmarried men are therefore restricted in their social interaction to their families, male age-mates, and older male friends. Recently married men are just beginning to feel the affinal stress which invariably accompanies marriage. This aura of bad feeling is first expressed in the shotgun shots that a potential father-in-law fires into the air as a groom's petitioning party arrives at his house. Even after bride-price is set and the marriage ritual is completed, hostile feelings between brothers-in-law are frequently such that they often ask each other to become the *padrinos* of their first children in order to turn what has been an avoidance relationship into one of respect and cooperation. Chamulas talk freely about this stress. They explain that a girl's brothers and father are angry about losing her in marriage, for the patriline thereby loses part of its numerical strength and workforce. Recently married men face still other frustrations. When finally able to finance marriage, they are often deeply in debt because of their expenses and therefore cannot begin a political or religious career and enter the ritual heirarchy. In addition, the period of bride service at the father-in-law's household lasts from several weeks to two years. Such factors combine to prolong and frustrate the process of becoming a socially mature man for several years. These problems are vividly dramatized in verbal dueling.

RULES AND STRUCTURE

Verbal dueling is based on a *minimum sound shift from word to word or phrase to phrase combined with a maximum derogatory or obscene attack on the opponent.* The subtler the sound and semantic shift required to throw the opponent's challenge back at him, the better the performance. Sometimes poor players cannot maintain the sound continuity very well but can sustain the exchange by semantic continuity alone. Observers consider this option extremely clumsy and ridicule it. In sum, consecutive items in a duel series must have semantic continuity; they should have phonological continuity as well.

Although only about twenty words or phrases were used to inaugurate those challenges of *truly frivolous talk* which I heard, there are more opening formulas. Because they are standardized, these "starter" words are effective in warning an individual that he is being challenged to a duel. Rules governing sound shift limit the number of proper responses to a "starter" word. For example, *k'elun,* "look at me," must retain at least one CV or CVC segment in the word or phrase which follows. Although I have never heard more than six different responses to any one "starter" word, there exist as many if not more alternatives for phonological shift at each node in the chain. Therefore, there is a substantial number of hypothetically possible decisions implied in a chain of two hundred exchanges. The number of alternative responses multiplies geometrically when whole morphemes are retained and combined with new morphemes. Alliteration is also a permitted, though not highly esteemed, form of phonological continuity. The numerous ways to follow the rules of minimal sound shift give the game many possibilities for innovative permutation and combination. Semantic continuity must, of course, always be maintained.

THE TEXT

The following example of a *truly frivolous talk* exchange illustrates several aspects of the genre. A Chamula assistant recorded it verbatim from a performance by his friends at the fiesta of *k'in santo* (equivalent to All Saints and All Souls Festivals in the Catholic calendar), October 30 and 31 of 1968. This text (65 exchanges) is but the first segment of a very long sequence (210 exchanges). The duel ended when one of the players gave up. The two performers were about seventeen and were bachelors and close friends. Their age implies the presence of the kind of joking relationship described above. In the following text, the numerals I and II refer to the two participants.

I have supplemented my free English translation of the text with explanatory notes when the pun and/or other meanings are not completely obvious. In the left column, boxes and arrows indicate the pattern of sound continuity in the duel. In brackets I note those points where phonological discontinuity or mere single-consonant alliteration

| | *Tzotzil* (Phonological continuity indicated by ☐ and ↓) | *English* | *Explanatory Notes* |
|---|---|---|---|
| 1. I. | k'el un | Look at me. | This is a standard initial phrase for *truly frivolous talk*. |
| 2. II. | k'el → ʔavahnil | Look at your wife. | That is, "I might do as your wife." or "My sister might do as your wife." |
| 3. I. | hel avanik | Let's go ahead. | |
| 4. II. | heč → ʔavalik | That's true, what you say. | |
| 5. I. | š'ʔeč → ʔavak'ik | It happens that you give it to her. | |
| 6. II. | š'ʔeč → ʔavok'ik | It happens that you break it. | That is, break her hymen. |
| 7. I. | š'ʔeč → ʔapokik | It happens that you wash it. | Sexual intercourse is thought of as a scrubbing motion, the sexual fluids being soap. |
| 8. II. | š'ʔeč → ʔapohik | It happens that you snatch her away. | |
| 9. I. | š'ʔeč → ʔanopik | It happens that you think about it. | |
| 10. II. | š'ʔeč → ʔamukik | It happens that you bury (it in her). | |

| Tzotzil | English | Explanatory Notes |
|---|---|---|
| 11. I. s-ʔečʔ ʔaʔvikač ʔapit kʔunik | It happens that you put down your load. | That is, relieve yourself sexually. |
| 12. II. yikʔ kas | Smell of gas. | That is, the odor of passing wind. |
| 13. I. yikʔ kas ʔanutiʔ | Smell of gas of your carrying net. | Carrying net is a hemp bag. Here it refers to the scrotum. |
| [Phonological discontinuity with semantic continuity and alliteration] | | |
| 14. II. poklo pokʔokʔ | Wash it. | That is, "Wash your scrotum." Also a play on the Spanish poco, "small amount," thus insulting the size of the other's scrotum. |
| 15. I. pokʔokʔ | Toad. | The scrotum, when swollen, is thought to look like a swollen toad. |
| 16. II. pokʔ sat | Swollen face. | An insult, for this is a species of fish. |
| 17. I. ʔat ot | Your father. | That is, "Your father has a fish face." |
| 18. II. ʔatol | Semen. | A play on the Spanish atole, "sweet corn gruel," which the Chamula say resembles sexual fluid. |

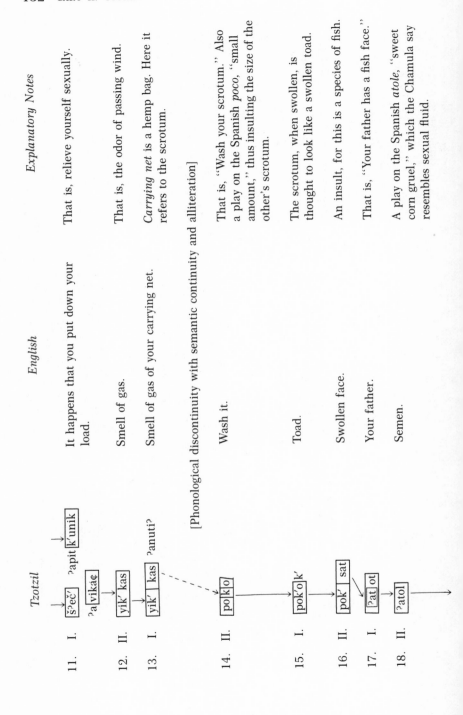

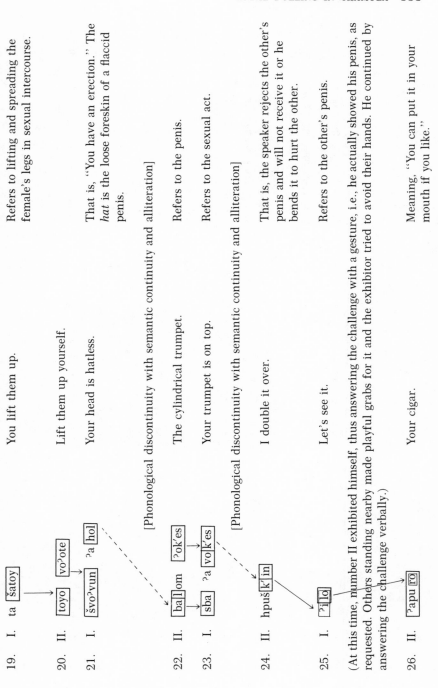

19. I. ta šatoy

You lift them up.

Refers to lifting and spreading the female's legs in sexual intercourse.

20. II. toyo voʔote

Lift them up yourself.

21. I. švoʔvun ʔa hol

Your head is hatless.

That is, "You have an erection." The *hat* is the loose foreskin of a flaccid penis.

[Phonological discontinuity with semantic continuity and alliteration]

22. II. baḷom ʔokʼes

The cylindrical trumpet.

Refers to the penis.

23. I. sba ʔa voḳes

Your trumpet is on top.

Refers to the sexual act.

[Phonological discontinuity with semantic continuity and alliteration]

24. II. hpuškʼin

I double it over.

That is, the speaker rejects the other's penis and will not receive it or he bends it to hurt the other.

25. I. ʔiḷo

Let's see it.

Refers to the other's penis.

(At this time, number II exhibited himself, thus answering the challenge with a gesture, i.e., he actually showed his penis, as requested. Others standing nearby made playful grabs for it and the exhibitor tried to avoid their hands. He continued by answering the challenge verbally.)

26. II. ʔapu ro

Your cigar.

Meaning, "You can put it in your mouth if you like."

| Tzotzil | English | Explanatory Notes |
|---|---|---|
| | | *Explanatory Notes* |
| | *English* | |
| *Tzotzil* | | |

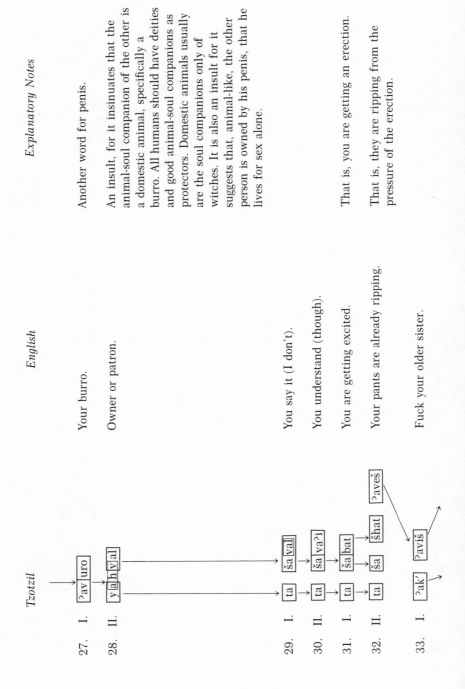

27. I. ʔav uro — Your burro. — Another word for penis.

28. II. y a h v al — Owner or patron. — An insult, for it insinuates that the animal-soul companion of the other is a domestic animal, specifically a burro. All humans should have deities and good animal-soul companions as protectors. Domestic animals usually are the soul companions only of witches. It is also an insult for it suggests that, animal-like, the other person is owned by his penis, that he lives for sex alone.

29. I. ta / ša val — You say it (I don't).

30. II. ta / ša vaʔi — You understand (though).

31. I. ta / ša bat — You are getting excited. — That is, you are getting an erection.

32. II. ta / ša / šhat / ʔaveš — Your pants are already ripping. — That is, they are ripping from the pressure of the erection.

33. I. ʔak' / ʔaviš — Fuck your older sister.

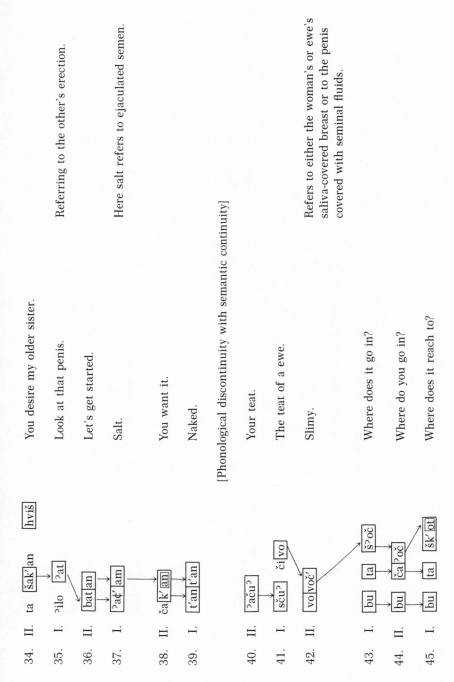

34. II. ta šak'an hviš — You desire my older sister.

35. I. ʔilo ʔat — Look at that penis. — Referring to the other's erection.

36. II. bat|an — Let's get started.

37. I. ʔaȼ'am — Salt. — Here salt refers to ejaculated semen.

38. II. ča k' am — You want it.

39. I. t'am t'am — Naked.

[Phonological discontinuity with semantic continuity]

40. II. ʔačuʔ — Your teat.

41. I. sčuʔ čivo — The teat of a ewe.

42. II. vo voč' — Slimy. — Refers to either the woman's or ewe's saliva-covered breast or to the penis covered with seminal fluids.

43. I. bu ta sʔoč — Where does it go in?

44. II. bu ča ʔoč — Where do you go in?

45. I. bu ta šk' ot — Where does it reach to?

| | *Tzotzil* | *English* | *Explanatory Notes* |
|---|---|---|---|
| 46. II. | | Where does it remain? | |
| 47. I. | | Where does it burst? | |
| 48. II. | | Where is there still room? | |
| 49. I. | | There isn't any. | |
| 50. II. | | It doesn't say so. | |
| 51. I. | | It doesn't weave. | Refers to the shuttle which is inserted through the warp in weaving. The meaning is also sexual. |
| 52. II. | | It isn't moving. | Also to be understood as an instruction given between partners during intercourse. |
| 53. I. | | Your damned sandal. | Context is amusing for it suggests that the man has inserted his sandal rather than his penis. |
| 54. II. | | Your side . . . | To be understood as an order given to a sexual partner. |
| 55. I. | | . . . is free. | Completes preceding phrase. |

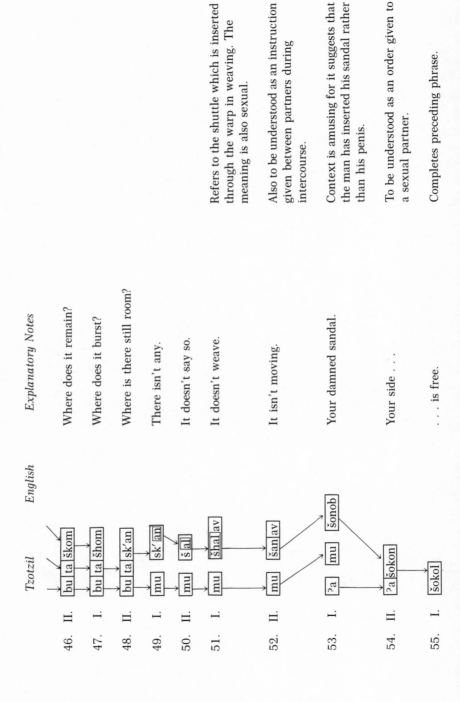

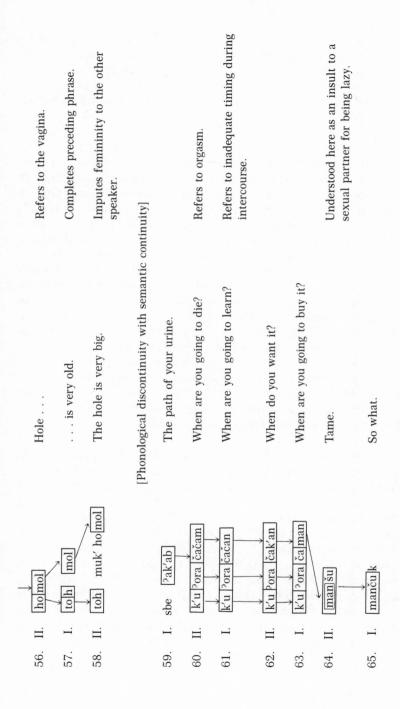

| | | | |
|---|---|---|---|
| 56. | II. | ho mol | Hole . . . | Refers to the vagina. |
| 57. | I. | to h  mol | . . . is very old. | Completes preceding phrase. |
| 58. | II. | toh  muk' ho mol | The hole is very big. | Imputes femininity to the other speaker. |

[Phonological discontinuity with semantic continuity]

| | | | |
|---|---|---|---|
| 59. | I. | sbe  ?ak'ab | The path of your urine. | |
| 60. | II. | k'u ?ora čačam | When are you going to die? | Refers to orgasm. |
| 61. | I. | k'u ?ora čačan | When are you going to learn? | Refers to inadequate timing during intercourse. |
| 62. | II. | k'u ?ora čak'an | When do you want it? | |
| 63. | I. | k'u ?ora čaman | When are you going to buy it? | |
| 64. | II. | man šu | Tame. | Understood here as an insult to a sexual partner for being lazy. |
| 65. | I. | mančuk | So what. | |

accompanies semantic continuity. Phonological discontinuity is a sign of inferior performance since ideally both sound and semantic continuity should be present. Player II, who performed clumsily four out of the five times (see below, items 14, 22, 24, 50), eventually lost the duel when he could not respond after the 210th exchange. In the analysis which follows the text, the numbers refer to the items in the exchange.

DISCUSSION

1.  WHAT DOES ONE LAUGH AT IN *truly frivolous talk?* The problems shared by adolescents and young married men are verbalized vividly in dueling sessions. Although competitive on the surface, verbal dueling also expresses solidarity in this male age-mate group. Never in the life cycle are men more *equal* in status and influence, or lack thereof, than at this stage. Joking expresses this solidarity. Yet the men *rank* each other by a methodical set of insults which impute progressively more asocial traits to the opponent as the game progresses. The improper behavior implied in the duel is precisely the opposite of the behavior which accords rank and status to adult men in real life. This can be seen in the text just given. The exchange begins with homosexual nuances and suggestions of incestuous or promiscuous sexual behavior on the part of the other's female siblings (items 1–11), continues with insults to the other's family, sexuality, and sexual apparatus (items 12–17), and concludes with a long exchange of directions between two sexual partners (items 18–65). Whether in the latter they are male/male instructions or male/female instructions is not entirely clear. Rapid sexual role reversal between the two players, however, appears throughout.

Most of the humorous items are unified by their stress on what brother-in-law relationship and the adult male sexual role should *not* be. Verbal dueling is thus a drama of asocial behavior acted out by individuals who are ambivalent because they are not yet able to assume full adult male roles. The themes of the joking relationship therefore emphasize by stylized breach and laughter just what an adult male *should* be. By analogy this also clarifies why *truly frivolous talk* so frequently occurs during transition points in fiestas (i.e., rest periods between segments of ritual action) among men of *all* ages, particularly among mature ritual officials. During ritual action, even older men may periodically enter *communitas,* a symbolic condition of stripped status and role, which contrasts with the ranked order of everyday life (see Turner, 1969). Expressive of the *communitas* ethos prevalent among ritual personnel is their abstention from sexual relations before, during, and after the fiesta. This abstention is analogous to the ideal celibacy of unmarried men. Furthermore, ritual personnel go deeply into debt in order to buy the food and goods which they need for fulfilling their cargoes properly. This too is analogous to the economic condition of unmarried and young married men. In sum, one of the main themes that one laughs at in *truly frivolous talk* is *male sexual and social immaturity*. Through this laughter, the mature male sexual role is publicly upheld and defended.

Another important duel theme is the contrast between the ideal of male dominance over the female and the reality of some male insecurity in this patrifocal society. In Chamula society the ideal residence is virilocal; father's two patronymics are kept by men and women for a lifetime; and the reckoning of descent is through the male line. Furthermore, men control the public ritual organization while women acquire rank through the ritual position and wealth of their husbands. Nonetheless, there is an important subterfuge of female power in Chamula society and men are very much aware of this. Some of the most noted and feared shamans are women. Furthermore, women inherit land and goods from their parents in the same portion as their brothers. Thus, it is sometimes the case that a woman is richer in potential land inheritance than her husband. In this case the ideal of virilocal residence is set aside for residence near the wife's patriline, close to most of the land parcels which the couple will eventually use. Also, if a husband does not provide well for his wife, Chamula law is quick to recognize a woman's right to immediate divorce, often without refund of bride-price to the man and with the woman taking all of the household goods with her. Thus, men are well aware that even social and ritual maturity will not guarantee them absolute dominance and authority.

Male insecurity in a patrifocal society is expressed frequently in the text above, especially in terms of sexual role reversal and covert homosexuality. In items 51–65, the players "one-up" each other by adopting the female role when chastising the male opponent for his inadequate sexual performance. They are dueling for *female* power as is also common in Chamula court cases, for example, when a woman asks for a divorce on the grounds that her husband does not give her adequate sexual attention. This publicly mortifies the husband, especially if the divorce is granted, and is but one way women wield power in Chamula society. Men laugh at this dilemma in the verbal duel as if to say, "We don't want it this way. It's the opposite of the way things should be." Again the ideal patrifocal order in the fourth creation is upheld by laughing at its inverse.

Principles of rank constitute still another theme in Chamula social life which is upheld by laughing at its inverse in verbal dueling. Chamula is a clearly ranked society. Men outrank women; age outranks youth; religious and political officials outrank laymen; officials with long service in the hierarchy outrank those who have just begun; officials with expensive ritual responsibility outrank those who must spend only a little money on their cargo; shamans with a good record of curing patients outrank (and charge more than) those who do not have so good a record; elder siblings outrank younger siblings. This is expressed in two pervasive classifying words: *bankilal*, "senior" and *ʔiȼ'inal*, "junior." These terms are used to rank everything from siblings to political power, mountains and rivers, even the animals of the forest. Greater size, age, distance, power, breadth, and strength are criteria for identifying something as *bankilal;* those things which possess lesser amounts of these traits are characterized as *ʔiȼ'inal*. (See Vogt, 1969: 238–245, for a more extensive discussion of this ranking principle in nearby Tzotzil-speaking Zinacantan.)

In Chamula life, a man or woman can become more *bankilal* than his fellows by virtue of increasing age, power, prestige, and wealth. For example, to be three time past-*Presidente* is a very *bankilal* trait. To be fifty years old, poor, and a non-cargoholder puts a man in an unquestionably *ʔiȼ'inal* position in relation to a past-*Presidente*. However humble, Chamula men strive as adults to become *bankilal* within some sphere, if only within their own descent line. Note that verbal dueling is most important at that stage of the male life cycle when men are relatively free of rank within their age grade. They continue to be *bankilal* or *ʔiȼ'inal* in relation to their sibling group, but the adult ranking criteria of power, prestige, and wealth are not yet operative, for the youths are not economically, socially, or ritually mature.

Verbal dueling may be seen therefore as a drama in which *bankilal ʔiȼ'inal* status is established in a pair of players who were not ranked before the duel. Ultimately, the victor wins by virtue of his mastery of language and social rules, as in adult life. But in *truly frivolous talk*, ranking is established by criteria which are the inverse of those in effect in adult settings. The duel does not state "How good I am" but rather "We are both bad, but you are worse." Verbal dueling is thus an effort to establish temporary ranked categories in a social group in which adult rank category boundaries are actually not yet clear. It uses much of the raw material from which adult rank derives—cleverness in the use of language, knowledge of social rules, and ability to manipulate them—to set up a temporary adult rank order between two players. Each player must know social rules very well in order to attribute their inverse to his opponent, thus drawing supportive laughter from onlookers. To use Mary Douglas's useful terminology, the two players enter the duel as anomalous beings—animal-like, bisexual, homosexual, immature, unranked, dangerous, and threatening—and emerge, temporarily, as pure ranked social beings (see Douglas, 1966). The winner is *bankilal* to his vanquished opponent. The loser must accept his temporary *ʔiȼ'inal* status, also a pure category. A ranked pair has been established.

By laughing at images of imperfect adult male behavior, Chamula males uphold and defend what a proper adult male should be and emphasize the inevitable stresses and points of ambivalence which men feel in Chamula society. Not all men can be *bankilal* in all spheres; women are by no means completely submissive to the ideal of male authority; and patrilines and male affines will never live in complete harmony.

2. WHAT DOES *truly frivolous talk* TEACH? Chamulas believe that verbal dueling, like other kinds of *frivolous language, games,* and *true recent narrative,* shows people how to act in the fourth creation. From observing "good" and "bad" performances of the genre, I believe that mastery of it is extremely important to the socialization process in general and to the learning of language in particular. Small boys suffer great ridicule from older boys who constantly beat them at *truly frivolous talk.* Among the reasons for this ridicule is the importance of eloquence in Chamula life. The Chamulas believe that they speak the only true language. Their word for Tzotzil is *baȼ'i k'op,* "true or genuine language," and they highly value the ability to speak well and persuasively. A man aspiring to be *bankilal* in any sphere of Chamula life must be eloquent. The ability to wage a good verbal duel serves as one of the earliest signs of social maturity, intelligence, and linguistic eloquence, traits which will be useful in a political or religious career. The man who jokes well with *truly frivolous talk* knows the cultural norms and the range of potential deviation from them very well. Virtuosity in verbal dueling is therefore a culturally significant sign of an excellent traditional education.

Verbal dueling also develops a consciousness of sound play. Minimal sound shift from one item to the next in the sequence of exchanges is as important to a good performance as semantic continuity. The most polished kind of sound shift in a good performance focuses upon one and not more than two phonemes per syllable in each of the words in the phrase. Although my sample of texts is too small to attempt a

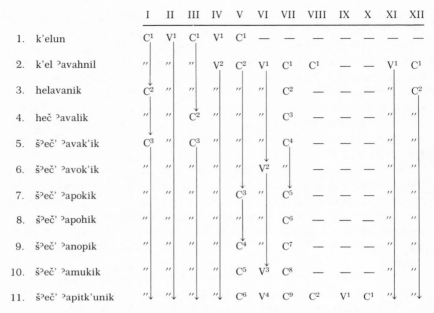

|  |  | I | II | III | IV | V | VI | VII | VIII | IX | X | XI | XII |
|---|---|---|---|---|---|---|---|---|---|---|---|---|---|
| 1. | k'elun | $C^1$ | $V^1$ | $C^1$ | $V^1$ | $C^1$ | — | — | — | — | — | — | — |
| 2. | k'el ʔavahnil | '' | '' | '' | $V^2$ | $C^2$ | $V^1$ | $C^1$ | $C^1$ | — | — | $V^1$ | $C^1$ |
| 3. | helavanik | $C^2$ | '' | '' | '' | '' | '' | $C^2$ | — | — | — | '' | $C^2$ |
| 4. | heč ʔavalik | '' | '' | $C^2$ | '' | '' | '' | $C^3$ | — | — | — | '' | '' |
| 5. | šʔeč' ʔavak'ik | $C^3$ | '' | $C^3$ | '' | '' | '' | $C^4$ | — | — | — | '' | '' |
| 6. | šʔeč' ʔavok'ik | '' | '' | '' | '' | '' | $V^2$ | '' | — | — | — | '' | '' |
| 7. | šʔeč' ʔapokik | '' | '' | '' | '' | $C^3$ | '' | $C^5$ | — | — | — | '' | '' |
| 8. | šʔeč' ʔapohik | '' | '' | '' | '' | '' | '' | $C^6$ | — | — | — | '' | '' |
| 9. | šʔeč' ʔanopik | '' | '' | '' | '' | $C^4$ | '' | $C^7$ | — | — | — | '' | '' |
| 10. | šʔeč' ʔamukik | '' | '' | '' | '' | $C^5$ | $V^3$ | $C^8$ | — | — | — | '' | '' |
| 11. | šʔeč' ʔapitk'unik | '' | '' | '' | '' | $C^6$ | $V^4$ | $C^9$ | $C^2$ | $V^1$ | $C^1$ | '' | '' |

FIGURE 2. Sound shift in *Truly Frivolous Talk*. Columns (I, II, etc.) indicate vowel-consonant slots. Raised numerals indicate number of times a vowel or consonant has shifted. Arrows indicate continuity of vowel or consonant.

generative rule for these exchanges, it is clear that verbal dueling constitutes an impressive living catalogue of minimal pairs. The sound continuity in an excerpt (nos. 1–11 above) is summarized in Figure 2.

Certain vowels and consonants are held constant (columns II and XI) throughout the eleven-item exchange. Others are held most of the time (columns I, IV, and XII). Other vowels and consonants shift slowly and at irregular intervals throughout the sequence. When the possibilities for a particular sound environment are exhausted, another syllable shifts in one or two phonemes.

I have heard feeble attempts at verbal dueling from children as young as two or three years who often try to challenge their older male siblings. At this stage they can seldom manage any accompanying semantic continuity. They do well to form minimal sound shifts which are phonologically possible and meaningful. At five or six, little boys become much more proficient in making accurate shifts, often with derogatory semantic continuity, but these tend to be rote sequences which do not involve improvisation. My own level of competence in performing the genre was at about the level of a six-year-old. Whenever they are challenged by older children, little boys tend to lose, like I nearly always did, for two reasons. First, they seldom succeed in going beyond a memorized sequence. An older boy would probably force the younger to make an unexpected sound shift by opting for a previous change that was not in the younger boy's memorized version of the exchange. The younger boy would then have to mobilize all of his energy to manage the appropriate sound shift, thereby losing control of the semantic continuity. Otherwise, he could opt for carrying only the insulting semantic aspect, while ignoring the sound continuity. Both would be inferior performances. Second, younger boys do not yet know social rules well enough to play with their inverse, especially in a humorous way which follows the sound rules. In early adolescence, truly good players begin to emerge, precisely at the time in the life cycle when they find themselves suspended between childhood and social maturity.

*Truly frivolous talk,* like other secular genres of *k'op,* prepares players for the phonological and syntactic rules, the structures and rhythms of the formal genres, *language for rendering holy, prayer, true ancient words,* and *song* (see *ancient words* in Figure 1). The elementary structure of *ancient words* is the metaphoric couplet. This is a more or less fixed sequence of two phrases each of which says approximately the same thing. In one type of metaphoric couplet, syntax remains constant from line 1 to line 2; only one word is changed from one line to the next. This example from a *prayer* illustrates this type of metaphoric couplet:

1. *lital ta yolon <u>ʔak'ob</u>*
   I have come before your hands.
2. *lital ta yolon <u>ʔavok</u>*
   I have come before your feet.

In a second type of metaphoric couplet, syntax need not remain constant, but the idea must be repeated in the second line, as this example from *true ancient narrative* shows:

1. *lok' la talel ti htotik e*
   The sun came out.
2. *sakhaman ša la talel ti šohobal e*
   Its rays came forth in soft white radiance.

The phonological, syntactic, and semantic aspects of formal metaphoric couplets are not only anticipated in but are actually taught in *truly frivolous talk.* For example (from text above), verbal dueling utilizes many of the same principles of form and sequence:

5.  *š⁷eč' ⁷avak'ik*
    It happens that you give it (to her).
6.  *š⁷eč' ⁷avok'ik*
    It happens that you break it (for her).

This sequence is similar in syntax to the formal metaphoric couplet, as in this example from a *song:*

1.  *sk'ak'alil la ⁷ak'inal e*
    It is the day of your festival.
2.  *sk'ak'alil la ⁷apašku⁷al e*
    It is the day of your passion.

There are of course important differences in mood between the two forms. *Truly frivolous talk* is secular, flexible (less fixed in rote forms), disjunctive (duel between two to eliminate one), non-normative (statement of inverse of norms) and derogatory (insulting); the formal metaphoric couplet is typically sacred, more or less fixed in form, conjunctive (stated by one person in an effort to link man to a sacred order), normative, and often laudatory. Nevertheless, there is an underlying unity of syntax and sound and semantic continuity which ties the forms, and indeed the whole of Chamula oral tradition, together. My observations indicate that the formal genres, which involve hundreds of formal couplets, are not effectively learned until the child reaches adolescence. However, when he does realize that knowledge of formal language is required to become a respectable adult, he will already know the underlying structure of the couplets from his experience with *truly frivolous talk* and other genres. This probably makes the formulas of *ancient words* much easier for the male adolescent to learn and perform. Furthermore, he has experimented with the normative order thousands of times by stating and laughing at its inverse in verbal dueling, thereby sensing the implicit rules of social, supernatural, and cosmological order which *ancient words* attempt to maintain formally.

It is for these reasons that virtuosity in *truly frivolous talk* bodes well for a boy's political and social future. With the reservoir of social rules and thorough knowledge of language which the genre inculcates, a consistent winner in verbal dueling is well equipped to begin the genuine play for rank and prestige which is an important aspect of adulthood.

3.   HOW DOES VERBAL DUELING FORM A PART OF A GENERIC CONTINUUM IN CHAMULA ORAL TRADITION? *Truly frivolous talk* is but one of five

kinds of *frivolous language.* These humorous verbal genres all provide entertainment and exercise informal social control in the fourth creation through stating the inverse of norms and laughing at them. Like all *recent words, truly frivolous talk* was learned for the first time in and refers to events of the fourth creation while maintaining a defensive orientation to it. Furthermore, *frivolous language* is a kind of *pure speech,* which is the supercategory which encompasses the spectrum of specialized and more or less fixed forms of verbal behavior. (See Gossen, 1972a, for a more detailed discussion of the generic continuum of Chamula oral tradition.)

Other genres are instrumental in preparing children for verbal dueling. The players learn about asocial and animal-like behavior from the two narrative genres, which together relate events spanning the four creations and mostly tell of the improper behavior of the ancients and of contemporary men. Children hear these stories from a very young age. It would be impossible to play *truly frivolous talk* without this information. Furthermore, the structure of verbal dueling has antecedent forms in young children's games; for example, the verbatim repetition of commands in *games* and the parallel syntax and use of insult in *angry speech.* Children master these forms before they control verbal dueling. Dueling syntax also has cognate structures in other kinds of *recent words* and is closely related to metaphoric couplets, which form the elementary building blocks of *ancient words.*

4.   WHY DOES VERBAL DUELING EXIST AT ALL IF SO MUCH OF WHAT IT IS AND DOES CAN BE FOUND ELSEWHERE IN CHAMULA LANGUAGE AND CUSTOM? Verbal dueling represents an intermediate stage in the acquisition of adult linguistic competence. For good performance, great mastery of sound discrimination and parallel syntax is required. Male children and adolescents develop many of these skills by dueling, which inculcates the principles of minimal sound shift, parallel syntax, rhythm, alliteration, and dyadic semantic sets in metaphoric couplets, the elementary form of formal adult speech. *No other nonformal genre of Chamula verbal behavior depends so completely on dyadic patterns of sound and meaning, and limits participation to two and only two persons.* Most of the other genres are typically performed by one person or by a small group. The emphasis on a specified pair of performers and on dyadic sets of linguistic and semantic exchange makes the ranking function of the genre very explicit. Much of the Chamula universe being classified into junior and senior aspects, the verbal duel serves as a crystalline form of this ranking principle; it is identified with a period of transition between childhood and adulthood when ranking becomes important to young men but when very few of the real criteria for adult

rank operate, with the exception of grace and power in the use of language. To use Tzotzil, *bac̆'i k'op,* "the true language," well constitutes a significant social asset. *Presidentes,* shamans, and cargoholders are constantly evaluated by their peers and by those beneath them as to whether "they know how to talk well" (*mi lek snaʔ šk'opoh*). This usually means, "How extensive is their knowledge of ritual speech and song, and how well do they perform them?" The same phrase is used in evaluating young men. The major arena and proving ground for the early evaluation of their potential is *truly frivolous talk.*

Verbal dueling also involves a systematic search through the cultural reservoir for insult, for ways to invert norms, for hundreds of examples of asocial behavior. Once the inverse of a rule is found, considerable skill is required to insert it according to the phonological, syntactic, and semantic rules. Although quite fluent in conversational Tzotzil, as I mentioned before, I never achieved even the level of a six-year-old in *truly frivolous talk.* The other genres of *recent words* and *speech for people whose hearts are heated* (transitional between *ordinary language* and *pure speech*) also constantly use negative examples to illustrate and teach norms, but they usually address specific cases of deviation which need righting and do not involve such strict formal requirements. *Angry speech,* for example, attributes animal-like qualities to an opponent or other person who is considered deviant, from the speaker's point of view. But this is spontaneous and is addressed to a specific situation; it need not follow inflexible rules of sound and syntax. The same is true of most of the other informal genres. It is the *systematic cataloguing of deviance according to strict phonological, semantic, and performance rules* which makes *truly frivolous talk* stand out as a very special kind of *recent words.*

Like verbal dueling in other cultures, *truly frivolous talk* draws its strength and popularity from factors that are not always apparent in the text alone, as Dundes, Leach, and Ozkök (1970), and Abrahams (1962, 1970b) have also observed. Chamula verbal dueling is more than a frivolous game. It is also more than an expression of male stress and anxiety, as one might assume in viewing the game as a drama of phallic attack and submission (see Dundes, et al. 1970). Although these elements are present, the role of Chamula verbal dueling is more complex than first meets the eye and ear. Its larger significance as a speech event becomes more intelligible within a holistic social and linguistic framework.

# Creativity: Institutional
# and Individual

PART III

ANTHONY E. BACKHOUSE

# How to Remember Numbers

# in Japanese*

CHAPTER SEVEN

## Introduction

The purpose of this article is to describe how one area of the Japanese vocabulary undergoes the application of a certain type of wordplay, and to illustrate the practical use to which this resource is put in everyday life. In Japanese, it is often possible to construct mnemonics for the memorization of numbers. The present attempt to account for the principles involved in their construction is based on the inspection of attested number mnemonics. The repertory of forms used can be accounted for in terms of the basic Japanese numerals and certain extensions effected on these which can be conveniently stated in terms of the Japanese writing system. This repertory of forms is used in constructing mnemonics in accordance with a wordplay technique known as *goroawase*, "matching of sounds." Number mnemonics are used publicly in two social domains: assigned to telephone numbers by certain types of commercial enterprises in advertising material and assigned to historical dates and other useful numbers in certain educational aids.

*Goroawase* is an extended punning technique in which a sequence of sounds (typically, a phrase or sentence) is associated with a similar sequence of sounds of different meaning. In the present case *goroawase* is applied to sequences of numeral forms to provide a mnemonic device for the memorization of numbers.

The single-digit numerals form the basic linguistic material to which the technique is applied. As is well known, Japanese is unusual in possessing two etymologically distinct series of such numeral forms, one comprising native Japanese elements (NJap), the other made up of

* The author wishes to thank Mr. Tatsuo Ban for help in providing data for this article.

Sino-Japanese elements originating as borrowings from Chinese (SJap). These may be set out, with their variants, as follows:

TABLE 1[1]

| | NJap | SJap |
|---|---|---|
| 1 | *hito* | *iti* |
| 2 | *huta* | *ni* |
| 3 | *mi* | *saN* |
| 4 | *yo/yoN* | *si* |
| 5 | *itu* | *go* |
| 6 | *mu* | *roku* |
| 7 | *nana* | *siti* |
| 8 | *ya* | *hati* |
| 9 | *kokono* | *kyuu/ku* |

The distributional restrictions on the occurrence of these forms in the normal use of the language are irrelevant to the operation of the mnemonic system.[2] The important point is that the forms in Table 1 represent material already available in the language, as distinct from material created specially for the operation of the mnemonic system, which we shall consider below.

At this point we can illustrate the technique with a simple example: the number 24, normally pronounced *nizyuusi* or *nizyuuyoN*, "twenty-four," can be memorized by pronouncing the SJap forms for 2 (*ni*) and 4 (*si*) in succession to give the word *nisi*, "west," it being easier to remember a word than a random number. Naturally, the technique is particularly useful if it can be successfully applied to longer numbers, but the example suffices to show how *goroawase* is applied here: the resources of homophony in the language are employed so as to construct a meaningful linguistic sequence from an original succession of sounds (i.e., a series of numerals).

Inspection of actual mnemonics shows that the forms in the list given in Table 1 undergo various extensions and modifications in the practical operation of the mnemonic system. What follows is an attempt at a principled explanation of the operations involved in these changes.

---

[1] Japanese forms are given in the Kunreisiki system of romanization, except that the mora nasal is represented by N and the mora geminate (i.e., the first element in a non-nasal geminate consonant) by Q.

[2] In general, the SJap forms are used in counting and in forming compound numerals. Both sets enter into compounds with numeral classifiers, the classifier concerned determining which set to use.

Examples of attested mnemonics, which constitute the justification for this explanation, are then given in the course of discussing the public use made of the mnemonic system.

## Construction of Number Mnemonics

One of the demands of a system of this kind is a large repertory of useful forms, to increase the possibility of forming a mnemonic in any given case. The extensions to the basic forms which occur constitute natural ways of satisfying this demand. We can distinguish three separate strategies under this heading, and in all three cases we are dealing with material introduced especially for the operation of the mnemonic system.[3] In considering the precise form which these extensions take it is useful to look at the language, as does the ordinary Japanese who intuitively controls and understands the principles involved here, via the writing system.

As is well known, the Japanese language is normally written by means of a combination of characters (*kaNzi*) and a syllabary (*kana*).[4] The following aspects of the *kana* syllabary are of importance here: firstly, it is based on the mora, i.e., the phonological unit intermediate between the phoneme and the syllable; secondly, it reflects certain morphophonemic correlations between sounds in the language; and thirdly, it reflects certain principles of syllable structure with regard to syllable-final morae. Let us consider each of these in turn.

In general, each *kana* symbol represents one mora. (The mora coincides with the syllable except for the following cases: a syllable containing a long vowel or diphthong contains two morae, as does a syllable containing a final nasal or other final consonant.[5] Thus in Table 1 the forms *iti, kyuu, saN* are all di-moric, i.e., *i-ti, kyu-u, sa-N*, although only *iti* is disyllabic.) The salient status thus accorded to the

---

[3] In fact the line here is somewhat difficult to draw. Some of our derived forms do occur elsewhere in the language in special circumstances: *hi* (1) and *hu* (2) are sometimes used in counting, and the form *ro* (6) appears in the series *ni, si, ro, ya* (2, 4, 6, 8) used in counting off pairs; some modifications are also made in reciting the multiplication table and in using the abacus. In none of these cases are the changes as thoroughgoing as here, however, and it seems reasonable to state the division as we do.

[4] In fact there are two syllabaries (*hiragana* and *katakana*), used in different circumstances. Both are based on the same principles. The basic tables of symbols for both are set out in Miller, 1967: 123.

[5] This statement holds for the forms that concern us here and generally, though not completely, for the language as a whole. For some exceptions, involving tri-moric syllables, see Wenck, 1966: 19, 85.

mora makes it the natural unit with which to operate in the intuitive analysis of longer forms on the part of literate speakers.

In the phonological system of Japanese, the consonant pairs $k/g$, $s/z$, $t/d$ and $h/b$ are morphophonemically correlated in that an initial voiceless member is often replaced by the corresponding voiced member of the pair in the second element of compounds: thus *kawa*, "river," but *o-gawa*, "stream." A similar relationship holds under certain conditions between the pair $h/p$.[6] These relationships are reflected in the *kana* syllabary as follows: morae with initial $k/s/t/h$ and the corresponding morae with initial $g/z/d/b$ are written with the same *kana* symbol, a diacritic being added in the case of the voiced members; morae with initial $p$ are also written with the same symbol as morae with initial $h$, in this case with a different diacritic added. The modified morae are known as *dakuoN*, "impure sounds," and *haNdakuoN*, "semi-impure sounds," respectively, and constitute a ready-made set of natural variants.

We have stated that in general the mora coincides with the syllable except in the case of syllables containing a long vowel or diphthong, a syllable-final nasal, or other syllable-final consonant (i.e., the first element of a non-nasal geminate consonant): the segmental structure of the Japanese syllable can in general be represented as $(C(J)) \, V \left( \left\{ \begin{matrix} V \\ N \\ Q \end{matrix} \right\} \right)$, where N represents the mora nasal and Q the mora geminate.[7] The *kana* syllabary handles these facts as follows: the second element of a long vowel (known as *nobasu oto*, "lengthening sound") is represented by a single special length symbol;[8] the mora nasal (*hana ni kakeru oto*, "nasal sound") has its own *kana* symbol; and the mora geminate (*tumaru oto*, "clipped sound") is everywhere represented by a single symbol. The second element of a diphthong is simply written with the relevant vowel symbol. Of the four types of syllable-final morae, three are thus given salient unitary status in the syllabary and constitute natural ways in which to extend single-mora syllables.

Given this information, we can state the extensions effected on the basic numeral forms in Table 1 as follows:

---

[6] For details and examples of the relationships concerned here, see Wenck, 1966: 16, 18.

[7] This statement is subject to the same reservations as those given in note 5, involving tri-moric syllables of the form C(J)VVN, C(J)VVQ, C(J)VNQ. J is a palatal element, represented by (non-initial) $y$ in the romanization used here.

[8] This applies especially to *katakana*.

(1a)   Where applicable, introduce additional abbreviated forms consisting of the initial mora of longer forms. Thus, on the basis of the form *saN* (3) we introduce the abbreviated form *sa*, etc.

(1b)   Where applicable, introduce additional morphophonemic variant forms containing the corresponding initial *dakuoN* and *haNdakuoN;* where the original form contains an initial *dakuoN*, introduce the corresponding non-*dakuoN* variant. Thus, on the basis of *saN* we introduce the voiced form *zaN*, etc.

(1c)   Where not already present, introduce additional extended forms of single-mora syllables formed by attaching unitary syllable-final morae. Thus, given *mi* (3), we introduce the extended forms *mii, miN, miQ*, etc.

These operations are cumulative: (1a) applies to the basic forms, given in Table 1, (1b) applies to the basic forms and also to the output of (1a), and so on. The enlarged list of forms obtained in this way is set out in the tables below; NJap forms are given in Table 2(a), SJap forms in Table 2(b), and column headings indicate the operations involved in the derivation. (Starred forms are phonologically odd and as such are to be regarded as excluded from the outset: i.e., (1a), (1b) and (1c) apply only insofar as the phonological constraints of the language are not broken.[9])

[9]*Kyu* and *gyu* occur only as the initial morae in the syllables *kyuu/kyuQ* and *gyuu/gyuQ*, respectively, never as whole syllables or followed by *N*. *Pito, puta*, and *gokono* constitute unnatural morpheme shapes: the *h/p* correlation (*pito, puta*) holds predominantly for SJap forms and is out of place here, and initial voiced consonants (*gokono*) are uncommon in NJap morphemes and tend to have special connotations (Wenck, 1966: 13).

## TABLE 2(a)

| Basic forms | (1a) | (1b) | (1c) |
|---|---|---|---|
| 1  *hito* | *hi* | *bito/*pito/ bi/pi* | *hii/hiN/hiQ/bii/biN/biQ/ pii/piN/piQ* |
| 2  *huta* | *hu* | *buta/*puta/ bu/pu* | *huu/huN/huQ/buu/buN/buQ/ puu/puN/puQ* |
| 3  *mi* | | | *mii/miN/miQ* |
| 4  *yo/yoN* | | | *yoo/yoQ* |
| 5  *itu* | *i* | | *ii/iN/iQ* |
| 6  *mu* | | | *muu/muN/muQ* |
| 7  *nana* | *na* | | *naa/naN/naQ* |
| 8  *ya* | | | *yaa/yaN/yaQ* |
| 9  *kokono* | *ko* | *\*gokono/go* | *koo/koN/koQ/goo/goN/goQ* |

TABLE 2(b)

| Basic forms | (1a) | (1b) | (1c) |
|---|---|---|---|
| 1  *iti* | *i* | | *ii/iN/iQ* |
| 2  *ni* | | | *nii/niN/niQ* |
| 3  *saN* | *sa* | *zaN/za* | *saa/saQ/zaa/zaQ* |
| 4  *si* | | *zi* | *sii/siN/siQ/zii/ziN/ziQ* |
| 5  *go* | | *ko* | *goo/goN/goQ/koo/koN/koQ* |
| 6  *roku* | *ro* | | *roo/roN/roQ* |
| 7  *siti* | *si* | *ziti/zi* | *sii/siN/siQ/zii/ziN/ziQ* |
| 8  *hati* | *ha* | *bati/pati* | *haa/haN/haQ/baa/baN/baQ/* |
| | | *ba/pa* | *paa/paN/paQ* |
| 9  *kyuu/ku* | *\*kyu* | *gyuu/gu/\*gyu* | *kuu/kuN/kuQ/\*kyuN/kyuQ/guu/* |
| | | | *guN/guQ/\*gyuN/gyuQ* |

We must also mention here the treatment of 0 (zero) in the system. This is irregular in that the sequence 10 may be assigned single forms for "ten" (NJap *too*/SJap *zyuu*), plus extensions of these; otherwise 0 is assigned the form *ree*, "zero," with extensions as usual. The relevant forms are set out below and take their place alongside those in Tables 2(a) and 2(b).

| | | | | |
|---|---|---|---|---|
| 0 | *ree* | *re* | | *reN/reQ* |
| 10 | *too/zyuu* | *to/zyu* | *doo/syuu/* | *toN/toQ/zyuN/zyuQ/doN/* |
| | | | *do/syu* | *doQ/syuN/syuQ* |

The nonstarred forms given above constitute the theoretical repertory of forms used in the construction of number mnemonics. In practice, this repertory is reduced in the public use of the mnemonic system as the result of two factors, one accidental, the other conventional. The accidental factor is that a few of the forms are of highly restricted occurrence in the language, and thus statistically unlikely to figure in mnemonics. More important is the conventional factor of the elimination of ambiguity. We have noted that a large repertory of useful forms is an essential property of a system such as the present one; clarity, which to some extent runs counter to this first requirement, is equally important. The list as it stands contains several cases of ambiguity, and inspection of attested mnemonics enables us to extract certain conventions which operate in elimination of such cases.

The most obvious cases of ambiguity are those in which the same form appears in different places: *i* and its (1c) variants under 1 and 5; *si/zi* and their (1c) variants under 4 and 7; and *go/ko* and their (1c) variants under 5 and 9. Here the convention is as follows:

(2a)   *i* and variants represent 1, *si/zi* and variants represent 4, *go/ko* and variants represent 5; i.e., where applicable, basic forms take precedence over derived forms.

Other cases of ambiguity arise when a form can be construed either as a single form or as a succession of shorter forms: *hito/bito* vs. *hi/bi + to*, *roku* vs. *ro + ku*, *nana* vs. *na + na*, *hii/bii/pii/ii/nii/mii/sii/zii* (i.e. all forms with long *i*) vs. *hi/bi/pi/i/ni/mi/si/zi + i*. The convention in this case generally operates as follows:

(2b)   Ambiguous long forms representing single numerals are dropped; i.e., shorter forms take precedence over longer forms. However, *hito/bito* are retained as forms representing 1, rather than being construed as *hi/bi + to*, i.e. 110; this is doubtless due to the usefulness of the forms (which mean "person," "man") and the unlikelihood of confusion given the status of *to*.

The list of forms which are actually available for public use (i.e., with phonologically irregular and ambiguous forms omitted) can finally be stated as Table 3:

## TABLE 3

| | |
|---|---|
| 0 | *ree/re/reN/reQ* |
| 1 | *hito/iti/hi/i/bito/bi/pi/hiN/hiQ/iN/iQ/biN/biQ/piN/piQ* |
| 2 | *huta/ni/hu/buta/bu/pu/huu/huN/huQ/buu/buN/buQ/puu/puN/ puQ/niN/niQ* |
| 3 | *mi/saN/sa/zaN/za/saa/saQ/zaa/zaQ/miN/miQ* |
| 4 | *yo/yoN/si/zi/yoo/yoQ/siN/siQ/ziN/ziQ* |
| 5 | *itu/go/ko/goo/goN/goQ/koo/koN/koQ* |
| 6 | *mu/ro/muu/muN/muQ/roo/roN/roQ* |
| 7 | *siti/na/ziti/naa/naN/naQ* |
| 8 | *ya/hati/ha/bati/pati/ba/pa/yaa/yaN/yaQ/haa/haN/haQ/baa/baN/ baQ/paa/paN/paQ* |
| 9 | *kokono/kyuu/ku/gyuu/gu/kuu/kuN/kuQ/guu/guN/guQ/kyuQ/gyuQ* |
| 10 | *too/zyuu/to/zyu/doo/syuu/do/syu/toN/toQ/zyuN/zyuQ/doN/doQ/ syuN/syuQ* |

This list forms the core of the repertory for the mnemonic system. Exceptionally, a few additional forms based on different principles are occasionally introduced; these will be commented on individually in discussing examples in which they occur.

We are now in a position to state the principles involved in encoding actual mnemonics. Given a number, let us say 2469, which we wish to memorize:

(3a)   Break the number down into its constituent digits: i.e., in constructing mnemonics we read the number as "two, four, six, nine," not as "two thousand four hundred and sixty-nine."

(3b)   Assign to each digit the set of forms listed against it in Table 3. In addition, assign to any sequence 10 the single forms listed against 10 in Table 3.

(3c)   Proceeding from the leftmost digit, try to find a combination of forms that will yield a homophonous meaningful linguistic sequence.

In the case of the number 2469, the combination *ni* (2) + *si* (4) + *mu* (6) + *ku* (9) yields the meaningful syntagm *nisi muku*, "face west," a serviceable mnemonic.

## Use of Number Mnemonics

As mentioned before, there are at least two social domains in which the public use of the system is well established: the first is the use by certain types of commercial enterprises of mnemonics for telephone numbers in advertising material, the second their use as educational aids for the memorization of historical dates and other useful numbers. In both cases it is normally demanded that, for maximum effectiveness, the mnemonic syntagm should not only be meaningful, but should have some close semantic connection with the significance of the original number.

The use of mnemonics for telephone numbers is particularly associated with the service and entertainment sectors of commerce, including restaurants, coffee shops, bars, and hotels. Given the important role played by such establishments in Japanese society, the possession of an easily remembered telephone number is a major asset, not only in itself but also for the publicity value of an ear-catching mnemonic. Indeed the larger enterprises are willing to pay the telephone companies high fees in exchange for the allocation of a number for which a particularly apt mnemonic can be constructed.[10] The mnemonic phrase is then printed in *kana* alongside the telephone number on business cards, matchboxes and other advertising material, and, in the case of larger concerns, often read out in television commercials.

The range of application here is effectively limited to numbers of four digits, since Japanese telephone numbers in general take the form of a three-digit exchange followed by a four-digit number (e.g., 123-

[10]It seems that a similar practice occurs in the United States. Telephone mnemonics can be constructed based on the distribution of letters and digits on the dial, and firms sometimes request numbers which will yield an appropriate word: *fotolab* is an attested example.

4567), and the mnemonic as assigned only to the latter part (i.e., to 4567 in the above example), knowledge of the exchange being taken for granted. This permits the associated convention that initial zero(s) in telephone numbers are ignored in constructing the actual mnemonic, the requisite number of initial zeros to make up the four-digit complement being supplied by the decoder. (See the examples 0039 and 0491 in (a) below, where the mnemonic is constructed on the digits 39 and 491, respectively.)

The following list of attested telephone mnemonics is grouped under three headings according to the nature of the connection between the mnemonic and the enterprise concerned.

(a)   The mnemonic relates to some aspect of the activity of the enterprise:

4126   *yoi huro* "good bath," for a health center
5189   *goiQpaku* "your overnight stay," for a hotel
1129   *ii niku* "good meat," for a steak restaurant
4989   *yoku yaku* "we cook well," for an eel restaurant
0039   *saNkyuu* "thank you" (i.e., for your patronage), for a bar
4951   *yoku koi* "come often" for a night club
0491   *siQkui* "putty," for a glazier's

(b)   The mnemonic names the type of enterprise concerned:

2983   *nikuyasaN* "Mr Butcher"
1028   *toohuya* "bean curd shop"
5298   *gohukuya* "draper's shop"
1058   *tokoya* "barber's shop"

(c)   The mnemonic names or is otherwise associated with the actual name of the enterprise:

0028   *futaba,* for a restaurant called "Futaba"
0101   *maruimarui,* for the Marui Department Store. (The assignment of the form *maru* to 0 depends on the association of the meaning of *maru,* "circle," with the graphic form of the digit 0.)
5656   *gorogoro* "rumblingly," for the Tokyo confectioner's called Kaminari Okosi "Kaminari Confectioneries." The connection here is that *kaminari* literally means "thunder" and *gorogoro* is the onomatopoeic form commonly applied to thunder in Japanese.)

It is perhaps worth noting that both alternate forms of the word "good," *ii* and *yoi,* provide clear mnemonics (11 and 41, respectively) and figure prominently in mnemonics of type (a) above.

The second main public use of the system is in connection with numbers such as historical dates which have to be memorized for educational purposes. Though not included in the official state textbooks, mnemonics of this type feature in educational guides marketed for use by schoolchildren. In the case of dates, the mnemonic phrase itself is normally contained in a larger phrase or sentence chosen for its semantic connection with the event concerned and memorized as a whole. The examples in the following list are grouped according to subject-matter.

(a)  Historical dates:

334  (B.C.) (Alexander invades Persian Empire)
*saa sa siQkari ArekisaN* "Go ahead, Alex!" (*saa sa siQ* is the mnemonic)

272  (B.C.) (Italy unified under Rome)
*haNtoo o bunaN ni tooitu Rooma ka na* "Rome, safely unifying the peninsula" (*bunaN ni*)

46  (B.C.) (Caesar assumes dictatorship)
*Siizaa wa PoNpeiusu no kokoro yomu* "Caesar reads Pompey's mind" (*yomu*)

476  (Fall of Western Roman Empire)
*Dairooma Nisirooma yori sinamu to su* "Great Rome begins to perish in the West" (*sinamu*)

1066  (Norman Conquest)
*NorumaNdii, irero muri de mo* "Normandy [cries], 'Let us pass, though you find it unreasonable'" (*irero mu*)

1096  (First Crusade)
*zyuuziguN tuitookuroo no daieNsei* "the Crusaders, great expedition of subjugation" (*tookuroo*)

1192  (Founding of Kamakura Shogunate)
*ii kuni tukuroo* "Let's build a good country" (*ii kuni*)

1215  (Magna Carta)
*hito ni igo oboerare* "learned by people thereafter" (*hito ni igo*)

1241  (Hansa League)
*akinau hito ni yoi sikumi* "a good arrangement for merchants" (*hito ni yoi*)

1338  (Hundred Years' War begins)
*Ei to Futu isamihayaru hyakuneNkaN* "A hundred years in which England and France show their spirit" (*isamiha*)

1492  (Discovery of America)
*iyoiyo kuni ga mieta* "At last a country was sighted" (*iyo kuni*)

1549  (St. Francis Xavier reaches Japan)
*igo yoku Zabieru kuru* "Thereafter Xavier comes often" (*igo yoku*)

(b)  Geographical data:

1592  (Height in meters of Mt. Aso, in Kyushu)
*Higo no kuni* "the province of Higo" (in which the mountain is

situated) (*Higo kuni* is the mnemonic, the relational particle *no* being irrelevant to the system.)

(c)   Other numbers:

1.732   (Square root of 3)

*hitonami ni* "like the ordinary run of men"

2.236   (Square root of 5)

*HuzisaNroku* "foothills of Mt. Fuji" (The assignment of the form *zi* to 2 is due to the fact that the form is sometimes written with the character for "two," e.g., in the male given name *Ziroo*. Since it conflicts with the normal $zi = 4$, it involves an additional memory burden, as does the use of *roku* for 6 which breaks ambiguity constraint [2b].)

2-4-6-9-11   (Numbers of the months having less than 31 days)

*nisi muku samurai* "a samurai facing west" (The assignment of the form *samurai* to 11 is based on the graphic similarity of the character for *samurai* ($\pm$) and the characters for *zyuuiti* "eleven" ($\pm$). This is the Japanese equivalent of the English mnemonic verse beginning "Thirty days hath September, . . ." Since the Japanese names of the months incorporate numbers, e.g., *itigatu* "January" is literally "one-month," this is an efficient way of memorizing the information.)

The lack of the normal semantic connection in examples (c) is naturally to be expected in view of the nature of the numbers concerned.

The mnemonic system cannot be successfully applied to all numbers, but the list of attested examples given above could be extended considerably. With the exception of occasional ambiguity (*HuzisaN-roku*) and introduction of extraneous forms (*maru* = 0, $zi = 2$, *samurai* = 11), they can all be explained on the basis of the basic numeral forms of the language and the rules and conventions we have set out above. The system is of course also available to individuals to apply for their private purposes, and in this case some of the constraints which are vital for public purposes can be lifted, resulting in a higher success rate: if one is determined to use the system to remember a friend's telephone number, for example, one can as often as not find some way of assigning a mnemonic if one is prepared to relax the constraint on close semantic relatedness and perhaps tolerate some ambiguity (and the increased memory burden involved).

## Summary

The essential aspects of the phenomenon discussed in this article are thus the wordplay technique of *goroawase*, the extension of the repertory of Japanese numeral forms, and their combination into a mnemonic system used in certain areas of Japanese society. The phenomenon forms part of Japanese linguistic culture and, as such, is intuitively controlled in all its aspects by any normal speaker of the language.[11] We hope to have brought out some of the principles implicit in the system as it works.

In conclusion it may be useful briefly to consider the system from a more general point of view. As a mnemonic system, it falls into the broad category of digit-letter systems, which Hunter (1964: 292 ff.) names as one of the three general types into which mnemonic systems can be divided; digit-letter systems are "designed to assist the memorizing of digit sequences by translating digits into code items which can easily be related together." Hunter mentions a typical system devised by Brayshaw, an English headmaster, who in 1849 published a work entitled "Metrical Mnemonics" containing rhymes incorporating dates and other numerical facts for memorization by schoolchildren. In Brayshaw's system, one or more consonants are assigned to each digit (vowels being left unassigned), and a word or phrase containing the relevant letters is built into a mnemonic verse appropriate to the date concerned. For example, his verse for 1837 (date of Queen Victoria's accession) is *Lastly, our hope rests on Victoria's will, where our hope* ($r = 8$, $h = 3$, $p = 7$; initial 1 is taken for granted) is the mnemonic phrase; this provides an interesting parallel to the way historical dates are handled in the Japanese system. A digit-letter system of wider currency, although not a mnemonic system as such, is gematria, the basis of which is that each letter of the alphabet is conventionally associated with a numerical value, the values of the letters in a given word being added together to give a numerical value for the word as a whole. Gematria gives rise to cryptographs in the form of a word which has the same numerical value as another word taken to be its hidden meaning, and it is especially associated with the cabalistic method of interpreting the Hebrew Scriptures.

However, gematria, like Brayshaw's system and the United States' telephone mnemonics mentioned in note 10, differs from the Japanese system described here in that the letter-digit assignment on which it is based is linguistically arbitrary and has to be specially learned. In the Japanese system, by contrast, the basic forms associated with the digits are given in the language, and once the general principles for extending this basic repertory are understood, the system is immediately available for use. Some of the general factors required for such a linguistically

---

[11] It seems that children typically become aware of the system in their early teens and in some cases then practice applying it to friends' telephone numbers and the like.

motivated system to operate are highlighted by comparison with English: as far as wordplay possibilities in the English numerals are concerned, only *two*, *four*, and *eight* suggest homophony, and the natural approach appears to be the acronym (i.e., an abbreviatory strategy based on the letter, as the Japanese system is based, in [1a], on the mora). However, acronyms depend heavily upon the presence of forms with initial vowels to yield a pronounceable sequence, and since the initial letters of the English single-digit numerals (o,t,t,f,f,s,s,e,n) contain only two such (and are in any case highly ambiguous), the possibilities are severely limited. In comparison, Japanese has two clear advantages: a salient sound unit larger than the single phoneme, and a large number of distinct numeral forms. As far as the second factor is concerned, Japanese is clearly unusual, but the role of the first factor in fostering the type of wordplay described here is a question that may repay further investigation.

DINA SHERZER

# Saying Is Inventing:
# Gnomic Expressions in *Molloy*

## CHAPTER EIGHT

S AMUEL BECKETT's novel *Molloy* (1955) contains such utterances as:

Saying is inventing. (Beckett, 1955: 32)
Precautions are like resolutions to be taken with precautions. (Beckett, 1955: 32)
For to know nothing is nothing, not to want to know anything likewise, but to be beyond knowing anything, to know that you are beyond knowing anything, that is when peace enters in, to the soul of the incurious seeker. (Beckett, 1955: 64)

The expression "once upon a time" indicates that a fairy tale is about to begin. "Ladies and gentlemen" precedes a formal speech. The formulas quoted above and other similar ones woven into the texture of the novel also belong to a special code, in this case, *the gnomic code,* which involves proverbs, aphorisms, maxims, and similar general sayings, all of which are *gnomic expressions.*

Because of their semantic, phonological, lexical, and syntactic properties, gnomic expressions are immediately recognizable in written texts and oral discourse. *Semantically,* gnomic expressions deal with basic aspects of life: love, health, age, poverty, riches, work, etc. They advocate strategies and give advice. In contrast with the specificity of the context in which they appear, gnomic expressions state a general truth, often by metaphorically referring to a range of experiences broader than their immediate context of use. Verb tense in gnomic expressions is almost always the present, an atemporal present, since it applies to any time; in contrast, the verbs in the context are situated

163

temporally, for example, in the past. *Phonologically*, gnomic expressions may exhibit alliteration, assonance, and other kinds of repetition. *Lexically*, they may use archaic words. The copula is frequently employed, as are the impersonal forms of pronouns and nouns: one, we, you, people. *Syntactically*, gnomic expressions are characterized by parallelism, symmetry, and other verbal dispositions, for example, *chiasmus*. (See Milner, 1969: 63.)

These features make gnomic expressions stand out as special linguistic entities. Lewis (1971: 135–136), discussing the maxims of La Rochefoucauld, notices that they entail a juggling of words, a manipulation of the constraints and potentialities of language. This is true of gnomic expressions generally. "Juggling words" is a way of playing with language, play being understood here as the juxtaposition of linguistic forms to create new relationships among them. Play can also imply fun, as in puns and *contrepets* or spoonerisms (François, 1966). Fun-oriented play, although present in gnomic expressions, is not essential to them. The ultimate purpose of gnomic expressions is to manipulate language, to create a striking disposition of verbal forms, in order to teach, to convey wisdom, or to express a particular philosophy.[1]

The gnomic expressions found in *Molloy* are Beckett's own invention. They are found neither in published collections of proverbs, maxims, or sayings, nor in everyday conversation. Yet they are felt to be gnomic expressions. How is this effect achieved? Why does Beckett invent gnomic expressions and what role do they play in the text? These questions will be discussed in terms of the different types of gnomic expressions. For each type I shall present the expressions in their context and then discuss their properties.

TYPE 1

Some gnomic expressions are uttered by a self-conscious narrator who expresses his awareness of the act of writing. For instance, the narrator says that it does not matter what he says because:

(1)   Saying is inventing. (Beckett, 1955: 32)

Later he warns the reader that he might write again about a sergeant (referring to the scene with the policeman in the street and at the police station, pp. 20–26) or that he might come back to the ditch that he has just mentioned (p. 27), adding that he does not know whether he will talk about these things or not. The following sentence then appears:

---

[1] For instance, La Rochefoucauld wrote maxims in which he expressed his pessimism concerning man. Thoreau revitalized proverbs in *Walden* to express his own transcendentalist philosophy (Moldenhauer, 1967).

(2) Not to want to say, not to know what you want to say, not to be able to say what you think you want to say, and never stop saying, or hardly ever, that is the thing to keep in mind, in the heat of composition. (Beckett, 1955: 28)

In another case Moran whimsically says that he had planned to describe in detail how he got to Ballyba, but now that it is the time to do so, "his intention is dead" and

(3) The moment is come and the desire is gone. (Beckett, 1955: 157)

These three examples contain elements which are characteristic of gnomic expressions. Example (1) immediately brings to mind the well-known "Seeing is believing" because it is built on the same model: both make use of the copula and are organized symmetrically. In both, the model is *A is B*[2] in which A and B are both present participles of verbs. Because of its involved construction, example (2) reminds one of sayings by Confucius (see later discussion). The repetition of words (*say* and *want*) and sounds (*ing* in *saying, thing; ever* in *never, ever*) combined with the length of this expression creates the effect of "verbal skidding." Beckett is very fond of such constructions and uses them elsewhere. For instance, he says that the modern artist "is helpless, cannot act, in the event cannot paint, since he is obliged to paint. The act of him, who, helpless, unable to act, acts, in the event paints, since he is obliged to paint" (Beckett, 1965: 119). Example (3) has the feel of a gnomic expression because it states the sort of general truth found in proverbs: "in life one never gets satisfaction of his desires at the right time." Furthermore, example (3) also exhibits a symmetrical syntactic construction: *is* is repeated; *come* and *gone* have similar sound structures and are semantic opposites. In addition, these three expressions are *used* as gnomic expressions. They sum up what has been said before and generalize about it.

Thus, verbal construction, particularly the conscious manipulation of forms, and role (summing up and generalizing) in specific contexts make Beckett's invented expressions strikingly gnomic in character. But Beckett uses the mold of *conventional forms,* gnomic expressions, to make *unconventional statements,* to *write overtly and idiosyncratically about writing.* Beckett thereby violates our expectations regarding gnomic expressions in three ways. First, we expect the subject of the expressions to be general truths about life rather than specific comments about the act of writing. Second, we anticipate that the idea

---

[2] This is one of the prototype forms discussed by Brunvand (1968) and Dundes (1962).

expressed, whatever the subject, will represent a consensus of opinion rather than personal feelings and attitudes. Third, Beckett's expressions generally have to be taken literally, in contrast with traditional gnomic expressions which tend toward metaphor. In addition, the "verbal skidding" expresses the antinomy which is the motto of Beckett's writing and which recurs in the trilogy (*Molloy, Malone Dies, The Unnamable*): impossibility of writing/obligation to write.

TYPE 2

Gnomic expressions are also used by the narrator when he describes a situation in which he himself was an actor. Molloy has been taken to the police station and, after the interrogation, a social worker gives him something to drink and eat. This situation prompts the narrator to comment on the plight of poor people who have to deal with social workers or Salvation Army devotees and he says:

(1) Against the charitable gesture there is no defense. (Beckett, 1955: 24)

A little further he adds:

(2) To him who has nothing it is forbidden not to relish filth. (Beckett, 1955: 24)

Moran is about to be beaten by a peasant because he is crossing the peasant's field. To justify his presence in this particular spot, Moran invents a reason (pilgrimage in honor of his dead wife) and then asks the peasant for a cup of tea. This request calms the peasant and Moran says:

(3) Humbly to ask a favor of people who are on the point of knocking your brains out, sometimes produces good results. (Beckett, 1955: 173)

These three expressions function as codas to particular scenes. They are general statements containing impersonal forms (him, your) and have the syntactic feel of gnomic expressions because of their symmetrical construction: in example (1), with X, Y is impossible; in example (2), no X, Y is forbidden; and in example (3), X produces Y. Semantically, they are also quite striking. In example (1), charity, conventionally a positive gesture, is presented in a negative way. Example (2) begins like a regular proverb "To him who has nothing it is forbidden," and one expects something like "to have lofty aspirations" to follow. Instead, one reads "not to relish filth." Syntactically, the rhythm is broken by the use of *not* and this negative creates an *anacoluthon.* Semantically, *to relish filth* is an unusual combination of lexical items because *to relish* is normally followed by a positive and desired element. Example (3) starts in the proverbial style, "Humbly to ask a favor . . . ," but concludes with a familiar and idiomatic expression, "knocking your brains out," which is too colloquial for the proverb. Here, Beckett is playing with register by juxtaposing the proverbial and the colloquial registers.

These three examples are gnomic because of their content (general statements about life) and symmetrical construction. Play is involved both when Beckett invents gnomic expressions and when he creates new relationships by combining verbal forms not usually employed together.

TYPE 3

In the above examples, Beckett manipulates the syntactic, semantic, and stylistic features of gnomic expressions. In the following examples, he plays with their context.

Molloy runs over a dog with his bicycle and the narrator remarks:

(1) Precautions are like resolutions to be taken with precautions. (Beckett, 1955: 32)

This statement serves as an introduction to the idea that Lousse had taken all the precautions to protect her dog, since she was walking on the pavement with him. Later, Molloy, describing how he used to make love to Edith, says their lovemaking was unsatisfactory and adds:

(2) Twixt finger and thumb tis heaven in comparison. (Beckett, 1955: 58)

Wandering in town, Molloy finds himself in a narrow alley with houses on each side. He deduces that the lights which he sees in the windows are lavatory lights and is prompted to say:

(3) There are things from time to time that impose themselves on the understanding with the force of axioms for unknown reasons. (Beckett, 1955: 60)

A similar example occurs apropos of the strange instrument that Molloy does not know how to use and has stolen from Lousse. Puzzling about this V-shaped object, he says:

(4) For to know nothing is nothing, not to want to know anything likewise, but to be beyond knowing anything, to know that you are beyond knowing anything, that is when peace enters in, to the soul of the incurious seeker. (Beckett, 1955: 64)

Moran has left his house with his son, in search of Molloy. He wants to carry his son's knife to "save him from getting lost" for:

(5)   Where a scout's knife is there will his heart be also. (Beckett, 1955: 130)

In another passage Moran mentions that his son might very well feel like killing him and it would be easy since they are isolated. But, Moran remarks, his son is too young, and because his son has a tender heart, he will not kill his father. To this Moran adds:

(6)   When you have the will you do not have the way. (Beckett, 1955: 131)

Example (1) is built like a proverb syntactically and semantically (it presents a general statement) as well as with respect to its short, laconic, and alliterative character. As in earlier examples, there is semantic play: one would expect that "resolutions are to be taken with precautions" rather than that "precautions" have "to be taken with precautions." In addition, there is phonological play. The gnomic expression appears just after the words *resolutions* and *precautions* have been mentioned several times. In the gnomic expression, these two words appear again, this time brought together in the same clause. Consequently, a *phonic field* is created on the page because of the repetition of the same sounds. Beckett plays here with elements shared by the gnomic expression and the context, in particular, the phonic elements,[3] and is therefore playing with the *relationship of the context and the expression.*

Example (2) contains archaic forms (*twixt, tis*) frequently found in proverbs. Archaisms are characteristic of old sayings, which generally convey very conventional, conservative, and traditional ideas. In example (2), however, these archaisms are associated with an unconventional statement. Although capable of several meanings, the expression, because of its context in the novel, acquires a very specific meaning: it graphically describes the gesture of masturbation. Here again, play is involved in the relationship of the gnomic expression to its context, but this time Beckett exploits the context's power to determine the meaning of the expression. Beckett is also playing when he creates an unconven-

[3]Beckett is extremely sensitive to the sounds of words. Ludovic Janvier (1969), translating *Watt* in collaboration with Beckett, mentions how the author tried to respect and render the effects of the sounds of English in French. *Bing* could be described as a permutation on a certain number of sounds.

tional combination of style and subject matter by using polite, quaint archaisms to talk about masturbation.

Example (3) is an impersonal statement which is used in a conventional way because it makes a general remark about a specific situation. What is unconventional is the discrepancy between the context, which deals with a banal, unimportant, and trivial fact (the deduction that the lights that Molloy sees are bathroom lights), and the gnomic expression, which, like a Cartesian meditation, is a praise on the power of understanding.

Example (4), which describes how one reaches ataraxy, recalls the following saying by Confucius: "When you know to know that you know, and when you do not know, to know that you do not know that is knowledge."[4] But the philosophical and metaphysical tone of Beckett's expression is not in keeping with the context in which the character puzzles over a strange thing, the V-shaped object which he stole. Thus in both examples (3) and (4), Beckett is playing with a discrepancy between the gnomic expression and the context in which it is used.

Example (5) is a revitalization of the well-known saying, "Where your treasure is there will your heart be also."[5] Again, the context is responsible for a shift in meaning. The heart, which in the traditional saying stands metaphorically for affection and love, stands metonymically for the presence of the body, in Beckett's expression. Moran's son will not leave his father, because Moran carries his son's knife, which his son treasures.

Example (6) is also a revitalization of a well-known saying, "Where there is a will there is a way." (See Stevenson, 1948: 2510.) But example (6) means the opposite of the traditional saying upon which it is based. In addition, Beckett uses it in a context which concerns the killing of one's father rather than in a more conventional and expected situation like wanting to accomplish a desired task. Once again, Beckett plays with the relationship between the expression and its context.

## Typology of Gnomic Play in MOLLOY

In establishing a typology of play which involves the gnomic expressions in *Molloy*, the notion of the paradigmatic and syntagmatic axes of language will be useful. (See Kristeva, 1968 and Milner, 1971.) First, the paradigmatic axis of language is involved when novel expressions

[4]Confucius, *Analects*, ii, ch. 17. (See Stevenson, 1948: 1324.)
[5]*New Testament*, Matthew, vi, 21. (See Stevenson, 1948: 2367.)

are formed by modifying a particular well-known expression X, which remains recognizable in the modification. Examples of Beckett's revitalization of well-known expressions include:

"Saying is inventing,"

which derives from

"Seeing is believing."

"Where the scout's knife is there will be his heart,"

which derives from

"Where your treasure is there will be your heart."

This operation forms a paradigmatic chain.

Second, Beckett plays with the syntagmatic aspect of language, which organizes the elements horizontally rather than vertically and governs their combination: he juxtaposes elements that do not usually appear together (e.g., a noun and a verb such as *to relish filth;* two registers, such as colloquial and proverbial) and accumulates elements with greater than normal frequency (e.g., the repetition of similar sounds in a particular expression, as in "to know nothing is nothing, not to want to know anything. . .").

Third, Beckett plays with the relationship between gnomic expressions and their context by (a) inserting a gnomic expression which contains and brings together sounds recurring in the context, (b) choosing an expression which is not in keeping with the triviality of the context, and (c) making the context modify the meaning of the expression itself.

In addition to creatively using the more general paradigmatic and syntagmatic properties of language, Beckett specifically employs gnomic expressions. This practice indicates his awareness of a special type of language, the gnomic code, and involves both the revitalization of well-known expressions and the invention of new ones which have the characteristics of those in tradition. Gnomic expressions are in themselves a form of language play. Since Beckett manipulates particular features of gnomic expressions from a paradigmatic, syntagmatic, or contextual point of view, in order to stress, elaborate, or transform those features, Beckett's invention and use of gnomic expressions can be said to involve play with play.

Another important aspect of gnomic expressions is their didactic or rhetorical function (see Burke, 1957: 253–255). It is difficult to define the particular philosophy that Beckett intends to convey through his gnomic expressions as there is no obvious unity among them. The narrator, a former tramp, has lost all sense of identity. He has been wandering in and out of a town, whose name he does not know. He writes to pass the time and just says whatever comes to his mind. The gnomic expressions, then, are not meant to teach something or to convey wisdom, but are rather a way of playing with verbal forms. That is the essence of Molloy's and Moran's life now that they are writers. Indeed, the profusion of linguistic play makes unimportant the distinction between gnomic expressions used specifically to talk about writing and gnomic expressions used to comment on other situations. In *all* cases, the narrator is consciously manipulating and playing with language, thereby drawing the reader's attention to the fact that he is writing. Therefore, Beckett's play with gnomic expressions always focuses on the act of writing, whether *overtly,* when the content of the gnomic expression refers to writing, or *covertly,* when the content of the gnomic expression does *not* refer to writing but the manipulation of form draws our attention to the creative process. This interaction between the overt and covert ways of referring to writing is in itself a form of play and that is why Beckett says, "Saying is inventing." Indeed, for Beckett we can say that "Saying is playing," because what he does with gnomic expressions and other devices is put language on display.

# Conclusion

PART IV

BARBARA KIRSHENBLATT-GIMBLETT

# Directions for Future Research

CHAPTER NINE

T HE STUDIES in this volume raise many questions for future research, which are outlined here and supplemented by the following Bibliographic Survey of the Literature on Speech Play and Related Subjects. Together with the Bibliography, the survey provides resources for studying speech play cross-culturally as it illuminates and is illuminated by language structure and acquisition, cognitive development and socialization, the ethnography of speaking in any given community, and the nature of (socio)linguistic creativity.

Fundamental questions include: How are the resources of any given speech community exploited for purposes defined as playful? How are speech play genres defined and located within a native taxonomy of discourse? Slobin (1967: 171) suggests

The value placed upon language and its use in any culture may be reflected in the accepted attitudes in the adult community with regard to the playing of these games by children. Are they encouraged, tolerated, discouraged? Are there sanctions for or against role-playing by children? The number and kinds of verbal games played in the sub-adult community and the ages at which verbal play is begun and terminated may be directly related to the importance of language in the adult speech community.

To what extent do adults eschew or prefer or transform or specialize for use forms of speech play they define as childish or childlike? The limerick revival discussed in Chapter 10 is instructive here.

Cross-cultural comparison is needed for determining the nature of forms of speech play and the special role they play in developing general language proficiency and eloquence in the use of verbal art forms. Developmental studies based on comparative data are needed in order to determine how the development of poetic discourse relates to

175

general language development in any given speech community and the extent to which stages and sequences in such development are language or culture bound. Cross-cultural research might explore how phonological, syntactic, and semantic relations of a given language determine structural realizations of poetic devices peculiar to that language. Do children's speech play forms in various languages exhibit the same stages of concern with the different components of their developing language structure and in what ways? What is the impact of different traditions of poetic forms on children's speech play? How is children's interest in phonological patterning expressed in traditions without rhyme? How does the presence of syllabic, stress, or foot meters affect children's speech play productions? Since modeling behavior based on adult nursery lore produced for children plays an important role in children's developing competence (See Pinon, 1965b), cross-cultural studies could illuminate just how this works in specific cases. Developmental stages need to be determined for children's speech play preferences cross-culturally and the findings in each case related to language development studies. An important avenue for research is the pedagogical role of speech play in the acquisition of literacy, especially in traditional educational systems (Jewish, Chinese, classical) which have literacy at the center of their curriculum. A related problem is the relation of the acquisition of literacy to the acquisition of language.

Slobin (1967: 169) suggests that children's imitative and modelling activity often involves miming adult behavior, and it therefore would be useful for determining

what, if any, are the children's conceptions of, for example, stress, intonation, and pitch used by adults in the roles taken by children. Additionally, children may take the roles of baby-talking parents and offer their conceptions of baby-talk itself. Attention should be given to the code used in two areas: lexicon and sentence length. Role playing may show children to be more competent in the forms of speech used by adults than their normal speech would show in nonrole-playing, nongame settings. Longer and syntactically more complex sentences and lexical items common to adult domains may be employed by children to achieve a closer approximation to adult speech habits.

Special attention should be devoted to those cases where children socialize each other into various linguistic and speech play forms.

Especially interesting is the view of the native system of patterns of speaking in terms of intergenre relationships and their role in the acquisition of verbal art in a given speech community. It appears in some cases that a given sequence may be institutionalized, for example, riddling may be the genre which develops metaphorical thought and may serve as a precursor to proverb learning. (Kulah 1973. See Chapter 10). The role of verbal dueling in Chamula or of riddles in Kpelle should be seen in the context of the native systems of discourse and traditional systems of education.

Directions for future research include the ethnographic description of the forms, learning, use, and social significance of speech play. This would form the basis for the comparative and typological study of the dimensions of speech play associated with culture areas, historical periods, and language types. How is speech play used in the formation of speech acts and codes valued for their incomprehensibility? What are the functions of unintelligibility in play, ritual, and other domains? To what extent and how may joking and other forms of speech play be used "to create interaction, not to produce substance" (Brukman, 1972: 220)? Adult-infant baby talk and dandling interactions might be examined in these terms, as might many kinds of adult-adult interactions. The relationship of speech play to verbal art and other kinds of talk, the impact of speech play on language evolution, the role of speech play in multilingual settings, and the function of speech play in literature and other media (theater, television, advertising, etc.) deserve further attention both in their own right and for what they can reveal about the workings of language. Many other avenues for study are offered in Chapter 10 and the Bibliography which conclude the volume.

BARBARA KIRSHENBLATT-GIMBLETT

# Bibliographic Survey of the
# Literature on Speech Play
# and Related Subjects

CHAPTER TEN

MATERIAL ON speech play is scattered across a variety of disciplines. The purpose of this guide is to provide a comprehensive introduction to the literature on speech play and on folklore, the discipline which has probably published most on speech play. The folkloristic literature may not be familiar to non-folklorists, and in addition to individual studies, the major bibliographic and reference tools for folklore are indicated. A more comprehensive list appears in the Bibliography.

As discussed in the Introduction, a general theory of the relations of speech play to verbal art and other kinds of speaking has hardly been broached. The scope of this guide is governed, therefore, not so much by any single definition of speech play as by the issues raised in the studies in this volume.

This guide is divided into two parts: general folklore bibliographies and guides to single folklore genres and special domains. Studies relating to children's lore are reviewed in this guide and in Chapter 4; additional works are listed in the Bibliography. The material is organized as follows:

1. General Folklore Bibliography
(a) comprehensive bibliographies
(b) indexes prepared for individual folklore journals
(c) area folklore bibliographies
2. Genre and Subject Bibliographies
(a) Concept of Genre

(b)   Play
(c)   Children's Play
(d)   Word Play
(e)   Nursery Lore
(f)   Nonsense and Limericks
(g)   Play Languages
(h)   Numbers, Letters, Mnemonics, and Counting Out Rhymes
(i)   Names
(j)   Humor
(k)   Joking Relationships and Interaction
(l)   Verbal Contests
(m)   Psycho-Ostensive Expression
(n)   Obscenity
(o)   Proverb and Speech Metaphor
(p)   Riddle
(q)   Narrative
(r)   Audio-Visual Resources

## 1.   General Folklore Bibliographies

No bibliography of folklore bibliographies has been published, although at least one is in progress (Borie). Nor is there an annual index to all the major folklore journals, comparable to *Readers' Guide to Periodicals* or *Social Sciences and Humanities Index*. Therefore we must turn to (a) comprehensive folklore bibliographies, some of which appear annually; (b) indexes prepared for individual folklore journals; (c) area folklore bibliographies.

An invaluable aid in locating material on any subject is Bestermann's comprehensive bibliography of bibliographies and other finding tools (Bestermann, 1965–1966).

### (a)   COMPREHENSIVE FOLKLORE BIBLIOGRAPHIES

General folklore bibliographies contain speech play entries under a variety of headings including children's lore, play and games, songs and rhymes, popular poetry, and specific genres—riddle, tongue twister, counting out rhymes, and other terms found throughout this volume.

Several comprehensive folklore bibliographies appear annually. One of the oldest, most ambitious and important is *Internationale Volkskundliche Bibliographie* which first appeared in 1919, as *Volkskundliche Bibliographie*. Currently edited by Wildhaber, it is organized by genre and geographical area and indexed by author and topic. The

*Modern Languages Association International Bibliography* now contains a large section devoted exclusively to folklore. The bibliography for 1970 contains over 1,600 folklore entries arranged under such headings as gnomic folklore (proverbs and sayings, riddles, names), folk poetry, folk games, and toys. The spring issue of *Southern Folklore Quarterly* consists of a bibliography of folklore studies published the previous year and is especially strong in studies published in Spanish. Issued since 1955 by UNESCO, *International Bibliography of Social and Cultural Anthropology* is a good source of folklore bibliography. From 1963–1975, the American Folklore Society published *Abstracts of Folklore Studies* quarterly. Folklore articles which appear in journals, especially nonfolklore ones, are abstracted. Periodically a detailed cumulative index to several volumes of *Abstracts* appeared.

Bibliography on a wide range of folklore subjects may be found at the end of many entries in M. Leach (1949–1950). The Library of Congress distributes mimeographed bibliographies on many folklore subjects. Jabbour (1970) provides a listing. For a guide to single folklore editions, see Ziegler (1973). White (1965) provides a catalog of the John G. White Collection. See also Diehl (1962), Noy (1955), and Brunvand (1976).

Bethke (1970) lists dissertations on folklore and related subjects at the University of Pennsylvania. Sanderson (1971) covers theses and dissertations in folklife at the University of Leeds. Many of them deal with children's folklore, play, and speech play. Dundes (in press) is the most ambitious listing of folklore theses and dissertations.

Ben-Amos (1975a) provides a bibliography on structural analysis of folklore.

(b) FOLKLORE JOURNALS

Several efforts have been made to compile listings of folklore journals. For Indiana University's excellent holdings see Grimshaw (1967). Hickerson (1974) lists thirty-five American folklore and folksong journals. Dundes (1965: 478–481), Hand (n.d.) and Kirshenblatt-Gimblett (in progress) cover non-Western folklore journals as well.

The process of tracking down collections and studies of speech play in the numerous folklore journals is greatly facilitated by a cumulative index. Cumulative indexes have been prepared for *Schweizerisches Archiv für Volkskunde* and for the following English-language folklore journals (this list is not complete):

*Journal of American Folklore* (Coffin, 1958)
*Hoosier Folklore Bulletin and Hoosier Folklore* (Posen, Taft, and Tallman, 1973)

*Folklore* (Bonser, 1961, 1969)
*Publications of the Texas Folklore Society* (Bratcher, 1973)
*Tennessee Folklore Society Bulletin* (indexed every twelve years)
*Western Folklore* (Perkal, 1969)
*New York Folklore Quarterly*
*Keystone Folklore Quarterly* (Barrick, 1970)
*Ulster Folklore*
*Folk Life*
*English Folk Song and Dance*
*Folklore Fellows Communications* (vols. 1–47, 1934)

(c)   AREA FOLKLORE BIBLIOGRAPHIES

Listed here for the most part are bibliographies dealing primarily with folklore. General bibliographies for each area should also be checked. Although they vary greatly in scope, bibliographies have been prepared for the following areas (this list is not complete):

**Africa**—*Africa: Journal of International African Studies* features a regular "Bibliography of Current Publications." Görög (1968, 1969, 1970), Ben-Amos (1974b), and Scheub (1971) provide general bibliography on African folklore. Warren and Taylor (1972) focuses on the Akan of Ghana and Delancey (1972) on Cameroun.

**Asia**—See Kirkland (1966) for South East Asia, Sen Greptar (1967) for India, and Arsenio (1965) for the Philippines.

**Latin America**—Boggs (1940) provides a general folklore bibliography. For Mexico, see Boggs (1939) and for Oaxaca, see Martinez (1961). Chile is covered by Carvalho-Neto (1968), Dannemann Rothstein (1970), Castro (n.d.), and Pereira Salas (n.d.). Castro deals specifically with "poesia vulgar." For Brazil, see Carvalho-Neto (1968) and Câmara Cascudo (1954). Chertudi (1963) and Carvalho-Neto (1968) deal with Argentina. See Arguedas (1960) for Peru, Paredes Candia (1961) for Bolivia, and Carvalho-Neto (1968) for Paraguay and Uruguay.

**Middle East**—For a recent bibliography organized by genre, see Baghban (1972).

**Jewish**—U. and B. Weinreich (1959) and Kirshenblatt-Gimblett (in progress) deal with Yiddish folklore. Schwarzbaum (1968) is the most comprehensive bibliographic survey of Jewish folklore to date.

**Europe**—Halpert (1964) surveys the British Isles and Ireland; Van Gennep (1937–1938, vols. 3 and 4) France; and Hautala (1947, 1957) some of the Finnish material. The most recent bibliographies of Slavic folklore include Oinas and Soudakoff (in press) and M. Z. Brooks (1975) for Polish and Russian material. Under the entry "Slavic," Svatava

Pirkova Jakobson (in M. Leach, 1950) provides bibliography for Russian, Ukrainian, Byelo-Russian, Polish, Kashubian, Polabian, Sorbian, Czech, Slovak, Slovenian, Serbo-Croatian, Macedonian, and Bulgarian folklore. See the entries for Lithuanian, Latvian, Finnish, and Estonian folklore by Balys in M. Leach (1949–1950). Jauksch-Orlovski (1974) provides 1,500 titles and annotations pertaining to Russian folklore in Siberia.

Bibliography on German folklore may be found in the general volumes by Bach (1960), Beitl (1955), and Pessler (1935–1938). Bianco (1970) covers Italian and Italian-American folklore. See Black (1914) for Gypsy material.

**North America**—Haywood (1961) provides general bibliography organized by state, occupation, and other features and includes Canada and Native Americans. E. K. Maranda (1974) covers Canada. For North American Indian material see Dundes (1967), J. F. Freeman (1966), and Marken (1973). Szwed and Abrahams (in press) cover Afro-Americans and include the Caribbean. See Bianco (1970) for Italian-Americans, Klymasz (1969) for Ukrainian folklore in Canada, and Tully (1950) for Spanish folklore in New Mexico and Colorado. Hand (1967) covers the southwest. Randolph (1972) deals with the Ozarks. See Burns (1968) for Missouri.

Dorson (1961) provides surveys of folklore research in Europe, America, Asia, Africa, Oceania, and Australia. Aceves and Einarsson-Mullarký (1968) provide addresses for folklore archives, listed by country.

## 2.  Genre and Subject Bibliographies

### (a)  CONCEPT OF GENRE

Ben-Amos (1975b) provides comprehensive bibliography on the concept of genre in folklore and literature. See also Ben-Amos (1974a) and the bibliographic note in Hymes (1964b: 352). For a rhetorical theory of genre see Abrahams (1968 and 1969a). Gossen (1970, 1972a, and 1974) provides a Chamula native taxonomy of discourse. Jolles (1956) is a classic work.

### (b)  PLAY

The subject of play, its definition, nature, and function, has been discussed for centuries and has recently provided the *raison d'être* for a new organization—Association for the Anthropological Study of Play, the first meeting of which was held in Detroit in 1975. Recent surveys of the literature include Alleman (1951), Berlyne (1969), Millar (1972), S. Miller (1973), Piaget (1962), and Sutton-Smith (1974b); see also the Introduction to this volume. Classic early theories of play include the notion that play is a way of releasing surplus energy, mastering skills which are later needed in adulthood, allowing the child to re-enact the forms of behavior that characterized earlier stages of human evolution, and refreshing a tired organism. See Berlyne (1969) for a discussion of additional play theories under the headings of phenomenological, historical, ethological, reflexicological, psychoanalytic, and developmental.

Sully (1902) discusses the "play-mood" and anticipates points in the later discussions of play by Huizinga, Caillois, Piaget, Turner, and Sutton-Smith. According to Sully, play contrasts with work: "Play is a free activity entered upon for its own sake. That is to say, it is not directed to any end outside itself, to the satisfaction of any want, save that of the play impulse itself; and so it is free of external restraint, and from the sense of compulsion. . . . The play impulse provides its own ends . . ." (146–147). Sully goes on to mention the "make-believe" quality of play, what he calls a double or divided consciousness, the value of play as training for the serious social activity of later years, and the importance in play of disorder, inversion, incongruity, and novelty (149–151).

A further development in the notion of play relates to Huizinga's and Caillois's interest in the relation of play to the sacred and to Sully's (1902) contrasting of play to work. Turner (1974) suggests that before the Industrial Revolution the salient distinction was between sacred and profane work whereas afterward the contrast set became work as opposed to leisure, and as part of leisure, play. Play according to Turner develops most fully in industrial and postindustrial societies. Both Turner and Sutton-Smith (1974b) see play as "seedbeds of cultural creativity," (Turner, 1974: 12), as an experimental region of culture "where not only new elements but also new combinatory rules may be introduced" (Turner, 1974: 13). The inversions and subversions of normative structure in play "can generate and store a plurality of alternate models for living" that can be drawn upon when needed (Turner, 1974: 19). Consistent with this view, Sutton-Smith (1974b: 3–4) suggests that societies that need novelty will promote playfulness in children since play and fantasy provide "the breeding ground for an overproductive stock of ideas which may subsequently be called into adaptive action."

While recognizing the ludic as an informing principle in ritual and in other domains of preindustrial societies, Turner diverges from Huizinga, who identifies play with the sacred and finds the origin of much contemporary play activities in sacred rituals of the past. For Huizinga, play, ritual, theater, work, war, poetry, philosophy, art, and law are all framed worlds, set apart, and governed by special rules. (Compare with Bateson [1955] and Goffman [1974].) In his chapter, "The Play-Concept as Expressed in Language," Huizinga recognizes that "a general play-category has not been distinguished with equal definiteness by all languages everywhere, nor expressed in one word. . . . The absence of a common Indo-European word for play also points to the late conception of a general play-concept" (Huizinga, 1955: 28–29). Turner is consistent with Caillois who insists that play and the sacred be clearly distinguished since man is at the mercy of the sacred but in control of play. Play for Caillois (1961: 159) is an area of "limited and provisional perfection . . . a haven in which one is master of destiny."

Influential in the recent work of Turner and Sutton-Smith is the notion of "flow" developed by Mihaly Csikszentmihalyi and John McAloon, and extended by them beyond play to creative experiences in the arts and religion. The distinctive features of flow, "the holistic sensation present when we act with total involvement," include: (1) self-awareness without self-consciousness; (2) centering of attention on a limited stimulus field either by a limited set of formal rules, which stipulate what is relevant and dismiss many of the stimuli normally bombarding us, or by motivational means such as competitiveness, and the concomitant experience of heightened intensity; (3) loss of ego by surrendering the self to rules which simplify, define, and clarify the reality experienced at the time by all the participants and create a sense of unity, solidarity, and acceptance; (4) being in control of one's actions and environment, a feature which is facilitated by the simplicity and clarity of the demands made by the activity; (5) explicit rules ensuring noncontradictory, unproblematic demands for action and providing for clear, unambiguous, and immediate evaluation of action; (6) activity as intrinsically rewarding, "auteolic" or seeming to need no goals or rewards outside itself (Turner, 1974: 52). Turner argues that the Industrial Revolution involved a major change in the primary cultural flow mechanisms. With the attrition of religious ritual, art and sport have largely taken over the flow function in much of Western culture.

The emphasis on simplifying and restricting the stimuli in this characterization of the flow experience needs to be seen in light of Freud's (1963) discussion of the brevity of wit and Sutton-Smith's notion of play as a "form of subjective abstraction. It is a condensation, distancing, and generalizing of particular experiences, without at the same time being remote" (1974b: 5). Sutton-Smith suggests that certain salient aspects of experience are summarized and crystallized so that the vividness or gripping involvement experienced during play may be attributed to the quick transport across high points of experience which are selected and reordered in play. At the same time, the selectivity works to reorder priorities, to overelaborate and deliberately complicate aspects of the activity, what S. Miller (1973) calls galumphing. The Bibliography contains many references to the literature on play.

(c)　CHILDREN'S PLAY

The most comprehensive bibliography on this subject appears in Herron and Sutton-Smith (1971), a volume devoted to comparative, cognitive, developmental, normative, ecological, and psychoanalytical studies of child's play. See also Herron et al. 1971. Groos (1901) covers the nineteenth-century literature and cites studies not listed in more recent bibliographies. For bibliography specifically on the related topics of leisure, games, and sports, both as practiced by adults and children, see Avedon and Sutton-Smith (1971). Sutton-Smith (1972a) contains reprints of many of his essays on children's game behavior. Piaget (1962) critically evaluates previous theories of play and includes his own classification and developmental theory of children's play, which have generated considerable debate (Herron and Sutton-Smith, 1971: 326–342). See Piaget (1965) for a brilliant analysis of the game of marbles and the development of moral judgment in the child.

Studies dealing with fantasy, play, and imagination include Stein (1975), Singer (1973), Klinger (1969), Piaget (1962), Piaget and Inhelder (1971), Gould (1972), Henry (1973), and Werner and Kaplan (1963). Singer (1973) reviews the literature. Nicolich (1975) relates representational play to language development.

Contributions to the study of sex roles in the play and games of children include Conn (1951), A. Haas (1972), Eckhardt (1975), Brady (1974, 1975), Hawes (1969), Jones and Hawes (1972), Moore (1964), Muir (1965), Rosenberg and Sutton-Smith (1960), and Smith (1909).

A portion of the literature on children's play, games, and lore has been surveyed in Chapter 4 above. Additional references may be found in the Bibliography.

(d)　WORDPLAY

Comprehensive inventories of various types of wordplay include *Word Ways: The Journal of Recreational Linguistics*, begun in 1968, Leide (1963), a classic discussion of the play element in literature and folklore, Alleau and Matignon (1964), Bombaugh (1905, 1961), Canel (1867), Disraeli (1791), Dobson (1880, 1882), Esar (1952), Espy (1972, 1975a, 1975b), Lake (1975), Lalanne (1845), Mautner (1931), Phillips (1945), Shipley (1972), Weis (1942, 1951, 1952, 1954), Wölfflin (1887). See also Eckhardt (1909), Gauthier (1915), Gerber (1885), Schultz (1927), Fisher (1973), and Spanke (1931). Kraepelin (1885: 144–160) is an important effort to classify the various types of wordplay in jokes. See also Borgmann (1965, 1967).

An important bibliographic contribution to the study of speech play, especially in non-Western languages, is Hymes (1964b); the section, "Speech Play and Verbal Art," includes articles by Conklin and M. Haas and extensive bibliographic notes on speech play—especially puns, humor in language, and verbal contest (299–300); children's games and speech play (303–304); the riddle and proverb (352–355); argots, slang, and special languages (403–406); and expressive language (274–288).

In recent years, general works on cultural anthropology, language, and folklore have devoted a specific section to speech play. Jacobs (1964: 119–120) briefly considers language incongruities and humor cross-culturally. Burling (1970: 134–150) devotes one chapter to verse and linguistic games in which he considers "linguistic virtuosity," with special reference to play languages, nursery rhymes (unfortunately not distinguished from children's lore), and adult poetry. Edmonson (1971: 165–194) devotes an entire chapter to "play" in which he considers rhymed dialogues, dozens, contest punning and riddling, and *piropos* or *coplas* as examples of folk drama. He also considers wordplay (88–90), primarily punning, humor (161–164), the lore of infancy, childhood, and adolescence (203–211), and pornography (214–220). Farb (1973), under the headings, "Verbal Dueling" (95–112) and "Playing with Language" (113–137), deals with riddles, proverbs, disguised speech, dozens, advertising jingles, political slogans, sound symbolism, poetry, children's verses, argot, jargon, and lies as examples of the creative use of language.

Studies of wordplay in non-Western languages include Arnott (1957), Conklin (1959), Emeneau (1948), Hoa (1955), Laycock, Lloyd, and Staalsen (1969), Lowie (1914), Pike (1945a, 1945b, 1946), Sapir (1932), Susman (1941), and Ogundipe (1972). See Driver (1967) on wordplay in Hebrew.

Discussions of speech play have appeared in treatises on wit and humor and in the ancient rhetoric handbooks, especially those of Cicero, Quintillian, and Hermogenes, who paid particular attention to rhetorical figures. Quintillian distinguishes figures of sense from figures of sound. Many of the entries in Shibles (1971) deal with the relation of speech play to such figures of sense as metaphor. Figures of sound consist of (1) variations in syntax; (2) modes of iteration; (3) wordplay; (4) balance and antithesis (Baldwin, 1959: 42–43). Numerous figures of sound are identified as *comic* techniques; for example, *acyrologia* (impropriety of speech, use of wrong term), *antimera* (substitution of one part of speech for another), *cacozelon* (affected or faulty diction), *diaeresis* (dividing a word and re-forming it in abnormal order), *tapinosis* (degradation by use of debasing terms, foul language), and others. See Sonnino (1968: 211–213).

When classical rhetoricians use the term wordplay in its narrowest sense, they mean punning. Early eighteenth century wits such as Swift and Sheridan wrote entire treatises on punning, defending it and providing rules for becoming a good punster, one of which is reminiscent of our groans: "Never speak well of another punster" (Shipley, 1972: 7–9). See also Andrée (1882–1883) and Sacks (1972), who deals with topical puns.

Curtius (1963: 282–292) discusses and provides examples and bibliography pertaining to how Mannerists play with rhetorical figures and carry them to extremes: "Mannerism can begin with linguistic form or with intellectual content. In its periods of florescence [Late Antiquity and the Middle Ages] it combines both" (282). He provides examples of the excesses of *hyperbaton*, or liberties taken with word order, circumlocution, puns, and metaphor. Formal mannerisms include (1) writing works in which one letter of the alphabet never appears, (2) pangrammatic affectations (*vers lettrisés*), (3) figure poems, (4) *technopaegnion,* "poems in which various ingenious methods of using monosyllables in verse are displayed" (284), including *versos de cabo roto,* (5) verse-filling asyndeton where one crams as many words into one line as possible, (6) *versus rapporti,* which involves symmetrical grammatical dovetailing, and (7) the summation schemes. Speech play in literature is discussed further in the Introduction to this volume. On speech play in Jewish literature, see Rothenberg (forthcoming).

Drawing examples from centuries of English usage, French, and on occasion, non-Western languages, Shipley (1972), an Old English scholar, describes riddles, conundrums, puns, rebuses, pangrams, alphabettors, lipograms, cryptograms, catches, acrostics, kangaroodles, tiegrams, palindromes, amphisbaenae, jumbles, addagrams, scrabblings, ghosts, hangman, and others. Some of these appear to be of his own invention while others are accompanied by brief though informative historical documentation. Esar (1952) includes wisecracks, epigrams, gags, chains, rounds, tangletalk, spoonerisms, fuddletalk, tongue twisters, baby talk, doubletalk, Wellerisms, malapropisms, limericks, Little Willies, and many others.

Important contributions have been made by C. G. Loomis to the collection, classification, and study of "traditional American wordplay" of the nineteenth century. From Loomis's remarks and those of Robbins (1966) on the spoonerism, Legman (1974) on the limerick, and Shipley (1972) on neologisms and punning, it emerges that various periods and places in the English-speaking world showed a distinct fondness for one kind of speech play over another. Thus, Shipley claims the Elizabethan age as the greatest period of word innovation in England. The seventeenth century may have been the golden age of English language speech play, judging from Ashton (1968) and the proliferation of terminology. (Among the terms indicating speech play in the seventeenth century are epigrams, wit and drollery, jests, smart repartees, witty sayings, notable bulls, outlandish proverbs, witty apothegms, conceits, quibling, catches, joques, merriments, merry tales, merry riddles, tricks, farces, clinches, flashes, whimsies, fancies, humorous discourses, and jovial poems.) Legman (1974) claims the seventeenth century as the heyday of the limerick and the latter half of the nineteenth century as the period of its revitalization. Others see the seventeenth and eighteenth centuries as partial to punning. According to Loomis (1949a), although no history of traditional punning exists for the American scene, the early decades of the nineteenth century were probably especially prolific in wordplay, the "punning contagion" being spread and encouraged from England. Loomis (1955a) claims that the golden age of American Wellerisms was the period between 1840 and 1870. Robbins (1966: 461) notes a fad for word transpositions ("Morrow-skying") popular among London medical students in the nineteenth century, and the later vogue of *The Pink 'Un* in the Edwardian period. Robbins (1966) defines and classifies spoonerisms, clarifies the history of the term, and provides some useful bibliography. He notes that in the 1880's, one writer indicated that "We used to spend hours in inventing 'spoonerisms,'" and several periodicals sponsored spoonerism contests. Spoonerism and other wordplay contests are a regular feature of *New York* magazine today.

Tongue twisters have been considered by Emrich (1970), Gowlett (1966), Mook (1959), Parkin (1969), Potter (1964), Potts (1892), and Schwartz (1972).

NURSERY LORE

In addition to the long standing interest in socialization, there is a growing literature on the history of the family and the concept of childhood (Ariès, 1962; Boas, 1966; Chamberlain, 1896, 1911; Dudycha, 1941; Goodman, 1970; Ojemann, 1953; Ploss, 1911; and deMause, 1974). Recent work on children's literature views it as a culturally specific statement on how adults perceive children and develop a literature for them (Ariès, 1972; Jan, 1972, 1974; Soriano, 1959, 1968, 1972; Hazard, 1944). Children's literature and nursery lore are both important in the study of child acquisition of poetic discourse. The Children's Literature Association, formed in 1972, issues the journal, *Children's Literature.*

Collections and studies of nursery lore include Barchilon and Pettie (1960), Baring-Gould (1962), Bett (1924), Eckenstein (1906), Green (1899), Halliwell (1842, 1849), Ker (1834), Montgomerie (1946, 1948, 1964), Neely (1966), Opie (1951), Potts (1830), Ritson (1810), Sackville-West (1947), Seeger (1948, 1950), Stevens (1968), Thomas (1930), Wood (1938). Metrical studies of nursery rhymes include Burling (1966, 1970), Guéron (1974), and Malof (1970). Work on lullabies includes Cass-Beggs (1969), Commins (1967), Daiken (1959), Hawes (1974), and Strettell (1896).

Important research is being done on the use of frightening figures to control children. See especially Widdowson (1971), which is based on his doctoral dissertation, Nunn (1964), Whiting (1963), Soriano (1972), Pickard (1961), and Gathorne-Hardy (1973, chapter 9).

In his study of *contes-enfantines*, short stories told by parents and adults to children, Pinon suggests that the stylistic devices used in them are playful in spirit and contribute to the child's developing ability to handle style. He refers to such devices as : *"des alphabets parlants, des combes, des couronnés, des kyrielles, des lapalissades, des rimes numériques et alphabetiques, des vers olorimes, des lipogrammaties"* which are discussed in Alleau and Matignon (1964). Pinon also discusses parody as play and identifies several kinds of playful and in some cases parodic tales for children: *fable rengaine, conte virelangue, conte à devinettes, conte à calembours, conte cumulatif, rallonges, conte sans fin, conte amphigourique, conte-randonnée.*

Cook (1971) identifies children's likes and dislikes with reference to stories according to age. See also Lanham and Shimura (1967). Ariès (1972) traces the development of children's culture in Western society and the passage of adult oral tales into children's books. Soriano (1972) examines the relationship of oral tradition to French children's literature and the impact of children's speech play on French Surrealist literature and contemporary poetry. Soriano (1972: 42), like Chukovsky (1971), claims that by using the procedures of popular poetry, the Surrealists were the only ones to create poems which children accepted.

For examples of children's verbal art, see Koch (1970). For the impact of children's preferences on the designing of television production for them, see Lesser (1973: 292): "Animation [is] a way of creating incongruity which Kael suggests is the visual equivalent of the illogic of their nursery rhymes, jingles, and word games." Programming for pre-schoolers thus capitalizes on children's love of speech play: "Although young children seem to enjoy wordplay, they do not respond well to puns" (Lesser, 1973: 298).

## (f) NONSENSE AND LIMERICKS

Liede (1963, 1: 157 ff.) surveys English language nonsense collections and relates English forms to crosscultural analogues. Liede (1963, vol. 2) surveys nonsense in French (257–263), Spanish (263–264), and Italian (264). Among the many anthologies of nonsense literature are Reed (1925), Arnaud (1942), Benayoun (1957), and Wells (1958). Folklore nonsense collections are also numerous and include Babcock (1886a, 1886b), Cazden (1961), Cohen (1966), Emrich (1970), which is especially rich in bibliography, and the many collections of children's and adult's folk poetry, rhymes, and lore listed in the Bibliography.

Nonsense has been discussed by literary critics concerned with Lewis Carroll, Edward Lear, the Surrealist and Dadaist poets (Roberts, 1938; Jan, 1974), and observers of child language and speech play (Chukovsky, 1971). Holquist (1972), one of the most suggestive literary studies, is indebted to the earlier work of Sewell (1970) and Liede (1963); see also Evans (1949). Cammaerts (1926) holds that adult literary nonsense derives from nursery rhymes and devotes a chapter each to "Nonsense and the Child" and the distinctions between nonsense and poetry. Deleuze (1969) and Shibles (1969) examine Carroll's significance for the study of language. See also Gardner (1963), Flescher (1972), and Jan (1974). Kirk (1962) and Fisher (1973) discuss word games apparently invented by Carroll, eg., "doublets," "mishmah," "syzygies," etc. Kirk's work on Carroll is of interest because he examines Carroll's total output, including the mathematical works, and sees as the unifying principle a semiotic preoccupation.

The interest of young children in sound play and nonsense has been observed often and commented upon by early observers of child development and play. Sully (1902: 112) observes that for children, "New words are for them sounds to be reduced to familiar ones, and the funnier the reduction the more they are pleased." Groos (1901) devotes an entire section of *The Play of Man* to "receptive and productive sound play" where he cites many of the earlier child biographies. Groos

sees in productive sound play "the beginnings of, or rather, the introduction to, art" (31); it is "undeniable that the repetition of meaningless rhymes, as well as of reasonable words and passages, is important
to poetry as a whole" (Groos, 1901: 35). Sound play for Groos includes
not only speech play but also music and other kinds of sound. (On play
and humor in music, see Mull, 1949 and Blacking, 1974. On acquisition of music, see Hopkins, 1975.)

An extremely suggestive, though subjective, work is Chukovsky
(1971), first published with great success in Russia in 1925. A popular
Russian poet and writer for children, Chukovsky devotes a chapter to
children and their poetry: "In the beginning of our childhood, we are
all 'versifiers'—it is only later that we begin to speak in prose. . . .
Making up verses begins when the aimless producing of rhymed and
other sounds stops and meaning is introduced" (64), an idea that may
be challenged in part by modern literary experiments. Chukovsky
characterizes children's nonsense verse as being spontaneous and
inspired by merriment; they are not so much songs as melodic exclamations and are not recited but spoken with an accompaniment of clap-
ping and dancing; their rhythm is trochaic; they are brief, not more
than two lines in length, and are repetitive; the rhyming is close
together since children eschew intermittent rhyming. Chukovsky also
discusses the child's passion for the absurd and incongruous, for
severing the ties between objects and their regular functions, and for
systematic disorder based on regular departures from everyday order.
According to Chukovsky, the child has a genius for classification.

The limerick, which occurs both as a folklore genre in oral tradition
and as a literary form, has been described as "primarily a vehicle of
nonsense" (Cammaerts, 1926: 5) and as such is an important example
of traditional adult speech play. Furthermore, the limerick's relation to
nursery rhymes suggests some important avenues for study.

Legman (1974) is the definitive collection of limericks. The seventeen hundred examples are annotated and accompanied by an historical
and interpretive introduction, an index of rhyming words, and a
bibliography of pertinent studies and collections. See also Baring-Gould
(1972), which is indebted to Legman, N. Douglas (1931) and La Barre
(1939). Legman claims that the limerick verse form is indigenous to the
English language and dates from the fourteenth century, when it began
as a bawdy "adult" genre (which it continues to be today). During the
early eighteenth century it faded from active adult use and was
specialized for the nursery. Edward Lear's clean limericks prompted a
limerick fad, which contributed to the revitalization of the oral bawdy
limerick tradition as well. Adult limericks were then called "nursery

rhymes" and "nonsense rhymes," suggesting their reappropriation from the nursery; for example, "Nursery Rhymes for the Army," the name of a nineteenth-century collection of limericks.

This and many other instances of formerly "adult" genres finding their way into and out of the nursery need to be reconsidered in light of Ariès's (1972) insights into the development of the concept of child and childhood in Western Europe in the late seventeenth century, first among the well-to-do, and later among the general population: "Books addressed to and reserved for children appear at the end of the seventeenth century, at the same time as the awareness of childhood" (Ariès, 1972: 5), as did specialized forms of dress, games, play, and lore. The history of the limerick thus reflects the distancing between the worlds of adults and children, the appropriation of themes and genres which became available for children as adults abandoned them, and adult reappropriation of children's verses.

### (g) PLAY LANGUAGES

Bibliographic guides to argots, slang, and ceremonial language can be found in Hymes (1964b: 403–406) and Brenni (1964). Relevant journals include *Dialect Notes, Publications of the American Dialect Society, American Speech,* and *Current Slang.* See Lasch (1907) for an unsurpassed study of many varieties of special languages. Van Gennep (1908) is an important early attempt at a theory of special language. See also Niceforo (1912) and Bächtold (1914). On glossolalia and other instances of codes valued for their "incomprehensibility," see Samarin (1973). An important reference tool is Wentworth and Flexner (1960) reviewed by Mathiot (1962), and Bischoff (1915).

In the most comprehensive survey of play languages to date, Laycock (1972) explains that while the literature on play languages is not extensive, brief note of them is made in many ethnographies under such key words as secret languages, jargon, cant, argot, children's languages, and dialects. Liede (1963, vol. 2: 221–255) discusses and provides bibliography on secret and play languages in the section on *"Lautdichtung,"* where he considers *"spielerische Lautdichtung"* and its literary exploitation in the work of Joyce and the Dadaist poets. For typologies of play languages see Haas (1967) and Laycock (1965, 1972). J. Sherzer (this volume), Laycock (1972), Halle (1962), and Burling (1970) discuss the theoretical issues raised by play languages and suggest future areas for research. See also Hale (1971).

Maurer (1949: 282–288) argues that the proclivity for coining and using argot goes far beyond any need for technical vocabulary and stems rather from a love of talk. For Maurer, con man argot is essentially playful, shows creativity and pleasure in toying with language, and delights in connotative metaphor formed on the basis of grotesque comparisons. Polsky (1971: 105–114) rejects the notion that the primary function of argots is secrecy. Rather, hustlers always use their argot among themselves, use argot less in the presence of others, and have special non-argot *ad hoc* signals for secretive communication in the presence of outsiders. Similarly hustler nicknames are not used for disguise but for esprit de corps and out of a playful impulse—"They lend a little color to the game." Instead, aliases are used to protect the hustler's identity in the outside world. Nor are hustlers protective of their argot which is an "open secret." Furthermore their argot is especially rich is obscene expressions and inventive nicknames and is surprisingly stable and uniform in contrast with the highly unstable nature of the argots of other social deviants. Increasingly stable are the argots of respectable trades, general slang, and the language at large, in that order.

Especially important are accurate recordings of the play languages being spoken since most accounts provide only the rules and sample utterances. Ethnographic accounts of how the languages are learned and used are also needed. For data on African secret languages see Leiris (1948), Delafosse (1922), and Trevor (1955). For English play languages, see Hirschberg (1913), Millard (1954), Berkovits (1970), Opie (1959), and Sherzer et al. (1971). For other areas, see Götz (1896), Pike (1945b), Vycichl (1959), Schlegel (1891), Laycock, Lloyd, and Staalson (1969), Weis (1952, 1954), Conklin (1956, 1959), M. Haas (1967, 1969), R. and S. Price (this volume), and J. Sherzer (this volume). C. Adams (1971) and E. and M. Anderson (1970) discuss Boontling, a local language that developed between 1880 and 1920 in Boonville, California. Lysing (1974) is a compendium of cryptograms, ciphers, and codes.

Yiddish play languages, codes, and ciphers have generally been overlooked. They are reported, and their contexts of acquisition and use described by the readers of W. Younin's weekly column in *The Forward*, a Yiddish daily newspaper, in response to my request for information (February 11, 1974). The respondants, mainly males, described a backwards language, number code, mirror writing, *tashrak-loshn* and *ayak bekhar galash*, a variant of the orthographic code based on the position of letters in a matrix described by Berkovits (1970: 141–143) and similar to one in Lysing (1974:41). Since the Jewish alphabet is used, the Yiddish code is an especially interesting case for comparison. U. and B. Weinreich (1959: 26–27) cite some studies of Yiddish social dialects and argots. On the history and playful uses of the Jewish alphabet, see Lipiner (1941). See Yakir (1973) for a suggestive study of seven play languages used by Israeli children.

Laycock (1972) mentions a secret language which "was either transforming Russian texts to Czech by keeping the Russian words but pronouncing them in Czech and Czech endings, or the other way around." Van Rooten (1968) is an interesting example of a similar phenomenon: *Mots d'heures: gousses, rames,* as the title indicates, is a collection of Mother Goose rhymes written so as to appear to be French but really intelligible only when read in English with a French accent. This "obscure French text" is glossed in what becomes a spoof of literary criticism. Related to *Mots d'heures* is "fractured French" (Pearson, 1950), which also involves bilingual punning (*"s'il vous plâit"* is understood as "silver plate"). "Franglish" is a game which involves an English stimulus word for which one must find an English synonym which is identical in spelling to a French word of a different meaning (Espy, 1972: 110): depression → *dent* 'tooth.' Latin-nonstandard English punning produces such delights as:

Civili derego fortibus inero
Demes nobus demes trux.

"See Willy, dere dey go, forty buses in a row
Dem is no buses, dem is trucks."
(Espy, 1972: 194)

Espy (1972: 195) also provides an example of a nursery rhyme in pseudo-Latin comparable to the *Mots d'heures* material. See Haas (1957) for bilingual punning in a Thai word game.

Laycock (1972: 62), who defines *ludlings* as a subset of play languages, distinguishes ludlings from deliberately speaking with a foreign accent and suggests that they are transmitted differently: "ludlings are probably learnt by conscious acquisition of the rule, while foreign accents are probably most often learned by imitation, and by unconscious acquisition of many rules simultaneously." In the bilingual punning discussed here, an additional set of rules is applied in order to establish game-specified relationships between two languages, one of them a nonstandard or foreign accent variety.

"Anguish languish" is based entirely on English and involves "replacing all the words of the story with others similar in sound but unrelated in meaning" (Espy, 1972: 48): "Ladle Rat Rotten Hut" is Little Red Riding Hood. In contrast with these imperfect homonyms are the perfect homonyms which form the basis for "Words wrong, pronunciation right" (Bombaugh, 1905: 104–105): "A rite suite little buoy, the sun of a grate kernal, with a rough about his neck, flue up the rode swift as eh dear. . . ." But these perfect homonyms are not perfect puns because only one reading, the one *not* suggested by the spelling of the words, qualifies syntactically as part of a grammatical sentence in English. In this case, spelling becomes an essential clue for perceiving the homonyms. This type of wordplay is by nature orthographic.

Nebesky (1971) explores the question of the constructs in formal scientific languages having potentially poetic aspects.

Lauder (1965, 1968) produces dialect humor based upon "strine" and "fraffy," varieties of English from Australia and London's West End respectively. Espy (1972: 38, 48, 78, 113, 164, 189, 233) provides examples of several other humorous varieties and their use in narrative and poetry. See Kirshenblatt-Gimblett (1971) for an analysis of code-switching in traditional narrative with special reference to the imitations of nonstandard varieties. See also K. M. Stein (1953), Dorson (1948, 1952), Gans (1953), Landon (1891), and Sandys (1831). Liede (1963, vol. 2: 205–214) discusses and provides copious bibliography on macronic poetry and *"andere Arten der Sprachmishung."* On the implications of *"Sprachmishung"* for linguistic creativity see Mackensen (1926).

(h)  NUMBERS, LETTERS, MNEMONICS, AND COUNTING OUT RHYMES

For bibliography pertaining to sacred or ritual numbers, see Hymes (1964b: 184). Granet (1930, chap. 3) discusses the role of numbers in Chinese culture. Menninger (1970) provides a monumental cultural history of numbers but cites none of his sources. Lotz (1955) discusses number as a semantic field and how the use of numbers and the existence of preferred numerical units can affect cultural aims and behavior. Dornseiff (1925) discusses the role of the alphabet in religious and magical practices. See Mayer (1975) on a semiotics of the alphabet.

Other number-letter systems which serve a variety of functions are gematria and notarikon, both based on the Jewish alphabet. Gematria is "a cryptograph which gives, instead of the intended word, its numerical value, or a cipher produced by the permutation of letters" (*s.v.*, gematria, *The Jewish Encyclopedia*, 1901; see also the entries for anagram, notarikon, and numbers and numerals). Gematria, often used as a mnemonic device, serves important exegetical purposes; a gematria might be calculated from a text in order to deduce its hidden, inner meaning. The use of gematria was greatly extended in the cabalistic literature which viewed the letters as dynamic powers and number as the essence of things. In modern times, gematria may be used in a playful fashion: "A person celebrating his seventieth birthday might be greeted with the wish that he would live long enough to change from "wine" (*yayin*, 70) to "water" (*mayim*, 90). Similar plays on numbers are made on names, festal occasions, or the inauguration of a new year" (*s.v.*, gematria, *Universal Jewish Encyclopedia;* see also the entries in the *Encyclopedia Judaica,* 1971).

Under the heading *"Buchstabenspiele,"* Liede (1963, vol. 2: 70–112) provides bibliography for and discusses in cross-cultural and historical perspective the folkloristic and literary uses of *"Anagram; Akro-, Meso-, Telestichund Notarikon; Chronogramm und Chronostich; der Aberedarius; das Lipogramm; das Tautogramm; das Palindrom; der Schüttelreim."* Canel (1867) is also an excellent source of bibliography on these forms. On the palindrome in ancient China, see Kuhn (1953).

Reiss (1970) provides copious bibliography on the use of numbers in literature, mysticism and other domains. He refers to the formal aspects of number as structure, for example, *Lahlens Komposition,* or understanding literary composition in terms of numerical symbolism, the aesthetic use of number, inherent number, stated number, and explicated number. See also Curtius (1963: 501–509).

Collections of number rhymes and number games include Boyce and Bartlett (1940), Gullen (1950), Lockhart et al. (1924), and G. Adams (1965). Lysing (1974) provides many number and letter codes, cryptograms, and ciphers, alphabet rhymes (*s.v.*, alphabet rhymes, M. Leach, 1949–1950), spelling riddles (Brewster, 1944), spelling and number games and puzzles (Ball, 1939; Lindley, 1897) may be found in many of the collections of wordplay and children's lore listed in the bibliography.

Many counting out rhymes are based on numerical and alphabetical sequences. Abrahams and Rankin (in press) provide a dictionary, annotations, and bibliography of major collections and studies of counting out rhymes. Baucomont et al. (1961) provide an excellent bibliography of children's folklore, including counting out rhymes, from throughout the French-speaking world. Bolton (1888) remains the classic study of counting out rhymes. See also Bolton (1897). Menninger (1970: 123–125) discusses children's counting out rhymes in terms of "semantic fading." For psychological analyses, see Ferdière (1947a, 1947b). Fleuret (1963) provides a pedagogical commentary. See Bodmer (1923) for a collection from French Switzerland and Lacourcière (1948) for the French Canadian material. Gregor (1891) provides counting out rhymes orally collected in the northeast of Scotland, classifies them, and discusses their use, meaning, history, origin, and form. See also

Daiken (1963) and Opie (1969). American material may be found in Babcock (1886a), Margott (1937), Brewster (1939a), and E. Adams (1947). Withers's (1946) collection is based on his childhood memories in Cedar Country, Missouri, between 1907 and 1913 and on Brooklyn students, 1936–1945 (see Abrahams and Rankin, in press).

Mnemonics have received almost no attention in linguistic, folklore, and anthropological literature, although studies of memory have long concerned folklorists dealing with transmission of oral tales and songs. The classic work on memory (Bartlett, 1972) does not deal with mnemonic devices *per se*. Hunter (1964: 164–171) discusses a variety of mnemonic systems including visual symbol, digit-letter, and successive comparison. Hunter provides bibliography on these systems in his article in Penguin *Science News* 39 (1956). See "mnemonic" in the eleventh edition (1911) of the *Encyclopedia Britannica* for a full survey and bibliography. See "mnemonic devices" in M. Leach (1949–1950) for a comprehensive survey which includes non-Western and non-literate societies but no bibliography. Dundes (1961) discusses traditional mnemonics and provides ample bibliography. Brayshaw (1849) discusses traditional mnemonic rhymes meant to aid the schoolchild in memorizing two thousand dates and numerical facts. Lockhart et al. (1924) provides a collection of number mnemonics.

See Vansina (1965: 36–39) for discussion and bibliography concerning various non-Western mnemonic systems, including the Peruvian quipu and several African mnemonics.

An important, as yet little explored avenue for research, is the role of speech play, particularly alphabet and number games, in the acquisition of literacy in a traditional educational system. Comparative education studies have generally focused upon non-Western, non-literate societies. An examination of traditional educational systems, which have literacy at the core of the curriculum, would lend itself to a study of the role of speech play in pedagogy and the relationship of the acquisition of literacy to the acquisition of language. The current research of D. K. Roskies on primary education among East European Jews is important in this regard. Roskies's preliminary findings will appear in the Max Weinreich Center Working Papers in Yiddish and East European Jewish Studies (YIVO Institute for Jewish Research).

(i) NAMES

*Names, Onoma, Namn og Bygd, Onomastica, Beitrage zur Namenforschung,* and *Revue Internationale d'Onomastique* are six of several periodicals devoted exclusively to research on names. Published irregularly, *Onoma* features copious bibliography for a given year covering many foreign publications as well as the proceedings of the International Congress of Onomastic Sciences. *American Speech* also publishes name studies. An excellent bibliographic guide to the anthropological and sociolinguistic study of names is Hymes (1964b: 225–227), who cites work which is important methodologically and with reference to the general relation of language to culture: these studies investigate "the complex involvements of naming and address with social structure and cultural values—often as part of broader systems of kinship and role terminology" (Hymes, 1964b: 225). Included are studies of the place of names in acculturation (see also Hewson, 1963). For a survey of non-Western naming practices and guide to the ethnographic literature, see N. Miller (1926–1927).

Algeo (1973), Gardiner (1954), and Zabeeh (1968) discuss and cite the studies pertinent to various theoretical aspects of proper names including the problem of definition. Brender (1963) considers the social and psychological basis for infant name selection in the United States. Rennick (1966, 1968) considers some traditions and name-changing efforts associated with unusual and obscene names in America and England. Pyles (1959) describes American Bible-Belt personal naming, which tends to be innovative, involving in many cases bisexual names and the use of nicknames, clipped forms, and diminutives as formal and legal personal names for adults. These types of names may be prefaced by honorifics. See Inez (1958) for Chippewa naming practices, Franklin (1967) for the Kewa, R. and S. Price (1972) for Saramaka, and Lauterbach (1932) and Bardis (1972) for Jewish material. A tragic episode in the cultural history of naming is studied by Rennick (1970).

Whereas considerable attention has been accorded kinship terminology (Levi-Strauss, 1943), the use of personal pronouns (Brown and Gilman, 1960), and ritual, personal and family names (Evans-Pritchard, 1948; Roys, 1940), it is only recently that serious anthropological and sociolinguistic attention has been devoted to informal and unofficial modes of address and reference, an area of considerable expressiveness, creativity, and playfulness. Worthy of study are nicknames and *blason populaire* (Roback, 1944).

Nicknames define and foreground social relationships, roles, and distinctions of age, sex, and status. See Yoder (1967) for a field guide. Nicknaming may be institutionalized (Bernard, 1968–1969), or nicknames may acquire formal and legal status (Pyles, 1959). Especially interesting is nicknaming as an informal and alternative system of address and reference which may become specialized for use in given contexts or may provide options to be exploited expressively in a variety of settings from informal conversational joking to ritualized verbal and song duels (Herndon and McLeod, 1972).

The creation and application of nicknames or informal appellations, when considered as a "system of communicative codes" (Collier and Bricker, 1970) and in terms of the social use and meaning of modes of reference and address (Bricker, this volume; Brandes, 1975) are an extremely interesting instance of linguistic and sociolinguistic creativity and play. Nicknames serve important functions in the formation and maintenance of friendship networks (Brandes, 1975). See Brandes (1975) for discussion and bibliography concerning the study of nicknaming in Spain: noteworthy are Pitt-Rivers (1961: 8, 160–169) and Freeman (1970). Antoun (1968) analyzes "the full range of terms of address and reference and examines them for the purpose of assessing their significance for ethical behavior and social control." He ranks terms by pejorative intention and discusses the structural significance of nicknames, and their use mainly to make ethical evaluations and exert social control. Collier and Bricker (1970) relate formal and informal naming practices to modern Zinacanteco social structure and Bricker (this volume) shows how discrepancies between systems of address and reference may be exploited in Zinacanteco ritualized verbal dueling. Dorian (1970) is an excellent study of a complicated system of by-names which, though unofficial, are used almost to the exclusion of the very limited range of official names in Gaelic-speaking communities. She discusses the entertainment value of by-names in addition to their other functions. See also Parman (1973). Herndon and McLeod (1972) consider Maltese nicknames as a means of indirectness and with special reference to their function in singing duels. Polsky (1971: 105–114) discusses hustler nicknames.

Children's naming, epithet hurling, jeers, torments, and sobriquet traditions are classified and discussed by Winslow (1969), Opie (1959: 154–205), and Wolfenstein (1954: 63–91). Winslow (1969) finds that the most offensive nicknames are ones based on physical features. Puns and parodies of a child's actual name ranked second. Third in offensiveness were epithets signifying demeaning social relationships and behavior, for example, Baby, Sissy, Fink. Least offensive were insults to one's intelligence such as Stupid, Idiot, Dumbass.

Wolfenstein considers name play as antecedent to wordplay. According to Wolfenstein the youngest children made up a joke of calling a girl a boy and a boy a girl. This was followed by making a joke of rearranging names, calling Johnny "Mary." Later they seized a new name, forced a meaning from it, and used it to attack the bearer. School-age children presented the ambiguous word in the joke as a proper name of sexual or aggressive significance (Heinie, Tits, Free Show, Shut Up) and used the proper name jokingly long before play on common names is mastered. Wolfenstein sees wordplay as an important element in the complex joke form and the development of the joke facade since wordplay becomes a significant form of indirectness, a fundamental notion in psychoanalytic analyses of speech play. (See Freud, 1963; Bergler, 1936; and Ferenczi, 1916.)

The University of Pennsylvania Folklore Archives contains a collection of "onomastic autobiographies" gathered from students in folklore classes. Some could recall as many as sixty distinct nicknames by which any one person had been known and the circumstances that precipitated their formation and use. Humor and playfulness were very much in evidence.

Curtius (1963: 300–301) discusses the literary use of playing on proper names in terms of the rhetorical figure, *agudeza nominal.* Playing on the alternate forms of names for God is especially developed in Jewish tradition.


(j)  HUMOR

An excellent annotated bibliography of humor research in the behavioral sciences from 1900 to 1971, but with special emphasis on empirical studies after 1950, may be found in Goldstein and McGhee (1972: 267–283). Entries are coded to indicate those studies which deal with humor in children, contain original data, use experiments, etc. Surveys of the scholarly literature on humor usually contain valuable bibliography and include Piddington (1933), Lauter (1964), Goldstein and McGhee (1972: 4–39, 243–267), Berlyne (1969), Flugel (1954), Fry (1968), Monro (1951), Milner (1972), Burns (1975), and the entry, "Humor," by Levine in *International Encyclopedia of the Social Sciences* (1968). Attempts at typologies of humor include Kraeplin (1885) and Esar (1952).

Humor studies have examined humor in relation to creativity, intelligence, affect, aesthetics, and play, as well as the cognitive and psychosocial development of humor, smiling, and laughter. Koestler (1964), Bateson (1953), Fry (1968), Chapman and Foot (1975), Levine (1969), Goldstein and McGhee (1972), and Jacobs (1964: 240–252) are examples of current research. McGhee (1971b) reviews developmental studies of humor which include among others Gorham (1958), Harms (1943), Kris (1938), Shaw (1960), McGhee (1971a, 1971c, 1972), Wolfenstein (1951, 1953, 1954), Zigler, Levine, and Gould (1966), Helmers (1965), Shultz and Horibe (1974), and Sully (1902). See

Zippin (1966) and Omwake (1937) for discussions of sex differences in humor. Sutton-Smith (1960) and Abrahams (1961) deal with cruel jokes. The relation of humor to the aesthetic is considered by Kallen (1911) and Koestler (1964). For a discussion of the joke as "playful judgment" and "playing with ideas" and of the analogy between joking and the aesthetic attitude which is also characterized as playful, see Freud (1963: 10–11) on K. Fischer. Humor and creativity are dealt with by Smith and White (1965), and Bateson (1953) and Fry (1968), who also relate humor to play. The incongruous nature of humor has been widely studied; see, for example, Bergson (1911), Clark (1970), and McGhee (1972).

Cross-cultural studies of humor include Milner (1968), Bowman (1939), and Jacobs (1960). Studies of American Indian humor include Bricker (1968, 1973b), Easton (1970), Hill (1943), Jacobs (1959), Skeels (1954a, b), and W. Miller (1967). On the subject of ritual clowns, see Levine (1969: 167–178) who provides bibliography, and Bricker (1973a).

Hymes (1964b: 299) provides a bibliographic note on humor in language. A classic study is Freud (1963). Freud's careful analysis of the linguistic techniques of jokes and his theory of wordplay have influenced subsequent psychoanalytic theory and analysis of humor, especially with reference to the role of language in the comic. Freud (1963: 11 ff.) also discusses the joke in terms of "sense in nonsense" and the "coupling of dissimilar things." Other studies of humor in language include Bergson (1911), who discusses humorous incongruities resulting from linguistic factors as one of three major causes of laughter, Estrich and Sperber (1952, chap. 15), and Greenwald (1975). On humor and semiotics, see Milner (1972), who attempts a theory of why so much of our laughter can be shown to be ultimately based on linguistic reversal and transposition. Especially interesting is his discussion of the pun, spoonerism (*contrepet, Schüttelreime*), and chiastic structure (often found in conundrums) as reversals which are paradigmatic, syntagmatic, and paragrammatic (from Kristeva, 1968) respectively. Milner (1968, chaps. 4 and 9) considers Samoan humor which is sociolinguistically generated. For a fascinating analysis of humor in literature, see Bakhtin (1968) on Rabelais in the history of laughter and the grotesque.

(k)  JOKING RELATIONSHIPS AND INTERACTIONS

As Goodchilds (1972: 176, 173) notes, humor is "preeminently interactive, immanent, impromptu," yet "that which is social about the funny, the amusing, the humorous, the witty remains an under-investigated, largely uncomprehended subject." Humor studies have thus tended to emphasize general theorizing about the nature of humor, experimental studies of the humor response, and analyses of joke content. The interest in the interactional nature of humor is more recent and includes studies of (a) conversational joking, teasing, playful insult, especially in the context of institutionalized joking relationships, and (b) ritualized verbal and song duels, to be discussed in the following section. Studies of conversational and ritual joking generally touch on the related subjects of "psycho-ostensive expression" (Matisoff, 1973), emotive speech and expressive language, speech taboo, insult, profanity, and obscenity, topics to be covered below. See Dryden (1968) for an attempt to distinguish humor, insult, and obscenity.

Informal conversational joking is discussed by Goffman (1974), Emerson (1953), Lindberg (1960), Hall (1974), Freud (1963), Bradney (1957), and Sykes (1966). Teasing, which is a combination of friendliness and antagonism, has been studied with special reference to children. See Babcock (1888), Froelich (1970), Opie (1959: 175–205), Stimson (1945), Brenman (1952), and Winslow (1969). See also the discussion of children's folklore in this volume, pp. 71–73.

Institutionalized joking relationships have received considerable attention from anthropologists who have approached the subject in general social structural and functional terms. The concern has been with *who* are doing the joking and their relationship rather than on how, about what, and to what various purposes they joke. Radcliffe-Brown (1965) was one of the first to view ritual joking relationships in general structural terms. He suggests a typology of joking relationships which he sees as a special form of alliance between families or clans or tribes. Joking relationships entail privileged disrespect, the only obligation being not to take offense so long as the disrespect stays within bounds. Thomson (1935) presents a classification of joking among the Wik Monkan people who distinguish *kul kentanak* or "unorganized" insult, swearing, and obscenity intended to arouse anger, from organized and licensed obligatory insult and swearing among *kintja* (certain kinship relations), which are "supposed to make everyone happy." The latter type is subdivided into genital and anal obscenity. See also Sharman (1969), Jacobs (1960), Rigby (1968), and Christensen (1963). Sykes (1966) and Bradney (1957) broaden the notion of joking relationships and examine them in contemporary Western society.

Brukman (1972: 158), in a discussion of joking relationships among the Koya, suggests that while such structural considerations may form the ground against which interpersonal, ritual joking is carried out, they do not by themselves determine the course or quality of the interaction. Brukman, who views joking behavior as one aspect of the ludic or play element in culture, is interested in the particulars of how the Koya joke, for example, how they use kinship terms to manipulate the structure of various encounters, and how the structure of the relationships of the participants affects the content of these interchanges. He suggests that social relationships are constantly being defined in particular situations and that playing with language is an important aspect of this process of definition. Brukman's close analysis of transcripts of joking sequences is of particular value, especially his explication of the background expectations upon which they are predicated and the context in which they are meaningful. Gossen and Bricker (this volume) are important in this context for their careful examination of the language, form, content, and social significance of particular joking routines.

Douglas (1968) distinguishes "community" (undifferentiated social relations, for example, friendship) from "structure" (differentiated social relations, for example, hierarchical ones) and suggests that joking, since it attacks classification can create community. See Rigby (1968) for a suggestive analysis along these lines. In contrast, Fry (1968: 147) suggests that humor is used primarily *to establish a pecking order*, a notion developed by Gossen (this volume). The positions of Douglas and Fry are only contradictory if either one is seen as accounting for all uses of humor. If, in contrast, they are seen as two different ways in which humor may be and is used, then joking relationships and verbal dueling (to be discussed below) would seem to be examples of each of these strategies respectively. Joking relationships, by allowing privileged disrespect, attack structure and create "community" whereas verbal dueling, by determining a winner, establishes a pecking order. This might illuminate why, in most reports of verbal dueling cross-culturally, the duelers are peers. Therefore, while joking relationships transform structure into community, verbal dueling would appear in many instances to transform community into structure, or in some of the cases cited by Bricker (this volume), to create an alternative structure of advantage to one player for the purposes of the game.

Brukman (1972: 159) suggests that it is "misleading to maintain a distinction between on the one hand an 'institutionalized' form of joking and on the other, all other kinds of joking," because "the play element can penetrate every form of social interaction and can reduce even the most formally prescribed and serious encounter among individuals to play, to the nonserious, and even therefore to the inherently humorous. Any social relationship has the potential to become ludicrous, and one might suggest that the serious nature of certain kinds of ritual encounters is maintained just because the ludicrous potential of any encounter must be guarded against, lest the denial of serious reality come to the fore." While Brukman's point regarding the pervasiveness of humor in interaction is well-taken, interactional joking does appear to take various forms, intra- and cross-culturally, and these forms appear to function differently.

## (1) VERBAL CONTESTS

Formal verbal contests take various forms and have been reported widely. See Farb (1974: 95–112) for a review of the subject. Gibson (1975: 9) suggests that verbal contests are public events, involve spectators, entail the social ranking of individuals on the basis of skill, use a verbal medium, are subject to evaluation by socially accepted rules, and are understood as nonserious or playful. Abrahams (1962) argues for a clear distinction between joking relationships and verbal dueling such as the Afro-American dozens. (See also Elliott, 1960.) If, as Douglas (1968) suggests, the privileged disrespect allowed by joking relationships converts structure into community, joking relationships would seem to stand in contrast to the verbal dueling defined by Gibson and described by Abrahams (1962), Gossen (this volume), Dundes, Leach, and Özkök (1970) and others. In verbal dueling like the dozens, adolescent male peers duel to establish a hierarchy, albeit a temporary and playful one. This point is discussed more fully in the section on joking relationships and interactions.

Dundes (1973: 295–297) provides a critical review of studies of African and Afro-American verbal dueling, also known as "playing the dozens," "sounding," "signifying," "woofing," "joning," "cutting," "capping," "chopping." Dundes also discusses the controversies regarding their origin. See Dollard (1939) for a classic though controversial study of the dozens in terms of race relations. Abrahams (1962, 1970a) interprets the dozens in terms of Afro-American family structure and the tensions experienced by males in a matriarchy. On the influence of dozens on poetry, see Rodgers (1969). Labov (1972a, 1974) sees sounding interactions as a way of socializing the process of insult and adapting it for play. He argues that unlike personal insult, ritual insult is not about individuals *qua* individuals but about roles or categories. Ritual insult is not intended as a factual statement and is therefore not denied but topped. Symbolic distance and highly patterned form (rhyming couplets, rules governing the content of each component of the couplet and the relationship between components) help insulate the exchange from further consequences. Labov (1972a, 1974) writes a formal description for the dozens. He also shows how children acquire competence. Abrahams (1962) also discusses the dozens in developmental terms, suggesting that interest drops off between the ages of sixteen and twenty-six. Proverbs come to serve as clever retorts. See Labov, Cohen, Robins, and Lewis (1968) for a discussion of competence with reference to black toasts. See also Legman (1975: 788–797).

Verbal duels have also been reported among Anglo-Americans (Ayoub and Barnett, 1965), Turks (Dundes, Leach, and Özkök, 1970), Ancient Aryans (Kuiper, 1960), the Chamula (Gossen, this volume), and the Waiwai (Fock, 1958). Devereux (1951: 105) mentions that Mohave have "humorous make-believe 'quarrels' among friends which are actually little more than contests of wit." Song duels have been reported among Eskimos (Elliott, 1960; Farb, 1968; Chamberlain, 1910), Annamites (Van Huyen, 1934), and in Malta (Herndon and McLeod, 1972).

See Huizinga (1955: 66–71) on play and contest as civilizing functions, especially for his mention of Chinese contests in politeness as an inverted boasting match; and of formal contests in invective and vituperation in pre-Islamic Arabia, in the context of the potlatch, among the ancient Greeks, and in Old Germanic and Old French traditions. Legman (1975: 782–788) discusses "contests-in-insult." See pp. 212, 218 below for references to riddling and proverb contests respectively. Edmonson (1971: 168–169) describes a distinctive kind of riddling and punning contest in Ethiopian Amharic. He also discusses Spanish *piropos* or *coplas*, flyting songs, and courtship games, and cites similar competitive phenomena among the Vietnamese and Araucanian Indians.

See Dondore (1930) for a discussion of contests of tales of prowess, Anglo-Saxon flyting, Old French boasting, and American frontier Big Talk. Dorson (1959: 39–73) and Blair (1960: 29–31) discuss contests involving tall tales, lying or boasting as part of the rise of native American humor. Dorson also sets these behaviors in the context of Chadwick's heroic age hypothesis. For a review of the literature on lying and tall tale telling and a discussion of their competitive nature, see Liede (1963, vol. 2, 38–42), Henningsen (1965), and the index to Dorson (1959). Farb (1974: 129 ff., 327) discusses the antinomy of the liar and cites the relevant literature.

Formal descriptions for verbal contests include Irvine (1974) on Wolof greeting routines, Salmond (1974) on a Maori ceremonial gathering which turns into an oratorical contest, and Labov (1972b, 1974) on the dozens.

(m)  PSYCHO-OSTENSIVE EXPRESSION

On expressive and emotive language, see Stankiewicz (1964), Werner (1955), and Hymes (1964b: 264–266, 280–282) for essays and bibliography. For the literature on oaths, profanity, and insult, see Hymes (1964b: 287). See also the bulletin and forthcoming publications of *Maledicta: International Research Center for the Study of Verbal Aggression.*

Basing his study on Yiddish data, mainly in the form of published collections of oral jests, Matisoff (1973) proposes a useful semantic classification of "psycho-ostensive expressions," a neologism he coined to refer to utterances "intended by the speaker to be accepted as the direct linguistic manifestation of his psychic state of the moment" (5). Included are thanks and congratulations; expressions of lamentation and sympathy; curses, taunts, and insults; and oaths. An excellent collection of Yiddish "psycho-ostensive expressions" is Bastomski (1920), who also proposes a classification and emic terminology. Montagu (1967) provides useful bibliography and attempts a typology and historical study of cursing, swearing, oaths, "expletives, maledictions, exclamations, imprecations of the immediately explosive or vituperative kind" (35).

On *blason populaire* or ethnic slurs, see Roback (1944) and Taylor (1962a). Leach (1964) examines speech taboo, animal categories, and verbal obscenity in terms of culturally specific systems of social classification. See also Swadesh (1933) for a comparative study of Chitimacha abusive language. Non-Western languages provide the data for studies of curses by Lowie (1959) and Evans-Pritchard (1949) and of insults by Bricker (1973b), Ritzenthaler (1945), and Samarin (1969).

Schaechter (1954) discusses Yiddish-speaking children's oaths in the context of speech taboo and the humorous use of language. He postulates that many of the oaths originated among adults who supplied children with gibberish forms "to restrain the children from using dangerous real oaths" (197). There also appears to be evidence of children creating nonsense oaths through punning on and altering oaths in phonologically determined ways. This may be attributable to a documented tendency in children's speech play and imitations of adult speech. (See Sanches and Kirshenblatt-Gimblett, this volume.)

(n)  OBSCENITY

General discussions of the nature of erotic folklore and problems in terminology and definition may be found in Legman (1964: 239–288; 1968; 1975), Dorson (1962), Hoffman (1973), Read (1934), Montagu (1967), Devereux (1951), Segal (1970), Kaplan (1955), La Barre (1955),

Reynolds (1943), Sagarin (1962), and "Obscenity and the arts," a special issue of *Law and Contemporary Problems* 22, 4 (1955). The great bibliographer of obscenity and its expressive use is Legman (1964). An important recent guide, Hoffman (1973), provides an analytical survey of the materials of erotic folklore and a supplement of six appendexes of annotated bibliographies and indices.

This kind of discourse has been variously referred to as scatological, erotic, sexual, pornographic, profane, improprietous, indecent, lewd, lascivious, bawdy, dirty, smutty, foul, abusive, locker room, and billingsgate. English, French, Latin, and other European languages exhibit a particular richness of vocabulary in the erotic domain as evidenced by the many special dictionaries and supplements. See, for example, Farmer's (1896) erotic supplement to Farmer and Henley (1890–1904) and Hoffman (1973: 36, 56, 106, 107, 301) for other such dictionaries. Bawdy songsters are a good source of erotic slang and other genres of obscene folklore—riddles, jokes, toasts, verse, puns on book titles, etc.—used as page and signature fillers. See Hoffman (1973: 48–51), who also notes the prevalence of dialect humor and wordplay in erotic joke books.

Whereas the literature on legal controversies surrounding obscenity is voluminous, basic groundwork remains to be done in the ethnographic study and analysis of eroticism in expressive language, folklore, and speech play. Due to the propriety of collectors and publishers, very little erotic lore has been recorded. If collected, this material has been published pseudonymously, in Latin, or privately in a limited edition, or not published at all. During the past century, scholars of the stature of F. S. Krauss, Gaston Paris, Henri Gaidoz, and Guiseppe Pitré have been responsible for the major publishing of erotic folklore materials, annotations, and studies, most of them Western European, especially French and German. The publication of English language material has been minimal in comparison. The major published collection of traditional erotic lore and studies is the thirty-nine volumes comprised by the three journals, *Kryptadia, Anthropophyteia,* and *Contributions au Folklore Erotique.* There have been some attempts to correct the paltry representation of erotic lore in children's collections, for example, Gaignebet (1974) and Borneman (1974); Wolfenstein (1954) is a classic study.

The culturally relative nature of obscenity, the extent to which it exists as a category at all, and what it encompasses have been hotly debated; see Honigman (1943). Most agree that obscenity is predicated on taboo. Read (1934: 264) distinguishes "taboo of concept and a taboo of word." He asks, "When a subject is admissable at all, why should not the plain outspoken terms be the best ones to use?" and cites many examples where a response to a taboo word is out of proportion to the semantic content of the word. Devereux (1951: 99) notes the importance, in psychoanalytic theories of obscenity, of the obscene word itself being tabooed and points out that this view assumes double-coding—decent and indecent terminology for a given phenomenon—which is not a cross-cultural universal. The Mohave, and other societies, have "no polite substitutes for colloquial terms designating the sexual and excretory organs and their functions" (99). The concept of obscenity among the Mohave involves the context and manner in which sexual and excretory matters are discussed rather than the terminology used. "A Mohave word is 'obscene' when uttered with obscene, aggressive or humorous intent." Hence, Devereux (1951: 100) distinguishes between obscene words and obscene speech and in this respect approaches Kaplan's (1955: 551) argument that "obscenity, like art itself, is not a matter of referential, but of expressive meanings."

On the historic transformations of speech norms in connection with obscenities, see Bakhtin (1968: 187–195). Important sociolinguistic questions arise in connection with the history and social implications of the components of a language and their relation to obscenity, for example, drawing the most powerful obscene terms in English from the Anglo-Saxon component.

Of major importance is Bakhtin's (1968: 145–195) discussion of marketplace and billingsgate elements in Rabelais. Bakhtin, who views abuses, curses, profanities, and improprieties as a breach of the established norms of official verbal address, sees in them great power of travesty. See Partridge (1960) on the bawdy in Shakespeare. Cray (1972) notes the prominence of parody in traditional bawdy song in English. See also the "Goose Mother" rhymes discussed by Dundes and Georges (1962). The literature on humor and verbal dueling, discussed above, deals with the use of obscenity in parody and playful insult.

The close association of obscenity and humor is essential to psychoanalytic theory and has been reported often cross-culturally, even though Freud's theory of humor and of obscene humor in particular has been attacked as ethnocentric. Milner suggests that "in spite of Freud's contribution to this problem, we still know very little of the reasons why possibly (or even probably) in every culture, language, and period, sex should be a major source of actual or potential laughter" (Milner, 1972: 22). Devereux (1951: 104) notes the importance of humorous obscenity in Mohave relations. Basing the argument primarily on Western, especially English language material, Legman (1968: 9) claims that erotic humor is the most popular of all types of humor. Hoffman (1974) notes that the primary vehicle of erotic folk narrative is humor. Cray (1972) also notes the ubiquity of erotic humor and, in addition, discusses the remarkable stability and continuity of bawdy song, which is humorous for the most part. Reuss (1965) finds that 40–60 percent of traditional college song lore on American campuses is bawdy. The paucity of published material therefore reflects the propriety of the academic and publishing worlds rather than of oral tradition.

Obscene lore, especially in the playful form of jokes, limericks, and humorous song, is of special value to psychoanalytic scholars for what it reveals about the content of the "normal" unconscious (La Barre, 1939) and the extent to which it can complement or corroborate clinical evidence from psychotic individuals, the basis for many psychoanalytic generalizations. In an analysis of folklore in which dreams are described, Freud and Oppenheim (1958: 65) find that "folklore interprets dream symbols in the same way as psychoanalysis." Dundes (1966) takes advantage of the collective nature of latrinalia to explore the relationships between personality and culture and to reveal aspects of American national character. La Barre (1939) distinguishes the obscene discourse preferences of various American subcultures and focuses on limericks recorded from "healthy and normal young men in secondary schools and colleges" (204).

The play element is highly developed in bawdy lore, the creative aspects of which have been explored to some extent in studies of obscene wit, humor, and speech play. Among the Koya, "sexual joking is one of the areas in which creativity in language is highly motivated as well, because a man's reputation as a "sweet" (K-tiiya) talker is closely related to his (putative) abilities as a seducer of women" (Brukman 1972: 174). Cray (1972), Legman (1974), La Barre (1939), and Dundes and Georges (1962) point to indications that many bawdy songs and limericks (see pp. 192–193 for an extended discussion) are the product of a literate group of carriers and display considerable wit, ingenuity, and sophistication. According to Hoffman (1973: 48), "Much of the bawdiness depends upon double entendre, implied meanings, and euphemistic language for its effects rather than upon direct or open statement." According to Cray (1972: xxxiii), bawdy song is "speech-oriented" music to a far greater extent than other forms of traditional singing; it is audience oriented and fundamentally a social experience.

Discussions of bawdy song (Cray, 1972: 264) and humor (Legman, 1968: 217) have stressed that this material is created by, for, and about male needs. An important contribution to our knowledge of a "female folk-literature of sexuality" (La Barre, 1939: 204) is Johnson (1973). Recent feminist literature has drawn attention to the male bias and verbal degradation of women in the English language generally and in much current sexual vocabulary in particular. See the annotated entries in the bibliography by Thorne and Henley (1974: 3–10).

Important studies of playful verbal obscenity in the form of graffiti include McLean (1970), Dundes (1966), Stocker, Dutcher, Hargrove, and Cook (1972), and Read (1935), who is presently revising this important early work. These works also contain the pertinent bibliography on the subject.

## (o) PROVERB AND SPEECH METAPHOR

*Proverbium*, the journal devoted to the study of the proverb, contains many important articles on proverb meaning, structure, style, classification, and history, and lists and describes new publications in the field. Major bibliographies of proverb collections and studies include Bonser and Stephens (1930) and Moll (1958). For the American proverb literature, see de Caro and McNeil (1970), who include general reference works, studies of non-American proverbs published in the United States as well as studies of American proverbs published elsewhere. Ferguson and Echols (1952) provide a critical bibliography of the Arabic proverb literature. General surveys, including some bibliography, are Taylor (*s.v.*, proverb, in M. Leach, 1949–1950), Taylor (1962a), and Abrahams (1972b). On the maxim, see Bénichou (1967), Rosso (1968), Starobinski (1966), Barley (1972, 1974a), Lewis (1971), and Aristotle (*Rhetoric* 2.21). See Shibles (1971) for a history and an annotated bibliography on metaphor and Crossan (1974) for a bibliography on parable research.

Recent studies of proverb structure include Cirese (1968–1969), Milner (1969, 1971), Dundes (1975), Gumpel (1975), Kuusi (1972), and Seitel (1972). For proverb form and style, see Rothstein (1968), especially for his discussion of the use of parallelism and ellipsis, and Silverman-Weinreich (1964). For ethnographic treatments of proverb use and discussions of the proverb in terms of socially situated meaning, see Seitel (1969, 1972), Arewa and Dundes (1964), Messenger (1959), and Kirshenblatt-Gimblett (1973b). An important recent work which discusses problems of proverb form, meaning, use, and function is Herzenstiel (1973).

African proverb scholarship is especially rich. Recent studies include Kulah (1973) for the Kpelle, Seitel (1972) for the Haya, and Boadi (1972) for the Akan. For a comparative study of European proverbs, see

Gluski (1971). A classic collection of Chinese proverbs (A. H. Smith, 1902) has recently been reprinted.

Playing with proverbs is dealt with by Kirshenblatt-Gimblett (1973a) and Brewster (1971: 41) who mention a variety of proverb games popular in nineteenth century America, Shakespeare's England, Bombay, and elsewhere. Lewis (1971: 133), in considering La Rochefoucauld's maxims, mentions the " 'charming game' of maxim making" so popular among the *précieux* and refers to Lanson's *L'art de la prose* which includes an "impressive enumeration of formulae for constructing maxims." See also Lewis (1969). Taylor (1962a: 182–183) discusses the *"proverbes dramatiques,"* a literary genre of the seventeenth and eighteenth centuries in which, "after the manner of a charade, the audience is led to guess the proverb on which the play depends for its point and purpose." On the use of proverbs in drama, see Liede (1963, vol. 2: 217–218) and Narciss (1927–1928).

The utilization of proverbs and related genres (maxims, aphorisms, apothegms, epigrams, etc.) in literary works has been widely researched. See Taylor (1962a: 171–183) for a survey. Curtius (1963: 292–293) discusses the epigram and the style of *pointes:*

No poetic form is so favorable to playing with pointed and surprising ideas as epigram—for which reason seventeenth and eighteenth-century Germany called it "Sinngedicht." This development of the epigram necessarily resulted after the genre ceased to be bound by its original definition (an inscription for the dead, for sacrificial offerings, etc.).

Curtius relates the interest in epigrams to the development of the "conceit" as an aesthetic concept. On the Priamel see Taylor (1962: 179–180) and Uhl (1897). A seminal study is Moldenhauer (1967) on *Walden*. Mieder (1972) reviews studies of the use of proverbs in German literature and has himself worked on Gotthelf, Immermann, Auerbach, Grass, Droste-Hülshoffs, and others. de Caro and McNeil (1970) provide a comprehensive listing of studies of the use of proverbs in American literature and cover, among others, Cooper, Emerson, Robinson, Flanagan, Melville, Faulkner, Sandburg, and O'Hara, and some figures from world literature, namely, Brecht and Kipling. Eberhard (1967) examines the use of proverbs in Chinese novels. Numerous studies of proverbs being used in French, Spanish, and other literatures appear in *Proverbium*.

There is a considerable literature on proverb tests, designed to tap verbal comprehension, especially in the area of abstraction. Some of these tests are intended for use for individual clinical evaluation by psychologists and as a screening test for mental hospitals and mental hygiene clinics. Gorham (n.d.) claims that the test can distinguish normal and schizophrenic populations with a high degree of reliability. This material is worth study in its own right as well as for its implications for the study of proverb meaning and comprehension more generally. The proverb test literature has been reviewed by Brewer (1973: 34–38) and includes Palmer (1956), Pounders (1956), Bass (1957, 1958), Gorham (1956a, b, c, d), Rabin and Broida (1948), Elmore (1957), and Reveal (1960).

Theory of metaphor is the subject of a special issue of *Poetics: International Review for the Theory of Literature*, vol. 4, nos. 2–3 (14–15). Work done on the development of symbolic thought includes Bruner and Olver (163), Werner and Kaplan (1963), Piaget and Inhelder (1971). On the development of the ability to understand and use figurative language, see H. Gardner (1973, 1974), Abou-Allam (1963), Horne (1966), A. S. Levine (1950), Stross (1972), Milchman (1974a, 1974b), Leondar (1975). Fewer studies have considered children's ability to understand such culturally specific uses of figurative language as proverbs (Richardson and Church, 1959) and parables (Beechick, 1974). Brewer (1973) examines the developing competence of Anglo- and Afro-American children in understanding and using proverbs. She finds that children normally acquire the ability to understand proverbs as social metaphor when seven- through nine-years-old but do not acquire the same degree of mastery in usage as in comprehension for at least three years. Kulah (1973) focuses on the acquisition of competence in the *use* of proverbs among Kpelle children and adults. A riddle-like game, *koloŋ*, played by children as young as six, as well as by adults, is an exercise in figurative language and metaphoric relationships which actually utilizes proverbs as responses to many of the riddles. The Kpelle even refer to the riddle responses as *saŋ*, "proverb," and the game can be seen in part as "playing with proverbs." Six- through nine-year-olds therefore first acquire a repertoire of proverbs through playing *koloŋ*, although at this stage these proverbs constitute riddle answers for them rather than social metaphors. Because of Kpelle rules for proverb usage, it is not until they are nineteen to twenty that they can use proverbs without a prefatory apology. These studies suggest the importance of examining the riddle as a "primary form" (Taylor, 1962b; Jolles, 1956) and cross-cultural differences in the role of the riddle and other speech play games in the acquisition of figurative speech generally and of other genres of poetic discourse, such as proverbs, parables, and jokes (see Wolfenstein, 1954), in particular.

Taylor (1938) and other scholars have explored riddle-proverb relations outside of a developmental context. First, the genres have been distinguished and their relations explored by Abrahams (1968, 1969a) and Barley (1974a). Second, Siddiqui (1961), Hamnett (1967), Kuusi (1969), Milner (1970), Hassell (1970, 1974), Basgöz (1972), and Hasan-Rock (1974) have examined the interchangeability of proverbs and riddles, especially in cases where the same metaphor is used in both a riddle and a proverb in a given speech community, often African, but also Samoan, Bengale, Turkish, Aramaic, and French. Kuusi (1974), for example, provides a substantial concordance of Ovambo riddles and proverbs. Third, a riddle may consist of two proverbs (Messenger, 1960; Simmons, 1961) or a proverb may constitute the answer to a riddle (Kuusi, 1969; Kulah, 1973) or a riddle may be embedded in a proverb (Kuusi, 1969). On the Wellerism as a mini-narrative form built upon proverbs and riddles and their trans-mutability, see Cirese (1969), Cray (1964), Mieder (1974), Loukatas (1972), and Taylor (1962a: 200–220; s.v., Wellerism, Leach, 1950). On the embedding of proverbs in traditional narratives, see Mieder (1974) for a listing of pertinent studies.

(p) RIDDLE

Bibliographies of riddle collections and studies include Taylor (1939) and Santi (1952) for worldwide coverage, Bhagwat (1965) for India, Hart (1964) for cross-cultural and Filipino materials, Hain (1966) for Germany, Bodker et al. (1964) for the Nordic riddle, Kuusi (1974) for Africa, Taylor (1951) for England and other traditions, Taylor (1948) for the literary riddle before 1600, and Hassell (1974) for French and other European collections, especially the early ones.

General surveys of the riddle, its nature, subgenres, and study, include Taylor (1938, 1962b), Abrahams and Dundes (1972), Brunvand (1968: 48–58), Bhagwat (1965), and Hain (1966). Hart (1964: 1–13, 24–75) is a pioneering review of anthropological, especially functional studies of riddles. Burns (in press) and Evans (1975) cover the more recent ethnographic contributions. On the koan, see Miura and Sasaki (1965) and Zug (1967). On ancient Greek riddles and games, see Ohlert (1886) and W. Schultz (1909–1912).

The development of riddle classifications began with a concern for devising an orderly arrangement of collected materials so that they might be easily catalogued, retrieved, and compared. Based on content features, the most influential etic scheme is Lehmann-Nitsche (1911) and Taylor (1951) which is derived from it. See also Williams (1963), Barrick (1964), and Hart (1964).

Lindley (1897) is extremely interesting for the classification of puzzles he designed to facilitate his study of puzzle preferences by age, and his historical notes on the evolution and revival of interest in various kinds of puzzles. Lindley classifies puzzles into five main groups: language and word; mechanical; mathematical; logical and philosophical; dilemmas of etiquette, ethics, etc. Language and word puzzles are further subdivided and include: riddles; rebuses; conundrums; enigmas; charades, word squares, and diamonds; acrostics; logograms, metagrams, decapitations, curtailments, retailments; hidden words, anagrams; doublets, etc. Lindley found that, among his subjects (American and mostly women), language puzzles were by far the most popular and that, among the subclasses, riddles led. He suggests that riddles represent the earliest and most rudimentary aspect of puzzle interest. See Bellamy (1894) and Ballard (1895) for collections of charades and their answers respectively. See Andrée (1882–1883) for rebuses in antiquity.

More recently, classification schemes have developed out of linguistic, stylistic, structural and logical analyses and, in some cases, reflect a concern with emic structure and classification, and, to a lesser extent, with an interest in developmental studies of child acquisition of riddles. A seminal and early contribution to the analysis of riddle structure and style is Petsch (1899). Georges and Dundes (1963) discuss types of Aristotelian logical oppositions utilized in riddle questions. Gowlett (1966) classifies Lozi riddles according to Georges and Dundes's scheme and finds that in Lozi, metaphorical nonoppositional riddles predominate, there being proportionately fewer oppositional riddles in Lozi than in English. Scott (1965, 1969) attempts a language-centered structural definition of the riddle based on Arabic and Persian riddles. Hamnett (1967), E. K. Maranda (1969, 1971a, 1971b), Todorov (1973), and Barley (1974b) are concerned with the structural relationships between the riddle and its possible answers. They deal with the riddle as an exercise in novel definition and classification expressed through radical metaphor, or what Todorov calls *"synonymie non institutionelle"* (1973: 141). In his important article, Todorov, responding to Maranda, and Dundes and Georges, first clarifies the relationships between the riddle question and answer: whereas paradox is contained within the question part of the riddle and establishes a relationship between two stated terms, metaphor establishes a relationship between question and answer and hence between a stated and an unstated term. Todorov then distinguishes among the various types of metaphor and paradox found in riddles and identifies the tropes and figures in riddles which have not usually been noted, among them synecdoche, antiphrasis, hyperbole, litote, syllepsis, enthymeme, and others.

Important analyses of riddle form and style include Bascom (1949) for Yoruba, Beuchat (1957) for Bantu, Cong-Huyen-Ton-Nu (1971) for Vietnamese, and Hacikyan (1966) for Old English. Hart (1964: 32–36) cites studies which discuss the use in Southeast Asian and African riddles of obscure language as a strategy for confusion, for example, nonsense, archaic or abstruse terms, meaningless names, baby talk, and ritual language. This suggests types of riddles where confusion is not so much the result of semantic oppositions as phonological, morphological, and syntactic obscurities and the use of special codes. Hart (1964: 33) cites Junod's study of Bathonga riddles, many of which "emphasize 'similitude in sound' instead of meaning, whereas some are 'altogether incomprehensible.'" Jordan (Hart, 1964: 33) reports a popular type of African riddle, *iquina*, "knot," which "is concealed under obscure language." See Hart for numerous other instances.

Studies of riddling contexts have emphasized general cultural setting and functional analysis. For Africa, see Blacking (1961), Harries (1971), Raa (1966), Simmons (1956, 1958b), and Redmayne and Ndulute (1970). Other studies of African riddles are listed in Ben-Amos (1974b) and Kuusi (1974). See Williams (1963) for an important account of the Tambunan Dusun riddling context, Hart (1964) for Filipino, Basgöz (1965) for Turkey, and Upadhyaya (1970) for Bojpuri.

More recently scholars have addressed themselves to the immediate social context of riddling and have examined particular riddling sessions (Goldstein, 1963) in terms of their interactional structure. Burns (1976) presents "a synthetic and comparative overview of the structure of the interaction in riddling from descriptions of diverse traditions in the literature." D. Evans (1975) is exceptional in providing a verbatim transcript of one complete riddling session. The data is from a black rural area in Mississippi. He analyzes the session in terms of the selection and sequence of riddles asked. Evans's (1975) data lends itself to the analysis of riddling as a special kind of interrogative routine, in which participants offer right, wrong, and logically possible but untraditional answers while the riddlers present clues and clarifications of the questions and exercise arbitrary power in deciding which answers they will accept. Ben-Amos (1974) discusses the importance of examining the attempted answers, often unacceptable because nontraditional, to riddles posed during an actual session. The total set of answers offered for any one riddle by the participants could provide the basis for analyzing the semantic set defined by a given riddle and the ways in which the participants proceed in resolving the ambiguities and logical problems presented therein. See also the work of Maranda (1971) on the importance of examining the multiple possible answers as a basis for a generative theory of riddles.

Recent sociolinguistic studies of riddling interaction include Roberts and Forman (1971), discussed by Sutton-Smith (this volume), and McDowell (1974), who examines Mexican-American children's interrogative routines. McDowell's typology of riddling behavior has developmental implications and includes (1) descriptive routines where language is used to reveal rather than conceal; (2) riddles proper, which are deliberately confusing; and (3) ludic routines of victimization, including tricks, pranks, and catches, which range from physical aggression to verbal abuse and embarrassment. "Descriptive routines center on the functional aspects of the code; riddles focus on those aspects which are nonfunctional from a purely referential point of view, its twists and wrinkles. Routines of victimization move away from the code itself, and focus on the dynamics of social intercourse" (p. 26).

Developmental studies of children's riddling interests and competence have focused upon appreciation and comprehension (Shultz, 1974; Prentice and Fathman, 1972) and upon production. Lindley (1897) questioned American adults, primarily women, about their puzzle preferences at different ages and found several trends: riddle interest began at four and culminated at eight, nine, and ten. This finding should be compared with later work of Sutton-Smith (this volume), Wolfenstein (1954), and others. Wolfenstein (1954) studied the riddle and joke repertoires of children in a New York school and, utilizing a psychoanalytic approach, analyzed generic shifts as well as the development of thematic concerns and formal complexity in their repertoires. Her work is discussed by Sanches and Kirshenblatt-Gimblett (this volume). Weiner (1970) collected the active riddle repertoire from Massachusetts schoolchildren and tabulates her findings by age and sex. Park (1972) and Sutton-Smith (this volume) analyze the riddle repertoire of American schoolchildren in terms of Piaget's theories of cognitive development.

Though often not directly concerned with riddles, studies on wit and humor, especially those dealing with incongruity, suggest important new avenues for riddle research. Rapp (1949) considers the role of riddles in the origin of wit. Freud (1963: 52, 67) discusses the complementary relationship of riddles and jokes. Similarly studies of symbolic thought and figurative language, especially those concerned with the proverb, are also important for riddle study. This is suggested above by the role riddles appear to play in the development of metaphoric thinking, figurative language, and the acquisition of proverbs (Kulah, 1973) and jokes (Wolfenstein, 1954). See above for the development of the ability to use and understand figurative language and for the literature on the relationships between riddles and proverbs. Shultz and Pilon (1973) deal with the development of the ability to detect linguistic ambiguity, an important prerequisite for riddle and proverb competence.

For a bibliography of the literary riddle, see Taylor (1948). Aristotle (*Rhetoric* 3.2) discusses the metaphor as enigma and the riddle as metaphor. Sebillet (1972, first published 1548) devotes chapter 11 of his *Art poétique françoys* to the riddle.

Abrahams (1972a) discusses Huizinga's (1955) and Caillois's (1968) theories of the riddle as examples of the problems raised by some practitioners of the "literary study of the riddle." Recent studies of the Anglo-Saxon riddle include Barley (1974) and Hacikyan (1966). For a fifteenth century French riddle collection see Hassell (1974), who cites other literary collections. Lindley (1897) suggests that the seventeenth century was the great riddle era in France and also refers to the interest in riddles on the parts of Menestrier, Swift, Cowper, Fox, and others. See also Schevill (1910–1912).

Caillois (1968) describes a riddle-like game popular in Surrealist circles. Breton called it "One in the Other." Consistent with Surrealist thought, Breton uses as the basis for the game the thesis that "a poetic image will be all the more effective as the terms which it joins increase in distance from each other." Any object might be described in terms of any other and any "action and also any person, even placed in a precise situation, might be described in terms of any object, and vice-versa." One person might pretend to be a staircase and be asked to describe himself as a bottle of champagne in such a way as to enable the players to guess that he was a staircase. Related to the conceits of the metaphysical poets, this game of correspondences played by the surrealist writers, might be compared to traditional riddling contests.

Curtius (1963: 275–278) explores the relationship between ritual language, artistic discourse, and speech play as they relate to the riddle. He suggests that some rhetorical figures, for example, periphrasis (circumlocution), may have their origin in cult languages. He distinguishes between circumlocution which is euphemistic (to preserve decorum) and circumlocution which is decorative or intended as a way of artistically inflating diction. When carried to extremes "periphrase passes into riddling" as in the case of early Greek poetry and Old Norse kennings. See J. A. MacCulloch's discussion in Hasting's *Encyclopaedia of Religion and Ethics* (1912), s.v., "Euphemism."

(q)  NARRATIVE

Narrative *per se* is not analyzed in this volume, but several papers have dealt with child acquisition of verbal art, and studies of children's developing narrative competence point to exciting avenues for research closely related to such concerns. Hence, resources for the study of narrative, especially children's storytelling, are provided here.

The major reference tools for traditional narrative, one of the most researched genres of verbal art, are Aarne and Thompson (1961) and Thompson (1946, 1966). For some current developments in the field, see *Fabula,* the journal devoted to folktale research; the proceedings of the International Congress for Folk Narrative Research, which meets every five years; and *Poetics: International Review for the Theory of Literature.* The general folklore bibliographies listed above provide copious references to folktale scholarship. For recent surveys see Colby and Peacock (1973) and Dorson (1972b: 54–83). Collections, bibliography, and surveys of the field may be found in individual volumes of the Folktales of the World series published by the University of Chicago Press. Thus far volumes have appeared for China, Japan, France, Hungary, Norway, Germany, Chile, Mexico, Israel, and England, among others.

Folktale scholars have focused upon problems of terminology and genre definition (Ben-Amos, 1974a, 1975b), classification (Aarne and Thompson, 1961; Thompson, 1946, 1966), diffusion (Thompson, 1946; Dundes, 1965: 414–474), function (Fischer, 1963; Jacobs, 1959) meaning (Emeneau, 1966; Hymes, 1971c), structure, ethnography of storytelling, and acquisition.

Seminal studies of the nature of narrative include Labov and Waletsky (1967) and Labov (1972b). Sacks (1972) should be read in conjunction with Speier (1970). Important recent contributions to the analysis of narrative structure are listed in Ben-Amos (1975: 8–14). Noteworthy are Bremond (1966, 1973), Dundes (1964a), Hendricks (1973), and Prince (1973). The pioneering study of narrative structure is Propp (1968, first published in 1928). Dundes (1964b) and Colby (1975) relate narrative structure to the organization of other domains.

Ethnographic treatments of storytelling include Finnegan (1967), Dégh (1969), Crowley (1966), Geddes (1957), Abrahams (1970b, 1970c), Dorson (1972a: 103–114), Sebeok (1960: 17–51), and Kirshenblatt-Gimblett (1974a, 1974b). A classic early work is Azadowski (1975).

Acquisition studies include Hrdličková (1965, 1968), Lord (1960), and an emerging literature on children's developing ability to comprehend and produce stories. The literature on stories produced for children is vast and will be discussed more fully in connection with nursery lore. Alvey (1974) examines organized storytelling to children, its historical development in the United States and its impact on other storytelling activities. He provides copious bibliography on the subject. The interest in children's own narrative productions has developed out of a diversity of concerns. Gardner (1971) uses the "mutual storytelling technique" as a therapeutic device and has produced a set of cassette tapes demonstrating his method. Cottle (1973) examines the recollections of the childhood of a twelve-year-old girl in the context of developmental perceptions of time. Compare Cottle with G. and M. Dudycha (1941), who review the literature on childhood memories. Colby et al. (1974) are concerned with narrative comprehension as part of their ongoing studies of narrative grammars.

Beechick deals with children's developing ability to comprehend religious parables or narrative analogies. She finds the following progression (1974: 86):

1.   Analogies of "actions" are understood first (age 7).
2.   Analogies of "actors" are understood next (ages 8–10).
3.   Analogies of "objects acted upon" are understood last (age 11).

Halliday (1974) traces the beginnings of narrative in the speech of his son Nigel, as an integral part of the development of linguistic competence. For Halliday, the building up of the relationships that constitute texts is an independent function, coordinate with the other functions, particularly the ideational and interpersonal, in terms of which language is to be analyzed and understood. Keenan (1974) considers narrative one of five elementary uses of language in the productions of her twin sons (alongside comments, questions, mands [directives], and speech play). Hymes (1975) postulates that narrative, and speech play, are fundamental to the nature of language, and hence are linguistic roots of folklore itself.

Brose's (1973) study is essentially thematic as she examines the impact of the mass media and other sources of information on California and Nebraska children's stories about the supernatural. She suggests the following issues be investigated in future research (161):

1.   the relationship between a child's exposure to traditional folk literature and his mastery of fundamental narrative structures, including cause and effect sequences;
2.   the relationship between a child's mastery of the narrative

structures and stereotyped characters of formula literature, including folktales, and his later enjoyment of literature of greater complexity and ambiguity;

3. the relationship between the child's mastery of the linguistic and rhetorical formulas of folk literature, and his ability to use more elaborate and complex linguistic structures in his own story writing.

Compare Brose with Virtanen (1972), who examines children's legend repertoires and performance contexts in Finland. In 1969 Virtanen gathered about five thousand descriptions of storytelling situations and tales from ten- to thirteen-year-olds. Gothic themes and traditional tale models were prevalent as were the pleasure-through-terror attitude and the use of parody.

The classic study of children's developing narrative competence, especially the mastery of traditional riddles and jokes and the emergence of the "joke facade" is Wolfenstein. Psychoanalytic in approach, she examines generic, thematic, and formal aspects of New York children's own productions primarily during the latency period. Pitcher and Prelinger (1963), in their study of New Haven children's fantasy as expressed in spontaneous original stories, analyze formal and thematic features using an Eriksonian approach to psychosocial development. Their rating categories (Appendix 1) should prove useful for future studies. Ames (1966) is a companion study which diverges from Pitcher and Prelinger in identifying clear-cut age trends in the stories told. Ames considers her data not in terms of fantasy but as "examples of the kinds of stories a child is able to tell at succeeding ages in the pre-school years." Ames's other findings are also suggestive.

More recently, Sutton-Smith (1974a, in press) has analyzed children's spontaneous original stories. Using E. and P. Maranda (1971), Sutton-Smith finds that between the ages of five and ten years, children go through the following stages:

1. tales in which one power overwhelms another and there is no attempt at response;
2. tales in which the minor power attempts a response but fails;
3. tales in which the minor power nullifies the original threat;
4. tales in which not only is the threat nullified but the original circumstances are substantially transformed.

Whereas the Marandas had used Bartlett's technique of presenting tales to subjects and examining how they transformed them on-retelling, Sutton-Smith analyzed spontaneous stories created by the children themselves. He finds interesting differences, according to age and sex, as regards length and complexity of plot structure, and the ways conflicts are defined and resolved. See also Labov, 1972b.

In contrast with these primarily psychosocial and cognitive developmental approaches to the thematic and formal features of children's stories is the sociolinguistic approach. K. Watson (1972, 1973), Watson and Boggs (1974), and Levitt (1974) emphasize the necessity for recording stories in natural contexts. Watson and Boggs analyze how stories are generated from various types of conversational routines and how children organize their interaction, evolve a norm of taking turns, and anticipate and collaborate in the narration. See also Sacks (1972) and Speier (1970). Levitt, Watson, and Boggs are also concerned with generic distinctions in the narrative productions of children. Working with "made up" and "true" stories, Levitt further investigates how children use narrative to "mediate the disjunctions of experience."

Narrative studies and materials may be found in many volumes cited in the bibliography of this volume in connection with other subjects: Abrahams (1970b, 1970c), Ashton (1968), Ben-Amos (1974b), Blümml and Polsterer (1908), Bombaugh (1961), Dorson (1972a), Dundes (1964a, 1965, 1973), Edmonson (1971), Freud (1963), Gossen (1970, 1974), Greenway (1964), F. Hoffman (1973), Hymes (1964b), Jacobs (1959, 1960, 1964), Jolles (1956), Jones and Hawes (1972), M. Leach (1949–1950), Legman (1964, 1968), E. and P. Maranda (1971), Oinas and Soudakoff (in press), Paredes and Bauman (1971), Rosenberg (1970), Rühmkorf (1972), Van Gennep (1937–1938).

(r) AUDIO-VISUAL RESOURCES

Of particular interest are two films which complement each other nicely: (1) *Pizza Pizza Daddy-O* which was made by B. L. Hawes in the late 1960s and is distributed by the University of California Extension Center. This film shows black girls playing singing-clapping games in a Los Angeles schoolyard. (2) *The Singing Street* (Norton Park Production, no. 2, 1951) shows children in Edinburgh playing singing games on the street.

A selective list of records follows:

Courlander, H. (Collector), 1953. *Ring Games: Line Games and Play Party Songs of Alabama.* Folkways #FP704.
    Contains record notes which provide song texts and game gestures.
MacColl, E. and Behan, D. 1958. *The Singing Streets: Childhood Memories of Ireland and Scotland.* Folkways #FW8501.

Kaplan, I. 1961. *When I Was a Boy in Brooklyn: An Autobiography.* Folkways #FG3501.
Includes games, sayings, name-calling, riddles, rhymes, sayings, limericks, and other lore, performed in the course of an autobiographical narrative.

Lomax, A. 1945–1946. *Afro-American Blues and Game Songs.* Library of Congress, AAFS L4.

———. 1947. *Bahamian Songs, French Ballads and Dance Tunes, Spanish Religious Songs and Game Songs.* Library of Congress, AAFS L5.
Contains Mexican children's games.

Schwartz, T. (Collector and Editor), 1953. *1, 2, 3, and a Zing Zing Zing: Street Games and Songs of the Children of New York City.* Folkways #FP703. In English and Spanish.

———. 1954. *New York 19.* Folkways #FP58.
Street calls, children's lore.

———. 1955. *Nueva York: A Tape Documentary of Puerto Rican New Yorkers.* Folkways #FP58/2.
Children's street games and songs; adult discourse on the streets.

Seeger, P. 1955. *Skip Rope Games Recorded in Edgewood, Illinois.* Folkways #FP729.
Contains texts and jumprope patterns.

Sorenson, E. R. 1959. *Street and Gangland Rhythms: Beats and Improvisations by Six Boys in Trouble.* Folkways #FD5589.

# Bibliography

PART V

# Bibliography

Aarne, A. and Thompson, S. 1961. *The Types of the Folktale.* (Folklore Fellows Communications, no. 184.) Helsinki: Suomalainen Tiedeakatemia.

Abou-Allam, A. M. 1963. "A Study of the Difficulty of Different Forms of Verbal Analogies." Ed.D. dissertation, Teachers College, Columbia University.

Abrahams, R. D. 1961. "Ghastly Commands: The Cruel Joke Revisited." *Midwest Folklore* 11: 235–246.

———. 1962. "Playing the Dozens." *Journal of American Folklore* 75: 209–220. (Reprinted in Dundes 1973: 295–309.)

———. 1966. "There's a Black Girl in the Ring." In Goldstein and Byington, 1966: 121–35.

———. 1968. "Introductory Remarks to a Rhetorical Theory of Folklore." *Journal of American Folklore* 81: 143–158.

———. 1969a. "The Complex Relations of Simple Forms." *Genre* 2: 104–128.

———, ed. 1969b. *Jump-rope Rhymes: A Dictionary.* (American Folklore Society Bibliographical and Special Series, vol. 20.) Austin: University of Texas Press.

———. 1970a. "Creativity, Individuality, and the Traditional Singer." *Studies in the Southern Literary Imagination* 3: 5–36.

———. 1970b. *Deep Down in the Jungle: Negro Narrative Folklore from the Streets of Philadelphia,* revised edition. Chicago: Aldine.

———. 1970c. "A Performance-centered Approach to Gossip." *Man* 5: 290–301.

———. 1970d. "Patterns of Performance in the British West Indies." In Whitten and Szwed, 1970: 163–179.

———. 1970e. *Positively Black.* Englewood Cliffs: Prentice Hall.

———. 1972a. "The Literary Study of the Riddle." *Texas Studies in Literature and Language* 14: 177–197.

————. 1972b. "Proverbs and Proverbial Expressions." In Dorson, 1972b: 117–127.

Abrahams, R. D. and Dundes, A. 1972. "Riddles." In Dorson, 1972b: 129–143.

Abrahams, R. D. and Rankin, L. In press. *Counting-out Rhymes: A Dictionary.* Austin: University of Texas Press for the American Folklore Society.

Aceves, P. and Einarsson-Mularký, M. 1968. *Folklore Archives of the World: A Preliminary Guide.* (Folklore Forum Bibliographic and Special Series, no. 1.) Bloomington, Indiana.

Adams, C. C. 1971. *Boontling: An American Lingo.* Austin: University of Texas Press.

Adams, E. H. 1947. *Jump-rope Rhymes.* Seattle: Silver Quoin.

Adams, G. B. 1965. "Counting-rhymes and Systems of Numerations." *Ulster Folklife* 11: 85–97.

Ainsworth, C. H. 1961. "Jump rope Verses around the United States." *Western Folklore* 20: 179–199.

Alexis, G. 1970. "Le parler Bolite." *Lecture en anthropologie haitienne,* pp. 203–207. Port-au-Prince: Presses Nationales d'Haiti.

Algeo, J. 1973. *On Defining the Proper Name.* Gainesville: University of Florida Press.

Alleau, R. and Matignon, R. 1964. *Dictionnaire des jeux.* Paris: Tchou.

Alleman, C. 1951. *Über das Spiel.* Zürich: Juris.

Alvey, G. 1974. "The Historical Development of Organized Storytelling in the United States." Ph.D. dissertation, folklore, University of Pennsylvania.

Ames, L. B. 1966. "Children's Stories." *Genetic Psychological Monographs* 73: 337–396.

Anderson, E. N., Jr., and M. L. 1970. "The Social Context of a Local 'Lingo.'" *Western Folklore* 35: 153–165.

Anderson, W. W. 1973. "Children's Play and Games in Rural Thailand: A Study in Enculturation and Socialization." Ph.D. dissertation, folklore, University of Pennsylvania.

Andrée, J. L. 1882–1883. "Puns and Rebuses in History and Archaeology." *Reliquary, Archaeological Journal and Review* 23: 169–173.

Antoun, R. T. 1968. "On the Significance of Names in an Arab Village." *Ethnology* 7: 158–170.

Appleton, L. E. 1910. *A Comparative Study of the Play Activities of Adult Savages and Civilized Children: An Investigation of the Scientific Basis of Education.* Chicago: University of Chicago Press.

Arewa, E. O. and Dundes, A. 1964. "Proverbs and the Ethnography of Speaking Folklore." In Gumperz and Hymes, 1964a: 70–85.

Arguedas, J. M., ed. 1960. *Bibliografía del folklore Peruano.* Lima and Mexico City: Instituto Panamericano de Geografía e Historia.

Ariès, P. 1962. *Centuries of Childhood: A Social History of Family Life,* trans. R. Baldrich. New York: Vintage.

————. 1972. "At the Point of Origin." In Brooks, 1972: 15–23.

Arnaud, L. E. 1942. *French Nonsense Literature in the Middle Ages.* New York: New York University Press.

Arnott, D. W. 1957. "Proverbial Lore and Word-play of the Fulani." *Africa* 27: 379–396.

Arsenio, M. E. 1965. *Philippine Folklore Bibliography: A Preliminary Survey.* Quezon City: Philippine Folklore Society.

Ashton, J. 1968. *Humor, Wit and Satire of the Seventeenth Century.* New York: Dover.

Atkinson, F. 1963. " 'Knur and Spell' and Allied Games." *Folk Life* 1:43–65.

Atkinson, R. M. 1967. "Songs Little Girls Sing: An Orderly Invitation to Violence." *Northwest Folklore* 2: 2–8.

Aufenanger, H. 1958. Children's Games and Entertainments among the Kumongo Tribe in Central New Guinea." *Anthropos* 53: 575–584.

Austin, M. H. 1930. *The American Rhythm: Studies in Re-expression of Amerindian Songs.* Boston: Houghton Mifflin.

Avedon, E. M. and Sutton-Smith, B., eds. 1971. *The Study of Games.* New York: Wiley.

Ayoub, R. and Barnett, S. A. 1965. "Ritualized Verbal Insult in White High School Culture." *Journal of American Folklore* 78: 337–344.

Azadowski, M. 1974. *A Siberian Tale Teller,* trans. J. R. Dow. (Center for Intercultural Studies in Folklore and Ethnomusicology, Monograph Series, no. 2.) Austin: University of Texas. (First published in German in 1926.)

Babcock, W. H. 1886a. "Song Games and Myth Dramas in Washington." *Lippincott's Magazine* 37: 239–257.

———. 1886b. "Carols and Child-lore at the Capitol." *Lippincott's Magazine* 38: 320–342.

———. 1888. "Games of Washington Children." *American Anthropologist* 1 (3): 243–284.

Babcock-Abrahams, B., ed. In press. *The Reversible World: Essays on Symbolic Inversion.* Ithaca, New York: Cornell University Press.

Bach, A. 1960. *Deutsche Volkskunde,* 3d edition. Heidelberg: Quelle and Meyer.

Bach, E. and Harms, R. T., eds. 1968. *Universals in Linguistic Theory.* New York: Holt, Rinehart and Winston.

Bächtold, H. 1914. "Geheimsprachen." *Schweizer Volkskunde* 4: 9–11, 22, 38.

[Baghban, H.] 1972. *Bibliography of Middle Eastern Folklore.* (Folklore Forum Bibliographic and Special Series, no. 9.) Bloomington, Indiana.

Bakhtin, M. 1968. *Rabelais and His World,* trans. H. Iswolsky. Cambridge, Mass.: M.I.T. (First published in Russian in 1965.)

Baldwin, C. S. 1959. *Medieval Rhetoric and Poetic (to 1400) Interpreted from Representative Works.* Gloucester, Mass.: Peter Smith. (First published 1928.)

Baldwin, G. C. 1969. *Games of the American Indian.* New York: Norton.

Ball, W. W. R. 1939. *Mathematical Recreations and Essays,* 11th edition. London: Macmillan.

Ballard, H. H. 1895. *Open Sesame.* Boston: Colonial.

Balzer, R. 1972. *Street Time.* New York: Grossman.

Bar-Adon, A. and Leopold, W. F., eds. 1971. *Child Language: A Book of Readings.* Englewood Cliffs: Prentice-Hall.

Barchilon, J. and Pettie, H. 1960. *The Authentic Mother Goose Fairy Tales and Nursery Rhymes.* Denver: Alan Swallow.

Bardis, P. D. 1972. "Social Aspects of Personal Onomastics among the Ancient Hebrews." *Social Science* 47: 100–109.

Baring-Gould, S. 1895. *The Book of Nursery Songs and Rhymes.* London: Methuen and Company (Reprinted, Detroit: Singing Tree, 1969.)

Baring-Gould, W. S. 1972. *The Lure of the Limerick.* London: Panther.

Baring-Gould, W. S. and C. 1962. *The Annotated Mother Goose.* New York: Clarkson N. Potter.

Barker, R. G. and Wright, H. F. 1955. *Midwest and Its Children: The Psychological Ecology of an American Town.* New York: Harper and Row.

Barley, N. 1972. "A Structural Approach to the Proverb and Maxim." *Proverbium* 20: 737–750.

———. 1974a. "The Proverb and Related Problems of Genre Definition." *Proverbium* 23: 880–884.

———. 1974b. "Structural Aspects of the Anglo-Saxon Riddle." *Semiotica* 10: 143–175.

Barrick, M. E. 1964. "The Shaggy Elephant Riddle." *Southern Folklore Quarterly* 28: 266–290.

———. 1970. "The Complete and Official Index of the First Fifteen Volumes." *Keystone Folklore Quarterly* 15, supplement.

———. 1974. "The Newspaper Riddle Joke." *Journal of American Folklore* 87: 253–257.

Barthes, R. 1953. *Le degré zéro de l'écriture.* Paris: Le Seuil.

Bartlett, F. C. 1972. *Remembering: A Study in Experimental Psychology.* Cambridge, England: Cambridge University Press. (First published 1932.)

Barton, F. R. 1908. "Children's Games in British New Guinea." *Journal of the Royal Anthropological Institute* 38: 259–279.

Bascom, W. R. 1949. "Literary Style in Yoruba Riddles." *Journal of American Folklore* 62: 1–16.

Basgöz, M. I. 1965. "Functions of Turkish Riddles." *Journal of the Folklore Institute* 2: 132–147.

———. 1972. "Riddle-Proverbs and the Related Forms in Turkish Folklore." *Proverbium* 18: 655–668.

Bass, B. M. 1957. "Validity of a Proverb Personality Test." *Journal of Applied Psychology* 41: 158–160.

———. 1958. "Famous Sayings Test: General Manual." *Psychological Reports* vol. 4, no. 3, Monograph Supplement 6: 479–497. Missoula, Montana: Montana State University.

Basso, K. 1972. "Ice and Travel among the Fort Norman Slave: Folk Taxonomies and Cultural Roles." *Language in Society* 1: 31–49.

Bastomski, Sh. 1920. *Baym kval: yidishe shprikhverter, vertlekh, glaykh-*

*vertlekh, rednsartn, farglaykhenishn, brokhes, vintshenishn, kloles, kharomes, simonim, sgules, zabobones.* Vilna: Naye yidishe folks-shul.

Bateson, G. 1953. "The Position of Humor in Human Communication." *Cybernetics: Circular Causal and Feedback Mechanisms in Biological and Social Sciences; Transactions of the Ninth Conference* (March 20–21, 1952), ed. H. von Foerster, pp. 1–47. New York: Josiah Macy, Jr., Foundation. (Reprinted in abridged form in Levine, 1969: 159–166.)

———. 1955. "A Theory of Play and Fantasy." *Psychiatric Research Reports* 2: 39–50. (Reprinted in Bateson, 1972: 177–193.)

———. 1972. *Steps to an Ecology of Mind.* New York: Ballantine.

Baucomont, J., Guibat, F., Lucile, T., Pinon, R., Soupault, P. 1961. *Les comptines de langue française.* Paris: Editions Seghers.

Bauman, R. 1971. "Differential Identity and the Social Base of Folklore." *Journal of American Folklore* 84: 31–41.

———. 1975. "Verbal Art as Performance." *American Anthropologist* 77: 290–312.

Bauman, R. and McCabe, N. 1970. "Proverbs in an LSD-cult." *Journal of American Folklore* 83: 318–324.

Bauman, R. and Sherzer, J., eds. 1974. *Explorations in the Ethnography of Speaking.* New York: Cambridge University Press.

Béart, C. 1955. *Jeux et jouets de l' Ouest Africain,* 2 vols. (Mémoires de l'Institut Français d' Afrique Noire, no. 42.) Dakar: IFAN.

Beckett, S. 1955. *Three Novels.* New York: Grove.

———. 1965. *Proust and Three Dialogues.* London: John Calder. (*Three Dialogues* [with Georges Duthuit] reprinted from *Transition '49,* no. 5, 1949.)

Beckett, S., et al. 1929. *Our Examination Round His Factification for Incamination of Work in Progress* [sic]. London: Faber and Faber.

Beckwith, M. W. 1922. *Folk-games of Jamaica.* (Publications of the Folk-Lore Foundation, no. 1.) Poughkeepsie: Vassar College.

Beechick, R. A. 1974. "Children's Understanding of Parables: A Developmental Study." Ed.D. dissertation, education, psychology, Arizona State University.

Behaghel, O. 1923. "Humor und Spieltrieb in der deutschen Sprache." *Neophilologus* 8: 180–193.

Beilin, H. 1972. "Colloquium Presentation." New York: Teachers College, Columbia University.

Beitl, R. 1955. *Wörterbuch der deutschen Volkskunde,* 2d edition. Leipzig: Kroner. (First published 1936.)

Bellamy, W. 1894. *Century of Charades.* Cambridge, Mass.: Houghton, Mifflin.

Ben-Amos, D. 1974a. "Catégories analytiques et genres populaires." *Poétique: Revue de Théorie et d'Analyse Littéraires* 19: 265–293.

———. 1974b. "African Folklore: Reading List." Philadelphia: University of Pennsylvania. Mimeo.

—————. 1974c. "Solutions to Riddles." Paper presented to the American Folklore Society, Portland, Oregon.

—————. 1975a. "Structural Analysis in Folklore: Preliminary Selected Bibliography." Philadelphia: University of Pennsylvania. Mimeo.

—————. ed. 1975b. *Folklore Genres.* Austin, Texas: University of Texas Press.

Benayoun, R. 1957. *Anthologie du nonsense.* Paris: J. J. Pauvert.

Bender, L. and Schilder, P. 1936. "Form as a Principle in the Play of Children." *Journal of Genetic Psychology* 49: 254–261.

Bénichou, P. 1967. "L'Intention des maximes." In *L'écrivain et ses travaux.* Paris: J. Corti.

Bergler, E. 1936. "Obscene Words." *Psychoanalytic Quarterly* 5: 226–248.

Bergson, H. 1911. *Laughter: An Essay on the Meaning of the Comic,* trans. C. Brereton and F. Rothwell. New York: Macmillan. (First published in French, 1900.)

Berkovits, R. 1970. "Secret Languages of School Children." *New York Folklore Quarterly* 26: 127–152.

Berlyne, D. E. 1969. "Laughter, Humor, and Play." In *Handbook of Social Psychology,* vol. 3, 2d ed., eds. G. Lindzey and E. Aronson, pp. 795–852. Reading, Mass.: Addison-Wesley.

Bernard, H. R. 1968–1969. "Paratsoukli: Institutionalized Nicknaming in Rural Greece." *Ethnologia Europaea* 2: 65–74.

Bernstein, B. 1960. "Review of *The Lore and Language of School Children* by I. and P. Opie." *British Journal of Sociology* 11: 178–181.

Bertholet, A. 1940. "Wortanklang und Volksetymologie in ihrer Wirkung auf religiösen Glauben und Brauch." *Preussiche Akademie der Wissenschaft.* Abhandlung Philosophisch- historische Klasse Nr. 6: 3 ff.

Best, E. 1925. *Games and Pastimes of the Maori.* (Dominion Museum Bulletin, no. 8.) Wellington, N.Z.: Whitcombe and Tombs.

Bestermann, T. 1965–1966. *A World Bibliography of Bibliographies and of Bibliographical Catalogues, Abstracts, Digests, Indexes and the Like,* 5 vols. Lausanne: Societas Bibliographica.

Bethke, R. D. 1970. "A Compilation by Department of University of Pennsylvania Theses and Dissertations of Relevance for Interdisciplinary Research in Folklore and Folklife," *Folklore Forum* 3: 59–64.

Bett, H. 1924. *Nursery Rhymes and Tales, Their Origin and History.* London: Methuen.

—————. 1929. *The Games of Children, Their Origin and History.* London: Methuen. (Reprinted, Detroit: Singing Tree, 1968.)

Beuchat, P. D. 1957. "Riddles in Bantu." *African Studies* 16: 133–149. (Reprinted in Dundes, 1965: 182–205.)

Bhagwat, D. 1965. *The Riddle in Indian Life, Lore and Literature.* Bombay: Popular Prakashan.

Bianco, C. 1970. *Italian and Italian-American Folklore: A Working Bibliography.* (Folklore Forum Bibliographic and Special Series, no. 5.) Bloomington, Indiana.

Bierce, A. 1925. *The Devil's Dictionary.* New York: A. and C. Boni.

Bierwisch, M. 1965–1967. "Poetik und Linguistik." In *Mathematik und Dichtung,* ed. H. Kreuzer and R. Gunzenhäuser, pp. 49–65. München: Nymphenburger Verlagshandlung. (English translation in Freeman, 1970: 96–115.)

Bischoff, E. 1915. *Wörterbuch der wichtigsten Geheimund Berufssprachen: Jüdisch-Deutsch, Rotwelsch, Kundensprache; Soldaten-, Seemans-, Weidmanns-, Bergmanns- und Komodiantensprache.* Leipzig: T. Grieben.

Black, G. F. [1914.] *A Gypsy Bibliography.* (Gypsy Lore Society, Monograph no. 1.) London: Bernard Quaritch for the Gypsy Lore Society.

Blacking, J. 1961. "The Social Value of Venda Riddles." *African Studies* 20: 1–32.

———. 1967. *Venda Children's Songs.* Johannesburg: Witwatersrand University Press.

———. 1974. *How Musical Is Man?* Seattle: University of Washington Press.

Blackowski, S. 1937. "The Magical Behavior of Children in Relation to School." *American Journal of Psychology* 50: 347–361.

Blair, W. 1960. *Native American Humor.* San Francisco: Chandler. (First published 1937.)

Bloch, B. 1953. "Linguistic Structure and Linguistic Analysis." *Report of the Fourth Annual Round Table Meeting on Linguistics and Language Teaching,* ed. A. A. Hill, pp. 40–44. (Georgetown University Monograph Series on Languages and Linguistics 4.) Georgetown, Maryland: Institute of Languages and Linguistics, Georgetown University.

Bloom, L. 1970. *Language Development: Form and Function in Emerging Grammars.* Cambridge, Mass.: M.I.T.

———. 1973. *One Word at a Time: The Use of Single Word Utterances before Syntax.* Hague: Mouton.

Blount, B. G. 1975. "Review Article: Studies in Child Language, An Anthropological View." *American Anthropologist* 77: 580–600.

Blümml, E. K. and Polsterer, J., eds. 1908. *Futilitates: Beiträge zur volkskundlichen Erotik,* 4 vols. Vienna: Dr. R. Ludwig Verlag.

Boadi, L. A. 1972. "The Language of the Proverb in Akan." In Dorson, 1972a: 183–191.

Boas, A. 1966. *The Cult of Childhood.* London: Warburg Institute, University of London.

Bødker, L. 1965. *Folk-literature (Germanic).* (International Dictionary of Regional European Ethnology and Folklore, vol. 2.) Copenhagen: Rosenkilde and Bagger.

Bødker, L., et al. 1964. *The Nordic Riddle: Terminology and Bibliography.* Copenhagen: Rosenkilde and Bagger.

Bodmer, E. 1923. *Empros oder Anzählreime der französischen Schweiz.* Halle (Saale): Karras, Kröber and Nietschmann.

Böhme, F. M. 1897. *Deutsches Kinderlied und Kinderspiel. Volksuber-*

*lieferungen aus allen Landen deutscher Zunge.* Leipzig: Breitkopf und Hartel. (Reprinted, Nendeln, Leicht.: Kraus Reprint, 1967.)

Boggs, R. S. 1939. *Bibliografía del folklore Mexicano.* (Separata del Boletín Bibliográfico de Antropología Americana, vol. 3, no. 3.) Mexico: Instituto Panamericano de Geografía e Historia.

———. 1940. *Bibliography of Latin American Folklore.* New York: Wilson.

Bolinger, D. 1950. "Ríme, Assonance and Morpheme Analysis." *Word* 6: 117–136.

Bolton, H. C. 1888. *The Counting-out Rhymes of Children, Their Antiquity, Origin, and Wide Distribution.* London: Elliot Stock. (Reprinted, Detroit: Singing Tree, 1969.)

———. 1897. "More Counting-out Rhymes." *Journal of American Folklore* 10: 313–321.

Bombaugh, C. C. 1905. *Facts and Fancies for the Curious from the Harvest-fields of Literature: A Melange of Excerpta.* Philadelphia: Lippincott. (Reprinted by Gale Research Co.: Detroit, 1968).

———. 1961. *Oddities and Curiosities of Words and Literature,* ed. M. Gardner. New York: Dover. (Reprinted from the third edition of *Gleanings for the Curious from the Harvest-fields of Literature: A Melange of Excerpta.* Philadelphia: Lippincott, 1890.)

Bonser, W. 1961. *A Bibliography of Folklore as Contained in the First Eighty Years of the Publications of the Folklore Society.* (Publications of the Folklore Society, no. 121.) London: W. Glaisher for the Folklore Society.

———. 1969. *A Bibliography of Folklore for 1958–1967. Being a Subject Index, Vols. 69–78 of the Journal,* Folklore. (Publications of the Folklore Society, no. 130.) London: Folklore Society.

Bonser, W. and Stephens, T. A. 1930. *Proverb Literature: A Bibliography of Works Relating to Proverbs.* London: W. Glaisher.

Bonte, E. P. and Musgrove, M. 1943. "Influences of War as Evidenced in Children's Play. *Child Development* 14: 179–200.

Borgmann, D. A. 1965. *Language on Vacation.* New York: Scribners.

———. 1967. *Beyond Language.* New York: Scribners.

Borie, B. In progress. "Bibliography of Folklore Bibliographies." Philadelphia: University of Pennsylvania.

Borneman, E. 1974. *Unsere Kinder im Spiegel ihrer Lieder, Reime, Verse und Rätsel: Studien zur Befreiung des Kindes,* Band 1. Olten, Freiburg i. Breisgau: Walter-Verlag.

Botkin, B. A. 1937. *The American Play Party Song, with a Collection of Oklahoma Texts and Tunes.* (University Studies of the University of Nebraska, vol. 38, nos. 1–4.) Lincoln: University of Nebraska. (Reprinted, New York: Ungar, 1963.)

———. 1944. "Play Rhymes and Catches." *A Treasury of American Folklore,* pp. 768–803. New York: Crown.

Bowman, H. A. 1939. "The Humor of Primitive People." In *Studies in the Science of Society,* ed. G. P. Murdock, pp. 67–84. New Haven: Yale University Press.

Boyce, E. R. and Bartlett, K. 1940. *Number Rhymes and Finger Plays*. London: Pitman.

Bradney, P. 1957. "The Joking Relationship in Industry." *Human Relations* 10: 179–187.

Brady, M. K. 1974. " 'Gonna shimmy shimmy 'til the sun goes down': Aspects of Verbal and Nonverbal Socialization in the Play of Black Girls." *Folklore Annual of the University Association*, no. 6: 1–16. Austin: University of Texas.

———. 1975. "This little lady's gonna Boogaloo": Elements of the Socialization in the Play of Black Girls. In Early Elementary Program 1975: 1–36.

Brailoiu, C. 1956. Le rythme enfantin: notions liminaires. *Les Colloques de Wéqimont*, vol. 1. Bruxelles: Elsevier.

Brandes, S. H. 1975. "The Structural and Demographic Implications of Nicknames in Navanogal, Spain." *American Ethnologist* 2 (1): 139–147.

Bratcher, J. T. 1973. *Analytical Index to Publications of the Texas Folklore Society, vols. 1–36*. Dallas: Southern Methodist University Press.

Brathwaite, E. 1971. *The Development of Creole Society in Jamaica*. London: Oxford University Press.

Brayshaw, T. 1849. *Metrical Mnemonics Applied to Geography, Astronomy and Chronology in which the Most Important Facts in Geography and Astronomy and Dates in Ancient and Modern Chronology are Expressed by Consonants Used for Numerals and Formed by the Aid of Vowels into Significant Words*. London: Simpkin, Marshall.

Bremond, C. 1966. "La logique des possibles narratifs." *Communications* 8: 60–76.

———. 1973. *Logique du recit*. Paris: Le Seuil.

Brendor, M. 1963. "Some Hypotheses about the Psychodynamic Significance of Infant Name Selection." *Names* 11: 1–9.

Brenman, M. 1952. "On Teasing and Being Teased: The Problem of Moral Masochism." *Psychoanalytic Study of the Child* 7: 264–285.

Brenni, V. J. 1964. *American English: A Bibliography*. Philadelphia: University of Pennsylvania Press.

Brewer, P. 1973. "Age, Language, Culture, Previous Knowledge and Proverb as Social Metaphor: A Study in Relationships." Ph.D. dissertation, folklore, University of Pennsylvania.

Brewster, P. G. 1939a. "Game-songs from Southern Indiana." *Journal of American Folklore* 49: 243–262.

———. 1939b. "Rope-skipping, Counting-out and Other Rhymes of Children." *Southern Folklore Quarterly* 3: 173–185.

———. 1944. " 'Spelling Riddles' from the Ozarks." *Southern Folklore Quarterly* 8: 301–303.

———. 1952. "Children's Games and Rhymes." *The Frank C. Brown Collection of North Carolina Folklore*, vol. 1, pp. 29–219. Durham, North Carolina: Duke University Press.

———. 1971. "Games and Sports in Shakespeare." In Avedon and Sutton-Smith, 1971: 27–47.

Bricker, V. R. 1968. "The Meaning of Laughter in Zinacantan: An Analysis of the Humor of a Highland Maya Community." Ph.D. dissertation, anthropology, Harvard University.

――――. 1973a. *Ritual Humor in Highland Chiapas.* Austin: University of Texas Press.

――――. 1973b. "Three Genres of Tzotzil Insult." In Edmonson, 1972: 183–203.

Britt, S. H. and Balcom, M. M. 1941. "Jumping-rope Rhymes and the Social Psychology of Play." *Journal of Genetic Psychology* 58, part 2: 289–306.

Britt, S. H. and Janus, S. Q. 1941. "Toward a Social Psychology of Human Play." *Journal of Social Psychology* 13, part 2: 351–384.

Brooks, M. Z. 1975. "Slavic Folklore: Part 1, Polish Folklore; Part 2, Russian Folklore." Philadelphia: University of Pennsylvania. Mimeo.

Brooks, P., ed. 1972. *The Child's Part.* Boston: Beacon Press. (First published as *Yale French Studies* no. 73, 1969.)

Brose, P. B. D. 1973. "An Analysis of the Functioning of Gothic Themes in the Folklore and Writing of Children in the Second and Fifth Grades." Ph.D. dissertation. Education, University of Nebraska.

Brown, R. W. 1973. *A First Language: The Early Stages.* Cambridge, Mass.: Harvard University Press.

Brown, R. W. and Berko, J. 1960. "Word Association and the Acquisition of Grammar." *Child Development* 31: 1–14.

Brown, R. W. and Fraser, C. 1964. "The Acquisition of Language." In *Report of the Fourth Conference, Committee on Intellective Processes Research of the Social Science Research Council,* eds. U. Bellugi and R. W. Brown, pp. 43–78. (Monographs of the Society for Research in Child Development, serial no. 92, vol. 29, no. 1.) Lafayette, Indiana: Purdue University.

Brown, R. W. and Gilman, A. 1960. "The Pronouns of Power and Solidarity." In Sebeok, 1960: 253–276.

Brown, W. K. 1974. "Cultural Learning Through Game Structure: A Study of Pennsylvania German Children's Games." *Pennsylvania Folklife* 22: 2–11.

Browne, R. B. 1955. "Southern California Jump-rope Rhymes: A Study in Variants." *Western Folklore* 14: 3–22.

Brukman, J. C. 1972. "Strategies of Ritual Interaction among the Koya of South India." Ph.D. dissertation, University of California, Berkeley.

――――. 1973. "Language and Socialization: Child Culture and Ethnographer's Task." In *Learning and Culture,* ed. S. T. Kimball and J. H. Burnett, 43–58. (Proceedings of the 1972 Annual Spring Meeting, American Ethnological Society.) Seattle: University of Washington Press.

Bruner, J. S. 1972. "Nature and Uses of Immaturity." *American Psychologist* 27: 687–708.

Bruner, J. S. and Olver, R. R. 1963. "Development of Equivalence Transformation in Children." *Basic Cognitive Processes in Children,* eds. J. Wright and J. Kagan, pp. 125–141. (Monographs of the Society for Research in Child Development 28.) Lafayette, Indiana: Purdue University.

Brunvand, J. H. 1968. *The Study of American Folklore: An Introduction.* New York: Norton.

────. 1976. *Folklore: A Handbook for Study and Research.* New York: St. Martin's Press.

Bryant, D. C. 1958. *The Rhetorical Idiom.* Ithaca: Cornell University Press.

Buckley, B. R. 1966. "Jump-rope Rhymes: Suggestions for Classification and Study." *Keystone Folklore Quarterly* 11: 99–111.

Bühler, C. and Bilz, J. 1961. *Das Märchen und die Phantasie des Kindes,* 2d edition. Munich: J. A. M. Barth.

Burgess, A. 1973. *Joysprick.* London: Andre Deutsch.

Burke, K. 1931. *Counterstatement.* New York: Harcourt Brace.

────. 1957. *The Philosophy of Literary Form,* revised edition. New York: Vintage.

────. 1958. "The Poetic Motive." *Hudson Review* 11: 54–63.

────. 1966. "Poetics in Particular, Language in General," *and* "Rhetoric and Poetics." In *Language as Symbolic Action,* pp. 25–43, 295–307. Berkeley: University of California Press.

Burke, W. J. 1939. *The Literature of Slang.* New York: The New York Public Library.

Burling, R. 1966. "The Metrics of Children's Verse: A Cross-Linguistic Study." *American Anthropologist* 68: 1419–1441.

────. 1970. *Man's Many Voices.* New York: Holt, Rinehart, and Winston.

Burns, T. A. 1968. "A Bibliographic Inventory of the Folklore of the State of Missouri." Bloomington: Indiana University Folklore Archive. Unpublished manuscript.

────. 1975. *Doing the Wash: An Expressive Culture and Personality Study of a Joke and Its Tellers.* Norwood, Pennsylvania: Norwood Editions.

────. 1976. "Riddling: Occasion to Act." *Journal of American Folklore* (forthcoming).

Butler, F. 1973. "The Poetry of Rope-skipping." *The New York Times Magazine,* December 16: 90, 92–95.

Caillois, R. 1955. "The Structure and Classification of Games." *Diogenes* 12: 62–75.

────. 1957. "Unity of Play: Diversity of Games." *Diogenes* 19: 92–121.

────. 1959. *Man and the Sacred,* trans. M. Barash. Glencoe, Illinois: Free Press.

────. 1961. *Man, Play and Games,* trans. M. Barash. New York: Free Press.

────. 1967. *Jeux et sports.* (Encyclopédie de la Pléiade, vol. 23.) Paris: Gallimard.

────. 1968. "Riddles and Images." In Ehrmann, 1971: 148–158.

Callaway, H. 1866–1868. *Nursery Tales, Traditions and Histories of the Zulus.* London: Trübner. (Reprinted, Hatboro, Pennsylvania: Legacy, 1970.)

Câmara Cascudo, L. da. 1954. *Dicionário do folclore brasileiro*. Rio de Janeiro: Instituto Nacional do Livro.

Cammaerts, E. 1926. *The Poetry of Nonsense*. New York: Dutton.

Canel, A. 1867. *Recherches sur les jeux d'esprit, les singularités et les bizarreries littéraires principalement en France*. Evereux: A. Herissey.

Cansler, L. D. 1968. "Midwestern and British Children's Lore Compared." *Western Folklore* 27: 1–18.

Cardona, M. 1956. *Algunos juegos de los niños de Venezuela*. Caracas: Ediciónes del Ministerio de Educación.

Carvalho-Neto, P. de. 1968a. "Bibliografía del folklore Paraguayo." *Estudios de folklore*, vol. 1: Brasil, Paraguay, pp. 237–376. Quito, Ecuador: Editorial Universitaria.

———. 1968b. "Bibliografía del folklore Paraguayo." *Estudios de folklore*, vol. 2: Argentina, Uruguay, Chile, pp. 159–193. Quito, Ecuador: Editorial Universitaria.

Cass-Beggs, B. and M. 1969. *Folk Lullabies: 77 Traditional Folk Lullabies from Every Corner of the World*. New York: Oak.

Cassidy, F. G. 1958. "Report of a Recent Project of Collecting." *Publication of the American Dialect Society* 29: 3–18.

Castro, R. S., n.d. "Notas Bibliográficas para el estudio de la 'poesia vulgar' de Chile." *Archvos del Folklore Chileno*, fascículo no. 2.

Cazden, N. 1961. *A Book of Nonsense Songs*. New York: Crown.

Chamberlain, A. F. C. 1896. *The Child and Childhood in Folk-thought*. New York: Macmillan.

———. 1910. "Nith-songs." In *Handbook of American Indians North of Mexico* (BAE—B 30), part 2, ed. F. W. Hodge, p. 77. Washington, D.C.: Smithsonian Institution.

———. 1911. *The Child: A Study in the Evolution of Men*, 2d ed. London: W. Scott.

Chamberlain, J. S. 1961. "The Development of Research into Children's Folklore in England." Master's thesis, folklife, University of Leeds.

Chambers, R. 1841. *Popular Rhymes of Scotland*, 3d edition. Edinburgh: W. and R. Chambers.

Chapman, A. and Foot, H., eds. 1975. *Research in Laughter and Humor*. New York: Wiley.

Chase, R. 1949. *Hullabaloo and Other Singing Games*. Boston: Houghton Mifflin.

Chateau, J. 1950. *L'enfant et le jeu*. Paris: Éditions du Scarabée.

———. 1955a. *Le réel et l'imaginaire dans le jeu de l'enfant*. Paris: Vrin.

———. 1955b. *Le jeu et l'enfant*. Paris: Vrin.

Chertudi, S. 1963. *El cuento folklórico y literario regional. (Bibliografía Argentina de artes y letras.)* Buenos Aires: Fondo Nacional de las Artes.

Chomsky, C. 1969. *The Acquisition of Syntax in Children from 5 to 10*. Cambridge, Mass.: M.I.T. Press.

Chomsky, N. 1957. *Syntactic Structures (Janua Linguarum*, series minor, 4.) Hague: Mouton.

——. 1964. "Current Issues in Linguistic Theory." In *The Structure of Language: Readings in the Philosophy of Language*, eds. J. A. Fodor and J. J. Katz, pp. 50–118. Englewood Cliffs: Prentice-Hall.

——. 1965. *Aspects of the Theory of Syntax*. Cambridge, Mass.: M.I.T.

——. 1972. *Language and Mind*. New York: Harcourt, Brace, Jovanovich.

Christensen, J. B. 1963. "Utani: Joking, Sexual License and Social Obligations among the Luguru." *American Anthropologist* 65: 1314–1327.

Chukovsky, K. 1971. *From Two to Five*, trans. and ed. M. Morton. Berkeley: University of California Press. (First published in Russian in 1925).

Cirese, A. M. 1968–69. *Prime annotazioni per una analisi strutturale dei proverbi*. Università di Cagliari.

——. 1969. "Wellérismes et micro—récits." *Proverbium* 14: 384–390.

Claparède, E. 1934. "Sur la nature et la fonction du jeu." *Archives de Psychologie* 24: 350–369.

Clark, M. 1970. "Humor and Incongruity." *Philosophy: Journal of the Royal Institute of Philosophy* 45: 20–32.

Cock, A. de and Teirlinck, I. 1902–08. *Kinderspel en Kinderlust in Zuid-Nederland*, 8 vols. (Koninklijke vlaamsche academie voor taal- en letterkunde. Uitagaven. 6 reeks. Bekroonde werken 29.) Gent: A. Siffer.

Coffin, T. P. 1958. *An Analytical Index to the Journal of American Folklore, vols. 1–70*. (American Folklore Society Bibliographical Series, vol. 7.) Philadelphia: American Folklore Society.

——. 1963. *The British Traditional Ballad in North America*, revised edition. (American Folklore Society Bibliographical Series, vol. 2.) Philadelphia: American Folklore Society. (First published 1950.)

Cohen, E. N. 1973. "A Community of Nicknames." Paper presented to the American Anthropological Association, New Orleans.

Cohen, M. 1966. *101 plus 5 Folk Songs for Camp: Sea Shanties, Story Ballads, Work Songs, Animal Songs, Spirituals, Songs for Fun and Nonsense*. New York: Oak.

Colby, B. N. 1975. "Culture Grammars." *Science* 14: 913–919.

Colby, B. N., Cooper, Carol G., and Rice, G. E. 1974. "A Study of Narrative Comprehension." Paper presented to the American Folklore Society, Portland, Oregon.

Colby, B. N. and Peacock, J. L. 1973. "Narrative." In *Handbook of Cultural and Social Anthropology*, ed. J. J. Honigman, pp. 613–635. Chicago: Rand McNally.

Collier, G. A. and Bricker, V. R. 1970. "Nicknames and Social Structure in Zinacantan." *American Anthropologist* 72: 289–302.

Collier, J. F. n.d. "Zinacanteco Kin Terms." Unpublished manuscript.

Commins, D. B. 1967. *Lullabies of the World*. New York: Random House.

Cong-Huyen-Ton-Nu, N.-T. 1971. "Poetics in Vietnamese Riddles." *Southern Folklore Quarterly* 35: 141–156.

Conklin, H. C. 1956. "Tagalog Speech Disguise." *Language* 32: 136–139.

——. 1959. "Linguistic Play in Its Cultural Context." *Language* 35: 631–636. (Reprinted in Hymes, 1964b: 295–300.)

Conn, J. H. 1951. "Children's Awareness of Sex Differences: Play Attitudes and Game Preferences." *Journal of Child Psychiatry* 2: 82–99.

Connolly, K. and Bruner, J. S., eds. 1974. *The Early Growth of Competence.* London: Academic Press.

Cook, E. 1971. *The Ordinary and the Fabulous: An Introduction to Myths, Legends, and Fairy Tales for Teachers and Storytellers.* Cambridge, England: Cambridge University Press.

Cooperative Research Project. 1968. *Rope Skipping Games: Language, Beliefs and Customs.* Tri-University Project in Elementary Education, University of Nebraska and U.S. Office of Education.

Cortazar, A. R. 1942. *Guía bibliográfica del folklore Argentino.* Buenos Aires: Instituto de literatura Argentina, Universidad de Buenos Aires.

Cottle, T. J. 1973. "Memories of Half a Life Ago." *Journal of Youth and Adolescence* 2: 201–211.

Cox, J. 1942. "Singing Games." *Southern Folklore Quarterly* 6: 183–261.

Cramer, M. W. 1950. "Leisure Activities of Privileged Children." *Sociology and Social Research* 34: 440–450.

Cray, E. 1964. "Wellerisms in Riddle Form." *Western Folklore* 23: 114–116.

———, ed. 1972. *The Erotic Muse.* New York: Pyramid Special Books.

Crossan, J. D. 1974. "A Basic Bibliography for Parable Research." *Semeia* 1: 236–274.

Crowley, D. J. 1966. *I Could Talk Old Story Good: Creativity in Bahamian Folklore.* (California Folklore Studies, no. 17.) Berkeley: University of California Press.

Csikszentmihalyi, M. 1969. "The Rigors of Play." *The Nation.* February 17: 210–213.

———. 1970. "Art and Life: An Existential Approach to the Psychology of Artistic Creation." Unpublished manuscript. Chicago: University of Chicago.

———. 1974. "Flow: Studies of Enjoyment." *P.N.S. Report.* Chicago: University of Chicago.

Csikszentmihalyi, M. and Bennett, S. 1971. "An Exploratory Model of Play." *American Anthropologist* 73: 45–58.

Culin, S. 1891. "Street Games of Boys in Brooklyn, N.Y." *Journal of American Folklore* 4: 221–237.

———. 1895. *Korean Games with Notes on the Corresponding Games of China and Japan.* Philadelphia: University of Pennsylvania Press. (Reprinted as *Games of the Orient: Korea, China, Japan.* Rutland, Vermont: Tuttle, 1958.)

———. 1907. *Games of North American Indians.* (Smithsonian Institution, Bureau of American Ethnology, Annual Report—1902–1903, vol. 24.) Washington, D.C.: United States Government Printing Office.

Curti, M. W. 1930. *Child Psychology.* New York: Longmans, Green.

Curtius, E. R. 1963. *European Literature and the Latin Middle Ages,* trans.

W. R. Trask. New York: Harper and Row. (First published in German 1948.)

Daiken, L. 1959. *The Lullaby Book*. London: Edmund Ward.

———. 1963. *Out Goes She*. Dublin: Dolman.

Dale, P. S. 1972. *Language Development: Structure and Function*. Hinsdale, Illinois: Dryden Press.

Dannemann Rothstein, M. 1970. *Bibliografía del folklore Chileno 1952–1965*. (Latin American Folklore Series, no. 2.) Austin, Texas: Center for Intercultural Studies in Folklore and Oral History, University of Texas.

Dean-Smith, M. 1954. *A Guide to English Folk Song Collections 1822–1952*. Liverpool: University Press.

de Caro, F. A. and McNeil, W. K. 1970. *American Proverb Literature: A Bibliography*. (Folklore Forum Bibliographic and Special Series, no. 6.) Bloomington, Indiana.

Dégh, L. 1969. *Folktales and Society: Storytelling in a Hungarian Peasant Community*, trans. E. Schossberger. Bloomington, Indiana: Indiana University Press.

Delafosse, M. 1922. "Langage secret et langage conventionnel dans l'Afrique noir." *L'Anthropologie* 32: 83–92.

Delancey, V. and M. 1972. *A Bibliography of Cameroun Folklore*. (An Occasional Publication of the Literature Committee of the African Studies Association.) Waltham, Mass.: African Studies Association.

Deleuze, G. 1969. *Logique du sens*. Paris: Éditions de Minuit.

deMause, L., ed. 1974. *The History of Childhood*. New York: The Psychohistory Press.

Denis, L. 1949. *Folklore enfantin: chants et jeux des enfants haitiens*. Haiti: Port-au-Prince.

Devereux, G. 1950. "Heterosexual Behavior of the Mohave Indians." *Psychoanalysis and the Social Sciences* 2: 85–128.

———. 1951. "Mohave Indian Verbal and Motor Profanity." In *Psychoanalysis and the Social Sciences*, vol. 3, ed. G. Roheim, pp. 99–127. New York: International Universities Press.

Diehl, K. S. 1962. *Religions, Mythologies, Folklores: An Annotated Bibliography*, 2d ed. New York: Scarecrow Press. (First published 1956.)

Disraeli, I. 1791. *Curiosities of Literature*. London: J. Murray.

Dobson, W. T. 1880. *Literary Frivolities, Fancies, Follies and Frolics*. London: Chatto and Windus.

———. ed. 1882. *Poetical Ingenuities and Eccentricities*. London: Chatto and Windus.

Dollard, J. 1939. "The Dozens: The Dialect of Insult." *American Imago* 1: 3–24. (Reprinted in Dundes, 1973: 277–294.)

Dondore, D. 1930. "Big Talk! The Flyting, the Gabe, and the Frontier Boast." *American Speech* 6: 45–55.

Donicie, A. and Voorhoeve, J. 1963. *De Saramakaanse woordenschat*. Amsterdam: Bureau voor Taalonderzoek in Suriname van de Universiteit van Amsterdam.

Dorian, N. C. 1970. "A Substitute Name System in the Scottish Highlands." *American Anthropologist* 72: 303–319.

Dornseiff, F. 1925. *Das Alphabet in Mystik und Magie,* 2d ed. Leipzig, Berlin: B. G. Teubner.

Dorson, R. M. 1948. "Dialect Stories of the Upper Peninsula: A New Form of American Folklore." *Journal of American Folklore* 61: 113–150.

———. 1952. *Bloodstoppers and Bearwalkers: Folk Tales of Canadians, Lumberjacks and Indians.* Cambridge, Mass.: Harvard University Press.

———. 1959. *American Folklore.* Chicago: University of Chicago Press.

———, ed. 1961. "Folklore Research around the World: A North American Point of View." *Journal of American Folklore* 74: 287–468. (Also issued as Indiana University Folklore Series no. 16. Bloomington.)

———, ed. "Symposium on Obscenity in Folklore." *Journal of American Folklore* 75: 189–265.

———, ed. 1972a. *African Folklore.* Garden City: Doubleday.

———. 1972b. *Folklore and Folklife: An Introduction.* Chicago: University of Chicago Press.

Douglas, M. 1966. *Purity and Danger.* New York: Praeger.

———. 1968. The Social Control of Cognition: Some Factors in Joke Perception. *Man* (n.s.) 3: 361–375.

Douglas, N. 1931. *London Street Games,* 2d ed. London: Chatto and Windus. (First published 1916. Reprinted, Detroit: Singing Tree Press 1968.)

Driver, G. R. 1967. "Playing on Words." *Fourth World Congress of Jewish Studies* 1: 121–129.

Dubois, J., Edelin, F., Klinkenberg, J. M., Minguet, P., Pire, F. and Trinon, H. 1970. *Rhétorique générale.* Paris: Larousse.

Dudycha, G. J. and M. M. 1941. "Childhood Memories: A Review of the Literature." *Psychological Bulletin* 38: 668–682.

Dundes, A. 1961. "Mnemonic Devices." *Midwest Folklore* 11: 139–147.

———. 1962. "Trends in Content Analysis: A Review Article." *Midwest Folklore* 12: 31–38.

———. 1964a. *The Morphology of North American Indian Tales.* (Folklore Fellows Communications 195.) Helsinki: Suomalainen Tiedeakatemia.

———. 1964b. "On Game Morphology." *New York Folklore Quarterly* 20: 276–288.

———, ed. 1965. *The Study of Folklore.* Englewood Cliffs: Prentice-Hall.

———. 1966. "Here I Sit: A Study of American Latrinalia." *Kroeber Anthropological Society Papers* 34: 91–105.

———. 1967. "North American Indian Folklore Studies." *Journal de la Société des Américanistes* 56: 53–79.

———. 1968. *Every Man His Way: Readings in Cultural Anthropology.* Englewood Cliffs: Prentice-Hall.

———, ed. 1973. *Mother Wit from the Laughing Barrel: Readings in the Interpretation of Afro-American Folklore.* Englewood Cliffs: Prentice-Hall.

———. 1975. "On the Structure of the Proverb." *Proverbium* 25: 961–973.

———. In press. *Folklore Theses in the United States*. Austin, Texas: University of Texas Press for the American Folklore Society.

Dundes, A. and Georges, R. 1962. "Some Minor Genres of Obscene Folklore." *Journal of American Folklore* 75: 221–226.

Dundes, A., Leach, J. W., and Özkök, B. 1970. "The Strategy of Turkish Boys' Verbal Dueling Rhymes." *Journal of American Folklore* 83: 325–349. (Reprinted in Gumperz and Hymes, 1972: 130–160.)

Early Elementary Program. 1973. *Children's Folklore Master Plan*. Austin, Texas: Southwest Educational Development Laboratory.

———. 1974. *Experiment in Children's Folklore*. Austin, Texas: Southwest Educational Development Laboratory.

———. 1975. *Black Girls at Play: Folkloric Perspectives on Child Development*. Austin, Texas: Southwest Educational Development Laboratory.

Eastman, M. 1937. *Enjoyment of Laughter*. London: Hamish Hamilton.

Easton, R. 1970. "Humor of the American Indian." *Mankind: The Magazine of Popular History* 2: 37–41, 72–73.

Eberhard, W. 1967. "Some Notes on the Use of Proverbs in Chinese Novels." *Proverbium* 9: 201–208.

Eckenstein, L. 1906. *Comparative Studies in Nursery Rhymes*. London: Duckworth and Co. (Reprinted, Detroit: Singing Tree Press, 1968.)

Eckhardt, E. 1909. "Über Wortspiele." *Germanisch-Romanische Monatsschrift* 1: 674–690.

Eckhardt, R. 1975. "From Handclap to Line Play." In Early Elementary Program, 1975: 57–101.

Edmonson, M. S. 1971. *Lore: An Introduction to the Science of Folklore and Literature*. New York: Holt, Rinehart and Winston.

———. 1973. *Meaning in Mayan Languages*. Hague: Mouton.

Ehrmann, J., ed. 1971. *Games, Play, Literature*. Boston: Beacon. (First published as *Yale French Studies*, no. 41, 1968.)

Eifermann, R. 1971. "Social Play in Childhood." In Herron and Sutton-Smith, 1971: 270–297.

Elder, J. D. 1965. *Song Games from Trinidad and Tobago*. (Bibliographical and Special Series, vol. 16.) Philadelphia: American Folklore Society.

Elliott, R. C. 1960. *The Power of Satire*. Princeton, New Jersey: Princeton University Press.

Ellis, M. J. 1974. *Why People Play*. New York: Prentice Hall.

Elmore, C. M. and Gorham, D. R. 1957. "Measuring the Impairment of the Abstracting Function with the Proverb Test." *Journal of Clinical Psychology* 13: 263–266.

Emeneau, M. B. 1948. "Homonyms and Puns in Annamese." *Language* 23: 239–44.

———. 1966. "Style and Meaning in an Oral Literature." *Language* 42: 323–345.

Emerson, J. P. 1963. "Social Functions of Humor in a Hospital Setting." Ph.D. dissertation. University of California at Berkeley.

Emrich, D. 1955. "The Ancient Game of Tongue-twisters." *American Heritage* 6: 119–120.

——. 1970. *The Nonsense Book of Riddles, Rhymes, Tongue Twisters, Puzzles and Jokes from American Folklore.* New York: Four Winds Press.

——. 1974. *American Folk Poetry: An Anthology.* Boston-Toronto: Little, Brown and Co.

Emrich, M. V. and Korson, G. 1947. *The Child's Book of Folklore.* New York: Dial Press.

Enäjärvi-Haavio, E. 1932. *The Game of Rich and Poor: A Comparative Study in Traditional Singing Games.* (Folklore Fellows Communications, no. 100.) Helsinki: Suomalainen Tiedakatemia.

Ervin-Tripp, S. 1967. "Sociolinguistics." *Working Paper,* no. 3. Berkeley: Language Behavior Research Laboratory, University of California.

——. 1973. *Language Acquisition and Communicative Choice.* Stanford, California: Stanford University.

Esar, E. 1952. *The Humor of Humor: The Art and Techniques of Popular Comedy Illustrated by Comic Sayings, Funny Stories, and Jocular Traditions Through the Centuries.* New York: Horizon Press.

Espy, W. R. 1972. *The Game of Words.* New York: Grosset and Dunlop.

——. 1975a. *An Almanac of Words at Play.* New York: Clarkson N. Potter.

——. 1975b. *Omak Me Yours Tonight or Ilwaco Million Miles For One of Your Smiles.* Seattle: Seattle Books.

Estrich, R. M. and Sperber, H. 1952. *Three Keys to Language.* New York: Rinehart.

Euling, K. 1905. *Das Priamel bis Hans Rosenplüt.* Breslau: M. & H. Marcus.

Evans, B. 1949. *The Natural History of Nonsense.* 4th edition. London: Michael Joseph.

Evans, D. 1975. "Riddling and the Structure of Context." Fullerton, California: California State University. Unpublished manuscript.

Evans, P. 1966. *Rimbles: A Book of Children's Classic Games, Rhymes, Songs, and Sayings.* Garden City, New York: Doubleday.

Evans-Pritchard, E. E. 1929. "Some Collective Expressions of Obscenity in Africa." *Journal of the Royal Anthropological Institute of Great Britain and Ireland* 59: 311–332.

——. 1948. "Nuer Modes of Address." *The Uganda Journal* 12: 166–171. (Reprinted in Hymes, 1964b: 221–227.)

——. 1949. "Nuer Curses and Ghostly Vengeance." *Sociologus* 4: 23–41.

——. 1956. "*Sangi,* Characteristic Feature of Zande Language and Thought." *Bulletin of the School of Oriental (and African) Studies* 18: 161–180.

Farb, P. 1968. *Man's Rise to Civilization as Shown by the Indians of North America from Primeval Times to the Coming of the Industrial State.* New York: Dutton.

————. 1974. *Word Play, What Happens When People Talk*. New York: Alfred A. Knopf.

Farmer, J. S. 1896. *Vocabula Amatoria*. London: Privately printed.

Feifel, H. and Lorge, I. 1950. "Qualitative Differences in the Vocabulary Responses of Children." *The Journal of Educational Psychology* 41: 1–18.

Ferdière, G. 1947a. "Intérêt psychologique et psychopathologique des comptines et formulettes de l'enfance." *L'Evolution Psychiatrique,* fasicule 3: 45–63.

————. 1947b. "Les comptines et formulettes étudiées par un psychologue du jeu de l'enfant, Jean Chateau." *L'Evolution Psychiatrique,* fasicule 4: 101–107.

Ferenczi, S. 1916. "Obscene Words." *Sex in Psychoanalysis*, trans. E. Jones. Boston: Gorham Press.

Ferguson, C. A. 1956. "Arabic Baby Talk." In *For Roman Jakobson*, eds. M. Halle, et al., pp. 121–128. Hague: Mouton.

————. 1964. "Baby Talk in Six Languages." In Gumperz and Hymes, 1964a: 103–114.

Ferguson, C. A. and Echols, J. M. 1952. "Critical Bibliography of Spoken Arabic Proverb Literature." *Journal of American Folklore* 65: 67–84.

Ferguson, C. A. and Slobin, D. I., eds. 1973. *Studies of Child Language Development*. New York: Holt, Rinehart, and Winston.

Ferretti, F. 1973. *The Great American Marble Book*. New York: Workman Publishing Company.

Fink, E. 1960. *Das Spiel als Weltsymbol*. Stuttgart: W. Kohlhammer.

Finnegan, R. 1967. *Limba Stories and Storytelling*. Oxford: Clarendon Press.

Fischer, J. L. 1963. "The Sociopsychological Analysis of Folktales." *Current Anthropology* 4: 235–296.

Fish, S. E. 1973. "How Ordinary is Ordinary Language?" *New Literary History* 5: 40–54.

Fisher, J., ed. 1973. *The Magic of Lewis Carroll*. New York: Simon and Schuster.

Flavell, J. H. 1968. *The Development of Role-taking and Communication Skills in Children*. New York: Wiley.

Flescher, J. 1972. "The Language of Nonsense in Alice." In Brooks, 1972: 57–72.

Fleuret, M. 1963. "Poésie, musique et magie des comptines; suivi d'un commentaire pédagogique de Jacques Caramella." *Le Français dans le Monde,* no. 21: 35–38.

Flugel, J. C. 1954. "Humor and Laughter." In *Handbook of Social Psychology*, vol. 2, Special Fields and Applications, ed. G. Lindzey, pp. 709–721. Cambridge, Mass.: Addison-Wesley Publishing Co.

Fock, N. 1958. "Cultural Aspects and Social Functions of the "oho" Institution among the Waiwai." *Proceedings of the Thirty-Second International Congress of Americanists* (Copenhagen, 1956), pp. 136–140. Copenhagen: Munksgaard.

Foley, L. 1971. "Green Talk: A Sociological and Linguistic Analysis." In J. Sherzer et al., pp. 14–23.

Fonagy, I. 1965. "Form and Function of Poetic Language." *Diogenes* 51: 72–110.

Foster, G. M. 1964. "Speech Forms and the Perception of Social Distance in a Spanish-speaking Mexican Village." *Southwestern Journal of Anthropology* 20: 107–122.

Foucault, M. 1963. *Raymond Roussel.* Paris: Gallimard.

Fowke, E., ed. 1969. *Sally Go Round the Sun: 300 Songs, Rhymes and Games of Canadian Children.* Toronto: McLelland and Stewart.

Frake, C. O. 1964. "How to Ask for a Drink in Subanum." In Gumperz and Hymes, 1964a: 127–132.

François, D. 1966. "Le contrepet." *La Linguistique* 2: 31–52.

Franklin, K. 1967. "Names and Aliases in Kewa." *Journal of the Polynesian Society* 76: 76–81.

Frazer, J. G. *Taboo and the Perils of the Soul.* London: Macmillan.

Freeman, D. C., ed. 1970. *Linguistics and Literary Style.* New York: Holt, Rinehart and Winston.

Freeman, J. F. 1966. *A Guide to Manuscripts Relating to the American Indians in the Library of the American Philosophical Society.* (Memoirs of the American Philosophical Society, vol. 61.) Philadelphia: American Philosophical Society.

Freeman, S. T. 1970. *Neighbors: The Social Contract in a Castilian Hamlet.* Chicago and London: University of Chicago Press.

Freud, S. 1963. *Jokes and Their Relation to the Unconscious,* trans. J. Strachey. New York: Norton.

Froehlich, T. 1970. "Children's Teasing: An Analysis of Performance." Austin, Texas: University of Texas. Unpublished manuscript.

Fry, W. F., Jr. 1968. *Sweet Madness, a Study of Humor.* Palo Alto, California: Pacific Books.

Gaignebet, C. 1974. *Le Folklore Obscène des Enfants.* Paris: G.-P. Maisonneuve et Larose.

Ganim, M. 1970. "A Study of Children's Folklore." *New York Folklore Quarterly* 25: 50–63.

Gans, H. J. 1953. "The 'Yinglish' Music of Mickey Katz." *American Quarterly* 5: 213–218.

García Ruíz, R. 1938. *Los juegos infantiles en las escuelas rurales.* Mexico City: El Nacional.

Gardiner, A. 1954. *The Theory of Proper Names,* 2d edition. London: Oxford. (First published 1940.)

Gardner, H. 1972. "Style Sensitivity in Children." *Human Development* 15: 325–338.

———. 1973. "Children's Metaphoric Productions and Preferences." Cambridge, Mass.: Harvard University. Unpublished manuscript.

———. 1974. "Metaphors and Modalities: How Children Project Polar Adjectives onto Diverse Domains." *Child Development* 45: 84–91.

Gardner, M. 1963. *The Annotated Alice:* Alice's Adventures in Wonderland *and* Through the Looking Glass. Cleveland: World Publishers.

Gardner, R. 1971. *Therapeutic Communication with Children: The Mutual Storytelling Technique.* New York: Science House.

Garth, R. 1920. "The Psychology of Riddle Solution: An Experiment in Purposive Thinking." *Journal of Educational Psychology* 11: 16–33.

———. 1935. "Riddles as a Mental Test." *American Journal of Psychology* 47: 342–344.

Gaskell, A. 1963. *"Those Were the Days": The Games and Jingles Played and Sung by the Children of a Lancashire Village, Fifty and More Years Ago.* Manchester, England: Swinton and Pendlebury Libraries. Mimeo. (Reprinted, *Transactions of the Historic Society of Lancashire and Chesire* 166, 1964: 207–222.)

Gathorne-Hardy, J. 1973. *The Unnatural History of the Nanny.* New York: Dial Press.

Gauthier, M. 1915. "De quelques jeux d'esprit." *Revue Hispanique* 33: 385–445; 35: 1–76.

Geddes, W. R. 1957. *Nine Dyak Nights.* Oxford: Clarendon Press.

Geertz, C. 1968. "Linguistic Etiquette." *Readings in the Sociology of Language,* ed. J. A. Fishman, pp. 282–295. Hague: Mouton.

Georges, R. A. 1969. "The Relevance of Models for Analysis of Traditional Play Activities." *Southern Folklore Quarterly* 23: 1–23.

Georges, R. A. and Dundes, A. 1963. "Toward a Structural Definition of the Riddle." *Journal of American Folklore* 76: 111–118.

Geracimos, A. 1970. "The Games New York City Children Play." *New York,* August 11: 24–29.

Gerber, G. 1885. *Die Sprache als Kunst,* 2 Auflage. Berlin: R. Gaertners Verlagsbuchhandlung, H. Heyfelder. (First published 1871.)

Gershman, H. S. 1971. "Children's Rhymes and Modern Poetry." *The French Review* 44: 539–548.

Gibson, L. 1975. "Some Thoughts on Verbal Contests." Unpublished paper. Philadelphia: University of Pennsylvania.

Gilchrist, A. G. 1915. "Notes on Children's Game-songs." *Journal of the Folk Song Society,* no. 19: 221–239.

———. 1916. "Forfeit Songs; Cumulative Songs; Songs of Marvels and of Magical Animals." *Journal of the Folk Song Society,* no. 20: 277–296.

———. 1919. "Note on the 'Lady Drest in Green' and Other Fragments of Tragic Ballads and Folk-tales Preserved amongst Children." *Journal of the Folk Song Society,* no. 22: 80–90.

Gilmore, J. B. 1966. "Play: A Special Behavior." In *Current Research in Motivation,* ed. R. N. Haber, pp. 343–355. New York: Holt.

Gluski, J. 1971. *Proverbs: A Comparative Book of English, French, German, Italian, Spanish and Russian Proverbs, with a Latin Appendix.* Amsterdam: Elsevier.

Görög, V. 1968. "Bibliographie analytique sélective sur la littérature orale de l'Afrique noire." *Cahiers d'Études Africaines* 8: 453–501.

———. 1969. "Littérature orale africaine: Bibliographie analytique (Périodiques)." *Cahiers d'Études Africaines* 9: 641–666.

———. 1970. "Littérature orale africaine: Bibliographie analytique (Périodiques)." *Cahiers d'Études Africaines* 10: 583–631.

Götz, G. 1896. "Über Dunkel- und Geheimsprachen im späten und mittelalterlichen Latein." *Berichte über die Verhandlungen der Königlich Sachsischen Gesellschaft der Wissenschaften, Philologisch-Historische Classe* (Leipzig) 48: 62–92.

Goffman, E. 1974. *Frame Analysis: An Essay on the Organization of Experience.* New York: Harper and Row.

Goldstein, J. H. and McGhee, P. E. 1972a. "An Annotated Bibliography of Published Papers on Humor in the Research Literature and an Analysis of Trends: 1910–1971." In Goldstein and McGhee, 1972b: 263–283.

———, eds. 1972b. *The Psychology of Humor: Theoretical Perspectives and Empirical Issues.* New York: Academic Press.

Goldstein, K. S. 1963. "Riddling Traditions in Northeastern Scotland." *Journal of American Folklore* 76: 330–336.

———. 1971. "Strategy in Counting Out: An Ethnographic Folklore Field Study." In Avedon and Sutton-Smith, 1971: 167–178.

Goldstein, K. S. and Byington, R. H. 1966. *Two Penny Ballads and Four Dollar Whiskey: A Pennsylvania Folklore Miscellany.* Hatboro, Pennsylvania: Folklore Associates for the Pennsylvania Folklore Society.

Gomme, A. B. 1894–1898. *The Traditional Games of England, Scotland, and Ireland,* 2 vols. London: David Nutt. (Reprinted, New York: Dover, 1964. Introduction by D. Howard.)

Gomme, A. B. and Sharp, C. J., eds. 1909–1912. *Children's Singing Games,* 5 vols. London: Novello.

Goodchilds, J. D. 1972. "On Being Witty: Causes, Correlates, and Consequences." In Goldstein and McGhee, 1972b: 173–193.

Goodenough, W. H. 1965. "Personal Names and Modes of Address in Two Oceanic Societies." In *Context and Meaning in Cultural Anthropology,* ed. M. Spiro, pp. 265–276. New York: Free Press.

Goodman, M. E. 1970. *The Culture of Childhood: Child's-Eye Views of Society and Culture.* New York: Teachers College, Columbia University.

Goodwin, J., Long, L., and Welch, L. 1945. "Generalization in Memory." *Journal of Experimental Psychology* 35: 71–79.

Gordon, M. W. 1951. "The Folklore of Vieques, Yauco, and Loquillo, Puerto Rico." *Journal of American Folklore* 64: 55–82.

Gorham, D. R. 1956a. *Clinical Manual for the Proverbs Test.* Louisville: Psychological Test Specialists.

———. 1956b. *Proverbs Test, Clinical Forms I, II, III. Best Answer Form. Manual.* Missoula, Montana: Psychological Test Specialists.

———. 1956c. "A Proverbs Test for Clinical and Experimental Use." *Psychology Reports.* (Monograph Supplement No. 1.)

———. 1956d. "Use of the Proverbs Test for Differentiating Schizophrenics from Normals." *Journal of Consulting Psychology* 20: 435–44.

Gossen, G. H. 1970. "Time and Space in Chamula Oral Tradition." Ph.D. dissertation, anthropology, Harvard University.

――――. 1972a. "Chamula Genres of Verbal Behavior." In Paredes and Bauman, 1972: 145–167.

――――. 1972b. "Temporal and Spatial Equivalents in Chamula Ritual Symbolism." In Lessa and Vogt, 1972: 135–149.

――――. 1972c. "Chamula Proverbs: Neither Fish nor Fowl." In Edmonson, 1972: 205–234.

――――. 1974. *Chamulas in the World of the Sun: Time and Space in a Maya Oral Tradition*. Cambridge, Mass.: Harvard University Press.

Gould, R. 1972. *Child Studies through Fantasy: Cognitive Affective Patterns in Development*. New York: Quadrangle.

Gowlett, D. F. 1966. "Some Lozi Riddles and Tongue-twisters Annotated and Analyzed." *African Studies* 25: 139–158.

Graham, L. R. 1958. "The Maturational Factor in Humor." *Journal of Clinical Psychology* 14: 326–328.

Granet, M. 1930. *Chinese Civilization*. New York: Knopf.

Grathoff, R. H. 1970. *The Structure of Social Inconsistencies: A Contribution to a Unified Theory of Play, Game and Social Action*. Hague: Martinus Nijhoff.

Grayson, M. F. 1962. *Let's Do Fingerplays*. Washington, D.C.: Robert B. Luce.

Green, P. B. 1899. *A History of Nursery Rhymes*. London: Greening.

Greenwald, D. 1975. "Language Impositions on Linguistic Humor." Paper presented to the Association for the Anthropological Study of Play. Detroit, Michigan.

Greenway, J. 1964. *Literature among the Primitives*. Hatboro, Pennsylvania: Folklore Associates.

Gregor, W. 1891. *Counting-out Rhymes of Children*. London: David Nutt. (Reprinted, Norwood, Pennsylvania: Norwood, 1972.)

Greimas, A. J. 1960. "Idiotismes, proverbes, dictons." *Cahiers de Lexicologie* 2: 41–61.

Grimes, J. E., ed. 1972. *Languages of the Guianas*. (Summer Institute of Linguistics Publications in Linguistics and Related Fields, no. 35.) Norman, Oklahoma: Summer Institute of Linguistics.

Grimshaw, P. 1967. "Journal and Monographic Series in the Indiana University Library Covering Anthropology, Folklore, and Sociology." Bloomington, Indiana: Indiana University. Mimeo.

Groos, K. 1901. *The Play of Man*, trans. E. Baldwin. London: William Heinemann. (First published in German in 1898.)

Gueron, J. 1974. "The Meter of Nursery Rhymes: An Application of the Halle-Keyser Theory of Meter." *Poetics: International Review for the Theory of Literature* 12 (3–4): 73–111.

Gullen, F. D. 1950. *Traditional Number Rhymes and Games*. (Publications of the Scottish Council for Research in Education, no. 32.) London: University of London Press.

Gump, P. V. and Sutton-Smith, B. 1955. "The 'It' Role in Children's Games." *The Group* 17 (3): 3–8. (Reprinted in Dundes, 1965: 329–336.)

Gumpel, L. 1975. "The Structure of Idioms." *Semiotica* 12: 1–40.

Gumperz, J. J. and Hymes, D., eds. 1964. *The Ethnography of Communication.* Washington, D.C.: American Anthropological Association. (First issued as *American Anthropologist* 66 (6), part 2.)

———, eds. 1972. *Directions in Sociolinguistics: The Ethnography of Communication.* New York: Holt, Rinehart & Winston.

Haas, A. 1972. "Male and Female Language as Reflected in the Play of Children." New York: Teachers College, Columbia University. Unpublished manuscript.

Haas, M. R. 1951. "Interlingual Word Taboos." *American Anthropologist* 53: 338–344.

———. 1957. "Thai Word Games." *Journal of American Folklore* 70: 173–175. (Reprinted in Hymes, 1964b: 301–304.)

———. 1967. "A Taxonomy of Disguised Speech." Paper presented to the Linguistic Society of America.

———. 1969. "Burmese Disguised Speech." *Bulletin of the Institute of History and Philology (Academia Sinica* 39, part 2): 277–285.

Hacikyan, A. 1966. *A Linguistic and Literary Analysis of Old English Riddles.* Montreal: Casalini.

Hain, M. 1966. *Rätsel, Realienbücher für Germanisten.* Stuttgart: J. B. Metzler.

Hale, K. 1971. "A Note on a Walbiri Tradition of Antonymy." In *Semantics,* eds. D. D. Steinberg and L. A. Jakobovits, pp. 472–482. Cambridge: Cambridge University Press.

Hall, F. 1974. "Conversational Joking: A Look at Applied Humor." *Folklore Annual of the University Association,* no. 6: 26–45. Austin: University of Texas.

Hall, S. 1940–1941. "That Spring Perennial—Rope Jumping." *Recreation* 34: 713–716.

Halle, M. 1962. "Phonology in Generative Grammar." *Word* 18: 54–72.

Halliday, M. A. K. 1974. *Explorations in the Development of Language.* London: Edward Arnold.

Halliwell, J. O. 1842. *The Nursery Rhymes of England.* (Early English Poetry, Ballads, and Popular Literature of the Middle Ages, Percy Society Publications, vol. 4.) London: T. Richards. (Revised and enlarged 1843, 1844, 1846, 1853, and circa 1860. Reprinted, Detroit: Singing Tree Press, 1969, from the American edition of 1843.)

———. 1849. *Popular Rhymes and Nursery Tales.* London: John Russell Smith. (The circa 1860 edition includes the work above.)

Halpert, H. 1964. *A Selected Bibliography of the Folklore of the British Isles [and Ireland].* Philadelphia: University of Pennsylvania. Mimeo.

Hammond, P. B. 1964. "Mossi Joking." *Ethnology* 3: 259–267.

Hamnett, I. 1967. "Ambiguity, Classification and Change: The Function of Riddles." *Man,* n.s., 2: 379–392.

Hand, W. 1967. *Eyes on Texas: Fifty Years of Folklore in the Southwest.* Austin, Texas: Texas Folklore Society.

———. n.d. "Folklore Journals, Folklore Societies, Monographic Series in Folklore." Los Angeles: University of California. Mimeo.

Harms, E. 1943. "The Development of Humor." *Journal of Abnormal and Social Psychology* 38: 351–369.

Harms, V. 1969. *Der Terminus "Spiel" in der Ethnologie. Eine Begriffskritische Untersuchung, Dargestellt Anhand von Berichten über die Kultur der Samoaner.* Hamburg: K. Renner.

Harries, L. 1971. "The Riddle in Africa." *Journal of American Folklore* 84: 377–393.

Hart, D. V. 1964. *Riddles in Filipino Folklore: An Anthropological Analysis.* Syracuse, New York: Syracuse University Press.

Hasen-Rock, G. 1974. "Riddle and Proverb: The Relationship Exemplified by an Aramaic Proverb." *Proverbium* 24: 936–940.

Hassell, Jr., J. W. 1970. "Proverbs in Riddles." *Proverbium* 15: 467–469.

———. 1974. *Amorous Games: A Critical Edition of* Les adevineaux amoureux. (Publications of the American Folklore Society Bibliographical and Special Series, vol. 25.) Austin: University of Texas Press for the American Folklore Society.

Hautala, J. 1947. "The Folklore Collections of the Finnish Literature Society." *Studia Fennica* 5 (6): 197–202.

———. 1957. "The Folklore Archives of the Finnish Literature Society." *Studia Fennica* 7 (2): 3–36.

Hawes, B. L. 1969. "Pizza Pizza Daddy-O. Film Notes." Berkeley: University of California Extension Media Center.

———. 1974. "Folksongs and Function: Some Thoughts on the American Lullaby." *Journal of American Folklore* 87: 140–148.

Hawkins, E. M. 1969. "The Folklore and Traditions of Schoolchildren in Hull and Beverley between 1890 and 1910." M. Phil. Folklife, University of Leeds.

Hawthorne, R. 1966. "Classifying Jump-rope Games." *Keystone Folklore Quarterly* 11: 113–126.

Haywood, C. 1961. *A Bibliography of North American Folklore and Folksong,* 2 vols., 2d edition. New York: Dover.

Hazard, P. 1944. *Books, Children, and Men.* Boston: The Horn Book. (First published in French in 1932.)

Heath, S. 1972. *The Nouveau Roman.* Philadelphia: Temple University Press.

Heck, J. O. 1927. "Folk Poetry and Folk Criticism, as Illustrated by Cincinnati Children in Their Singing Games and Their Thoughts about These Games." *Journal of American Folklore* 40: 1–77.

Helmers, H. 1965. *Sprache und Humor des Kindes.* Stuttgart: E. Klett.

Hendriks, W. O. 1973. *Essays on Semiolinguistics and Verbal Art.* Hague: Mouton.

Henius, F. 1943. *Songs and Games of the Americas.* New York: Charles Scribner's Sons.

Henningsen, G. 1965. "The Art of Perpendicular Lying." *Journal of the Folklore Institute* 2: 180–219.

Henry, W. E. 1973. *The Analysis of Fantasy: The Thematic Apperception Technique in the Study of Personality.* Huntington, New York: Robert E. Krieger. (First published 1965.)

Heppenstall, R. 1967. *Raymond Roussel: A Critical Study.* Berkeley: University of California Press.

Herndon, M. and McLeod, N. 1972. *The Use of Nicknames as Evaluators of Personal Competence in Malta.* (Texas Working Papers in Sociolinguistics, no. 14.) Austin: University of Texas.

Herron, R. E. and Sutton-Smith, B., eds. 1971. *Child's Play.* New York: Wiley.

Herron, R. E. et al. 1971. *Children's Play: A Research Bibliography.* Illinois: Wiley.

Herskovits, M. J. 1958. *The Myth of the Negro Past.* Boston: Beacon Press.

Herzenstiel, W. R. 1973. *Erziehungserfahrung im deutschen Sprichwort.* Saarbrücken: Universitäts- und Schulbuchverlag.

Hetzer, H. 1959. *Spiel und Spielzeug für jedes Alter,* 6th edition. Lindau/Bodensee: Verlag Kleine Kinder.

Hetzer, H., Benner, L., and Pée, L. 1966. *Kinderspiel im Freien.* Munich and Basel: E. Reinhardt.

Hewson, R. H. 1963. "Armenian Names in America." *American Speech* 38: 214–219.

Hickerson, J. C. 1970. *A Selected List of Materials Relating to Games and Play.* Washington, D.C.: Archive of Folksong, Music Division, Library of Congress. Mimeo.

———. 1974. "A Bibliography of American Folksong in the English Language." In Emrich, 1974: 777–816.

Hilger, Sister M. I. 1958. "Naming a Chippewa Indian Child." *Wisconsin Archaeologist* 39: 120–126.

———. 1966. *Field Guide to the Ethnological Study of Child Life.* 2d revised edition. (Behavior Science Field Guides, vol. 1.) New Haven: Human Relations Area Files Press.

Hill, W. W. 1943. "Navaho Humor." *General Series in Anthropology* 9: 1–28.

Hirn, Y. 1926. *Les jeux d'enfants,* 4th edition. Paris: Stock.

Hirschberg, L. R. 1913. " 'Dog Latin' and Sparrow Languages Used by Baltimore Children." *Pedagogical Seminar* 20: 257–258.

Hoa, N. D. 1955. "Double Puns in Vietnamese, a Case of 'linguistic play.' " *Word* 11: 237–244.

Höfer, L. 1954. "Notizen zur wiener Kindersprache." *Osterreichischer Zeitschrift für Volkskunde* 8: 33–42.

Hoenigswald, H. 1959. "Some Uses of Nothing." *Language* 35: 409–421.

Hofer, M. R. 1901. "Singing Games and Their Sources." *Kindergarten Magazine* 12: 449–471.

Hoffman, D. G. 1948. "Half a Dozen Repeating Games." *New York Folklore Quarterly* 4: 207–212.

Hoffman, F. 1973. *Analytical Survey of Anglo-American Traditional Erotica.* Bowling Green, Ohio: Bowling Green University Popular Press.

Hollander, R. 1975. "Babytalk in Dante's *Commedia.*" *Mosaic: A Journal for the Comparative Study of Ideas* 8 (4): 73–84.

Holquist, M. 1972. "What Is a Boojum? Nonsense and Modernism." In Brooks, 1972: 145–164.

Honigman, J. J. 1944. "A Cultural Theory of Obscenity." *Journal of Criminal Psychopathology* 5: 715–733.

Hopkins, P. 1975. "Approaches to the Study of Musical Development." Philadelphia: University of Pennsylvania. Unpublished manuscript.

Horne, R. N. 1966. "A Study of the Use of Figurative Language by Sixth Grade Children." Ph.D. dissertation, University of Georgia.

Howard, D. M. 1938. "Folk Rhymes and Jingles of American Children." Ph.D. dissertation, New York university.

———. 1949. "The Rhythms of Ball-bouncing and Ball-bouncing Rhymes. *Journal of American Folklore* 62: 166–172.

———. 1959. "Ball Bouncing Customs and Rhymes in Australia." *Midwest Folklore* 9: 77–87.

———. 1965. "Folklore of Australian Children." *Keystone Folklore Quarterly* 10: 99–115.

Howes, R. F., ed. 1961. *Historical Studies of Rhetoric and Rhetoricians.* Ithaca: Cornell University Press.

Hrdličková, V. 1965. "The Professional Training of Chinese Storytellers and Storytelling Guild." *Archiv Orientalni* 33: 225–246.

———. 1968. "Zenza, the Storyteller's Apprentice." *Transactions of the International Conference of Orientalists in Japan* 13: 31–41.

Huizinga, J. 1955. *Homo Ludens: A Study of the Play-element in Culture.* Boston: Beacon Press. (First published in German in 1938.)

Hummel, S. and Brewster, P. G. 1963. *Games of the Tibetans.* (Folklore Fellows Communications, vol. 77 (2), no. 187.) Helsinki: Suomalainen Tiedeakatemia.

Hunter, I. M. L. 1964. *Memory,* revised edition. Harmondsworth: Penguin Books.

Hurault, J. 1961. *Les noirs réfugiés Boni de la Guyane française.* (Mémoires de l'Institut Français d'Afrique Noire, no. 63.) Dakar: IFAN.

———. 1970. *Africains de Guyane: la vie matérielle et l'art des noirs réfugiés de Guyane.* La Haye-Paris: Mouton.

Hurvitz, N. 1954. "Jews and Jewishness in the Street Rhymes of American Children." *Jewish Social Studies* 16: 135–150.

Huxley, R. and Ingram, E., eds. 1971. *Language Acquisition: Models and Methods.* New York: Academic Press.

Hymes, D. 1962. "The Ethnography of Speaking." In *Anthropology and human behavior,* eds. T. Gladwin and W. C. Sturtevant, pp. 13–53. Washington, D.C.: Anthropological Society of Washington.

———. 1964a. "Introduction: Toward Ethnographies of Communication." In Gumperz and Hymes, 1964: 1–34. (Reprinted in revised form in Hymes, 1974: 3–27.)

———., ed. 1964b. *Language in Culture and Society: A Reader in Linguistics and Anthropology.* New York: Harper and Row.

———. 1967. "Models of the Interaction of Language and Social Setting." *Journal of Social Issues* 23: 8–28. (Reprinted in Gumperz and Hymes, 1972: 35–71.)

———. 1968. "Review of *Language as Symbolic Action* by K. Burke." *Language* 44: 664–69. (Reprinted in Hymes, 1974: 135–141.)

———. 1970. "Linguistic Theory and the Functions of Speech." In *Proceedings of International Days of Sociolinguistics,* pp. 111–144. Rome: Instituto Luigi Sturzo.

———. 1971a. "The Contribution of Folklore to Sociolinguistic Research." *Journal of American Folklore* 84: 42–50. (Reprinted in Hymes, 1974a: 125–134.)

———. 1971b. "Sociolinguistics and the Ethnography of Speaking." In *Social Anthropology and Language,* ed. E. Ardener, pp. 47–93. (ASA Monographs 10.) London: Tavistock.

———. 1971c. "The 'Wife' who 'Goes Out' Like a Man: Reinterpretation of a Clackamas Chinook Myth." In *Structural Analysis of Oral Tradition,* eds. P. and E. K. Maranda, pp. 49–80. Philadelphia: University of Pennsylvania Press.

———. 1974a. *Foundations in Sociolinguistics: An Ethnographic Approach.* Philadelphia: University of Pennsylvania Press.

———. 1974b. "Ways of Speaking." In Bauman and Sherzer, 1974: 433–451.

———. 1975. "Folklore's Nature and the Sun's Myth." *Journal of American Folklore* 88: 345–369.

Irvine, J. T. 1974. "Strategies of Status Manipulation in the Wolof Greeting." In Bauman and Sherzer, 1974, pp. 167–191.

Jabbour, A. 1970. "An Inventory of the Bibliographies and Other Reference Aids Prepared by the Archive of Folksong, Library of Congress." *Folklore Forum* 3: 66–69.

Jablow, A. and Withers, C. 1965. "Social Sense and Verbal Nonsense in Urban Children's Folklore." *New York Folklore Quarterly* 21: 243–257.

Jackson, H., ed. 1951. *The Complete Nonsense of Edward Lear.* New York: Dover.

Jacobs, M. 1959. *The Content and Style of an Oral Literature.* Chicago: University of Chicago Press.

———. 1960. "Humor and Social Structure in an Oral Literature." In *Culture in History,* ed. S. A. Diamond, pp. 181–189. New York: Columbia University Press.

———. 1964. *Pattern in Cultural Anthropology*. Homewood, Illinois: Dorsey Press.

Jakobson, R. 1941. *Kindersprache, Aphasie und Allgemeine Lautgesetze. (Uppsala Universitets Arsskrift,* no. 9.) Uppsala, A.B.: Lundequistska Bokhandeln. (English translation: *Studies in Child Language and Aphasia,* trans. A. R. Keiler. Hague: Mouton, 1971.)

———. 1960. "Closing Statement: Linguistics and Poetics." In Sebeok, 1960: 350–377.

———. 1968. "Poetry of Grammar and Grammar of Poetry." *Lingua* 21: 597–609.

Jan, I. 1972. "Children's Literature and Bourgeois Society since 1860." In Brooks, 1972: 57–72.

———. 1974. *On Children's Literature.* New York: Schocken. (First published in French in 1969).

Janvier, L. 1969. "Au travail avec Beckett." *Quinzaine Litteraire,* February: 16–28.

Jauksch-Orlovski, C. 1974. "Analytical and Chronological Bibliography of Russian Folklore in Siberia." Laval, Quebec: Université Laval. Unpublished manuscript.

Johnson, N. 1971. "You Can Say S F D in Corsicana, Texas." In Sherzer, et al. 1971: 8–13.

Johnson, R. B. 1973. "Folklore and Women: A Social Interactional Analysis of the Folklore of a Texas Madam." *Journal of American Folklore* 86: 211–224.

Johnson, Sister C. 1971. "Doggie Language." In Sherzer, et al. 1971: 4–7.

Johnson, T. F. 1973. "Tsonga Children's Folksongs." *Journal of American Folklore* 86: 225–240.

Jolles, A. 1956. *Einfache Formen: Legende, Sage, Mythe, Rätsel, Spruch, Kasus, Memorabil, Märchen, Witz,* ed. A. Schossig. Halle (Saale): Max Niemeyer. (First published 1930. French translation, 1972. *Formes simples.* Paris: Seuil.)

Jones, B. and Hawes, B. L. 1972. *Step It Down: Games, Plays, Songs, and Stories from the Afro-American Heritage.* New York: Harper and Row.

Kallen, H. M. 1911. "The Aesthetic Principle in Comedy." *American Journal of Psychology* 22: 137–157.

Kaper, W. 1959. *Kindersprachforschung mit Hilfes des Kindes.* Groningen: J. B. Wolters.

Kaplan, A. 1955. "Obscenity as an Esthetic Category." *Law and Contemporary Problems* 20: 544–559.

Keenan, E. 1974. "Conversational Competence in Children." *Journal of Child Language* 1: 163–183.

Keenan, E. and Klein, E. 1974. "Coherency in Children's Discourse." Paper presented to the Linguistic Society of America (summer meetings). Amherst, Mass.

Ker, J. B. 1834. *An Essay on the Archaiology* [sic] *of Popular English Phrases and Nursery Rhymes.* London: Whittaker and Co. (Enlarged edition, 2 vols. London: Longman, Rees, Orme, Brown, Green, and Co., 1937.)

Kessel, F. S. 1970. *The Role of Syntax in Children's Comprehension from Ages Six to Twelve.* (Monographs of the Society for Research in Child Development, serial no. 139, vol. 25, no. 6.) Chicago: University of Chicago Press for the Society for Research in Child Development.

Kirk, D. F. 1962. *Charles Dodgson, Semeiotician.* University of Florida Humanities Monograph no. 11. Gainesville: University of Florida Press.

Kirkland, E. C. 1966. *A Bibliography of South Asian Folklore.* Hague: Mouton.

Kirshenblatt-Gimblett, B. 1971. "Multilingualism and Immigrant Narrative: Code-switching as a Communicative Strategy in Artistic Verbal Performance." Austin: University of Texas. Mimeo.

———. 1973a. "A Playful Note: 'The Good Old Game of Proverbs.' " *Proverbium* 22: 860–861.

———. 1973b. "Toward a Theory of Proverb Meaning." *Proverbium* 22: 821–827.

———. 1974a. "The Concept and Varieties of Narrative Performance in East European Jewish Culture." In *Explorations in the Ethnography of Speaking*, eds. R. Bauman and J. Sherzer, pp. 283–308. New York: Cambridge University Press.

———. 1974b. "A Parable in Context: A Social Interactional Analysis of Storytelling Performance." In *Folklore: Performance and Communication*, eds. D. Ben-Amos and K. S. Goldstein, pp. 105–130. Hague: Mouton.

———. In progress a. "Bibliography of Folklore Journals." Philadelphia: University of Pennsylvania.

———. In progress b. "Working Annotated Bibliography of Yiddish Folklore: Part I, Sources in English, French, and German." New York: Max Weinreich Center for Advanced Jewish Studies, YIVO.

Klinger, E. 1969. "Development of Imaginative Behavior: Implications of Play for a Theory of Fantasy." *Psychological Bulletin* 72: 277–298.

Klymasz, R. B. 1969. *A Bibliography of Ukrainian Folklore in Canada, 1902–64.* (Anthropology Papers: The National Museum of Canada, no. 21.) Ottawa, Ontario: The Queen's Printer.

Knapp, M. and H. 1973. "Tradition and Change in American Playground Language." *Journal of American Folklore* 86: 131–142.

Knight, H. R. 1914. *Play and Recreation in a Town of 6,000 (A Recreation Survey of Ipswich, Mass.)* New York: Department of Recreation, Russell Sage Foundation.

Knortz, K. 1896. *Folklore: amerikanische Kinderreime.* Dresden: Glöss.

Koch, K. and Students of P.S. 61, New York City. 1970. *Wishes, Lies, and Dreams: Teaching Children to Write Poetry.* New York: Vintage Books.

Koch, M. 1961. "Folk Verse." In *Kansas Folklore,* ed. S. J. Sackett and W. Kock, pp. 116–124. Lincoln, Nebraska: University of Nebraska Press.

Kochman, T., ed. 1972. *Rappin' and Stylin' out: Communication in Urban Black America.* Urbana, Illinois: University of Illinois Press.

Koestler, A. 1964. *The Act of Creation.* London: Hutchinson.

Kohlberg, L., Yaeger, J., and Hjentholm, E. 1968. "Private Speech: Four Studies and a Review of Theories." *Child Development* 37: 691–736.

Kornbleuth, I. and Aynor, S. 1973. "A Study of the Longevity of Hebrew Slang." In *Language-Behavior Papers,* no. 2, pp. 3–28. Jerusalem, Israel: Language-Behavior Section, The School of Education and the Ministry of Education and Culture.

Kraepelin, E. 1885. "Zur Psychologie des Komischen," parts 1 and 2. In *Philosophische Studien,* vol. 2, ed. W. Wundt, pp. 128–160, 327–361. Leipzig: Verlag von Wilhelm Englemann.

Krappe, A. H. 1964. *The Science of Folklore.* New York: Norton. (First published 1930.)

Krejci, F. 1889. "Das charakteristische Merkmal der Volkspoesie." *Zeitschrift für Volkerpsychologie und Sprachwissenschaft* 19: 115–141.

Kristeva, J. 1968. "Poésie et négativité." *L'Homme* 8: 36–63.

Kuhn, F. 1953. "Palindrom: Eine literarische Spielerei in alten China." *Weltwoche* 21, no. 1013 (10. 4. 1953): 5.

Kuiper, F. B. J. 1960. "The Ancient Aryan Verbal Contest." *Indo-Iranian Journal* 4: 217–281.

Kulah, A. 1973. "The Organization and Learning of Proverbs among the Kpelle of Liberia." Ph.D. dissertation, anthropology, University of California, Irvine.

Kuusi, M. I. 1969. "Southwest African Riddle-proverbs." *Proverbium* 12: 305–312.

———. 1972. *Towards an International Type-system of Proverbs.* (Folklore Fellows Communications, no. 211) Helsinki: Suomalainen Tiedeakatemia.

———. 1974. *Ovambo Riddles with Comments and Vocabularies.* (Folklore Fellows Communications, no. 215.) Helsinki: Suomalainen Tiedeakatemia.

La Barre, W. 1939. "The Psychopathology of Drinking Songs: A Study of the Content of the 'Normal' Unconscious." *Psychiatry: Journal of the Biology and the Pathology of Interpersonal Relations* 2: 203–212.

———. 1955. "Obscenity: An Anthropological Appraisal." *Law and Contemporary Problems* 20: 533–543.

Labov, W. 1972a. "Rules for Ritual Insults." In *Studies in Social Interaction,* ed. D. Sudnow, pp. 120–169. New York: Macmillan. (Reprinted in revised form in Labov, 1972: 297–353.)

———. 1972b. "The Transformation of Experience in Narrative Syntax." *Language in the Inner City,* pp. 354–396. Philadelphia: University of Pennsylvania Press.

———. 1974. "The Art of Sounding and Signifying." In *Language in Its Social Setting,* ed. W. W. Gage, pp. 84–116. Washington, D.C.: Anthropological Society of Washington.

Labov, W., Cohen, P., Robins, C., and Lewis, J. 1968. "Toasts." *A Study of the Non-standard English of Negro and Puerto-Rican Speakers in New York,* vol. 2, *The Use of Language in the Speech Community,* pp. 55–75.

(Cooperative Research Project No. 3288.) New York: Columbia University. Mimeo. (Reprinted in Dundes, 1973: 329–347.)

Labov, W. and Waletsky, J. 1967. "Narrative Analysis: Oral Versions of Personal Experience." In *Essays on the Verbal and Visual Arts*, ed. J. Helm, pp. 12–44. (Proceedings of 1966 Spring Meeting, American Ethnological Society.) Seattle: University of Washington Press.

Lacourcière, L. 1948. *Comptines canadiènnes*. Montreal: Fides.

la Fontaine, E. de. 1877. *Die luxemburger Kinderreime*. Luxemburg: Buck.

Lake, A. B. 1975. *A Pleasury of Witticisms and Word Play: A Collection of Immortal Wit, Whimsical Verse, and Other Literary Tours de Force*. New York: Hart.

Lalanne, L. 1845. *Curiosités littéraires*. Paris: Paulin.

Lambert, L. 1906. *Chants et chansons populaires du Languedoc*, 2 vols. Paris, Leipzig: Welter.

Landon, M. D. 1891. *Wit and Humor of the Age Comprising Wit, Humor, Pathos, Ridicule, Satires, Dialects, Puns, Conundrums, Riddles, Charades, Jokes and Magic by Mark Twain, Robert J. Burdette, Josh Billings, Alex Sweet, Eli Perkins, with the Philosophy of Wit and Humor by Melville D. Landon, A.M.* Chicago: Star Publishing Co. (First published 1883.)

Langstaff, J. and C. 1973. *Shimmy Shimmy Coke-ca-pop! A Collection of City Children's Street Games and Rhymes*. Garden City, New York: Doubleday.

Lanham, B. B. and Shimura, M. 1967. "Folktales Commonly Told Japanese and American Children." *Journal of American Folklore* 80: 34–48.

Lanson, G. 1968. *L'art de la prose*. Paris: A. G. Nizet. (First published 1905–1907.)

Lasch, R. 1907. Über Sondersprachen und ihre Entstehung." *Mitteilungen der anthropologischen Gesellschaft in Wien* 37: 89–101, 140–162.

LaSorsa, S. 1937. *Come giuacano i fanciulli d'Italia*. Napoli: Editrice Rispoli Anónima.

Lauder, A. (A. Morrison). 1965. *Let's Stalk Strine*. Sydney: Ure Smith.

———. 1968. *Fraffly Well Spoken*. Sydney: Ure Smith.

Laughlin, R. M. 1968. "The Tzotzil." In *Handbook of Middle American Indians: Ethnology*, vol. 7, eds. R. Wauchope and E. Z. Vogt, pp. 152–194. Austin: University of Texas Press.

Lauter, P. 1964. *Theories of Comedy*. New York: Doubleday.

Lauterbach, J. Z. 1932. "The Naming of Children in Jewish Folklore, Ritual and Practice." *Central Conference of American Rabbis* 42: 316–360.

Laycock, D. 1965. "Back and fill: A Cross-Linguistic Look at Ludlings." Paper delivered to the Australian and New Zealand Association for the Advancement of Science, Hobart.

———. 1972. "Towards a Typology of Ludlings, or Play-Languages." *Linguistic Communications, Working Papers of the Linguistic Society of Australia* 6: 61–113. Clayton, Victoria: Monash University.

Laycock, D., Lloyd, R. G., and Staalsen, P. 1969. "Sub-languages in Buin:

Play, Poetry, and Preservation." *Papers in New Guinea Linguistics* 10 (Series A—Occasional Papers 22): 1–23.

Lazarus, M. 1883. *Über die Reize des Spiels.* Berlin: F. Dümmler.

Leach, E. R. 1964. "Anthropological Aspect of Language: Animal Categories and Verbal Abuse." In *New Directions in the Study of Language*, ed. E. H. Lenneberg, pp. 23–63. Cambridge: M.I.T. (Reprinted in Lessa and Vogt, 1972: 206–220.)

Leach, M., ed. 1949–50. *Funk and Wagnalls Standard Dictionary of Folklore, Mythology, and Legend*, 2 vols. New York: Funk and Wagnalls.

——. 1961. *Noodles, Nitwits, and Numskulls.* Cleveland: World.

Leech, G. 1965. " 'This Bread I Break': Language and Interpretation." *Review of English Literature* 6: 66–75. (Reprinted in Freeman, 1970: 119–128.)

Legman, G. 1964. *The Horn Book: Studies in Erotic Folklore and Bibliography.* New York: University Books.

——. 1968. *Rationale of the Dirty Joke: An Analysis of Sexual Humor.* New York: Grove Press.

——, ed. 1974. *The Limerick: 1700 Examples, with Notes, Variants and Index.* New York: Bell Publishing.

——. 1975. *Rationale of the Dirty Joke: An Analysis of Sexual Humor, Second Series.* New York: Breaking Point.

Lehmann-Nitsche, R. 1911. *Folklore Argentino*, vol. 1. *Adivinanzas rio-platenses.* Buenos Aires: Coni Hermanos.

Leiris, M. 1948. "La langue secrète des Dogons de Sanga." (*Soudan Français*). (Travaux et Mémoires de l'Institut d'Ethnologie, 50.) Paris: Université de Paris.

——. 1948–1966. *La règle du jeu*, 3 vols. Paris: Gallimard.

Leondar, B. 1975. "Metaphor and Infant Cognition." *Poetics: International Review for the Theory of Literature* 4, 2–3 (14–15): 273–288.

Lessa, W. A., and Vogt, E. Z., eds. 1972. *Reader in Comparative Religion: An Anthropological Approach*, 3rd edition. New York: Harper and Row.

Lesser, G. S. 1973. "Learning, Teaching, and Television Production for Children: The Experience of *Sesame Street*." In *Childhood and Socialization*, ed. H. P. Dreitzel, pp. 265–310. (Recent Sociology, no. 5.) New York: Macmillan.

Leventhal, N. and Cray, E. 1963. "Depth Collecting from a Sixth Grade Class." *Western Folklore* 22: 159–163, 231–257.

Levi-Strauss, C. 1943. "The Social Use of Kinship Terms among Brazilian Indians." *American Anthropologist* 45: 398–409.

Levine, A. S. 1950. "Construction and Use of Verbal Analogy Items." *Journal of Applied Psychology* 34: 105–107.

Levine, J., ed. 1969. *Motivation in Humor.* New York: Atherton.

Levitt, A. 1974. " 'Has the Cat Got Your Tongue?' Observations on Generic Distinctions in Children's Narratives." Philadelphia: University of Pennsylvania. Unpublished manuscript.

Lewalter, J. and Schläger, G. 1911. *Deutsches Kinderlied und Kinderspiel.* Kassel: K. Vietor.

Lewis, P. E. 1969. "La Rochefoucauld: Fragmentation and Formulation." Ph.D. dissertation, Yale University.

――――. 1971. "La Rochefoucauld: The Rationality of Play." In Ehrmann, 1971: 133–147.

Library of Congress, 1942. *Check-list of Recorded Songs in the English Language in the Library of Congress Archive of American Folksong to July, 1940*. Washington, D.C.: Library of Congress, (Reprinted New York: Arno Press, 1971.)

Lieberman, J. 1965. "Playfulness and Divergent Thinking: An Investigation of Their Relationship at the Kindergarten Level." *Journal of Genetic Psychology* 107: 219–224.

Liede, A. 1963. *Dichtung als Spiel; Studien zur Unsinnspoesie an den Grenzen der Sprache*, 2 vols. Berlin: De Gruyter.

Liliental, R. 1908. "Das Kind bei den Juden." *Mitteilungen zur jüdischen Volkskunde* 25: 1–24; 26: 41–55.

Lindley, E. H. 1897. "A Study of Puzzles with Special Reference to the Psychology of Mental Adaptation." *The American Journal of Psychology* 7: 431–493.

Lipiner, A. 1941. *Oysyes dertseyln; vor un legende in der geshikhte fun yidishn alefbeys*. São Paulo, Brazil: Bukhhandlung Mozayic.

List, G. 1963. "The Boundaries of Speech and Song." *Ethnomusicology* 7: 1–16.

Lockhart, L., Eldredge, A. C., and Brown, J. C. 1924. *Number Helps Including Number Games, Number Rhymes, Number Songs, Sense-training Exercises and Speed and Accuracy Tests*. Chicago: Rand McNally and Co.

Loomis, C. G. 1947. "Jonathanisms: American Epigrammatic Hyperbole." *Western Folklore* 6: 211–227.

――――. 1949a. "Traditional American Word Play: Wellerisms or Yankeeisms." *Western Folklore* 8: 1–21.

――――. 1949b. "Traditional American Word Play: The Conundrum." *Western Folklore* 8: 235–247.

――――. 1949c. "Traditional American Word Play: The Epigram and Perverted Proverb." *Western Folklore* 8: 348–357.

――――. 1949d. "A Handful of Tongue Twisters." *Western Folklore* 8: 373–375.

――――. 1950. "Traditional American Word Play." *Western Folklore* 9: 147–152.

――――. 1955a. "Wellerisms in California Sources." *Western Folklore* 14: 229–245.

――――. 1955b. "Rhymed Proverbial Comparisons." *Western Folklore* 14: 282–285.

――――. 1958. "Mary Had a Parody: A Rhyme of Childhood in Folk Tradition." *Western Folklore* 17: 45–51.

――――. 1964. "Proverbial Phrases in Journalistic Word Play." *Western Folklore* 23: 187–189.

Lord, A. B. 1960. *The Singer of Tales*. Cambridge, Massachusetts: Harvard University Press.

Lotz, J. 1955. "On Language and Culture." *International Journal of American Linguistics* 21: 187–189. (Reprinted in Hymes, 1964b: 182–184.)

Loukatas, D. S. 1972. " 'Citations proverbiales' plutôt que 'wellerismes latents.' " *Proverbium* 20: 759.

Lowie, R. H. 1914. "Crow Rapid Speech Puzzles." *Journal of American Folklore* 27: 330–331.

———. 1959. "Crow Curses." *Journal of American Folklore* 72: 105.

Lundberg, C. G. 1969. "Person-focused Joking: Pattern and Function." *Human Organization* 28: 22–28.

Lyons, J. 1968. *Introduction to Theoretical Linguistics*. Cambridge, England: Cambridge University Press.

Lysing, H. (J. L. Nanovic). 1974. *Secret Writing: An Introduction to Cryptograms, Ciphers and Codes*. New York: Dover. (First published 1936.)

McAllester, D. P. 1964. "Riddles and Other Verbal Play among the Comanches." *Journal of American Folklore* 77: 251–257.

McDowell, J. H. 1974. *Interrogative Routines in Mexican-American Children's Folklore*. (Working Papers in Sociolinguistics, no. 20.) Austin, Texas: Southwest Educational Development Educational Laboratory.

McGee, B. 1968. *Jump-rope Rhymes*. New York: Viking.

McGhee, P. E. 1971a. "Cognitive Development and Children's Comprehension of Humor." *Child Development* 42: 123–138.

———. 1971b. "The Development of the Humor Response: A Review of the Literature." *Psychological Bulletin* 76: 328–348.

———. 1971c. "The Role of Operational Thinking in Children's Comprehension and Appreciation of Humor." *Child Development* 42: 733–744.

———. 1972. "On the Cognitive Origins of Incongruity Humor: Fantasy Assimilation versus Reality Assimilation." In Goldstein and McGhee, 1972: 61–80.

McLean, W. 1970. *Contribution à l'étude de l'iconographie populaire de l'érotisme*. (Collection l'Érotisme Populaire, 1.) Paris: Maisonneuve et Larose.

McLuhan, M. 1964. *Understanding Media: The Extensions of Man*, 2d edition. New York: McGraw Hill.

Mack, D. 1975. "Metaphoring as Speech Act: Some Happiness Conditions for Implicit Similes and Simple Metaphors." *Poetics: International Review for the Theory of Literature* 4, 2–3 (14–15): 221–256.

Mackensen, L. 1926. "Sprachmischung als Wortsbildungsprinzip." *Zeitschrift für deutsche Philologie* 51: 406–412.

Mahood, M. M. 1968. *Shakespeare's Wordplay*. London: Methuen and Co.

Malof, J. 1970. *A Manual of English Meters*. Bloomington, Indiana: Indiana University Press.

Maranda, E. K. 1969. "Structures des énigmes." *L'Homme* 9: 5–48.

———. 1971a. "The Logic of Riddles." In P. and E. K. Maranda 1971: 189–232.

————. 1971b. "Theory and Practice of Riddle Analysis." *Journal of American Folklore* 84: 51–61.

————. 1971c. "A Tree Grows: Transformations of a Riddle Metaphor." In E. and P. Maranda, 1971: 116–139.

————. 1974. "Bibliography of Folklore in Canada." Vancouver: University of British Columbia.

Maranda, E. K. and P. 1971. *Structural Models in Folklore and Transformational Essays*. (Approaches to Semiotics, no. 10.) Hague: Mouton.

Maranda, P. and E. K., eds. 1971. *Structural Analysis of Oral Tradition*. (University of Pennsylvania Publications in Folklore and Folklife, no. 3.) Philadelphia: University of Pennsylvania Press.

Margolis, J. S. and Clorfene, R. 1973. *A Child's Garden of Grass: The Official Handbook for Marijuana Users*. New York: Pocket Books.

Margott, F. 1937. "Nebraska Counting-out Rhymes." *Southern Folklore Quarterly* 1 (4): 39–62.

Marken, J. W. 1973. *The Indians and Eskimos of North America: A Bibliography of Books in Print through 1972*. Vermillion: University of South Dakota Press.

Marrus, M. R. 1974. *The Emergence of Leisure*. New York: Harper and Row.

Marshall, H. 1931. "Children's Plays, Games and Amusements." In *A Handbook of Child Psychology*, ed. C. Murchison, pp. 515–526. Worcester, Mass.: Clark University Press.

Mártinez Ríos, F. 1961. *Bibliografía antropológica y sociológica del estado de Oaxaca, segunda parte, materiales para el estudio del folklore*. Mexico: Instituto de Investigaciónes Sociales de la Universidad Nacional Autónoma de México.

Marvin, D. E. 1930. *Historic Child Rhymes: A Monograph on the Origins and Growth of the Rhymes that Children Use and Love*. Norwell, Mass.: The Ross Bookmakers.

Mathias, E. 1974. "The Game as Creator of the Group in an Italian-American Community." *Pennsylvania Folklife* 23: 22–30.

Mathiot, M. 1962. "Review of Wentworth and Flexner, *Dictionary of American Slang*." *American Anthropologist* 64: 672–676.

Matisoff, J. A. 1973. *Psycho-ostensive Expressions in Yiddish*, second draft. Berkeley: University of California. Mimeo.

Maurer, D. W. 1949. *The Big Con*. New York: Pocket Books.

Mautner, F. H. 1931. "Das Wortspiel und seine Bedeutung." *Deutsche Vierteljahrsschrift für Literaturwissen-schaft und Geistesgeschichte* 9: 679–710.

Mayer, P. 1975. "Semiotics of the Alphabet." *Sociolinguistics Newsletter* 4 (1): 12–13.

Mead, M. and Wolfenstein, M., eds. 1966. *Childhood in Contemporary Cultures*. Chicago: University of Chicago Press.

Menninger, K. 1970. *Number Words and Number Symbols: A Cultural History of Numbers*, trans. P. Broneer. Cambridge, Mass.: M.I.T. (Revised German edition, 1958.)

Mercier, D., Brown, K., Varesano, A. 1974. " 'Nipsy': The Ethnography of a Traditional Game of Pennsylvania's Anthracite Region." *Pennsylvania Folklife* 23: 12–21.

Messenger, J. C. 1959. "The Role of Proverbs in a Nigerian Judicial System." *Southwestern Journal of Anthropology* 15: 64–73. (Reprinted in Dundes, 1965: 299–307.)

———. 1960. "Anang Proverb-riddles." *Journal of American Folklore* 73: 225–235.

Metzger, D. and Williams, G. E. 1963. "A Formal Ethnographic Analysis of Tenejapa Ladino Weddings." *American Anthropologist* 65: 1076–1101.

Micheli, P. 1900. *Letteratura che non ha senso.* Livorno: Raffaelo Giusti.

Mieder, W. 1972. "Das Sprichwort und die deutsche Literatur." *Fabula* 13: 135–149.

———. 1974. "The Essence of Literary Proverb Studies." *Proverbium* 23: 888–894.

Milchman, M. 1974a. "On the Acquisition of Relational Concepts in Language and the Development of Simile and Metaphor in Child Lore." New York: Teachers College, Columbia University. Unpublished manuscript.

———. 1974b. "The Relation between the Development of Metaphor and Concept Development in Children." New York: Teachers College, Columbia University. Unpublished manuscript.

Millar, S. 1972. *The Psychology of Play.* Harmondsworth, England: Penguin.

Millard, E. 1951. "Children's Rhyming Games and Other Verses in New York State." Ph.D. dissertation, Cornell University.

———. 1954. What Does It Mean? The Love of Secret Languages." *New York Folklore Quarterly* 10: 103–110.

———. 1959. "Racing, Chasing, and Marching with the Children of the Hudson-Champlain Valleys." *New York Folklore Quarterly* 15: 132–150.

Miller, D. L. 1973. *Gods and Games: Toward a Theology of Play.* New York: Harper and Row.

Miller, R. A. 1967. *The Japanese Language.* Chicago: University of Chicago Press.

Miller, N. 1926–1927. "Some Aspects on the Name in Culture-history." *American Journal of Sociology* 32: 585–600.

Miller, S. 1973. "Ends, Means, and Galumphing: Some Leitmotifs of Play." *American Anthropologist* 75: 87–98.

Miller, W. B. 1967. "Humor in a Chippewa Tribal Council." *Ethnology* 6: 263–271.

Milner, G. B. 1968. "Problems of the Structure of Concepts in Samoa: An Investigation of Vernacular Statement and Meaning." Thesis. London: University of London.

———. 1969. "De l'armature des locutions proverbiales: essai de taxonomie sémantique." *L'Homme* 9 (3): 49–70.

———. 1970. "From Proverb to Riddle and Vice Versa." *Proverbium* 15: 500–502.

———. 1971. "The Quartered Shield: Outline of a Semantic Taxonomy." In *Social Anthropology and Language*, ed. E. Ardener, pp. 243–269. (ASA no. 10.) New York: Tavistock.

———. 1972. "Homo Ridens: Towards a Semiotic Theory of Humor and Laughter." *Semiotica* 5: 1–30.

Mints, T. 1966. "The Psychology of a Nursery Rhyme: One, Two, Buckle My Shoe." *American Imago* 23: 22–47.

Mitchell-Kernan, C. 1971. "Signifying." *Language Behavior in a Black Urban Community*. (Monographs of the Language Behavior Laboratory, No. 2.), pp. 87–129. Berkeley: University of California. (Reprinted in Dundes, 1973: 310–328.)

———. 1972. "Signifying and Marking: Two Afro-American Speech Acts." In Gumperz and Hymes, 1972: 161–179.

Miura, I. and Sasaki, R. 1965. *The Zen Koan: Its History and Use in Rinzai Zen*. New York: Helen and Kurt Wolff.

Moldenhauer, J. 1967. "The Rhetorical Function of Proverbs in *Walden*." *Journal of American Folklore* 80: 151–159.

Moll, O. E. 1958. *Sprichworter-Bibliographie*. Frankfurt am Main: V. Klostermann.

Monod, J. 1968. *Les Barjots*. Paris: Julliard.

Monro, D. H. 1951. *Argument of Laughter*. Melbourne: University Press.

Montagu, M. F. A. 1942. "On the Physiology and Psychology of Swearing." *Psychiatry* 5: 189–201.

———. 1967. *The Anatomy of Swearing*. New York: Macmillan.

Montgomerie, N. and W., eds. 1946. *Scottish Nursery Rhymes*. London: Hogarth Press.

———, eds. 1948. *Sandy Candy, and Other Scottish Nursery Rhymes*. London: Hogarth Press.

———. 1964. *The Hogarth Book of Scottish Nursery Rhymes*. London: Hogarth Press.

Montiero, G. 1964. "Parodies of Scripture, Prayer, and Hymn." *Journal of American Folklore* 77: 45–52.

Mook, M. 1959. "Tongue Tanglers from Central Pennsylvania." *Journal of American Folklore* 72: 291–296.

Moore, G. L. 1964. "My Childhood Games." *Pennsylvania Folklife* 13: 42–57.

Morrison, L. 1955. *A Diller, a Dollar: Rhymes and Sayings for the Ten O'clock Scholar*. New York: Crowell.

Morrissette, B. 1971. "Games and Game Structures in Robbe-Grillet." In Ehrmann, 1971: 159–167.

Muir, W. 1965. *Living with Ballads*. London: Oxford University Press.

Mukařovský, J. 1964. "Standard Language and Poetic Language." In *A Prague School Reader on Esthetics, Literary Structure, and Style*, ed. and trans. P. L. Garvin, pp. 17–30. Maryland: Georgetown University Press. (Reprinted in Freeman, 1970: 40–56.)

———. 1970 *Aesthetic Function, Norm and Value as Social Facts*, trans. M. E. Suino. (Michigan Slavic Contributions, no. 3.) Ann Arbor: University of Michigan.

Mull, H. K. 1949. "A Study of Humor in Music." *American Journal of Psychology* 62: 560–566.

Musick, R. A. and Randolph, V. 1950. "Children's Rhymes from Missouri." *Journal of American Folklore* 63: 425–437.

Narciss, G. H. 1927–1928. *Studien zu den Frauenzimmergesprächsspielen Georg Philipp Harsdörffers.* Dissertation, Greifswald/Leipzig.

Nebesky, L. 1971. "On the Potentially Poetic Aspects of Artificial Languages." *Poetics: International Review for the Theory of Literature* 2: 87–90.

Neely, K. 1966. "A Content Analysis of the *Oxford Dictionary of Nursery Rhymes.*" M.S. thesis, Bowling Green State University.

Newell, W. W. 1883. *Games and Songs of American Children.* New York: Harper and Row. (Second edition of 1903 reprinted, New York: Dover, 1963, with new introduction and index by C. Withers.)

———. 1906. "Note on the Interpretation of European Song-games." In *Boas Anniversary Volume: Anthropological Papers Written in Honor of Franz Boas . . .* , ed. B. Laufer, pp. 404–409. New York: G. E. Stechert.

Niceforo, A. 1912. *Le génie de l'argot.* Paris: Mercure de France.

Nicolich, L. M. 1975. "A Longitudinal Study of Representational Play in Relation to Spontaneous Imitation and Development of Multi-word Utterances." (Final report.) Rutgers, New Jersey: National Institute of Mental Health.

Northall, G. F. 1892. *English Folk-rhymes: A Collection of Traditional Verses Relating to Places and Persons, Customs, Superstitions, etc.* London: Kegan Paul, Trench, Trübner and Co. (Reprinted, Detroit: Singing Tree Press, 1968.)

Noy, D. 1955. *Study of Folk Literature: A Selected Bibliography of Recent Years.* Israel: Haifa School of the Humanities.

Nulton, L. 1948. "Jump-rope Rhymes as Folk Literature." *Journal of American Folklore* 61: 53–67.

Nunn, C. Z. 1964. "Child-control through a Coalition with God." *Child Development* 35: 417–32.

Nuyts, E. H. J. 1930. *Folkloristische Sprokkelingen uit de Kinderwereld: Rijmkes en Licdjes uit Kinderspelen le Turnhout verzameld.* Turnhout: Lumen.

O'Connell, W. E. 1969. "Creativity in Humor." *Journal of Social Psychology* 78: 237–241.

Ogundipe, A. 1972. "Yoruba Tongue Twisters." In Dorson, 1972: 211–220.

Ohlert, K. 1886. *Rätsel und Gesellschaftsspiel der alten Griechen,* 2 Auflage. Berlin: Mayer & Müller.

Oinas, F. J. and Soudakoff, S., eds. In press. *The Study of Russian Folklore.* Hague: Mouton.

Ojemann, R. H. 1953. *The Child's Society.* Chicago: Science Research Associates.

Omwake, D. 1937. "A Study of the Sense of Humor in Relation to Sex, Age and Personal Characteristics." *Journal of Applied Psychology* 21: 688–704.

Opie, I. and P. 1947. *I Saw Esau: Traditional Rhymes of Youth*. London: Williams and Norgate.

———. 1951. *The Oxford Dictionary of Nursery Rhymes*. Oxford: Clarendon Press.

———. 1959. *The Lore and Language of Schoolchildren*. Oxford: Clarendon Press.

———. 1969. *Children's Games in Street and Playground*. Oxford: Clarendon Press.

———. 1973. *The Oxford Book of Children's Verse*. Oxford: Clarendon Press.

———. 1974. *The Classic Fairy Tales*. London: Oxford Press.

Otsikrev, A. 1963. *Play Languages and Language Play*. Hillsboro, Oregon: Esperanto.

Palakornkul, A. 1971. "Some Linguistic Games in Thai." In Sherzer et al, 1971: 25–31.

Palmer, G. 1956. "Discriminations of Psychopaths, Normal Prisoners, and Nonprisoners Using a Disguised Objective Personality Test." Master's thesis, Louisiana State University.

Paredes, A. 1964. "Some Aspects of Folk Poetry." *Texas Studies in Language and Literature* 6: 213–225.

Paredes, A. and Bauman, R., eds. 1972. *Toward New Perspectives in Folklore*. (Publications of the American Folklore Society Bibliographical and Special Series, vol. 23.) Austin, Texas: University of Texas Press for the American Folklore Society. (First appeared as *Journal of American Folklore*, vol. 84, no. 331, 1971.)

Paredes Candia, A. 1961. *Bibliografía del folklore Boliviano*. La Paz, Bolivia.

Park, R. R. 1972. "An Investigation of Riddles of Children, Ages Five through Fourteen, Using Piaget Derived Definitions." Ed.D. dissertation, Teachers College, Columbia University.

Parker, R. B. 1958. "Lebanese Proverbs." *Journal of American Folklore* 71: 104–114.

Parkin, K. 1969. *Anthology of British Tongue-twisters*. London: Samuel French.

Parman, S. 1973. "Patterns of Naming among Bilingual Scottish Crofters." Paper presented to the Southwest Anthropological Association, San Francisco.

Parrott, S. 1972. "Games Children Play: Ethnography of a Second-grade Recess." In *The Cultural Experience: Ethnography in Complex Society*, eds. J. P. Spradley and D. W. McCurdy, pp. 207–220. Chicago: Science Research Associates.

Partridge, E. 1950. *The Nonsense Words of Edward Lear and Lewis Carroll: Here, There and Everywhere, Essays upon Language*. London: Macmillan.

———. 1960. *Shakespeare's Bawdy: A Literary and Psychological Essay and a Comprehensive Glossary*. New York: Dutton (First published 1948.)

Pearson, F. S. 1950. *Fractured French*. Garden City, New York: Doubleday.

Perceau, L., ed. 1959. *La redoute des contrepéteries*. Paris: G. Briffaut.

Pereira Salas, E. n.d. "Guía bibliográfica para el estudio del folklore Chileno." *Archivos del Folklore Chileno*, Fascículo no. 4.

Perkal, J. R. 1969. *Western Folklore* and *California Folklore Quarterly*, *Twenty-five-Year Index, vols. I–XXV, 1942–1966*. Berkeley: University of California Press for the California Folklore.

Perrow, E. C. 1913. "Songs and Rhymes from the South." *Journal of American Folklore* 26: 123–173.

Pessler, W., ed. 1935–1938. *Handbuch der deutschen Volkskunde*, 3 vols. Potsdam: Akademische Verlagsgesellschaft Athenaion m.b.h.

Petsch, R. 1899. *Neue Beiträge zur Kenntnis des Volksrätsels*. (Palaestra 4.) Berlin: Mayer and Müller.

———. 1938. *Spruchdichtung des Volkes, Vor- und Frühformen der Volksdichtung. Ruf, Zauber- und Weisheitsspruch, Rätsel. Volks- und Kinderreim*. Halle (Saale): Max Niemeyer.

Phillips, H. 1945. *Word Play*. Harmondsworth, England: Ptarmigan Books, Penguin.

Piaget, J. 1954. *The Construction of Reality in the Child*, trans. M. Cook. New York: Basic Books. (First Published in French in 1936.)

———. 1962. *Play, Dreams and Imitation in Childhood*, trans. C. Gattegno and F. M. Hodgson. New York: Norton. (First published in French in 1946.)

———. 1965. *The Moral Judgment of the Child*, trans. M. Gabain. New York: Free Press. (First published in French in 1932.)

Piaget, J. and Inhelder, B. 1971. *Mental Imagery in the Child: A Study of the Development of Imaginal Representation*. New York: Basic Books. (First published in French in 1966.)

Pickard, P. M. 1961. *I Could a Tale Unfold: Violence, Horror, and Sensationalism in Stories for Children*. New York: Humanities Press.

Piddington, R. 1933. *The Psychology of Laughter: A Study in Social Adaptation*. London: Figurehead.

Pike, K. N. 1945a. "Tone Puns in Mixteco." *International Journal of American Linguistics* 11: 129–139.

———. 1945b. "Mock Spanish of a Mixteco Indian." *International Journal of American Linguistics* 11: 219–229.

———. 1946. "Another Mixteco Tone Pun." *International Journal of American Linguistics*. 12: 22–24.

Piña Chan, R. 1969. *Spiel und Sport in alten Mexico*. Leipzig: Edition Leipzig.

Pinon, R. 1941. *Questionnaire des Jeux et divertissements enfantins*. Charleroi: Imprimerie Aimé Pinon.

———, ed. 1965a. *Chansons populaires de la Flandre Wallone*. Bruxelles: Commission Royale Belge de Folklore.

———. 1965b. "Les contes-enfantines et l'apprentissage du style." *IV Inter-*

*national Congress for Folk-Narrative Research in Athens 1964,* ed. G. H. Megas, pp. 364–380. Athens: Laographia.

Pitcher, E. G. and Prelinger, E. 1963. *Children Tell Stories: An Analysis of Fantasy.* New York: International Universities Press.

Pitt-Rivers, J. A. 1961. *The People of the Sierra.* Chicago: Phoenix.

Ploss, H. 1911. *Das Kind in Brauch und Sitte der Völker,* 2 vols., 2d edition. Leipzig: Th. Grieben Verlag.

Polsky, N. 1971. *Hustlers, Beats and Others.* Harmondsworth, England: Penguin.

Pop, M. 1968. "Der formelhafte Charakter der Volksdichtung." *Deutsche Jahrbuch für Volkskunde* 14: 1–15.

Porter, K. 1958. "Circular Jingles and Repetitious Rhymes." *Western Folklore* 18: 107–111.

———. 1965. "Racism in Children's Rhymes and Sayings, Central Kansas, 1910–1918." *Western Folklore* 24: 191–196.

Posen, I. S., Taft, M., Tallman, R. S., comps. 1973. *Index to Hoosier Folklore Bulletin (1942–1945) and Hoosier Folklore (1946–1950).* (Folklore Forum Bibliographic and Special Series, no. 10.) Bloomington, Indiana.

Postal, P. 1974. *On Raising.* Cambridge, Mass.: M.I.T.

Potter, C. F. 1964. *More Tongue Tanglers and a Rigamarole.* Cleveland: World Publishing.

Potts, J. W. 1892. "Peter Piper's Proper Pronunciation of Perfect English versus Peter Pipernus." *Journal of American Folklore* 5: 74–76.

Potts, W. 1930. *Banbury Cross and the Rhyme.* Banbury: The Banbury Guardian.

Pounders, C. J. 1956. "A Study of the Proverbs Test as a Measure of the Abstract Level of Concept Formation." Master's thesis, Baylor University.

Pozas Arciniega, R. 1959. *Chamula, un pueblo indio de los altos de Chiapas.* (Memorias del Instituto Nacional Indigenista, vol. 8.) Mexico: Instituto Nacional Indigenista.

———. 1962. *Juan the Chamula: An Ethnological Recreation of the Life of a Mexican Indian,* trans. L. Kemp. Berkeley: University of California Press. (First published in Spanish, 1959.)

Prentice, N. M. and Fathman, R. E. 1972. "Joking Riddles: A Developmental Index of Children's Humor." *Proceedings of the 80th Annual Convention of the American Psychological Association* 7: 119–120.

Price, R. 1970a. "Saramaka Emigration and Marriage: A Case Study of Social Change." *Southwestern Journal of Anthropology* 26: 157–89.

———. 1970b. "Saramaka Woodcarving: The Development of an Afro-American Art." *Man* 5: 363–78.

———. 1972. "The Guiana Maroons: Changing Perspectives in 'Bush Negro' Studies." *Caribbean Studies* 11 (4): 82–105.

———. 1975a. "KiKoongo and Saramaccan: A Reappraisal." *Bijdragen tot de Taal-, Land- en Volkenkunde 131.*

———. 1975b. *Saramaka Social Structure: Analysis of a Maroon Society in*

*Surinam.* (Caribbean Monograph Series 12.) Rio Piedras: Institute of Caribbean Studies of the University of Puerto Rico.

———. 1976. *The Guiana Maroons: A Historical and Bibliographical Introduction.* Baltimore: Johns Hopkins University Press.

Price, R. and Price, S. 1972. "Saramaka Onomastics: An Afro-American Naming System." *Ethnology* 11: 341–367.

Price, T. J. 1970. "Ethnohistory and Self-image in Three New World Negro Societies." In Whitten and Szwed, 1970: 63–73.

Prince, G. 1973. *A Grammar of Stories: An Introduction.* Hague: Mouton.

Propp, V. 1968. *The Morphology of the Folktale,* 2d edition, trans. L. Scott. Austin: University of Texas Press. (First published in Russian in 1928.)

Pyles, T. 1959. "Bible Belt Onomastics or Some Curiosities of Anti-pedobaptist Nomenclature." *Names* 7: 84–100.

Quirk, R. 1951. "Puns to Sell." *Studia Neophilologica* 23: 81–86.

Raa, E. T. 1966. "Procedure and Symbolism in Sandawe Riddles." *Man,* n.s., 1: 391–397.

Rabin, A. and Broida, D. 1948. "Projection via Proverbs: Follow-up of a Suggestion." *Journal of Consulting Psychology* 12: 246–250.

Radcliffe-Brown, A. R. 1965. "On Joking Relationships" and "A Further Note on Joking Relationships." *Structure and Function in Primitive Society,* pp. 90–116. New York: Free Press.

Ramsey, E., comp. 1952. *Folklore for Children and Young People: A Critical and Descriptive Bibliography for Use in the Elementary and Intermediate School.* (American Folklore Society Bibliographical and Special Series, vol. 3.) Philadelphia: American Folklore Society. (Reprinted, New York: Kraus, 1970.)

Randolph, V. 1972. *Ozark Folklore, a Bibliography.* (Indiana University Folklore Institute Monograph Series, no. 24.) Bloomington, Indiana.

Randolph, V. and Wilson, G. P. 1953. *Down in the Holler: A Gallery of Ozark Folk Speech.* Norman, Oklahoma: University of Oklahoma Press.

Rapp, A. 1949. "A Phylogenetic Theory of Wit and Humor." *Journal of Social Psychology* 30: 81–96.

Razran, G. 1961. "The Observable Unconscious and the Inferable Conscious in Current Soviet Psychophysiology." *Psychological Review* 68: 81–147.

Read, A. W. 1934. "An Obscenity Symbol." *American Speech* 9: 264–278.

———. 1935. *Lexical Evidence from Folk Epigraphy in Western North America: A Glossarial Study of the Low Element in the English Vocabulary.* Paris: Privately printed.

———. 1949. "The Nature of Obscenity." *Neurotica* 5: 23–40.

Redl, F. 1959. "The Impact of Game Ingredients on Children's Play Behavior." *Transactions of the Fourth Conference on Group Processes,* ed. B. Schaffner, pp. 33–81. New York: Josiah Macy, Jr. Foundation.

Redmayne, A. and Ndulute, C. M. 1970. "Riddles and Riddling among the Hehe of Tanzania." *Anthropos* 65: 794–813.

Reed, L. 1925. *Nonsense Verses, an Anthology.* London: Jarrolds.

Reisman, K. 1970. "Cultural and Linguistic Ambiguity in a West Indian Village." In Whitten and Szwed, 1970: 129–144.

Reiss, E. 1970. "Number Symbolism and Medieval Literature." In *Medievalia et Humanistica: Studies in Medieval and Renaissance Culture*, n.s., no. 1, ed. P. M. Clogan, pp. 161–174. Cleveland: Case Western Reserve University.

Rennick, R. M. 1966. "The Folklore of Curious and Unusual Names (a brief introduction to the folklore of onomastics)." *New York Folklore Quarterly* 22: 5–14.

————. 1968. "Obscene Names and Naming in Folk Tradition." *Names* 16: 207–229.

————. 1970. "The Nazi Name Decrees of the Nineteen Thirties." *Names* 18: 65–88.

Reuss, R. 1965. "An Annotated Field Collection of Songs from the American College Student Oral Tradition." M.A. thesis, Indiana University.

Reveal, R., Jr. 1960. "The Development and Validation of a Proverbs Test for the Selection of Supervisors." Ph.D. dissertation, University of Southern California.

Reynolds, R. 1946. *Cleanliness and Godliness*. New York: Doubleday.

Ricardou, J. 1967. *Problèmes du nouveau roman*. Paris: Seuil.

————. 1971. *Pour une théorie du nouveau roman*. Paris: Seuil.

Richardson, C. and Church, J. 1959. "A Developmental Analysis of Proverb Interpretation." *Journal of Genetic Psychology* 94: 169–179.

Riedl, A. and Klier, K. M. 1957. *Lieder, Reime und Spiele der Kinder im Burgenland*. Eisenstadt: Burgenländisches Landesmuseum.

Riess, B. F. 1946. "Genetic Change in Semantic Conditioning." *Journal of Experimental Psychology* 36: 143–152.

Rigby, P. 1968. "Joking Relationships, Kin Categories and Clanship among the Gogo." *Africa* 38: 133–155.

Ritchie, J. T. R., 1964. *The Singing Street*. Edinburgh: Oliver and Boyd.

————. 1965. *The Golden City*. Edinburgh: Oliver and Boyd.

Ritson, J. 1810. *Gammer Gurton's Garland: or, the Nursery Parnassus. A Choice Collection of Pretty Songs and Verses, for the Amusement of All Little Good Children Who Can Neither Read nor Run*, enlarged edition. London: R. Triphook. (First published 1784.) (Reprinted, Norwood, Pennsylvania: Norwood, 1973.)

Ritzenthaler, R. 1945. "Totemic Insult among the Wisconsin Chippewa." *American Anthropologist* 47: 322–324.

Roback, A. A. 1944. *A Dictionary of Ethnic Slurs (Ethnophaulisms)*. Cambridge, Mass.: Sci. Art. Publishers.

Robbe-Grillet, A. 1963. *Pour un nouveau roman*. Paris: Gallimard.

Robbins, R. H. 1966. "The Warden's Wordplay: Toward a Redefinition of Spoonerisms." *The Dalhousie Review* 46: 457–465.

Robe, S. 1963. *Hispanic Riddles from Panama, Collected from Oral Tradition*. (University of California Folklore Studies, no. 14.) Berkeley: University of California Press.

Robert, M. 1972. "The Grimm Brothers." In Brooks, 1972: 44–56.

Roberts, D. K. 1938. *Nonsensical and Surrealist Verse.* London: The Bodley Head.

Roberts, J. M., Arth, M. J. and Bush, R. R. 1959. "Games in Culture." *American Anthropologist* 61: 597–605.

Roberts, J. M. and Forman, M. L. 1971. "Riddles: Expressive Models of Interrogation." *Ethnology* 10: 509–533. (Reprinted in revised form in Gumperz & Hymes, 1972: 180–209.)

Roberts, J. M. and Sutton-Smith, B. 1962. "Child training and Game Involvement." *Ethnology* 1: 166–185.

———. 1964. "Rubrics of Competitive Behavior." *Journal of Genetic Psychology* 105: 13–37.

———. 1966. "Cross-cultural Correlates of Games of Chance." *Behavior Science Notes* 3: 131–144.

Roberts, J. M., Sutton-Smith, B. and Kendon, A. 1963. "Strategy in Games and Folk Tales." *Journal of Social Psychology* 61: 185–189.

Roberts, J. M., Sutton-Smith, B. and Kozelka, R. M. 1967. "Studies in an Elementary Game of Strategy." *Genetic Psychological Monograph* 75: 3–42.

Rochholz, E. L. 1857. *Alemannisches Kinderlied und Kinderspiel aus der Schweiz. Gesammelt und sitten- und sprachgeschichtlich erklart.* Leipzig: J. J. Weber.

Rodgers, C. M. 1969. "Black Poetry—Where It's At." *Negro Digest* 18: 7–16.

Roheim, G. 1943. "Children's Games and Rhymes in Duau (Normandy Island)." *American Anthropologist* 45: 99–119.

Rolland, E. 1967. *Rimes et jeux de l'enfance.* Paris: G. P. Maisonneuve et Larose. (First published in the series, Les Littératures Populaires de Toutes les Nations, vol. 14, 1883.)

Romney, A. K. and D'Andrade, R. G. 1964. "Cognitive Aspects of English Kin Terms." In *Transcultural Studies in Cognition,* ed. A. K. Romney and R. G. D'Andrade, pp. 146–170. (*American Anthropologist* 66, no. 3, part 2.) Washington, D.C.: American Anthropological Association.

Rosenberg, B. A. 1970. *The Art of the American Folk Preacher.* New York: Oxford University Press.

Rosenberg, B. G., and Sutton-Smith, B. 1960. "A Revised Conception of Masculine-feminine Differences in Play Activities. *Journal of Genetic Psychology* 96: 165–170.

Rosso, C. 1968. *La maxime: saggi per una tipologia critica.* (Testi e saggi di letteratura francese, saggi 2.) Naples: E.S.I.

Rothenberg, J. Forthcoming. *A Big Jewish Book: Poems and Other Visions of the Jews.* New York: Doubleday.

Rothstein, R. A. 1968. "The Poetics of Proverbs." In *Studies Presented to Professor Roman Jakobson by His Students,* ed. C. E. Gribble, pp. 265–274. Cambridge, Mass.: Slavica Publications.

Roy, C. 1954. *Trésor de la poésie populaire française.* Paris: Seghers.

Roys, R. L. 1940. "Personal Names of the Maya of Yucatan." In *Carnegie In-*

*stitution of Washington Contributions to American Anthropology and History* 6: 31–48.

Rubin, R. 1952. "Nineteenth Century Yiddish Folksongs of Children in Eastern Europe." *Journal of American Folklore* 65: 227–254.

Rühmkorf, P. 1972. *Über das Volksvermögen: Exkurse in den litterarischen Untergrund.* Hamburg: Rowohlt.

Rutherford, F. 1971. *All the Way to Pennywell: Children's Rhymes of the North East.* Durham, England: University of Durham Institute of Education.

Sackett, S. J. 1964. "Poetry and Folklore: Some Points of Affinity." *Journal of American Folklore* 77: 143–153.

Sacks, H. 1972. "On the Analyzability of Stories by Children." In Gumperz and Hymes, 1972: 325–345.

———. 1973. "On Some Puns with Some Intimations." In *Sociolinguistics,* ed. R. W. Shuy, pp. 135–144. (Report of the Twenty-Third Annual Roundtable Meeting on Linguistics and Language Studies.) Washington, D.C.: Georgetown University Press.

Sackville-West, V. M. 1947. *Nursery Rhymes.* (Dropmore Essays, no. 4.) London: Dropmore.

Sadtono, E. 1971. "Language Games in Javanese." In Sherzer et al., 1971: 32–38.

Sagarin, E. 1962. *The Anatomy of Dirty Words.* Secaucus, New Jersey: Lyle Stuart.

Salmond, A. 1974. "Rituals of Encounter among the Maori: Sociolinguistic Study of a Scene." In Bauman and Sherzer, 1974, pp. 192–212.

Samarin, W. 1969. "The Art of Gbeya Insults." *International Journal of American Linguistics* 35: 323–329.

———. 1972. *Tongues of Men and Angels.* New York: Macmillan.

Sanches, M. and Blount, B. 1975. *Sociocultural Dimensions of Language Use.* New York: Academic Press.

Sanderson, S. F. 1971 *A Catalogue of Theses and Dissertations in Folk Life Studies in the University of Leeds 1961–1970.* (Institute of Dialect and Folk Life Studies, University of Leeds. Occasional Paper, no. 1.) Yorkshire, England: Scolar Press.

Sandys, W., ed. 1831. *Specimens of Macronic Poetry.* London: Richard Beckley.

Santi, A. 1952. *Bibliografia della enigmistica.* (Biblioteca Bibliografica Italica, 3.) Firenze: Sansoni.

Sapir, E. 1915. *Abnormal Types of Speech in Nootka.* (Canada, Department of Mines, Geological Survey, Memoir 62; Anthropological Series No. 5.) Ottawa: Government Printing Bureau.

———. 1920. "The Heuristic Value of Rhyme." *Queen's Quarterly* 27: 309–312.

———. 1932. "The Navaho Puns." *Language* 8: 217–219.

Schaechter, M. 1954. "On Children's Nonsense Oaths in Yiddish." In *The Field of Yiddish: Studies in Yiddish Language, Folklore, and Literature,* ed. U. Weinreich, pp. 196–198. (Linguistic Circle of New York Publications, no. 3.) New York: Linguistic Circle of New York.

Schaffner, H. R. 1971. *The Growth of Sociability*. London: Penguin.

Schegloff, E. A. 1968. "Sequencing in Conversational Openings." *American Anthropologist* 70: 1075–1095.

Scheub, H. 1971. *Bibliography of African Oral Narratives*. (Occasional Paper no. 3) Madison, Wisconsin: African Studies Program, University of Wisconsin.

Schevill, R. 1910–1912. "Some Forms of the Riddle Question and the Exercise of Wits in Popular Fiction and Formal Literature." *Publications in Modern Philology* (University of California) 2: 183–287.

Schlegel, G. 1891. "Secret Languages in Europe and China." *T'oung Pao* 2: 161.

Schultz, J. 1927. "Psychologie des Wortspiels." *Zeitschrift für Aesthetik und allgemeine Kunstwissenschaft* 21: 16–37.

Schultz, W. 1909–1912. *Rätsel aus dem hellenischen Kulturkreise*. Leipzig: Einrich.

Schwartz, A. 1972. *A Twister of Twists, a Tangler of Tongues*. Philadelphia: Lippincott.

———. 1973a. *Tomfoolery: Trickery and Foolery with Words*. Philadelphia: Lippincott.

———. 1973b. "Witcracks, Jokes and Jests from American Folklore." Philadelphia: Lippïncott.

———. 1974. *Cross Your Fingers, Spit in Your Hat: Superstitions and Other Beliefs*. Philadelphia: Lippincott.

Schwarzbaum, H. 1968. *Studies in Jewish and World Folklore*. Berlin: de Gruyter.

Schwendener, N. 1932. *Game Preferences of 10,000 Fourth Grade Children*. New York: Columbia University.

Sciacca, G. M. 1957. *Il fanciullo e il folklore*. Bologna: Edizioni Giuseppe Malipiero.

Scott, C. T. 1965. *Persian and Arabic Riddles: A Language-centered Approach to Genre Definition*. (Indiana University Research Center in Anthropology, Folklore and Linguistics Publication 39: also *International Journal of American Linguistics* 31 [4], part 2.) Bloomington, Indiana: Indiana University.

———. 1969. "On Defining the Riddle: The Problem of a Structural Unit." *Genre* 2: 129–142.

Seagoe, M. V. 1962. "Children's Play as an Indicator of Cross-cultural and Intra-cultural Differences." *Journal of Educational Sociology* 35: 278–283.

———. 1970. "An Instrument for the Analysis of Children's Play as an Index of Degree of Socialization." *Journal of School Psychology* 8: 139–144.

Sebeok, T. A., ed. 1960. *Style in Language*. Cambridge, Mass.: M.I.T.

Sebillet, T. 1972. *Art poétique françoys*. Genève: Slatkine Reprints. (Reprint of 1555 edition. First published 1548.)

Secretaría de Industria y Comercio. 1963. *VIII censo general de población, 1960, 8 junio, Estado de Chiapas*. Mexico, D. F.

Seeger, R. C. 1948. *American Folk Songs for Children in Home, School and Nursery School: A Book for Children, Parents and Teachers*. Garden City: Doubleday.

———. 1950. *Animal Folksongs for Children: Traditional American Songs*. Garden City: Doubleday.

Segal, A. 1970. "Censorship, Social Control and Socialization." *British Journal of Sociology* 21: 63–74.

Seitel, P. 1969. "Proverbs: A Social Use of Metaphor." *Genre* 2: 143–161.

———. 1972. "Proverbs and the Structure of Metaphor among the Haya of Tanzania." Ph.D. dissertation, folklore, University of Pennsylvania.

Sen Greptar, S. 1967. *A Bibliography of Indian Folklore and Related Subjects*. Calcutta: Indian Publications.

Sewell, E. 1970. *The Field of Nonsense*. London: Folcroft.

Shankle, G. E. 1937. *American Nicknames: Their Origin and Significance*. New York: H. W. Wilson.

Sharman, A. 1969. " 'Joking' in Padhola: Categorical Relationships, Choice and Social Control." *Man 4: 103–117*.

Sharman, J. 1884. *A Cursory History of Swearing*. New York: Burt Franklin.

Shaw, F. 1970. *You Know Me, Aunt Nelly? Liverpool Children's Rhymes*, 2d edition. London: Wolfe.

Shaw, F. J. 1960. "Laughter: Paradigm of Growth." *Journal of Individual Psychology* 16: 151–157.

Sherzer, D. 1976. *"Circus: An Exercise in Semiotics." Sub-Stance* (forthcoming).

———. In press. "De-Construction in *Waiting for Godot*." In Babcock-Abrahams, in press.

Sherzer, D. and Sherzer, J. 1972. "Literature in San Blas: Discovering Cuna *Ikala*." *Semiotica* 6: 182–199.

Sherzer, J. 1970. "Talking Backwards in Cuna: The Sociological Reality of Phonological Descriptions." *Southwestern Journal of Anthropology* 26: 343–353.

———. 1971. "Five Cuna Linguistic Games." (Penn-Texas Working Papers in Sociolinguistics 6.) Austin: University of Texas.

Sherzer, J., Foley, L., Johnson, Sister C., Johnson, N. A., Palakornkul, A. and Sadtono, E. 1971. *A Collection of Linguistic Games*. (Penn-Texas Working Papers in Sociolinguistics 2.) Austin: University of Texas.

Shibles, W. 1969. "A Philosophical Commentary on *Alice's Adventures in Wonderland*." *Wittgenstein Language and Philosophy*, pp. 14–45. Dubuque, Iowa: Brown.

———. 1971. *Metaphor: An Annotated Bibliography and History*. Whitewater, Wisconsin: The Language Press.

Shipley, J. T. 1972. *Word Play*. New York: Hawthorne.

Shiver, S. M. 1941. "Finger Rhymes." *Southern Folklore Quarterly* 5: 221–234.

Shultz, T. R. 1974. "Development of the Appreciation of Riddles." *Child Development* 45: 100–105.

Shultz, T. R. and Horibe, F. 1974. "Development of the Appreciation of Verbal Jokes." *Developmental Psychology* 10: 13–20.

Shultz, T. R. and Pilon, R. 1973. "Development of the Ability to Detect Linguistic Ambiguity." *Child Development* 44: 728–733.

Siddiqui, A. 1961. "Bengali Riddles from Oral Tradition, from Riddles to Proverb." *Journal of the Asiatic Society of Pakistan* 6: 262–263.

Silverman-Weinreich, B. 1964. "Formale problemen baym forshn dos yidishe shprikhvort." In *For Max Weinreich on His Seventieth Birthday: Studies in Jewish Languages, Literatures, and Society*, pp. 398–383. Hague: Mouton. (To appear in English translation in *Journal of American Folklore*.)

Silverstein, M. 1972. "Linguistic Theory, Syntax, Semantics, Pragmatics." *Annual Review of Anthropology* 1: 349–382.

Simmons, D. C. 1956. "Erotic Ibibio Tone Riddles." *Man* 56 (article 78).

———. 1958a. "Efik Games." *Folklore* 69: 26–33.

———. 1958b. "Cultural Functions of the Efik Tone Riddle." *Journal of American Folklore* 71: 123–138.

———. 1960. "Ibibio Topical Ballads." *Man* 60 (article 73).

———. 1961. "Efik Tone Riddles and Anang Proverb Riddles. *Journal of American Folklore* 74: 245–246.

Singer, J. L. 1973. *The Child's World of Make-believe: Experimental Studies of Imaginative Play*. New York: Academic Press.

Skeels, D. 1954a. "A Classification of Humor in Nez Perce Mythology." *Journal of American Folklore* 67: 57–64.

———. 1954b. "The Function of Humor in Three Nez Perce Indian Myths." *American Imago* 11: 248–261.

Skolnik, P. L. 1974. *Jump Rope*. New York: Workman.

Slobin, D., ed. 1967. *A Field Manual for the Cross-cultural Study of the Acquisition of Communicative Competence*. Berkeley: University of California Language-Behavior Development Laboratory.

Smilansky, S. 1968. *The Effects of Sociodramatic Play on Disadvantaged Preschool Children*. New York: Wiley.

Smith, A. H. 1902. *Proverbs and Common Sayings from the Chinese, Together with Much Related and Unrelated Matter, Interspersed with Observations on Chinese Things-in-general*, revised edition. Shanghai: American Presbyterian Mission Press. (First published 1882–1885. Reprint of 1914 edition, New York: Dover.)

Smith, E. C. 1952. *Personal Names: A Bibliography*. New York: New York Public Library. (Reprinted, Detroit: Gale Research Co., 1965.)

Smith, E. E. and White, H. L. 1965. "Wit, Creativity and Sarcasm." *Journal of Applied Psychology* 49: 131–134.

Smith, P. A. 1909. "Some Phases of the Play of Japanese Boys and Men." *Pedagogical Seminary* 16: 256–267.

Sonnino, L. A. 1968. *A Handbook to Sixteenth Century Rhetoric*. London: Routledge and Kegan Paul.

Soriano, M. 1959. *Guide de la littérature enfantine*. Paris: Flammarion.

———. 1968. *Les contes de Perrault, culture savante et traditions populaires*. Paris: Gallimard.

———. 1972. "From Tales of Warning to Formulettes." In Brooks, 1972: 24–43.

Spamer, A., ed. 1934–35. *Die deutsche Volkskunde*, 2 vols. Leipzig: Bibliographischer Institut.

Spanke, H. 1931. "Klangspielereien im mittelalterlichen Liede." In *Studien zur lateinischen Dichtung des Mittelalters, Ehrengabe für Karl Strecker*, eds. W. Stach and H. Walther. Dresden: Baensch, pp. 171–183.

Speier, M. 1970. "The Everyday World of the Child." In *Understanding Everyday Life: Toward the Reconstruction of Sociological Knowledge*, ed. J. D. Douglas, pp. 188–217. Chicago: Aldine.

Spence, L. 1947. *Myth and Ritual in Dance, Game, and Rhyme*. London: Watts.

Speroni, C. 1942. "Some Rope-skipping Rhymes from Southern California." *California Folklore Quarterly* 1: 245–252.

Spitzer, L. 1910. "Die Wortbildung als stilistisches. Mittel exemplifiziert an Rabelais." *Zeitschrift für romanische Philologie*, Beiheft 29: 1–157.

Stankiewicz, E. 1964. "Problems of Emotive Language." In *Approaches to Semiotics* (Transactions of the Indiana University Conference on Paralinguistics and Kinesics.), ed. T. A. Sebeok, A. S. Hayes, and M. C. Bateson, pp. 239–264. (Janua Linguarum, series maior 15.) Hague: Mouton.

Starobinski, J. 1966. "La Rochefoucauld et les morales substitutives." *Nouvelle Revue Française* 14: 16–34, 211–229.

Steadman, J. M., Jr., 1936. "Tongue-twisters: Difficult Pronunciation as a Source of Verbal Taboos." *American Speech* 11: 203–204.

Stein, K. M. 1953. *Die allerschönste Lengevitch (Die schönste Lengevitch mit gemixte Pickles und limberger Lyrics zusammen downgeboilt, und plenty gesasont mit Additions von neugehachter Nonsense)*. New York: Crown.

Stein, M. 1975. *Stimulating Creativity*. New York: Academic Press.

Stevens, A. M. 1968. *The Nursery Rhyme: Remnant of Popular Protest*. Lawrence, Kansas: Colorado Press.

Stevenson, B. 1948. *The Home Book of Proverbs, Maxims, and Familiar Phrases*. New York: Macmillan.

Stimson, A. 1945. "Cries of Defiance and Derision, and Rhythmic Chants of West Side New York City, 1893–1903." *Journal of American Folklore* 58: 124–129.

Stocker, T. L., Dutcher, L. W., Hargrove, S. M., and Cook, E. A. 1972.

"Social Analysis of Graffiti." *Journal of American Folklore* 85: 356–366.

Stoeltje, B. 1974. "Mischief-makers and Marginality in Children's Folklore." Austin: University of Texas. Unpublished manuscript.

Straw, S. B., ed. 1974. "Identifying Oral Literary Patterns in Children's Creative Writing." Paper presented to the Canadian Council of Teachers of English, Saskatoon.

Streamer, D. [pseud. of H. Graham] [1899], *Ruthless Rhymes for Heartless Homes*. London: E. Arnold.

Strettell, A. 1896. *Lullabies of Many Lands,* 2d edition. London: G. Allen.

Stross, B. 1970. "Elicited Imitations in the Study of Tenejapa Tzeltal Language Acquisition." *Anthropological Linguistics* 12: 319–325.

———. 1972. "Metaphor in the Speech Play of Tzeltal Children." Unpublished paper. Austin: University of Texas.

Strutt, J. 1801. *The Sports and Pastimes of the People of England*. London: Methuen. (Reprinted, Detroit: Singing Tree Press, 1968.)

Stückrath, O. 1931. *Nassauisches Kinderlied und Kinderspiel in Sitte und Brauch*. Wiesbaden: Veröffentlichungen des Volksliedausschusses für das Land Nassau, USW.

Sully, J. 1902. *An Essay on Laughter, Its Forms, Its Causes, Its Development, and Its Value*. London: Longmans, Green, and Co.

Surrick, J. E. and Conant, L. M. 1927. *Laddergrams*. New York: Sears.

Susman, A. 1941. "Word Play in Winnebago." *Language* 17: 342–344.

Sutton-Smith, B. 1951. "The Meeting of Maori and European Cultures and Its Effects upon the Unorganized Games of Maori Children." *Journal of the Polynesian Society* 60: 93–107. (Reprinted in Sutton-Smith, 1972a: 317–330.)

———. 1953. "The Game Rhymes of New Zealand Children." *Western Folklore* 12: 411–423.

———. 1959a. "A Formal Analysis of Game Meaning." *Western Folklore* 18: 13–24. (Reprinted in Sutton-Smith, 1972a: 491–505.)

———. 1959b. *The Games of New Zealand Children*. (University of California Folklore Studies, no. 12.) Los Angeles: University of California Press. (Reprinted in Sutton-Smith, 1972a: 1–295.)

———. 1959c. "Some Comments on the Class Diffusion of Children's Lore." *Midwest Folklore* 9: 225–228.

———. 1960. " 'Shut Up and Keep Digging': The Cruel Joke Series." *Midwest Folklore* 10: 11–22.

———. 1967. "The Role of Play in Cognitive Development." *Young Children* 6: 361–370. (Reprinted in Herron and Sutton-Smith, 1971: 252–260.)

———. 1968a. "The Folk Games of the Children." In *Our Living Traditions: An Introduction to American Folklore,* ed. T. P. Coffin, pp. 179–191. New York: Basic Books.

———. 1968b. "Novel Responses to Toys." *Merrill-Palmer Quarterly of Behavior and Development* 14: 151–158.

————. 1970a. "Psychology of Childlore: Bibliography." New York: Teachers College, Columbia University. Mimeo.

————. 1970b. "Psychology of Childlore: The Triviality Barrier." *Western Folklore* 29: 1–8.

————. 1971a. "A Developmental Psychology of Play and the Arts." *Perspectives on Education* (spring): 8–17. New York: Teachers College, Columbia University.

————. 1971b. "Children at Play." *Natural History* 80: 54–59.

————. 1971c. "The Expressive Profile." *Journal of American Folklore* 84: 80–92. (Reprinted in Sutton-Smith, 1972a: 521–540.)

————. 1972a. *The Folkgames of Children.* (American Folklore Society Bibliographical and Special Series, vol. 24.) Austin, Texas: University of Texas Press.

————. 1972b. "The Published Works of Brian Sutton-Smith: A Chronological Bibliography." In Sutton-Smith, 1972a: 541–546.

————. 1974a. "Children's Narrative Competence: The Underbelly of Mythology." Paper presented to the American Folklore Society. Portland, Oregon.

————. 1974b. "Current Research in Children's Play." Paper presented to the American Psychological Association. New York, New York.

————. 1975. "Current Research and Theory on Play, Games and Sports." *Developmental Studies.* New York: Department of Psychology, Teachers College, Columbia University. (Paper presented to the First National Conference on the Mental Health Aspects of Sports, Exercise, and Recreation. *American Medical Association,* Atlantic City.)

————. In press. *The Dialectics of Play: Integration–Innovation.* Tübingen: Sportwissenschaft Institut.

————. n.d. "The Games of Two Cultures." New York: Teachers College, Columbia University. Unpublished manuscript.

Sutton-Smith, B., et al. In press. "The Importance of the Storytaker: An Investigation of the Imaginative Life." *Urban Review.*

Sutton-Smith, B., Crandall, V. J., and Roberts, J. M. 1971. "Achievement and Strategic Competence." In Avedon and Sutton-Smith, 1971: 488–497. (An abridged version of Roberts, Sutton-Smith, and Kozelka, 1967.)

Sutton-Smith, B. and Gump, P. V. 1955. "Game and Status Experience." *Recreation* 48: 172–174.

Sutton-Smith, B. and Lazier, G. 1971. "Psychology and Drama." *Empirical Research in Theater* 1: 38–46.

Sutton-Smith, B. and Roberts, J. M. 1964. "Rubrics of Competitive Behavior." *Journal of Genetic Psychology* 105: 13–37.

————. 1967. "Studies of an Elementary Game of Strategy." *Genetic Psychology Monographs* 75: 3–42.

Sutton-Smith, B., Roberts, J. M. and Kozelka, R. M. 1963. "Game Involvement in Adults." *Journal of Social Psychology* 60: 15–30.

Sutton-Smith, B. and Rosenberg, B. G. 1961. "Sixty Years of Historical Change in the Game Preferences of American Children." *Journal of*

*American Folklore* 74: 17–46. (Reprinted in Sutton-Smith, 1972: 258–294.)

Swadesh, M. 1933. "Chitimacha Verbs of Derogatory or Abusive Connotation with Parallels from European Languages." *Language* 9: 192–201.

Sykes, A. J. M. 1966. "Joking Relationships in an Industrial Setting." *American Anthropologist* 68: 188–193.

Szwed, T. and Abrahams, R. In press. *Afro-American Folk Culture: An Annotated Bibliography of Materials from North, Central and South America.* Austin, Texas: University of Texas Press for the American Folklore Society.

Talbot, T., ed. 1968. *The World of the Child: Birth to Adolescence from the Child's Viewpoint.* Garden City: Anchor.

Talley, T. W. 1922. *Negro Folk Rhymes: Wise and Otherwise.* New York: Macmillan. (Reprinted, Port Washington, New York: Kennikat, 1968.)

Taylor, A. 1938. "Problems in the Study of Riddles." *Southern Folklore Quarterly* 2: 1–9.

———. 1939. *A Bibliography of Riddles.* (Folklore Fellows Communications, no. 126.) Helsinki: Suomalainen Tiedakatemia.

———. 1948. *The Literary Riddle before 1600.* Berkeley: University of California Press.

———. 1951. *English Riddles from Oral Tradition.* Berkeley: University of California Press.

———. 1954. "An Annotated Collection of Mongolian Riddles." *Transaction of the American Philosophical Society* 44: 321–425.

———. 1960. "Wellerisms and Riddles." *Western Folklore* 19: 55–56.

———. 1962a. *The Proverb and an Index to the Proverb.* Hatboro, Pennsylvania: Folklore Associates. (First published 1931 and 1934.)

———. 1962b. "The Riddle as a Primary Form." In *Folklore in Action: Essays for Discussion in Honor of MacEdward Leach,* ed. H. P. Beck, pp. 200–207. (American Folklore Society Bibliographical and Special Series, vol. 14.) Philadelphia: American Folklore Society.

Taylor, A. and Hand, W. D. 1968. "Twenty-five Years of Folklore Study in the West." *Western Folklore* 25: 229–245.

Thomas, J. 1895. *Randigal Rhymes and a Glossary of Cornish Words.* Penzance, Cornwall: F. Rodda.

Thomas, K. E. 1930. *The Real Personages of Mother Goose.* Boston: Lothrop, Lee and Shepard.

Thompson, F. 1945. *From Lark Rise to Candelford: A Trilogy.* London: Oxford.

Thompson, S. 1946. *The Folktale.* New York: Holt, Rinehart and Winston.

———. 1966. *Motif-index of Folk Literature: A Classification of Narrative Elements in Folktales, Ballads, Myths, Fables, Medieval Romances, Exempla, Fabliaux, Jest-books and Local Legends.* Bloomington, Indiana: Indiana University Press.

Thomson, D. F. 1935. "The Joking-relationship and Organized Obscenity in North Queensland." *American Anthropologist* 37: 460–490.

Thorne, B. and Henley, N. 1974. "Sex Differences in Language, Speech, and Nonverbal Communication: An Annotated Bibliography." East Lansing, Michigan, photocopy.

Todorov, T. 1971. "Meaning in Literature." *Poetics: International Review for the Theory of Literature* 1: 8–15.

———. 1973. "Analyse du discours: l'example des devinettes." *Journal de Psychologie Normale et Pathologique* 1–2: 135–155.

Touny, A. D. and Wenig, S. 1969. *Sport in Ancient Egypt.* Leipzig: Edition Leipzig.

Treadwell, Y. 1967. "Bibliography of Empirical Studies of Wit and Humor." *Psychological Reports* 20: 1079–1083.

Trevor, J. C. 1955. "Backwards Languages in Africa." *Man* 55: 111.

Tully, M. F. 1950. *An Annotated Bibliography of Spanish Folklore in New Mexico and Southern Colorado.* Albuquerque: University of New Mexico Press.

Turner, I., ed. 1969. *Cinderella, Dressed in Yella.* Melbourne: Heinemann Educational.

Turner, V. 1969. *The Ritual Process: Structure and Anti-structure.* Chicago: Aldine.

———. 1974. "Liminality, Play, Flow, and Ritual: An Essay in Comparative Symbology." Unpublished paper. Austin: University of Texas.

Tyler, P. 1972. "Forms in Common in the Oral Literatures of the World." Paper presented to the Humanities Conference of the National Council of Teachers of English, New Orleans.

Tyler, S. A. 1966. "Context and Variation in Koya Kinship Terminology." *American Anthropologist* 68: 693–707.

Uhl, W. 1897. *Die deutsche Priamel, ihre Enstehung und Ausbildung.* Leipzig: S. Hirzel.

Upadhyaya, H. S. 1970. "Indian Family Structure and the Bojpuri Riddles." *Folklore* 81: 115–131.

van der Elst, D. H. 1971. "The Bush Negro Tribes of Surinam, South America: A Synthesis." Ph.D. dissertation, anthropology, Northwestern University.

Van Gennep, A. 1908. "Essai d'une théorie des langues spéciales." *Revue des Études Ethnographiques et Sociologiques* 1: 327–337.

———. 1937–1938. *Manuel de folklore français contemporain*, 9 vols. Paris: Picard.

Van Huyen, N. 1934. *Les chants alternés des garçons et des filles en Annam.* Paris: P. Geuthner.

Van Rooten, Luis d'Antin. 1968. *Mots d'heures: gousses, rames.* London: Angus and Robertson. (American edition, New York: Grossman Publishers, 1967.)

Vansina, J. 1965. *Oral Tradition: A Study in Historical Methodology.* London: Routledge and Kegan Paul.

Vetterl, K. 1966. *A Select Bibliography of European Folk Music.* Prague: Institute for Ethnography and Folklore of the Czechoslovak Academy of Sciences in cooperation with the International Folk Music Council.

Virtanen, L. 1972. "Sagentraditionen bei Kindern." In *Probleme der Sagen-forschung,* ed. L. Rohrich. Freiburg im Breisgau: Deutsche For-schungsgemeinschaft.

Vogt, E. Z. 1969. *Zinacantan: A Maya Community in the Highlands of Chia-pas.* Cambridge, Mass.: Belknap Press of the Harvard University Press.

Voorhoeve, J. 1959. "An Orthography for Saramaccan." *Word* 15: 436–445.

———. 1961. "Le ton et al grammaire dans le Saramaccan." *Word* 17: 146–163.

———. 1971. "Church Creole and Pagan Cult Languages." *Pidginization and creolization of languages.* ed. D. Hymes, pp. 305–315. Cambridge, England: Cambridge University Press.

Voorhoeve, J. and Donicie, A. 1963. *Bibliographie du Négro-Anglais du Surinam, avec une appendice sur les langues créoles parlées a l'intérieur du pays.* 's-Gravenhage: Martinus Nijhoff.

Vycichl, W. 1959. "A Forgotten Secret Language of the 'Abbādi Sheiks and the Slang of the Halab isSudān." *Kush* 7: 222–228.

Vygotsky, L. S. 1962. *Thought and Language,* trans. E. Hanfmann and G. Vakar. Cambridge, Mass.: M.I.T.

Wagenwood, J. 1974. *Hangin' Out: City Kids, City Games.* Philadelphia: Lip-pincott.

Walker, B. 1946. "Folklore in the Schools: Collecting by Seventh Graders." *New York Folklore Quarterly* 2: 228–236.

Warren, D. M. and Taylor, A. R. 1972. *The Akan Literature of Ghana: A Bib-liography.* (An Occasional Publication of the Literature Committee of the African Studies Association.) Waltham, Mass.: African Studies Associa-tion, Brandeis University.

Watson, K. A. 1972. "The Social Context of Narrative Performance among Hawaiian Children: A Sociolinguistic Approach." Paper presented to the American Anthropological Association, Toronto.

———. 1973. "The Rhetoric of Narrative Structure: A Socio-linguistic Analy-sis of Stories Told by Part-Hawaiian Children." Ph.D. dissertation, Uni-versity of Hawaii.

Watson, K. A. and Boggs, S. T. 1974. "From Verbal Play to Talk Story: The Role of Routines in Speech Events among Hawaiian Children." Paper presented to the American Anthropological Association, Mexico City.

Watson, W. 1952. "The Street Games and Rhymes of Scottish Children." *Folklore* 63: 397–410.

Weiner, M. 1970. "The Riddle Repertoire of a Massachusetts Elementary School." *Folklore Forum* 3: 7–38.

Weinreich, M. 1968. "*Yidishkayt* and Yiddish: On the Impact of Religion on Language in Ashkenazic Jewry." In *Readings in the Sociology of Lan-guage,* ed. J. A. Fishman, pp. 382–413. Hague: Mouton.

Weinreich, U. 1966. "Explorations in Semantic Theory." In *Theoretical Foundations,* ed. T. A. Sebeok, pp. 395–477. (Current Trends in Linguistics, vol. 4.) Hague: Mouton.

Weinreich, U. and B. 1959. *Yiddish Language and Folklore: A Selective Bibli-ography for Research.* (Janua Linguarum, NR. 10.) Hague: Mouton.

Weir, R. 1962. *Language in the Crib*. (Janua Linguarum, series maior, 14.) Hague: Mouton.

Weis, H. 1942. *Curiosa, noch einmal lateinische Sprachspielereien,* 3 Auflage. München: R. Oldenbourg.

————. 1951. *Bella Bulla, lateinische Sprachspielereien*. Bonn: F. Dümmler.

————. 1952. *Jocosa: lateinische Sprachspielereien*. 5th edition. München: R. Oldenbourg.

————. 1954. *Spiel mit Worten; deutsche Sprachspielereien,* 3d enlarged edition. München: R. Oldenbourg.

Wells, C. 1905. *A Satire Anthology*. New York: Scribner's.

————. 1906a. *At the Sign of the Sphinx: A Book of Charades*. New York: Duffield & Co.

————. 1906b. *A Whimsey Anthology*. New York: Scribner's.

————. 1910. *A Parody Anthology*. New York: Scribner's.

————, ed. 1932. *An Outline of Humor: Being a True Chronicle from Prehistoric Ages to the Twentieth Century*. New York: Putnam's.

————. 1958. *A Nonsense Anthology*. New York: Dover.

Welsch, R. 1966. "Nebraska Finger Games." *Western Folklore* 25: 173–194.

Wehrhan, K. 1909. *Kinderlied und Kinderspiel*. Handbücher zur Volkskunde, vol. 4. Leipzig.

Wenck, G. 1966. *The Phonemics of Japanese: Questions and Attempts*. Wiesbaden: Otto Harrassowitz.

Wentworth, H. and Flexner, S. B. 1960. *Dictionary of American Slang*. New York: Crowell.

Werner, H., ed. 1955. *On Expressive Language*. Worcester, Mass.: Clark University. (Reviewed in *Language* 31 [1955]: 543–549.)

Werner, H. and Kaplan, B. 1963. *Symbol Formation*. New York: Wiley.

White, J. G. 1965. *John G. White Collection of Folklore, Orientalia, and Chess*, 2 vols. (Catalogue of Folklore and Folksongs, John G. White Department, Cleveland Public Library.) Boston.

Whiting, B., ed. 1963. *Six Cultures: Studies of Child-rearing*. New York: Wiley.

Whiting, J. W. M., Child, I. L. and Lambert, W. W. 1966. *Field Guide for a Study of Socialization*. New York: Wiley.

Whitten, N. E., Jr. and Szwed, J. F., eds. 1970. *Afro-American Anthropology: Contemporary Perspectives*. New York: Free Press.

Widdowson, J. D. A. 1971. "The Bogeyman: Some Preliminary Observations on Frightening Figures." *Folklore* 82: 99–115.

————. 1975. "The Language of the Child Culture: Pattern and Tradition in Language Acquisition and Socialization." St. John's, Newfoundland: Memorial University of Newfoundland. Unpublished manuscript.

Wildhaber, R., ed. *Internationale volkskundliche Bibliographie. International Folklore and Folklife Bibliography. Bibliographie internationale des arts et traditions populaires*. Bonn: Rudolf Habelt Verlag.

Wilgus, D. K. 1959. *Anglo-American Folksong Scholarship since 1898*. New Brunswick, New Jersey: Rutgers University Press.

Williams, T. R. 1963. "The Form and Function of Tambunan Dusun Riddles." *Journal of American Folklore* 76: 95–110.

Winslow, D. J. 1966a. "An Introduction to Oral Tradition among Children." *Keystone Folklore Quarterly* 11: 43–58.

———. 1966b. "The Collecting of Children's Lore." *Keystone Folklore Quarterly* 11: 89–98.

———. 1966c. "An Annotated Collection of Children's Lore." *Keystone Folklore Quarterly* 11: 151–202.

———. 1969. "Children's Derogatory Epithets." *Journal of American Folklore* 82: 255–263.

Withers, C. A. 1946. *Counting Out.* New York: Oxford.

———. 1947a. "Current Events in New York City Children's Folklore." *New York Folklore Quarterly* 3: 213–222.

———. 1947b. *Ready or Not Here I Come.* New York: Crowell. (Reprinted as *A Treasury of Games, Riddles, Mystery Stunts, Tricks, Tongue Twisters, Rhymes, Chanting, Singing.* New York: Grosset and Dunlap, 1974.)

———. 1948. *A Rocket in My Pocket: The Rhymes and Chants of Young Americans.* New York: Henry Holt.

———. 1965. *I Saw a Rocket Walk a Mile.* New York: Holt, Rinehart and Winston.

Wölfflin, E. 1887. "Das Wortspiel im Lateinischen." *Sitzungsberichte der bayerische Akademie Wissenschaften,* Philosophisch-historische Klasse II, 187ff.

Wolfenstein, M. 1951. "A Phase in the Development of Children's Sense of Humor." *The Psychoanalytic Study of the Child* 6: 336–350.

———. 1953. "Children's Understanding of Jokes." *Psychoanalytic Study of the Child* 9: 162–173.

———. 1954. *Children's Humor: A Psychological Analysis.* Glencoe, Illinois: Free Press.

Wolford, L. J. 1916. *The Play-Party in Indiana.* Indianapolis: Indiana Historical Commission. (Edited and revised by W. E. Richmond and W. Tillson. Indiana Historical Society Publications 20 [2]: 1959.)

Wood, R. 1938. *The American Mother Goose.* New York: Lippincott.

———. 1952. *Fun in American Folk Rhymes.* New York: Lippincott.

Wood, R. W. 1959. *How to Tell the Birds from the Flowers, and Other Woodcuts; A Revised Manual of Flornithology for Beginners.* New York: Dover.

Yakir, R. 1973. "Secret Languages of Israeli Children." In *Language-Behavior Papers,* no. 2, pp. 29–39. Jerusalem, Israel: Language-Behavior Section, The School of Education of the Hebrew University and the Ministry of Education and Culture.

Yoder, D. 1967. "Nicknames: Folk-cultural Questionnaire No. 3." *Pennsylvania Folklife* 21: inside back cover.

———. 1970. "Children's Games: Folk-cultural Questionnaire no. 16." *Pennsylvania Folklife* 19: inside front cover.

Yoder, E. 1974. "Nicknaming in an Amish-Mennonite Community." *Pennsylvania Folklife* 23: 30–37.

Yoffie, L. R. C. 1947. "Three Generations of Children's Singing Games in St. Louis." *Journal of American Folklore* 60: 1–51.

Zabeeh, F. 1968. *What Is in a Name? An Inquiry into the Semantics and Pragmatics of Proper Names.* Hague: Nijhoff.

Zenner, W. P. 1970. "Ethnic Stereotyping in Arabic Riddles." *Journal of American Folklore* 83: 417–429.

Ziegler, E. B. 1973. *Folklore: An Annotated Bibliography and Index to Single Editions.* Westwood, Mass.: Faxon.

Zigler, E., Levine, J., and Gould, L. 1966. "Cognitive Processes in the Development of Children's Appreciation of Humor." *Child Development* 37: 507–518.

Zim, H. S. 1948. *Codes and Secret Writing.* New York: Morrow.

Zippin, D. 1966. "Sex Differences and the Sense of Humor." *Psychoanalytic Review* 53: 209–219.

Zug, C. G., III. 1967. "The Non-rational Riddle: The Zen Koan." *Journal of American Folklore* 80: 81–88.

Züricher, G. 1926. *Kinderlieder der deutschen Schweiz.* Basel: Schriften der schweizerischen Gesellschaft für Volkskunde. Publications de la Société Suisse des Traditions Populaires.

# Contributors

Anthony E. Backhouse, Lecturer in Japanese at the University of Adelaide, South Australia, is completing a Ph.D. in Linguistics at the University of Edinburgh. His dissertation is a semantic study of the lexical field of gustatory taste terms in modern Japanese.

Victoria Reifler Bricker, Associate Professor of Anthropology, Tulane University, received her Ph.D. in Social Anthropology from Harvard University in 1968. She is the author of *Ritual Humor in Highland Chiapas* (University of Texas Press, 1973) and numerous scholarly articles. Her research interests include Mayan languages, relationships between oral tradition and written history, Indian rebellions in Latin America, and ceremonial humor and joking behavior.

Gary H. Gossen, Associate Professor of Anthropology at the University of California, Santa Cruz, received his Ph.D. in Social Anthropology from Harvard University in 1970. He is the author of *Chamulas in the World of the Sun: Time and Space in a Maya Oral Tradition* (Harvard University Press, 1974), which won an award in the Chicago Folklore Prize Competition for 1974. He is currently working on a textbook on the intellectual history of folkloristics and on a book-length collection of Maya oral narratives. His research interests include anthropological folklore, sociolinguistics and symbolic interpretation of myth, ritual, and cosmology, with an areal specialization in Meso-America.

Barbara Kirshenblatt-Gimblett, Associate Professor of Folklore and Folklife, University of Pennsylvania, and Visiting Associate Professor of Yiddish Studies at Columbia University and the Max Weinreich Center for Advanced Jewish Studies, YIVO, received her Ph.D. in Folklore from Indiana University in

1972. She is the author of "A Parable in Context: A Social Interactional Analysis of Storytelling Performance," *Folklore: Performance and Communication*, edited by D. Ben-Amos and K. S. Goldstein (Mouton, 1975) and "The Concept and Varieties of Narrative Performance in East European Jewish Culture," *Explorations in the Ethnography of Communication*, edited by R. Bauman and J. Sherzer (Cambridge University Press, 1974). She is currently working on the social systematization of song performance in East European Jewish society. Her research interests include children's folklore, historical ethnography, and social interactional analysis of expressive behavior.

Richard Price, Professor of Anthropology at The Johns Hopkins University, received his Ph.D. in Social Anthropology from Harvard University in 1970. He edited *Maroon Societies: Rebel Slave Communities in the Americas* (Doubleday, 1973), and is the author of *Saramaka Social Structure* (University of Puerto Rico Press, 1975), *The Guiana Maroons* (Johns Hopkins University Press, 1976), and numerous scholarly papers. He is currently working on a historical reconstruction of eighteenth-century maroon life in Suriname and, with Sally Price, on a general ethnography of the Saramaka.

Sally Price is a graduate student in the Department of Anthropology, The Johns Hopkins University. She has conducted field research in Martinique, Spain, and Mexico, and among the Saramaka Maroons of Suriname, and has coauthored a number of papers, including "Saramaka Onomastics: an Afro-American Naming System" (*Ethnology*, 1972) and "*Kammbá:* The Ethnohistory of an Afro-American Art" (*Antropologica*, 1972). She is currently working on an analysis of the visual arts of the Saramaka.

Mary Sanches, Assistant Professor of Anthropology at the University of Texas, Austin, received her Ph.D. in Anthropology from Stanford University in 1969. She is the author of *Features in the Acquisition of Japanese Grammar* (Stanford University Press, 1976) and edited *Sociocultural Dimensions of Language Use* (Academic Press, 1975) with Ben Blount. Her research interests include language acquisition, sociolinguistics, and metacommunication, her areal specialization being Japan.

Dina Sherzer, Assistant Professor of French and Italian at the University of Texas, Austin, received her Ph.D. in Romance Languages in 1970 from the University of Pennsylvania. She is the author of *Structure de la Trilogie de Beckett: Molloy, Malone Meurt, L'Innommable* (Mouton, 1976) and numerous scholarly articles. Her major research interests include the *nouveau roman*, theater of the absurd, and Samuel Beckett.

Joel Sherzer, Associate Professor of Anthropology at the University of Texas, Austin, received his Ph.D. in Linguistics from the University of Pennsylvania in 1968. He is the author of *An Areal-Typological Study of the American Indian Languages North of Mexico* (North Holland, 1975) and numerous scholarly articles. His research interests include sociolinguistics, the ethnography of speaking, and North and South American Indians.

Brian Sutton-Smith, Professor of Psychology and Education and Program Head of Developmental Psychology, Teachers College, Columbia University, received his Ph.D. in Educational Psychology in 1954 from the University of New Zealand in Wellington. He is the author of *The Folkgames of Children* (University of Texas Press, 1972) and edited *Child's Play* (John Wiley, 1971) with R. E. Herron and *The Study of Games* (John Wiley, 1971) with E. M. Avedon. His research interests include expressive structures in art and play.

# Index

# Persons

Abrahams, Roger, 65 n, 74, 112-113, 115, 205, 206, 218
Abrahams, R. D. and A. Dundes, 112-113
Ames, L. B., 221
Ariès, P., 193
Arth, M. J., 4-5

Backhouse, A. E., 14
Bakhtin, M., 202, 209
Ban, Tatsuo, 148 n
Barker, R. G. and H. F. Wright, 117
Bartlett, F. C., 221
Bateson, G., 5, 6
Beckett, Samuel, 15 n, 162-171
Beechick, R. A., 220
Ben-Amos, D., 216
Berko, J., 83-84, 91
Bernstein, Basil, 73-74
Bertholet, A., 10 n
Blair, W., 206
Blount, B., 77
Boggs, S. T., 222
Brayshaw, T., 160
Breton, A., 218
Bricker, V. R., 5, 12, 14, 16, 121 n
Brose, P. B. D., 220
Brown, R. and J. Berko, 83-84, 91
Browne, R. B., 67, 90
Brukman, J. C., 6 n, 14, 203-204, 205
Bruner, J. S. and R. R. Olver, 79

Burling, R., 75, 187
Bush, R. R., 4-5

Caillois, R., 4, 5, 6, 184-185, 218
Cammaerts, E., 191
Carroll, Lewis, 10, 11, 93, 191
Chomsky, N., 31 n
Chukovsky, K., 190-191, 192
Cicero, 187
Conklin, Harold, 75
Cray, E., 210
Csikszentmihalyi, Mihaly, 185
Curtius, E. R., 8 n, 188, 218

Dante, 8 n
Devereux, G., 209
Dorian, N. C., 200
Dubois, J. et al., 24, 25
Dundes, A., 112-113, 205, 215

Edmonson, M. S., 187, 206
Erikson, E. H., 221
Esar, E., 188-189

Feifel, H. and I. Lorge, 82-84
Fish, S. E., 2 n, 15 n
Foley, L., 26 n
Franszoon, Adiante, 40
Freud, S., 185, 202, 209
Fry, W. F., 5
Frye, N., 8 n

# Languages, Groups, Places

# Subject

abusive language, 207. *See also* insult
acculturation, 199
acronym, 15, 161
acrostic, 188, 215
adolescents, 34, 35, 39, 40, 69, 127 passim, 187, 205
advertising jingles, 187
aesthetic function, 8 n
alias, 194
*Alice's Adventures in Wonderland,* 9, 11 n
alliteration, 23, 101, 130, 164
allusion, 72
alphabet. *See also* orthography
  playful uses of Jewish, 195, 196-197
  role of, in religious and magical practices, 196
  semiotics of, 196
ambiguity, 112, 115, 119, 154-155, 200, 218
amphisbaenae, 188
anacoluthon, 167
anagram, 196-197, 215
anecdote, 71-72. *See also* joke, humor, narrative
anguish languish, 195
antimony, 166, 206
antithesis, 100, 103, 108
aphorism, 162. *See also* proverb, gnomic expression
apothegm, 189. *See also* proverb, gnomic expression

archaism, 168, 216
argot, 12, 34, 35, 187, 193, 195
  as essentially playful, 194

babbling, 105
baby talk, 8 n, 66, 176, 177, 189, 216
backwards language, 21-23, 24-27, 30, 31, 32, 33, 34
ballad, 68, 69, 86
bawdy songsters, 208. *See also* obscenity
billingsgate, 208, 209. *See also* obscenity
*blason populaire,* 199, 207
boasting, 206
by-names, 200

Carroll as a semiotician, 191
catch, 188, 189
ceremonial language, 193
Chamula world view, 121
charades, 215
chiasmus, 164, 202
child and childhood, concept of, 190, 193
child language, 75-85
  compared with adult language, 76 passim
  generative models for, 76-77
  priority of phonological component in, 77-79, 86, 105, 176
  semantic system of, 79-84